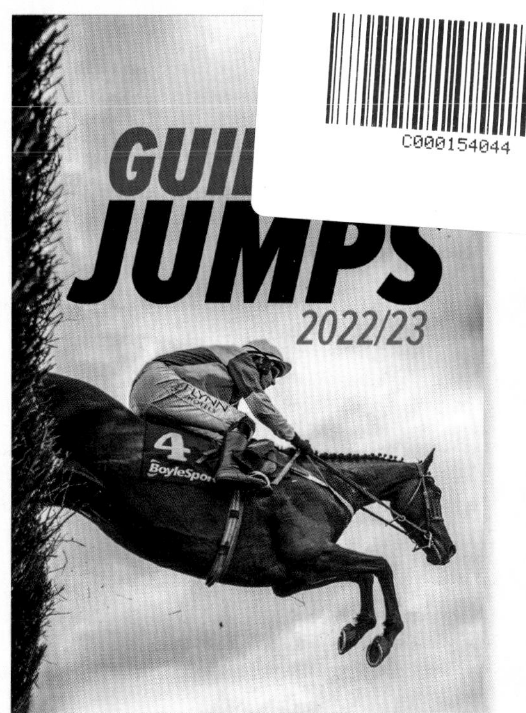

Edited and designed
by David Dew

Contributors

Richard Birch
James Burn
Ian Greensill
Dylan Hill
Paul Kealy
Lawrie Kelsey
Craig Thake
Nick Watts
Robbie Wilders

Cover artwork by Duncan Olner
Inside artwork by Stefan Searle

Published in 2022 by Pitch Publishing on behalf of Racing Post, A2 Yeoman Gate, Yeoman Way, Worthing, Sussex, BN13 3QZ.

ISBN: 978-1839501098

Printed by Buxton Press Ltd

RACING POST GUIDE TO THE JUMPS 2022-23

PAUL NICHOLLS

Established stars and big names of the future primed to do battle

46 47

RACING POST GUIDE TO THE JUMPS 2022-23

ANTHONY HONEYBALL

Numbers up and hopes are high

22 23

RACING POST GUIDE TO THE JUMPS 2022-23

EMMA LAVELLE

Expect more staying power from Paisley

30 31

RACING POST GUIDE TO THE JUMPS 2022-23

NICKY HENDERSON

Plenty of confidence in Constitution's bid for hurdles greatness

14 15

LOWDOWN FROM THE TRAINERS

Harry Fry Higher Crockermoor, Corscombe, Dorset **4-11**
Nicky Henderson Seven Barrows, Upper Lambourn, Berkshire **14-21**
Anthony Honeyball Potwell Farm Stables, Beaminster, Dorset **22-29**
Emma Lavelle Bonita Racing Yard, Marlborough, Wiltshire **30-37**
Charlie Longsdon Hull Farm Stables, Chipping Norton, Oxfordshire **38-45**
Paul Nicholls Manor Farm Stables, Ditcheat, Somerset **46-55**
Ben Pauling Naunton Downs Estate, Cheltenham, Gloucestershire **56-63**
Jamie Snowden Folly House, Upper Lambourn, Berkshire **64-70**
Evan Williams Fingerpost Farm, Llancarfan, Vale of Glamorgan **72-80**
Venetia Williams Aramstone, Kings Caple, Herefordshire **82-87**

RACING POST EXPERTS

Paul Kealy Festival fancies **89-97**
Nick Watts Ante-post analysis **98-100**
Richard Birch My ten for the season **102-105**
Robbie Wilders Below the radar **106-108**

THIS SEASON'S KEY HORSES

Key horses who can make a mark this season **110-198**
Key horses listed by trainer **198-199**
British fixtures 2023 **200-205**
Index of horses **206-208**

Love is in the air with Cheltenham mission

HARRY FRY is likely to target the mares' hurdle at the Cheltenham Festival for his stable star **Love Envoi**, who won the novice mares' equivalent race in March.

That was the last of five successive victories in Britain for the mare, winner of her only Irish point-to-point and subsequently bought for £38,000.

Love Envoi has already won more than three times her auction price,

WINNERS IN LAST FIVE SEASONS 38, 31, 30, 47, 53

Love Envoi: Mares' Hurdle the big target

> He needs to improve but he's got the potential to do that and we'll see if he makes into a Stayers' Hurdle contender

Might I: second to Constitution Hill last season

In charge of Paul Nicholls' satellite yard at Seaborough in Dorset, Harry Fry was widely credited with preparing Rock On Ruby to win the 2012 Champion Hurdle. The horse was then transferred to Fry as he began his own training career seven months later.

which was modest compared with the six-figure prices many winners from the Irish pointing field have fetched in the last few years.

She was a shrewd purchase for the former jockey Noel Fehily syndicate and did nothing to dent her growing reputation when finishing second to Brandy Love in the mares' novice hurdle championship final at Fairyhouse in April.

Love Envoi's season will be tailored to Cheltenham but becoming head girl will be tough with the likes of reigning British and Irish champion Marie's Rock and the Willie Mullins amazons being prepared for battle.

"She went from strength to strength throughout the season, winning her first five, and lost nothing in defeat in her final outing at Fairyhouse where she was beaten by a better horse on the day," says Fry.

"She'd run every month from December and we knew she might not be at her absolute best in Ireland, but she was good enough to finish second in a Grade 1.

"We're looking to stay over hurdles with her this season and we'll work back from the mares' hurdle in March."

Love Envoi needs cut in the ground, so Fry will wait for a good soaking of rain before deciding where her campaign begins.

"There's a two-mile Listed mares' hurdle at Wetherby on Charlie Hall day, and you've got a Listed mares' hurdle at Kempton at the end of November, but the options this side of Christmas are few and far between.

"So we might go into a handicap or take on the boys, which I'm not keen on. So it's a bit of a head-scratcher at the moment where we're going to start her, but from the turn of the year the races are there.

"She's a lovely tough mare who loves soft ground. She's rated 139 and has to improve again, but who's to say she won't."

Another in the same "exciting second-season hurdler" bracket is **Might I**, who ran with great credit behind Nicky Henderson hotpots Constitution Hill and Jonbon at Sandown and Haydock after rocketing home in a novice hurdle at Newton Abbot by 11 lengths.

He ended a season packed with promise by chasing home Irish raider Three Stripe Life in the Grade 1 Mersey Novices' Hurdle at Aintree.

"I can't believe we only won one race, to be honest," says Fry. "He tried mission impossible by trying to concede weight to Constitution Hill, then we thought we had the ideal profile horse for the Martin Pipe at Cheltenham. Unfortunately, he wasn't quite right and we couldn't get him there, so we waited for Aintree.

"He's a half-brother to Stattler, who won the National Hunt Chase in March, so there should be more to come once we step him up in trip.

"He needs to improve but he's got the potential to do that and we'll see if he makes into a Stayers' Hurdle contender. I've got a three-mile handicap hurdle at Haydock on Betfair Chase day in mind and we'll see if he can go down that route."

The key to **Metier**, who has a 50 per cent strike-rate having won four from eight since moving from Ireland, is "very testing conditions to put it mildly," says Fry.

"We're in two minds what to do with him: whether we stay over hurdles and possibly step him up in trip, or think about jumping fences. But either way, we'll be looking for his favoured ground, that's for sure.

"We'll be schooling him over fences and see if he takes to them, then making a decision whether we send him novice chasing or stay over the smaller obstacles."

Gin Coco won a novice hurdle nicely at Fontwell on debut for Fry in March and was taken to Punchestown the following month when he finished runner-up in a big-field handicap hurdle.

"I thought we had the race won jumping the last, but unfortunately he got battled out of it.

"He remains a novice until the end of

November, so we'll try to exploit that. We have in mind a crack at the Greatwood at the Cheltenham November meeting, and there are lots of good handicaps after that he could run in."

Lady Adare won three out of three and was on course for the mares' novice at the Cheltenham Festival until a setback the week before ruled her out.

"She's done well over the summer and at the moment she'll stay over hurdles and possibly go for the mares' hurdle at Wetherby on Charlie Hall Chase day," says Fry.

"Alternatively, we might go to Wincanton a week later for a mares' handicap hurdle over two miles five run in memory of Richard Barber [Fry's mentor in his early days], which is a race we like to win.

"She's on an upward curve and you never know, she might progress into a mares' hurdle candidate herself.

"She needs to improve further, but who's to say she won't. We'll take it one step at a time and see how we get on this side of Christmas and then make plans from there."

Ask Me Early had the "perfect prep" in the run-up to the Welsh National last year, winning two small hurdle races and being backed into 5-1, then a schooling fall put him out of contention.

"He made a similar mistake at Wincanton next time out and unseated Sean Bowen," says Fry. "He'll stay over fences and we'll see if we can get his confidence back. He jumps well, which makes the fall at home all the more frustrating. He's always been foot-perfect, but even the best can make mistakes.

"He needs cut in the ground, so we'll be waiting for the rain and getting him back on an even keel for those staying handicap chases."

Revels Hill could develop into a fine staying chaser having won his last two starts

Fry has a fine record on Kempton's all-weather surface – six winners from 11 runners (+£66.25)

Revels Hill: staying handicap chases will be on his agenda

> He's a second-season chaser we're really looking forward to in the better staying handicaps

at Taunton over two miles seven furlongs, then over five and a half furlongs further.

"He's a second-season chaser we're really looking forward to in the better staying handicaps, although he wouldn't want the ground too testing."

Boothill went hurdling and chasing last season and left his trainer frustrated that he didn't manage to get a win out of him in the last 12 months.

"We're set to go back over fences with him in early October and hopefully he can make a good novice chaser over two and a half miles," says Fry.

Ree Okka won twice over hurdles last season but is now poised to go novice chasing.

"He won over three miles at Kempton but I think we'll step back in trip over fences. I'm sure he can prove to be progressive over the bigger obstacles."

Dubrovnik Harry has a similar profile to Ree Okka, having won by 25 lengths over hurdles at Exeter and also being placed over hurdles, including a "very pleasing" third in a competitive Grade 3 at Sandown in March.

"That's a race which has produced good chase winners in the past and hopefully he can be another. He'll start over two and a half miles but I'm sure he'll stay further. He wants soft ground."

Deeper Blue, like Gin Coco, is a novice until the end of November, and could be aimed at the Persian War Novices' Hurdle at Chepstow's October meeting.

"He was second behind Stage Star at Chepstow last season [he went on to win the Grade 1 Challow Hurdle], so we have course form. We'll decide after that whether to stay over hurdles or go novice chasing."

Fairy Gem got her career off to a flying start when landing a mares' bumper at Plumpton on her debut and was then placed in Listed mares' bumpers at Cheltenham and Sandown and looks a very promising recruit to the hurdling ranks.

"She'll start out over hurdles in maiden novice company and hopefully she can win her share of mares' races and be contesting black-type races come the spring," says Fry.

Hymac was twice runner-up in Irish point-to-points and made an impressive winning debut for Fry in a Newton Abbot bumper in late March.

"He'll go straight over hurdles, probably two and a half miles to begin with, and he'll get further in time. It'll be a bonus what he does over hurdles because he'll be chasing in 12 months' time."

Hot Rod Lincoln is a winning Irish point-to-pointer by Westerner whom Fry hoped to run in the spring, but failed to get the ground he needed.

"He's a typical Westerner who wants cut in the ground, and it dried up on us, so he didn't get to run.

"He'll go novice hurdling and be starting out over two and a half. He looks an out-and-out galloper, certainly when he won his point-to-point.

"He just galloped and jumped, and the runner-up that day went on to win a Leopardstown maiden hurdle back in the spring. So we're hopeful that he can be a good novice hurdler for this season."

High Fibre was bought out of Ralph Beckett's yard after winning once on the Flat as a two-year-old last October and was then pipped on the post over 1m2f at Newmarket this spring.

"We're hoping he can make into a high-class juvenile hurdler this winter," says Fry. "Hopefully, if he takes to hurdling, he'll be contesting some of the better juvenile hurdle races come the spring."

Altobelli was hot favourite to win his bumper on his debut at Exeter in February and did so in the manner of a class horse.

Connections will no doubt hope he can score as regularly as his namesake, Alessandro Altobelli, the 1982 World Cup winner with Italy for whom he was a prolific goalscorer.

"We'll probably stick to bumpers initially, maybe even look at a better bumper, such as

From top: Boothill, Ree Okka and Forever Blessed

HARRY FRY

CORSCOMBE, DORSET

RECORD AROUND THE COURSES

	Total W-R	Per cent	Non-hcp Hdle	Non-hcp Chase	Hcp Hdle	Hcp Chase	N.H. Flat	£1 level stake
Exeter	45-143	31.5	23-60	8-21	5-34	5-13	4-15	+73.40
Taunton	33-153	21.6	16-64	0-3	7-50	4-14	6-22	-44.22
Wincanton	32-173	18.5	7-60	2-8	10-53	4-24	9-28	-12.82
Uttoxeter	28-107	26.2	6-21	1-10	6-28	11-33	4-15	+23.69
Newton Abbot	22-87	25.3	9-23	1-5	7-40	2-7	3-12	-8.71
Ascot	21-93	22.6	12-25	1-7	4-26	4-25	0-10	-3.67
Newbury	20-106	18.9	6-26	2-8	2-31	4-24	6-17	-22.51
Kempton	19-101	18.8	7-28	1-6	6-26	4-27	1-14	-25.45
Fontwell	18-71	25.4	6-26	1-4	8-25	3-6	0-10	-9.88
Plumpton	15-34	44.1	4-8	3-6	4-12	1-3	3-5	+25.40
Cheltenham	15-129	11.6	7-35	0-12	3-43	3-29	2-10	-49.24
Warwick	12-71	16.9	5-26	3-11	2-11	1-6	1-17	-12.94
Bangor	11-38	28.9	4-22	2-4	1-4	0-2	4-6	+9.26
Ludlow	11-50	22.0	4-14	1-3	2-11	2-13	2-9	-9.96
Doncaster	10-34	29.4	1-8	6-9	0-6	1-6	2-5	-1.46
Southwell	10-36	27.8	3-12	0-0	2-8	3-10	2-6	+7.89
Market Rasen	10-45	22.2	4-11	1-3	1-15	1-10	3-6	-4.67
Sandown	10-60	16.7	8-18	0-4	1-20	0-13	1-5	-13.28
Ffos Las	9-45	20.0	1-14	3-7	2-7	1-5	2-12	-1.57
Aintree	9-73	12.3	2-21	1-5	3-20	2-16	1-11	-19.27
Huntingdon	7-42	16.7	1-10	2-8	2-9	0-3	2-12	-18.48
Chepstow	7-61	11.5	3-23	0-2	1-12	3-14	0-10	-39.18
Kempton (AW)	6-11	54.5	0-0	0-0	0-0	0-0	6-11	+66.25
Stratford	6-35	17.1	2-6	3-5	1-15	0-6	0-3	-19.20
Leicester	4-12	33.3	2-6	1-1	0-2	1-3	0-0	+4.08
Lingfield	4-12	33.3	3-5	0-0	1-5	0-2	0-0	+3.17
Haydock	4-27	14.8	1-5	0-0	3-15	0-7	0-0	-1.20
Worcester	4-38	10.5	3-19	0-3	0-5	1-5	0-6	-27.05
Wetherby	3-17	17.6	2-8	1-2	0-3	0-2	0-2	-7.75
Hereford	3-23	13.0	1-8	2-6	0-4	0-4	0-1	-10.55
Carlisle	1-2	50.0	0-0	1-2	0-0	0-0	0-0	+3.00
Fakenham	1-2	50.0	0-0	0-0	0-0	1-2	0-0	+0.25
Newcastle	1-2	50.0	1-2	0-0	0-0	0-0	0-0	-0.60
Kelso	1-6	16.7	0-2	0-1	1-3	0-0	0-0	-0.50
Sedgefield	0-1	0.0	0-1	0-0	0-0	0-0	0-0	-1.00
Musselburgh	0-2	0.0	0-0	0-0	0-2	0-0	0-0	-2.00
Perth	0-3	0.0	0-1	0-1	0-1	0-0	0-0	-3.00
Ayr	0-4	0.0	0-0	0-0	0-2	0-2	0-0	-4.00
Lingfield (AW)	0-4	0.0	0-0	0-0	0-0	0-0	0-4	-4.00

a Listed bumper at Cheltenham's November meeting. We'll see on the back of that whether we stick to bumpers or kick on over hurdles," says the trainer.

Since coming over from France, **Fortunes Melody** has finished second seven times in ten outings, five of them in her last six starts over fences.

"On the one hand it was frustrating, but she bumped into some good horses," says Fry. "On the other hand she got some good experience over fences. So we'll be trying to make use of that in mares' novice company and hopefully she can get her head in front sooner rather than later."

Forever Blessed won his first two juvenile hurdles before being pulled up in the Grade 1 Juvenile Hurdle at Chepstow in December.

"It took him a long time to get over that and when he was ready the ground had gone against us," says Fry. "He should be competitive off his current hurdles rating of 124. He'll start off over hurdles but we may send him over fences to use his four-year-old allowance."

Finally, take close note of three former Irish point-to-pointers of whom plenty is expected: the winners **Credrojava** and **Carrigmoorna Rowan**, and runner-up **Goodtimecrew**.

Interview by Lawrie Kelsey

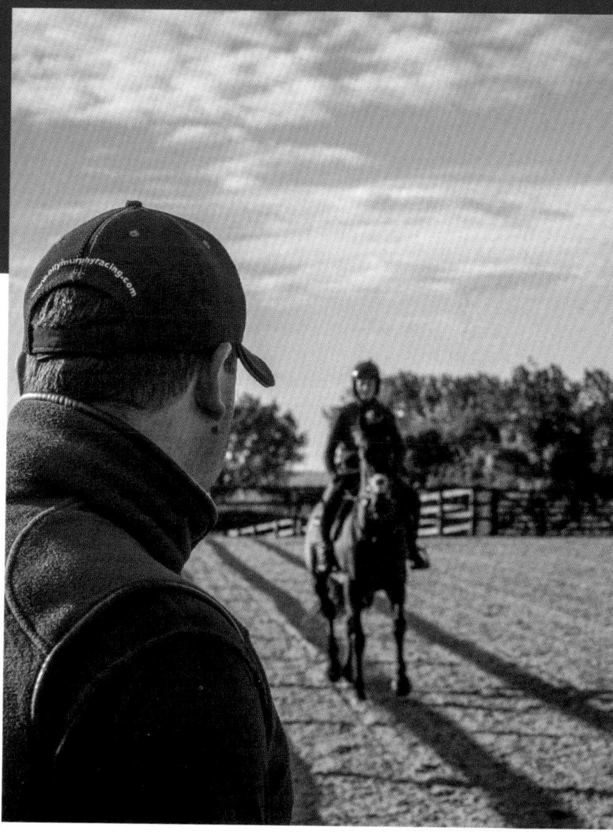

Plenty of confidence in Constitution's bid for hurdles greatness

AS THE starter drops his flag and the field jumps off for the fourth race on the opening day at next spring's Cheltenham Festival, it will herald the start of the most anticipated Champion Hurdle for almost half a century.

Not since the mid-70s when Night Nurse, Monksfield and Sea Pigeon were beating each other as they carved up the Champion Hurdle between them over six thrilling years has a hurdling showdown been as anticipated as this season's.

The remarkable Irish mare Honeysuckle, unbeaten in 16 races, will set out on her journey for a third successive hurdles title to join Hatton's Grace, Sir Ken, Persian War, See You Then and Istabraq in the pantheon of hurdling legends to have achieved the hat-trick.

Standing in the supermare's way, however, will be **Constitution Hill**, a bull of a horse who has won three out of three over hurdles by a total of 48 lengths.

Honeysuckle has already carved out her niche in hurdling history but will the Hill at Cheltenham prove too much for her this time?

Nicky Henderson thinks so and he sounds as bullish as his horse looks. "It was

WINNERS IN LAST FIVE SEASONS 120, 103, 118, 141, 141

phenomenal what he did last season and you've just got to hope and pray it wasn't a dream, and that he comes back as good as he was," says the master of Seven Barrows unusually optimistically.

"I hesitate to say better because I can't see how he can be. As long as he is as good as he was, that would appear to be enough."

Does he think that will be enough to beat Honeysuckle? "The book says it is, and by quite a long way," adds Henderson.

Two hours before Honeysuckle landed her second Champion Hurdle title in March, Constitution Hill sauntered away with the Supreme Novices' Hurdle by an

Constitution Hill and Sean O'Briain on the sand ring at Seven Barrows

Henderson also has Epatante, who won the Champion Hurdle in 2020 and was second in last year's race after a mistake at the last cost her any chance she had (right)

astonishing 22 lengths to earn an official rating of 170, 5lb higher than Honeysuckle, who will receive the mares' 7lb allowance next March.

Constitution Hill could reappear this season in the Ascot Hurdle, a race won by the likes of Faugheen, Annie Power and Rock On Ruby before their Champion Hurdle victories.

"It's possible we will look at the Ascot Hurdle. That's an idea that appeals to us; it's a good track, good place and two-mile-three and a bit is not going to worry him," says Henderson.

"It will either be Ascot [Hurdle] or the Fighting Fifth at Newcastle, which would lead him into the Christmas Hurdle [at Kempton on Boxing Day]. Then, if all's well, there is the Kingwell and Contenders' Hurdle, which I like, before Cheltenham."

Describing Constitution Hill, Henderson says: "He's completely different to my other [a record eight] Champion Hurdlers. He's a great big chaser who could go over fences tomorrow. We're not going to, but he's a big, strong horse – massive – but more so in thickness, he's balled up everywhere.

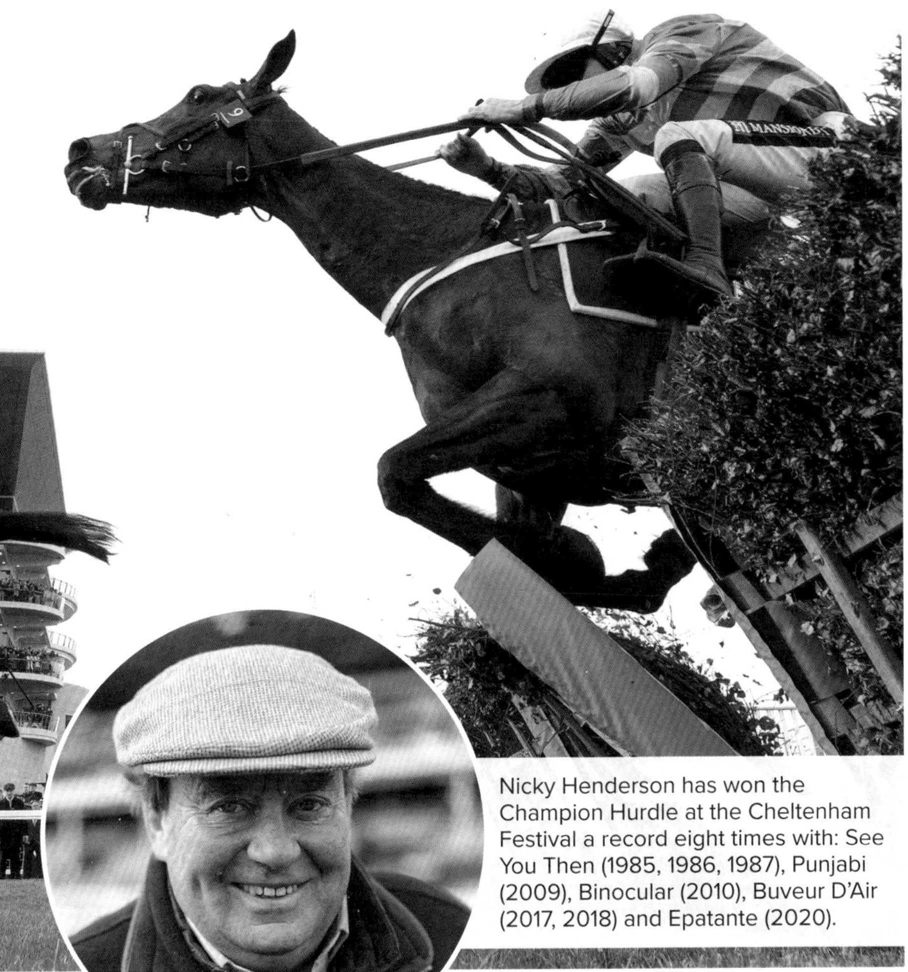

Nicky Henderson has won the Champion Hurdle at the Cheltenham Festival a record eight times with: See You Then (1985, 1986, 1987), Punjabi (2009), Binocular (2010), Buveur D'Air (2017, 2018) and Epatante (2020).

"The two things he's got are his engine and his mind. I think he's typical of Blue Bresil, who is a very good stallion and seems to stamp his stock with fantastic temperaments.

"You could do anything with this horse, which is why I thought he was no good; he wasn't fussed about anything. He doodles around and when you press the button, the turbo kicks in."

Intriguingly, Henderson also has **Epatante**, who won the Champion Hurdle in 2020 and was second in last year's race after a mistake at the last cost her any chance she had. It was some season for the mare who landed Grade 1 victories in the Fighting Fifth, Christmas Hurdle and Aintree Hurdle.

Henderson says: "She had a great season, while she proved she stays two and a half miles at Aintree, which opens up options, including the Mares' Hurdle at Cheltenham.

"That's a possibility if it says she isn't going to beat Honeysuckle and Constitution Hill, and she was brilliant at Aintree, but she also ran wonderfully at Cheltenham, and missed the last when she was only a length down."

Henderson also has the reigning Mares' Hurdle heroine in the yard in **Marie's Rock**, also a winner at the highest level at the Punchestown Festival in April.

She could step into the staying hurdle division, which is where last year's Long Walk winner Champ is likely to feature.

"Marie's Rock was a revelation," the Lambourn trainer said. "I knew she was good, but I didn't know she was that good!

"Her progress was incredible and they've all got to go down their own roads, but I think she could go three miles easily, while I imagine **Champ** will stay hurdling and he was very good in the Long Walk. He's had more work done on his back and we have to play with it every year, but JP's [McManus] team are very good at it."

Well-regarded duo **Walking On Air** and **Wiseguy** are winning, but inexperienced, hurdlers, whose chasing careers could be put on hold.

"I might just see where Walking On Air belongs over hurdles and it's the same for Wiseguy," says Henderson. "He's had some time off with a silly injury, but he's repaired and could be quite good."

Top of Henderson's list of seasoned chasers is **Shishkin**, who has a tasty return match being lined up next spring with reigning Champion Chase titleholder Energumene, but Henderson's star faces a race against time to make the Tingle Creek at Sandown on December 3 for his seasonal opener.

The Supreme Novices' Hurdle and Arkle winner seemed set to follow former stablemates Sprinter Sacre and Altior by becoming a Champion Chase hero after he beat Energumene in an epic Clarence House Chase at Ascot in January.

However, a rare bone condition meant Shishkin was pulled up at Cheltenham in March leaving the Willie Mullins-trained raider to coast home.

Henderson says: "It's been well documented, but the scans say it's all gone and apparently there's no higher chance of it coming back to him than any other horse in the country having it.

"I'm not going to rush him just because it's the Tingle Creek and then, like last year, him not be ready, and we go to Kempton for the Desert Orchid. He's cantering away but is a bit behind because we gave him longer in rehab.

"There's no reason the talent we know he's got won't still be there. The plan is to end up in the Champion Chase and get our own back on Energumene. We beat him once and I know he beat us, but it wasn't really a fair

Henderson has a 26% strike-rate in Listed races over the last five years – and a level-stake profit of £43.10

Chantry House: Henderson reports him to have grown considerably

fight because we never took part."

Henderson has been surprised by the physical progression of **Chantry House**, the Cotswold Chase winner who flopped in the Cheltenham Gold Cup.

"Believe it or not, he's grown considerably and he's a massive beast. If you saw him now, you'd be amazed," says the six-time champion trainer.

"It's slightly surprising at the age of eight, but he's developed and done everything right, although we've done quite a lot to him as well. He's had a wind operation and a full MOT, and I'm excited because I know he's very good.

"We did put him in the Grand National last season and I don't know if that's an option, but he's a staying chaser and the Coral Gold Cup at Newbury is a possibility as Newbury would be a great track for him."

That Newbury race, formerly the Hennessy, is a possibility for **Dusart** and Henderson says: "He's had some surgery on his back, which I hope will help him, while he could start in the intermediate chase we've used so successfully at Sandown in November. He's good."

Mister Fisher will be aimed at classy chases on decent ground before a possible tilt at the American Grand National Hurdle this time next year, while **Fusil Raffles** could attempt successive victories in the Charlie Hall at Wetherby on October 29, although the card's Grade 2 staying hurdle is also an option.

Caribean Boy could return at Aintree over the National fences in December's Becher Chase. "Some day there's going to be a big race in him," according to Henderson, who might also have strapping novice **Mister Coffey** for jump racing's most famous event.

"He's still a novice, but I'm not saying he'll stay in that division," he says. "He could end up in anything and the Grand National isn't fanciful."

Henderson, who hopes second-season novice chasers **Valsheda** and **Bothwell Bridge** can step up, is also thrilled by **Allarts** imminent comeback after a 20-month layoff.

Henderson has produced some top-flight novice hurdlers down the years, so take note of several he has picked out from what he calls "an exciting line-up", notably **Firestep**, whom he expects to be among the best novices this season.

"I stood here 12 months ago thinking Firestep was going to be one of the top dogs," he says. "He looks fantastic, but I thought him and **Russian Ruler** would be stars last season and you hardly saw them.

"It might be a blessing Firestep didn't run as he's a massive horse now. **Swapped** is

another quality horse for novice hurdles, as is **Attacca**, a distant relation to Altior.

"We like **Bold Reaction** a lot and **Boom Boom** is promising, while **Westwood Ryder** is more than capable. **Park Hill Dancer** is an interesting point-to-point bumper winner who probably didn't beat much but was wildly impressive and I think **Royal Max** is good. I thought he was a machine, but he had issues."

Henderson is also keen on several others, including **Issuing Authority**, who, like many of his team of novices, looks a future chaser. "He should have a lucrative time over hurdles first," says the trainer, who adds "the good-looking" **Petrossian** to his long list of talent.

"From the pointing ranks, **Jet Powered** is lovely, **Ballyhigh** does everything nicely, **Private Ryan** and **Persian Time** appear ready-made types, and **Amrons Sage** and **Jemura** are exciting embryonic chasers, while I can't wait to see **The Brew Master** in action.

"**Impose Toi**, **Iberico Lord**, **Easy Rider**, **Cadell**, **Immortal** and **Iolaos Du Mou** haven't run but should be in people's trackers. I can't help but be excited about that line-up."

The Seven Barrows maestro is also well known as a trainer of brilliant novice chasers, having saddled no fewer than seven Arkle Chase winners.

Topping his team this season is **Jonbon**, runner-up to stablemate Constitution Hill in the Supreme Novices' Hurdle, then followed up by winning a Grade 1 at Aintree.

"I don't think I've a better candidate. Without Constitution Hill he'd have been a good Supreme winner, but he backed it up at Aintree. That was a good performance and he seems to have settled down over the summer, while he's strengthened up enormously too."

Prominent in the betting at 5-1 for the Arkle, Jonbon is among several promising sorts for fences.

"**Balco Coastal** is one to look forward to as well," adds Henderson, "as is **City Chief** and **Kincardine** comes into the staying bracket. I'll be disappointed if **Captain Morgs** doesn't shine, while **No Ordinary Joe**, **The Bomber Liston**, **Full Of Light** and **Surrey Quest** are other fine prospects.

"**Will Carve**r is another to note and **Craigneiche** should be high class, but he's had issues and been off since last year's festival. **Rathmacknee** is actually a novice over hurdles, but could switch to fences."

A hurdle outing before his chasing debut is planned for **Broomfield Burg** and the returning **Pentland Hills** could follow the same path.

He has been off since the 2020 Champion Hurdle and Henderson said: "He's rated 150 over hurdles and 69 on the Flat and they say the gap is meant to be 40, so he'd have 41lb in hand if we ran him on the Flat!

"We've been waiting on the ground, but he could start over hurdles now, and his biggest weapon is his jumping – he's brilliant – so he will go chasing at some stage."

Ahorsewithnoname has two objectives this season: the Cesarewitch and the Mares' Novices' Hurdle at Cheltenham, in which she was second last season.

She also won two handicaps on the Flat, leaving her with a rating of 96, not far below Listed class.

"There's no doubt she improved considerably in the spring and her Cheltenham run and two Flat wins were way above anything she'd done before," says Henderson.

Among Henderson's enviable team of female performers for the novice hurdle division is **Luccia**, a spectacular Listed winner at Sandown in March.

"She could be anything," he said. "When she won at Sandown it was the best performance in a mares' bumper all season. She was incredible. Let's hope she's as good as we thought but she's not the only one as I adore **Lightfoot Lady**, a half-sister to Firestep.

"**Touchy Feely** might have disappointed after a good first run, but has had a wind op

From top: Jonbon, Pentland Hills and Ahorsewithnoname

NICKY HENDERSON

UPPER LAMBOURN, BERKSHIRE

RECORD AROUND THE COURSES

	Total W-R	Per cent	Non-hcp Hdle	Non-hcp Chase	Hcp Hdle	Hcp Chase	N.H. Flat	£1 level stake
Kempton	121-472	25.6	47-161	28-69	23-116	11-72	12-54	-5.40
Newbury	98-441	22.2	54-159	8-24	17-115	8-95	11-48	-50.01
Cheltenham	84-696	12.1	34-214	27-106	15-214	5-138	3-24	-224.79
Sandown	73-296	24.7	29-77	18-50	19-106	4-52	3-11	-11.45
Ascot	66-305	21.6	28-103	15-44	11-89	8-48	4-21	-34.09
Doncaster	56-186	30.1	34-87	10-27	7-34	3-24	2-14	+14.35
Huntingdon	55-189	29.1	31-82	12-24	4-36	4-14	4-33	-48.95
Ludlow	54-213	25.4	29-94	3-14	2-31	6-33	14-41	-61.49
Warwick	50-186	26.9	21-75	4-10	10-39	7-16	8-46	+4.51
Aintree	49-287	17.1	20-87	9-33	11-76	7-67	2-24	-40.71
Worcester	43-163	26.4	20-50	5-19	7-47	2-13	9-34	+18.55
Market Rasen	40-151	26.5	18-43	2-10	6-49	5-23	9-26	-11.95
Uttoxeter	40-159	25.2	17-53	6-18	6-47	4-24	7-17	-34.35
Southwell	37-127	29.1	13-42	1-7	3-28	1-10	19-40	-22.71
Ffos Las	29-74	39.2	16-30	2-6	5-21	1-4	5-13	+19.26
Fakenham	25-72	34.7	14-35	2-9	2-13	1-4	6-11	-17.29
Bangor	24-102	23.5	12-34	2-10	5-23	1-13	4-22	-31.08
Fontwell	22-78	28.2	10-30	4-8	5-17	1-5	2-18	-8.69
Newton Abbot	21-65	32.3	8-19	2-8	6-25	2-7	3-6	+8.43
Stratford	20-96	20.8	2-15	3-8	9-39	3-19	3-15	-32.15
Plumpton	19-54	35.2	5-17	5-10	7-18	2-4	0-5	+29.01
Taunton	19-74	25.7	10-31	2-4	4-26	1-8	2-5	-17.39
Haydock	19-91	20.9	9-27	3-14	3-40	3-8	1-2	-29.11
Chepstow	17-79	21.5	9-32	2-7	2-17	1-14	3-9	-9.07
Wetherby	14-36	38.9	7-12	5-9	0-7	0-4	2-4	-0.88
Hereford	13-35	37.1	9-18	1-4	2-8	0-0	1-5	-5.22
Exeter	13-58	22.4	6-24	1-8	2-10	2-7	2-9	-15.05
Wincanton	13-85	15.3	6-35	3-6	3-23	0-11	1-10	-34.81
Newcastle	12-17	70.6	10-12	0-0	0-0	1-4	1-1	+5.15
Musselburgh	11-35	31.4	8-16	1-4	2-12	0-2	0-1	-8.85
Ayr	11-66	16.7	1-5	2-5	2-30	4-20	2-6	-27.99
Kelso	9-16	56.2	3-3	2-2	1-4	1-2	2-5	+7.18
Kempton (AW)	9-24	37.5	0-0	0-0	0-0	0-0	9-24	+9.44
Lingfield (AW)	9-44	20.5	0-0	0-0	0-0	0-0	9-44	-9.66
Leicester	8-37	21.6	4-16	2-6	0-3	2-12	0-0	-4.02
Hexham	6-15	40.0	1-2	1-2	1-6	1-2	2-3	+1.98
Perth	6-28	21.4	3-9	0-2	0-5	3-10	0-2	-13.60
Lingfield	4-13	30.8	3-9	1-3	0-0	0-1	0-0	-7.25
Catterick	3-11	27.3	0-3	3-5	0-1	0-1	0-1	-2.27
Sedgefield	2-2	100.0	2-2	0-0	0-0	0-0	0-0	+0.71
Carlisle	2-3	66.7	1-1	0-0	0-1	1-1	0-0	+4.41
Cartmel	1-5	20.0	0-1	1-1	0-2	0-1	0-0	-2.80
Wolverhampton (AW)	1-6	16.7	0-0	0-0	0-0	0-0	1-6	-4.27

and is bred for jumping, while **Queens Rock** is a nice mare who should have won her bumper.

"**Treyarnon Bay** did win hers and has a touch of class, and **Lady D'Arbanville** has taken time, but is worth waiting for."

Of those yet to run for the yard, Henderson adds: "**Bombay Sapphire** is a lovely, big, scopey mare and **Love Bite** is simply sensational. She's a drop-dead gorgeous sister to Beat That and half-sister to Might Bite, and brilliantly named by me!

"You won't, however, see a better-looking filly than **Between Waters**, who was impressive in her point-to-point."

Also make a close note of the "incredibly progressive" **Theatre Glory** and the "interesting" **On My Command**, who will take the senior mares' hurdle route, while the chasing team includes **Tweed Skirt**, **Fable** and **Fantastic Lady**, who unseated in the Topham "but can usually jump with her eyes closed".

"They're fantastic," says Henderson. "You won't see a better bunch."

Interview by James Burn

ANTHONY HONEYBALL

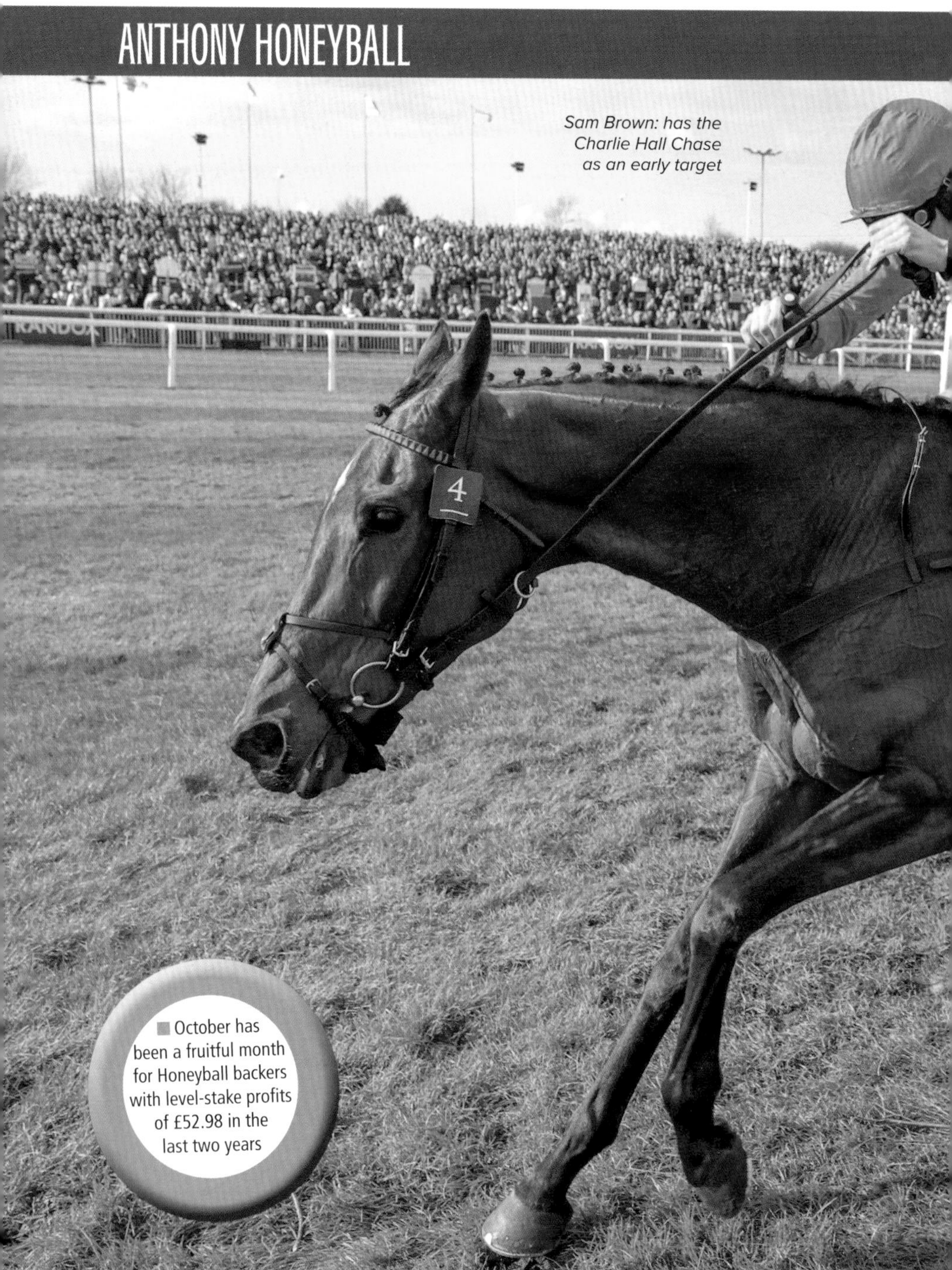

Sam Brown: has the Charlie Hall Chase as an early target

■ October has been a fruitful month for Honeyball backers with level-stake profits of £52.98 in the last two years

WINNERS IN LAST FIVE SEASONS 35, 27, 36, 15, 34

Numbers up and hopes are high

THEY'RE pothunting at Potwell Farm and Anthony Honeyball is sweet on his team's prospects this season.

Not only does his Dorset stable house more horses than at any time since taking out a licence 16 years ago, the standard is the highest since the likes of Regal Encore in his early days, Acey Milan and Ms Parfois were winning good races four or five years ago.

"It's a slow and relentless progression but we're going in the right direction," says Honeyball.

We had a nice batch a few years ago, then we had a bit of a lull, and now

Lilith (near): ended her last campaign with victory at Punchestown and will be back there in the spring

hopefully we've got another crop that we can get some Saturday horses from.

"We had a good season last year with 35 winners and a winner at two festivals, Aintree and Punchestown. We've had 30-odd winners several times but this season we'd like to have 40 or 50 and a few more high-profile winners to push our name and the yard forward.

"We've built a 25-box barn and we have an overflow yard, predominantly for three-year-olds. So we have about 70 horses, which is ten to 15 more than last year. We've never had so many."

The Potwell pothunters' flagbearer is **Sam Brown**, who is being aimed at the Grade 2 Charlie Hall Chase at Wetherby in late October, then possibly the Grade 2 Many Clouds Chase at Aintree in early December in which he finished third last year.

"The Aintrees, Newburys and Haydocks suit him well, so we have all sorts of options. We could go back for the Peter Marsh at Haydock off a higher weight if we want. We'll wait to see what he develops into.

"If he takes another step forward, then we'll run him in the top races. He's done really well in the summer and seems in really good order. We're very happy with him.

"He's ten but he has very low mileage, so he has plenty left in the tank. He's at the peak of his powers now. He'll be our flag-bearer for sure this season."

Lilith is a hardy type who ran nine times

She's qualified for a £35,000 race at Hereford in December, so that will be the early target
BETVICTOR
BETVICTOR
BETVICTOR
BETVICT

last season, culminating in a novice mares' handicap chase at Newbury before an even better victory in a mares' chase at Punchestown at the end of April.

"She liked dropping from three miles to two miles five and jumped like a buck at Punchestown. That was the second year in a row we'd had a Punchestown Festival winner after Sull D'Oc AA in 2021," says Honeyball.

"She's qualified for a £35,000 race at Hereford in December, so that will be the early target, then we'll plan to go back to Punchestown if all goes well."

Serious Charges won three times over hurdles last season and looked particularly impressive in handicap company at Uttoxeter, where he won by six and a half lengths. He then went to Aintree where he was made 9-2 joint favourite for a Grade 3 handicap hurdle and finished a creditable sixth of 21.

"We had entered him for the Grade 1 novice hurdle at Aintree, and he wasn't a silly price for that, but we thought we'd better go for the handicap after looking at the ratings," says Honeyball.

"We were a tad disappointed with him but he was only five and taking on battle-hardened handicappers. He didn't disgrace himself and we took a load of positives from his run.

"He could be a big player in novice chase ranks this season because he jumps hurdles beautifully and he was second in an Irish point-to-point.

"Jumping is his forte and I'm hoping he can win a little novice handicap chase, then graduate to Graded novice chases. He will be ready by late October or early November. I'm hoping he could be good enough for something like the Grade 2 Reynoldstown at Ascot in February.

"I'm quite sweet on him. He's a chaser in the making and everything else has been a bonus."

Gustavian was a classy hurdler who won three times and finished second three times, but he couldn't manage to win over fences during his novice season. However, he was never out of the first three every time he finished, including being runner-up three times.

"He nearly got it together last time out when he was second in a £40,000 novice handicap chase at Uttoxeter," says Honeyball. "We took the view that if he can win it's not a bad way to lose his novice status, and if not he'll be a good novice for the next season.

"He jumps well in the main and is a nice horse to go novice chasing with this season. If he can just clean up those mistakes he can progress through the season and perhaps go for the 3m6f novice chase at the Cheltenham Festival. That would be my dream scenario with him."

Norton Hill is a new recruit from Jack Barber, who left training this spring. He won a Wincanton bumper before going hurdling and, although he was finishing off well, his jumping wasn't slick enough to win.

"Once he gets his jumping together he could progress into a really good novice hurdler," says Honeyball. "With his mark of 111, I think he could be well handicapped because he's got a decent amount of ability. He could win a maiden hurdle, although with his mark you'd think he ought to go straight into a handicap. So we'll see."

Breaking Cover finished second in an Irish point-to-point and cost Honeyball £95,000 at the sales, while the winner was bought by Willie Mullins for £150,000.

"He looks a straightforward horse who will be one for bumpers early on. He's breezing along nicely and I hope he'll be a nice novice hurdler eventually," says Honeyball.

Former winning Irish pointer **Kilbeg King** cost a more modest £45,000 but was a runaway winner of his bumper on debut in March last year, then tweaked a tendon and missed the whole of last season.

"The form of that bumper has worked out quite well. Some of the horses behind him have run over hurdles and are rated in the 120s, so I'm quite keen on him and hope he can make into a nice novice hurdler when the mud's flying in the winter."

Honeyball won four races with Midnight Minx, three of them bumpers, and he's hoping the winning family trait is passed to her son **Cape Vidal**.

"He won a bumper at Ffos Las very impressively first time out in May, which we thought he might do. We think he's a very nice horse indeed for this season.

"There's a Listed bumper at Cheltenham in November he might run in. He jumps very well, so he'll probably go hurdling by mid-season."

Marco Island is posing Honeyball a dilemma. He knows the five-year-old has talent after he won a bumper on debut and his second outing over hurdles.

"His jumping was very good early in the season but by the end of it he'd got a bit lost," says Honeyball.

"I'm half thinking of giving him one more race hurdling, then go novice chasing. I really am undecided. I'm going to school him over fences in October and see how easy he finds that."

Firestream is an interesting character who won one of the four bumpers he contested last season.

"We thought he'd win every bumper he ever ran in," recalls Honeyball. "He ended up running in four but no way did we set out to do that. It just worked out that way.

"He's very well bred by Yeats and has

ANTHONY HONEYBALL

BEAMINSTER, DORSET

From top: Serious Charges, Gustavian and Regal Encore

RECORD AROUND THE COURSES

	Total W-R	Per cent	Non-hcp Hdle	Non-hcp Chase	Hcp Hdle	Hcp Chase	N.H. Flat	£1 level stake
Fontwell	54-166	32.5	12-40	1-7	16-53	10-32	15-34	+41.79
Plumpton	28-111	25.2	7-21	1-3	8-43	5-28	7-16	-10.46
Exeter	21-99	21.2	7-36	2-9	8-29	2-19	2-6	+22.25
Uttoxeter	20-107	18.7	3-23	2-6	10-44	0-18	5-16	-10.96
Taunton	17-95	17.9	1-35	0-0	11-31	2-16	3-13	+15.42
Ffos Las	17-96	17.7	3-20	1-3	3-26	4-21	6-26	-24.07
Wincanton	17-124	13.7	4-48	2-5	3-26	5-28	3-17	+1.18
Worcester	14-79	17.7	5-28	1-3	5-23	3-18	0-7	-33.59
Chepstow	11-73	15.1	3-26	0-1	4-17	1-18	3-11	-9.24
Warwick	7-36	19.4	1-9	2-3	0-4	3-12	1-8	-11.08
Ludlow	6-13	46.2	1-2	0-2	1-2	1-3	3-4	+48.00
Ascot	6-40	15.0	0-1	0-2	1-4	5-26	0-7	+29.25
Newbury	6-52	11.5	0-12	1-5	1-8	2-14	2-13	-22.75
Market Rasen	5-16	31.2	0-1	1-2	2-6	2-5	0-2	+3.12
Stratford	5-16	31.2	1-2	1-1	3-5	0-5	0-3	+1.91
Lingfield	5-25	20.0	0-5	1-1	3-7	1-12	0-0	+0.30
Newton Abbot	5-34	14.7	0-10	1-3	3-11	1-6	0-4	-16.11
Hereford	4-12	33.3	1-3	0-0	2-4	0-4	1-1	+5.28
Aintree	4-28	14.3	0-1	0-2	1-7	2-7	1-11	+22.00
Cheltenham	4-43	9.3	0-3	0-1	1-7	2-15	1-17	-20.50
Wetherby	3-6	50.0	0-2	2-2	0-0	0-1	1-1	+9.95
Catterick	3-7	42.9	0-1	1-2	0-1	1-1	1-2	+0.61
Kempton	3-11	27.3	0-1	0-2	1-3	1-3	1-2	-3.47
Southwell	3-24	12.5	0-4	1-3	0-7	1-4	1-6	-11.38
Carlisle	2-7	28.6	1-2	0-2	0-0	1-3	0-0	-1.42
Huntingdon	2-16	12.5	0-4	0-1	0-1	0-1	2-9	-7.25
Sandown	2-23	8.7	1-6	0-0	0-4	1-6	0-7	-14.00
Cartmel	1-2	50.0	0-0	1-1	0-1	0-0	0-0	+0.75
Leicester	1-9	11.1	0-2	0-2	0-2	1-3	0-0	-4.00
Bangor	1-18	5.6	1-4	0-0	0-3	0-10	0-1	-15.00
Haydock	1-22	4.5	0-2	1-1	0-6	0-13	0-0	-18.75
Doncaster	1-24	4.2	1-6	0-2	0-9	0-2	0-5	-22.75
Ayr	0-1	0.0	0-0	0-0	0-0	0-1	0-0	-1.00
Newcastle	0-1	0.0	0-0	0-0	0-0	0-1	0-0	-1.00
Musselburgh	0-1	0.0	0-0	0-0	0-0	0-1	0-0	-1.00
Kelso	0-1	0.0	0-0	0-0	0-0	0-0	0-1	-1.00
Folkestone	0-3	0.0	0-2	0-0	0-0	0-0	0-1	-3.00
Lingfield (AW)	0-4	0.0	0-0	0-0	0-0	0-0	0-4	-4.00
Hexham	0-11	0.0	0-5	0-0	0-3	0-0	0-3	-11.00

always given us a good feel. We think a lot of him. He'll go novice hurdling over two and a half miles in the hope we can see there's a proper horse there. We just feel we haven't seen the spark on the racecourse we were thinking we might see.

"We think he might develop into a three-mile Albert Bartlett type of horse. I'm not for a moment thinking he's a Supreme or even a Ballymore type, but there's an engine in there."

Regal Encore may be 14 rising 15 but still shows plenty of zest at home and on the racecourse, and is being prepared for a tilt at a £100,000 handicap at Ascot in late October, a race in which he finished second in 2019, won in 2020 and was third last season.

"The handicapper is dropping him quite quickly," says Honeyball. "He's down to 136 now, so that is a big help at his age. He's in great order and still tanks up the gallops like an eight-year-old.

"He'll go straight to Ascot without a prep race, then after that there's another £100,000 race at Ascot before Christmas. If he doesn't show anything in those two, though, I think he'll be retired."

But as Regal Encore is prepared for his 11th season, Honeyball knows the old boy owes the Potwell Farm team nothing after earning just over £347,000 prize-money

Anthony Honeyball's father John was master of the Taunton Vale Hunt and trainer in the early part of the career of Cheltenham Gold Cup winner The Dikler by training him to win his first point-to-point.

World Of Dreams (left): could prove very well treated in handicaps

since winning a Southwell bumper on his racecourse debut in 2012.

I Giorni is a winning Irish pointer who will be aimed at a mares' bumper and if she wins that she'll go for a Listed mares' bumper in mid-November at Cheltenham or a similar one at Huntingdon in December.

"She wouldn't be far off. She looks a decent mare," says Honeyball.

Doyen For Money is another winning Irish pointer for whom hopes are high. "He's a nice athletic horse who looks a good prospect. We'll run him in a bumper in October and if he wins there's a Listed bumper at Ascot we'd like to target. He jumps well, so there'll be no bother going hurdling with him."

Trojan Horse was rated 78 on the Flat with Charlie and Mark Johnston and has been sent by owner Ron Huggins [of Double Trigger fame] to Honeyball to be trained as a juvenile hurdler.

"If he takes to jumping he could become a smart juvenile hurdler. He has a decent level of Flat form and a good pedigree and could make into a Fred Winter-type horse."

Fortuitous Favour was "green as grass" for her debut in a Wetherby bumper in December but eventually flew home.

"She's a genuine, plucky filly who jumps particularly well at home. She's not that big, so I think we'll look at an ordinary mares' bumper with her. She's got a bit of oomph about her; she's not just a plodder."

World Of Dreams won two bumpers and was fifth in a Grade 2 bumper at Aintree before a long break after a setback, then a return last season brought two more wins in novice hurdles.

"He's definitely a horse with a really decent engine and fairly workable handicap mark of 120," says Honeyball.

"He'll be going down the handicap hurdle route and he'll be very dangerous off his mark. He'll probably be out some time in November."

Interview by Lawrie Kelsey

EMMA LAVELLE

Expect more staying power from Paisley

POPULAR old boy **Paisley Park** is back for his sixth season and, although the fire is burning a little less intensely than it was at its scorching zenith in his *annus mirabilis* of 2018-19, he's in fine fettle and ready to take on the leading stayers.

That's the bulletin from Wiltshire trainer Emma Lavelle, who says: "He's in great order. He looks really well and is as enthusiastic as ever. He's cantering away and we're really happy with how he is at this stage and, while he keeps telling us that's the way he is, we'll keep going until he tells us he doesn't want to."

In the season he hit the headlines, he won the Grade 1 Long Walk Hurdle at Ascot and ended it with a superb victory in the Grade 1 Stayers' Hurdle at the Cheltenham

Paisley Park: former Stayers' Hurdle winner

WINNERS IN LAST FIVE SEASONS 42, 32, 29, 35, 28

February is a good time of year to back runners from the Lavelle stable: (+£81.79) for the last four years

Festival as the likes of Faugheen, Bacardys and Supasundae floundered forlornly in his wake.

He won the Long Walk again in 2020 and was third in it last season, one of four third-placed finishes he had. In fact, the only time he was out of the frame was an honourable fifth in the Champion Stayers' Hurdle at Punchestown at the end of April when the track didn't play to his strengths.

"I hadn't been to Punchestown for several years and I'd forgotten how short the run-in was," says Lavelle.

"He travelled really well in the race, which always tells us they haven't gone quick enough, and when they quickened he got done for toe. So rather than it being a race too far, I think the configuration of the track was not in his favour."

As a staying hurdler near the top of the tree, he will tackle some of the same races he has for the last three years and face some of the same old rivals.

"There's no variation over hurdles – those are our options – and the weather will dictate where we start off. Last year we started at Wetherby and if it was soft enough we might do the same. I'm not saying Wetherby is the ideal place to go with him, but you can only run where the races are. I also wouldn't mind winning the Cleeve Hill again [for the fourth time after victories in 2019/20/22]."

Punchestown will definitely not be his final destination this season. Its short run-in precludes that as Paisley Park likes an uphill finish or long run from the final flight.

Nor will Aintree's flat circuit suit him. So the Cheltenham Festival is likely to bring down the curtain on his season.

"I imagine Cheltenham would be our target for the end of the season, but there's a lot of water to flow under the bridge before we worry about what his final race will be.

"It's more about how the season progresses and what we're likely to be aiming for."

Also back for more is **De Rasher Counter** after his unfortunate unseating of Adam Wedge at the Canal Turn on the first circuit of April's Grand National when badly hampered by a faller.

"It was just so frustrating. He'd come back from injury and had a lovely prep run at Newbury in the Denman," recalls Lavelle.

"He jumped well all the way at Newbury and just got tired, but it was the perfect prep run and he was really enjoying the first few fences in the National; he just got wiped out at the Canal Turn. It was game over, which was a shame because he was really enjoying it. We thought he'd run really well. It was a bit of a gutter.

"This year he's eligible for veterans' races and the plan is to start him at Chepstow in the veterans' qualifier series. They're for horses rated 0-150 and he's rated 149, then we'll just see where the season takes us.

"Whether we look at something like the Becher Chase at Aintree or the Coral Gold Cup at Newbury, there are some big chases out there. Although he's ten years old, he hasn't got many miles on the clock. He looks great and is in great shape.

"I wouldn't rule out Aintree again. Whereas last year was all about the National because of his injury, this year we'll have a season of racing before we think about it."

Killer Clown was unplaced in last season's Topham Handicap and could return to Aintree for another crack at the course, but the Grand National will not be the race. That's been ruled out because he wouldn't stay.

"He loved jumping the Aintree fences, so we would consider the Topham again," says Lavelle, but that's a long way off and I'd hope off 148 he could win another decent handicap chase before then.

"When he's good, he's very, very good, and he's been very impressive around Kempton. He's a quick horse and he's a very good jumper. We hope to have him out relatively early because we don't think he wants the ground too soft."

Hang In There won his last three outings

De Rasher Counter: will have veterans' chases on his schedule

at Uttoxeter, Worcester and Market Rasen in the Paisley Park colours, but is probably better than merely a "summer jumper", according to the trainer.

"He's a smashing horse. He's not very big but he's athletic and was very good jumping round Market Rasen.

"The ground has meant he's been able to gain valuable experience all summer without necessarily tackling the toughest opposition," says Lavelle. "I'm not saying that's been good for British racing, but it has been for him and he's learned an awful lot in the process.

"Ground is important for him. There's a novice chase at the end of September at Newton Abbot and if we don't get loads of rain in the early part of the season.

"He's the sort of horse you'd love to have a look at also running in something like the Rising Stars Chase at Wincanton [in early November] as his finale before the ground goes completely, then look at something in the spring."

Red Rookie had an impressive win at Hereford, then fell at the last fence in the Arkle at the Cheltenam Festival but is worth following.

"He was raised 4lb for that to 140. I'm hoping now he's getting a bit older he'll finish up getting a little bit further than two miles.

"There are lots of quality two-mile, two-mile-two and two-and-a-half handicap chases and I think that even off 140 he's got plenty of wriggle room with his mark. I think he's a potentially really smart horse. He just hasn't had all the luck so far. There are plenty of options but he's a proper mudlark, so ground is going to be key. I'd love to look at something like the Haldon Gold Cup at Exeter with him, but we'll see."

If **Tarahumara** is anywhere near as good as his brother, See The World – who led, almost ran out, lost at least 15 lengths and still bizarrely won going away in a bumper at Wincanton in 2015 – he should be worth following.

"He's a lovely young horse. He was second in a bumper at Wincanton in January, then absolutely dotted up in a novice hurdle at Chepstow," says the trainer. "I'm not saying it was the strongest race in the world, but the way he did it was deeply impressive.

"His owner-breeders have given him loads of time to strengthen up and he'll go over fences this season. I think he's a lovely horse for the future. He's potentially smart and hopefully pretty well handicapped."

Shang Tang won a small novice chase at Newton Abbot in September last year before a niggling injury kept him off the track, but Lavelle managed to get a run into him over fences at Aintree, which should have set him up for this season.

He jumped so fluently that she describes him as "a smart horse with some very good form".

Top Dog was placed in two bumpers before landing a Listed bumper at Newbury in February. He was tried in the Champion Bumper at the Cheltenham Festival but failed to handle the heavy ground and was not given a hard race by Tom Bellamy.

"He's schooled well and will start off in a two-mile novice hurdle, possibly at the Cheltenham October meeting, although it may be that he comes to hand a bit sooner and goes somewhere else," says Lavelle.

"I love him. He's out of a sister to Altior, so he's entitled to be a nice horse. He's done it on the track so far and he's only learning and getting stronger."

Young Butler is a big, raw, half-brother to Put The Kettle On who won twice over hurdles and was placed twice last season.

"He's a work in progress who just got better and better. It was a lovely education last season and he's ready to go over fences this season. He's done well through the summer and looks a really promising horse for jumping fences this time around. We'll start him in a novice handicap chase and there are lots of options for him."

Voice Of Calm is described by her trainer as "a tough mare with a great attitude".

Lavelle says: "She had a good season over hurdles, winning and being placed and she's now ready to go and jump a fence. She's got plenty of size and scope and seems to act on pretty much any ground. There are some decent mares' novice chases around and there's a mares' programme in place, so why not use it. We'll look to try and get some black type with her."

Wouldubewell has won three times and never been out of the first four since coming from Ireland in 2020, taking her rating to 132. If she can win again and improve her rating into the high 130s, she could creep into the Welsh Grand National, a race which Lavelle feels is within her compass.

"She's a genuine mare who gallops, jumps, stays and has a great attitude," says the trainer.

Expect improvement from **Mumbo Jumbo**, who was repeatedly placed without winning last season but has grown up a lot over the summer, says Lavelle, who will send him novice handicap chasing.

"He's a fine, big, strapping horse who will be a different kettle of fish once we get him over fences."

Tedwin Hills finished fourth in his only bumper last season, then had a setback. It was nothing serious but it meant he couldn't get back on to the track.

From top: Killer Clown, Red Rookie and Top Dog

EMMA LAVELLE

MARLBOROUGH, WILTSHIRE

RECORD AROUND THE COURSES

	Total W-R	Per cent	Non-hcp Hdle	Non-hcp Chase	Hcp Hdle	Hcp Chase	N.H. Flat	£1 level stake
Wincanton	23-139	16.5	4-37	1-6	9-39	5-37	4-20	+12.91
Worcester	21-106	19.8	5-23	2-5	5-30	9-37	0-11	+18.27
Kempton	21-134	15.7	4-45	1-5	4-30	9-43	3-11	+97.40
Doncaster	19-80	23.7	5-23	0-1	5-16	6-27	3-13	-0.11
Newton Abbot	17-66	25.8	5-17	1-5	5-23	4-17	2-4	+66.00
Stratford	17-89	19.1	4-19	0-5	6-24	5-29	2-12	-5.03
Exeter	17-132	12.9	3-39	0-9	4-30	9-42	1-12	-35.75
Market Rasen	15-76	19.7	3-7	1-2	5-27	5-31	1-9	+11.95
Chepstow	14-99	14.1	8-37	1-4	3-18	1-26	1-14	-33.51
Uttoxeter	13-108	12.0	3-22	2-10	2-40	4-24	2-12	-49.14
Fontwell	12-90	13.3	2-23	0-2	6-29	3-29	1-7	-28.88
Taunton	11-66	16.7	1-15	0-1	6-23	4-21	0-6	-14.60
Plumpton	8-53	15.1	3-15	0-1	0-15	5-18	0-4	-26.48
Warwick	8-95	8.4	2-26	0-5	2-25	4-22	0-17	-24.67
Cheltenham	8-106	7.5	5-20	2-13	0-28	1-42	0-3	-68.63
Sandown	7-57	12.3	2-7	0-3	1-25	3-19	1-3	-22.33
Lingfield	6-25	24.0	3-11	1-2	0-1	2-11	0-0	+10.00
Haydock	6-39	15.4	1-7	0-5	4-20	1-6	0-1	+7.50
Southwell	6-45	13.3	2-12	0-0	1-14	2-12	1-7	-7.80
Huntingdon	6-70	8.6	3-18	1-5	2-20	0-13	0-14	-44.42
Newbury	6-113	5.3	1-28	0-5	1-31	3-33	1-16	-69.97
Hereford	5-35	14.3	2-9	1-1	1-13	1-7	0-5	-13.88
Ludlow	5-45	11.1	0-14	0-0	2-11	3-18	0-2	-20.00
Ascot	5-71	7.0	3-13	1-4	0-19	1-27	0-8	-47.75
Leicester	4-20	20.0	3-8	0-0	0-1	1-11	0-0	-7.77
Bangor	4-22	18.2	0-3	0-0	1-3	2-10	1-6	-1.75
Fakenham	3-12	25.0	2-4	0-0	0-2	1-6	0-0	-0.38
Ffos Las	3-34	8.8	2-13	0-1	0-12	1-5	0-3	-25.34
Aintree	3-39	7.7	0-6	0-2	2-9	0-18	1-4	-3.50
Lingfield (AW)	2-16	12.5	0-0	0-0	0-0	0-0	2-16	+0.50
Cartmel	1-1	100.0	0-0	0-0	1-1	0-0	0-0	+2.50
Kempton (AW)	1-8	12.5	0-0	0-0	0-0	0-0	1-8	+9.00
Musselburgh	0-1	0.0	0-0	0-0	0-1	0-0	0-0	-1.00
Kelso	0-1	0.0	0-0	0-0	0-0	0-1	0-0	-1.00
Ayr	0-3	0.0	0-0	0-0	0-1	0-2	0-0	-3.00
Sedgefield	0-4	0.0	0-0	0-0	0-1	0-3	0-0	-4.00
Newcastle	0-4	0.0	0-0	0-0	0-0	0-4	0-0	-4.00
Wetherby	0-7	0.0	0-3	0-0	0-2	0-2	0-0	-7.00

"He'll go novice hurdling. He is a natural jumper and has a lovely way of going. He travels well and looks like a horse who should make trade in novice hurdles before he goes chasing."

The goal for **Jemima P**, winner of four of her last five races, will be to earn some black type. "She's a beautiful, big mare who has rattled up through the ratings to a mark of 142."

Lavelle has taken delivery of several Irish point-to-pointers and is keen to extol their promise, and none is pleasing her more than **Tightenourbelts**. He was placed in a point-to-point at the end of December, the winner of which, Weveallbeencaught, was sold for £210,000 and has already won a bumper at Newbury.

"He's just got a bit of class about him. Everything he does at home just makes you smile. He'll start out in a novice hurdle and looks one of the exciting youngsters showing lots of promise."

Another ex-pointer to be followed closely is **Porter In The Park**, a winner and runner-up in two runs in Ireland this spring.

"She has a very nice way of going. She's very tough and will go straight into novice hurdles."

Two dark horses to follow are: **Dream In The Park** and **Hunting Brook**.

Interview by Lawrie Kelsey

Emma Lavelle and husband Barry Fenton keep an eye on a schooling session

After Emma Lavelle moved into her historic Bonita Stables at Ogbourne Maizey in Wiltshire, a little more than five miles from the stables of Alan King and Neil King, she described herself as "a queen among two kings".

CHARLIE LONGSDON

Why we can expect Snow in spring

WINNERS IN LAST FIVE SEASONS 47, 31, 29, 36, 44

SNOW LEOPARDESS has another date with the Grand National after the heavily backed mare caused a collective nationwide groan when pulled up in last season's race.

Five days before the National the mare, who spent two years out of racing to have a foal, was backed from 14-1 to 7-1 favourite as the mare's story caught the imagination of the betting public.

Owned and bred by Marietta Fox-Pitt, whose Olympic eventer son William is married to ITV's Alice Plunkett, the story resonated with the public, whose backing was a one-way stream of hard cash.

Being a dashing grey helped, as did the way she held on bravely to win the 3m2f Becher Chase over the National fences in December.

She'd won three out of three last season before lining up in the Grand National, not quite as elusive as the eponymous and endangered Himalayan cat, but a sight not to

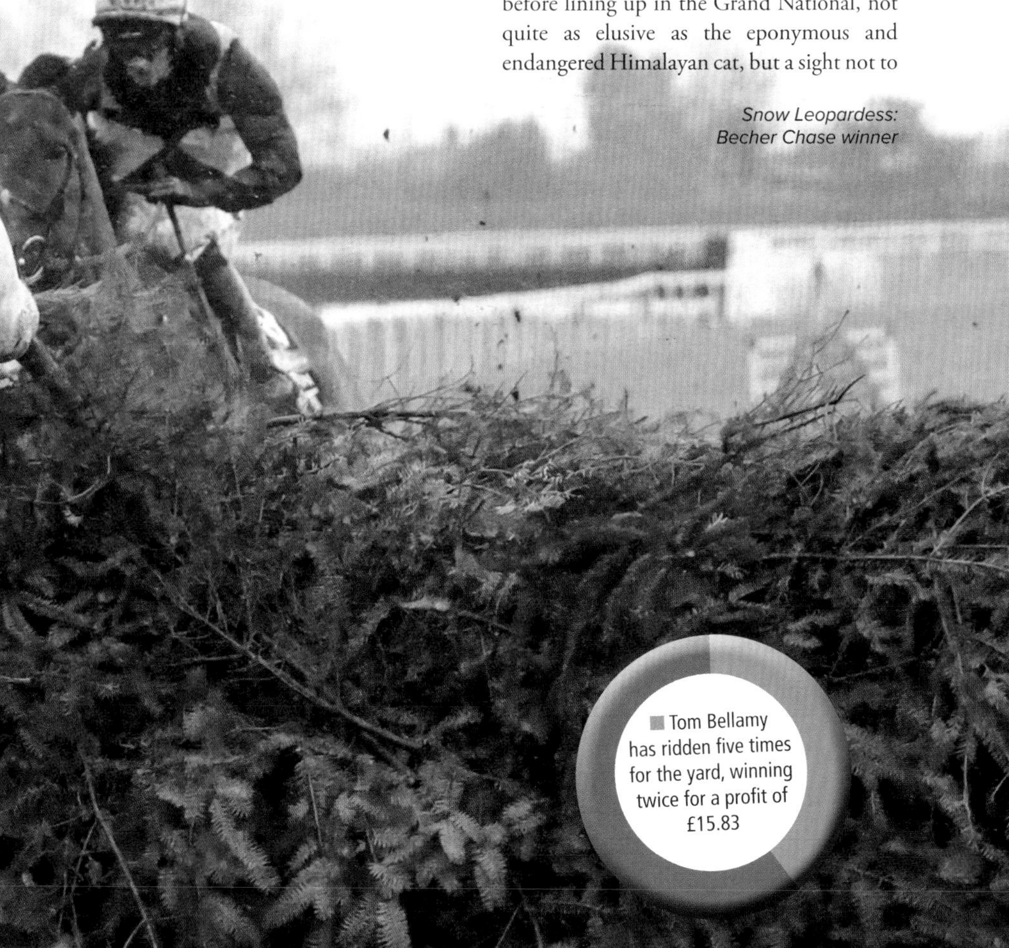

Snow Leopardess: Becher Chase winner

■ Tom Bellamy has ridden five times for the yard, winning twice for a profit of £15.83

be missed whenever she appears on the track.

"She'll probably have two or three runs by the end of January and that'll be it before the National," says her trainer Charlie Longsdon. "We'll go down the Becher Chase route, try and defend that, and we'll also try and get her qualified for the veterans' series in early November.

"There's one at Sandown on the sixth and another at Warwick on the 16th with the final at Sandown on Tolworth Hurdle day in early January."

The one thing ten-year-old Snow Leopardess needs above anything else is soft ground, which was her undoing at Aintree where Aidan Coleman was forced to pull her up at the 16th fence.

"In the week leading up to the National the ground was going against her and we knew it would be too quick; she needs to get her toe in," says Longsdon. "We dared to hope but we knew she needed more rain.

"The one thing we won't do this year is run her if the ground's not right; she won't go near the race if it's not soft. If that were the case, she'd probably go to stud."

Snow Leopardess's half-brother **Parramount** is also worth watching this year, not least because Longsdon reckons he's a far more talented individual.

"He didn't run last season but won a bumper the year before and was second in a couple of other bumpers.

"I've always said he's got more natural talent than his sister but not many would be as hard as she is.

"If we can get him to the track healthy and fit, there are some good novice hurdle races to be won with him. He's got more natural speed than she has and a higher cruising speed. My only worry is that he's not as tough as she is."

Castle Robin won three out of five outings in his first season over fences, winning at Exeter first time out and ending the campaign with victories at Doncaster and Wetherby.

"He looks after himself and only does just enough, which is quite good when it comes to the handicapping. I do think there's a decent handicap in him this season if we play our cards right," says Longsdon.

"There's a three-mile amateur riders' race at Cheltenham he might run in. I'll probably give him one simple run, then up him in class after that. I don't say he's ahead of the handicapper but off 134, he's one who can sneak into the bottom of a handicap and go and win a nice one somewhere."

Glimpse Of Gala won three of her seven appearances over hurdles and could go novice chasing this season.

"She's not very big but she's tough and as hard as nails. She just loves the game and is a pleasure to have around.

"She likes good ground and, although she's not that big, she'll jump a fence. She could be out in October. We'll take it one step at a time but there's the mares' challenger chase series we could go for."

Scene Not Herd won three of his four races last season, rising 21lb to a mark of 133 and could still be reasonably handicapped to win again.

"He can certainly win races where he is at the moment. He won't be out until the middle of November at the earliest and he'll have one of the spring festivals as a target when he'll get decent ground."

Rare Edition looks a class act and is confidently expected to win races in whatever discipline he takes part. He was second in an Irish point-to-point in December from which winners of bumpers and hurdle races have already emerged.

The winner Kalanisi Star was a runaway winner of a bumper at Gowran Park in March, and fifth-placed Path D'Oroux beat 22 rivals in a good Punchestown bumper. So there was no surprise when Rare Edition won a Southwell bumper on his debut for Longsdon.

"The form of his point-to-point race has worked out extremely well. The question now is whether we run him in another

CHARLIE LONGSDON

CHIPPING NORTON, OXFORDSHIRE

From top: Castle Robin, Scene Not Herd and Almazhar Garde

RECORD AROUND THE COURSES

	Total W-R	Per cent	Non-hcp Hdle	Non-hcp Chase	Hcp Hdle	Hcp Chase	N.H. Flat	£1 level stake
Uttoxeter	40-234	17.1	11-58	4-11	12-63	13-88	0-14	-40.15
Market Rasen	35-215	16.3	8-35	2-7	10-65	12-84	3-24	-86.59
Fontwell	31-142	21.8	10-28	0-2	6-43	11-50	4-19	-22.94
Worcester	31-212	14.6	5-41	1-14	12-64	9-69	4-24	+6.76
Southwell	30-173	17.3	8-40	2-6	9-57	6-45	5-25	+6.80
Huntingdon	30-210	14.3	7-53	4-11	8-73	9-53	2-20	-39.90
Stratford	25-134	18.7	3-29	2-6	11-41	6-48	3-10	+24.61
Warwick	25-192	13.0	6-55	1-9	5-56	8-49	5-23	-27.03
Wetherby	18-106	17.0	5-29	2-9	1-23	8-36	2-9	-27.41
Bangor	18-109	16.5	6-29	2-9	2-25	6-37	2-9	-28.62
Doncaster	18-160	11.2	4-47	0-7	4-41	8-55	2-10	-27.55
Ludlow	17-136	12.5	7-42	0-4	3-31	7-48	0-11	-42.22
Plumpton	14-89	15.7	5-32	0-2	2-20	6-31	1-4	-36.83
Towcester	13-81	16.0	1-24	4-10	2-20	5-21	1-6	-31.19
Kempton	13-117	11.1	2-17	1-5	3-35	7-54	0-6	-27.05
Carlisle	10-46	21.7	5-9	2-6	0-7	2-19	1-5	-25.58
Sandown	9-92	9.8	1-6	1-4	0-23	7-56	0-3	-3.00
Musselburgh	8-33	24.2	6-11	0-0	0-8	2-14	0-0	+12.87
Hereford	8-43	18.6	2-11	1-1	0-9	4-20	1-2	-15.40
Ascot	7-85	8.2	0-16	0-7	2-28	3-24	2-10	-8.50
Newcastle	6-19	31.6	2-5	0-0	2-3	1-9	1-2	-1.51
Lingfield	6-37	16.2	1-11	1-3	1-7	3-16	0-0	+0.74
Exeter	6-44	13.6	0-5	2-3	2-16	2-18	0-2	-7.13
Haydock	6-64	9.4	1-5	1-2	2-22	1-30	1-5	-10.50
Chepstow	6-85	7.1	1-15	0-3	1-26	4-38	0-3	-53.77
Aintree	6-90	6.7	1-17	0-3	3-25	2-32	0-13	-58.97
Sedgefield	5-22	22.7	0-4	1-2	1-4	3-10	0-2	-6.81
Newton Abbot	5-33	15.2	1-2	1-3	1-13	2-14	0-1	-16.55
Leicester	5-45	11.1	0-16	2-3	0-4	3-22	0-0	-18.40
Wincanton	5-51	9.8	0-5	1-2	1-21	3-21	0-2	-8.50
Newbury	5-104	4.8	0-18	0-6	2-20	3-49	0-11	-69.63
Cartmel	4-14	28.6	0-1	0-0	1-5	3-8	0-0	+10.00
Hexham	4-17	23.5	1-6	2-3	1-1	0-5	0-2	-7.28
Fakenham	4-28	14.3	0-8	0-2	1-7	3-11	0-0	-16.16
Cheltenham	4-146	2.7	1-17	0-10	2-42	1-63	0-14	-116.00
Perth	3-11	27.3	0-0	1-2	0-4	2-5	0-0	+3.73
Southwell (AW)	2-7	28.6	0-0	0-0	0-0	0-0	2-7	+2.50
Kempton (AW)	2-15	13.3	0-0	0-0	0-0	0-0	2-15	-10.33
Kelso	2-18	11.1	0-2	0-0	0-3	2-13	0-0	-8.25
Catterick	2-22	9.1	1-7	0-0	0-7	1-7	0-1	-15.46
Ffos Las	2-26	7.7	0-4	0-1	2-9	0-10	0-2	-11.50
Ayr	1-15	6.7	1-2	0-2	0-5	0-6	0-0	-13.90
Taunton	1-28	3.6	0-3	0-0	1-13	0-12	0-0	-23.00
Lingfield (AW)	0-7	0.0	0-0	0-0	0-0	0-0	0-7	-7.00

bumper under a penalty or go jumping," says Longsdon.

"He jumps great. He's quite a big horse and can win his novice hurdle before he goes on to better things. He's only five, so I'm not in a hurry with him.

"I'd like to hope he can run in a couple of nice novices. But, like all novices, they need to go and win, then win with a penalty before they step up in grade. He's certainly one of the youngsters who I think is good enough to do that."

Everyonesgame won his bumper at Doncaster last season and was then second in a decent bumper at Warwick under a penalty.

"He's like Rare Edition, a nice horse and definitely above average. He'll run in a novice hurdle, then hopefully in better novice races later on in the season."

Gaelic Park is a half-brother to high-class chaser Chantry House and the useful chaser The Last Day of whom big things are expected.

"He won his bumper at Warwick and was

Ardbraccan: looks to have a future in juvenile hurdles

third at Uttoxeter where he probably paid for taking on a 300-grand horse [Master Chewy] up the home straight. He beat that but then got collared close home by two others, giving a penalty away as well.

"He's a nice horse from a good family and I'd like to think over two and a half miles on soft ground he could be running in a decent novice hurdle towards the end of the season after winning a couple."

Almazhar Garde was Longsdon's only runner at the Cheltenham Festival last season when finishing 11th of 20 in the Kim Muir.

"He wasn't disappointing, he ran a grand race. He probably wants three and a half miles round Cheltenham, to be honest.

"He ran very well in a lot of those big staying races. He was placed in three of them."

One of those was the Southern National at Fontwell in November and that could be one of his targets this season.

"He'll probably start out at the Cheltenham meeting in October in a three-mile handicap chase, and once he's done that we'll probably look at some of those regional Nationals like the Southern National.

"He was second in that last year and was probably a little unlucky not to win. He could go to Wetherby again for the North Yorkshire Grand National as well. He was second in that too and again was probably unlucky not to win.

"He's an experienced old handicapper who's near the top of the handicap. So we should play our cards right and probably take some weight off his back."

Ardbraccan is a recruit from Richard Hannon's Flat team for whom she won at Newmarket over seven furlongs as a two-

year-old a fortnight after being beaten a length and a half by Inspiral over course and distance.

"She's ready to go juvenile hurdling. She's got a good attitude, jumps well and could be a fun one to follow. Her main target will be the Listed race for fillies only at Aintree's Becher Chase meeting in early December."

Guetapan Collonges won two chases last season, then fell in a two-runner race at Sedgefield.

"He's a horse who was unlucky last season. I'd like to think he can progress and could be one for those regional staying races."

Hector Javilex won two novice hurdles in March quite nicely but is still a novice until November and Longsdon will take advantage by aiming him at the Persian War Novices' Hurdle at Chepstow in early October.

"It's a Grade 2 but it's not the strongest race in the world because a lot of the better hurdlers are not ready yet," says Longsdon.

Little Bruce: missed last season but is back for long-distance chases

Charlie Longsdon gained experience with Nicky Henderson and in the USA with Todd Pletcher before taking out his licence to train in 2006.

Little Bruce didn't run last season and returned in July at Uttoxeter with a promising second.

"He'll go to Warwick in late September and then go for a cross country race. He's a stayer, so he has options and might go for some of those regional Nationals," says Longsdon.

Tea For Free took a bit of time to get going last season but was placed in four of his five outings over hurdles. It was when he was sent over fences, however, that he really came alive and won readily over just short of three miles at Huntingdon in May.

"He looks a nice horse to go chasing with off his mark of 112," says Longsdon. "He's an improver and there's plenty of room for improvement. He'll be out either at Southwell at the end of September or he could wait for Chepstow in October."

The Mighty Arc won a couple of "not that great races" over fences at Worcester and Sedgefield last season and rose 13lb to a mark of 123.

"He's a horse you have to admire; he always tries his heart out and is a really genuine, honest, likeable horse who probably punches above his weight a little.

"He'll go for two and a half to three-mile novice chases and be out in November."

Western Zephyr is an interesting hurdling recruit. After winning his only English point-to-point unchallenged in December, he landed a 13-runner bumper in January, then led for a long way in a strong Aintree bumper before finishing tailed off.

"He's a nice horse who'll be running in a novice hurdle come the end of October and I'll be disappointed if he can't be competing at a higher level further down the road."

Realisation is another of Longsdon's group of promising youngsters who is expected to step up on her second in a four-year-old mares' point-to-point in Ireland in February. She is expected to go down the mares' bumper route.

Stroll On By is another who can be followed confidently as he goes hurdling after finishing second in his first two bumpers at Carlisle and Sedgefield.

"He probably should have won one of them when beaten a nose and he looks a nice horse for the future," says Longsdon.

"He'll go novice hurdling in October and is one of a team of bumper horses from last year who look as nice a crew as we've had in a long time."

Interview by Lawrie Kelsey

PAUL NICHOLLS

WINNERS IN LAST FIVE SEASONS 143, 176, 96, 135, 127

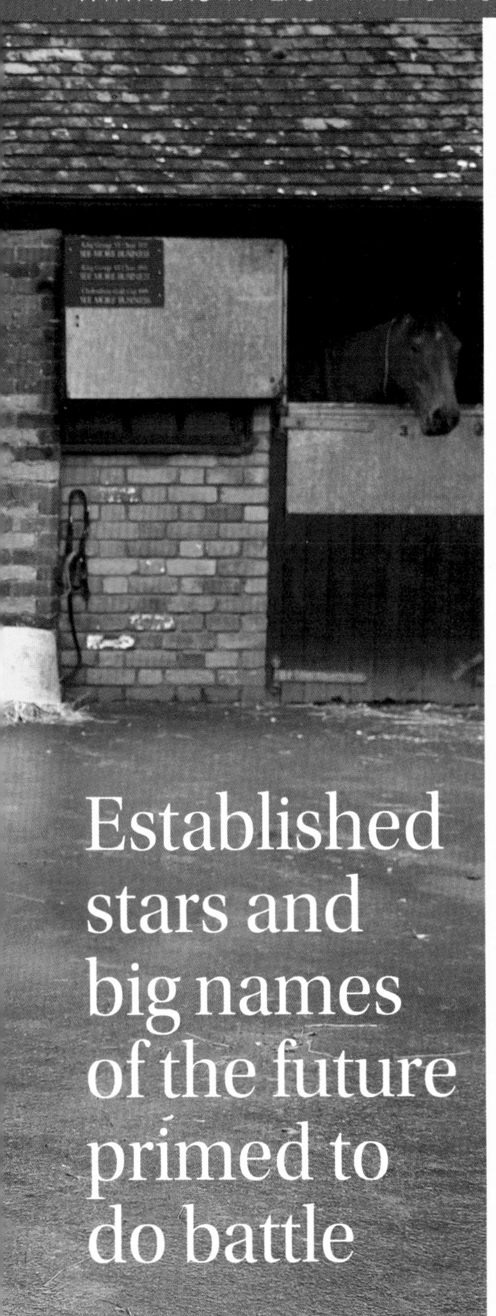

Established stars and big names of the future primed to do battle

PAUL NICHOLLS turned 60 in the spring but he displays the high-octane drive and restless enthusiasm of someone half his age and it is going to take a mighty effort from Nicky Henderson or Dan Skelton to stop the 13-times champion from marching to another trainers' title.

While the Irish may be dominant in the Gold Cup nowadays, when it comes to the King George, Nicholls is king, and he is already lining up a formidable team for Kempton on Boxing Day in his bid to put win No. 13 on the board.

Leading the charge will be **Bravemansgame** and the brilliant seven-year-old is described as "the ideal sort for the race in his second season over fences". This silky-slick jumper lost his unbeaten record over fences at Aintree, after being pulled out of Cheltenham at the last minute. And that no-show may have contributed to his downfall, his trainer reckons. "We trained him to peak at the Festival and by the time he got to Aintree he was over the top. It was as if he'd had a run at Cheltenham." And he added: "Defeat does not diminish his potential in the slightest and I retain the utmost faith in him. He could prep for Kempton in Ascot's 1965 Chase."

Other King George probables are established stars **Clan Des Obeaux** (big-race form figures 132) and **Frodon**, the 2020 winner, and despite the fact both are rising 11 their form last season suggests they are as good as ever. Clan may kick off shouldering top weight in the Coral Gold Cup (old Hennessy) but he is being trained to peak in the spring. "His big objective will be Aintree, when he'll try to win the Grade 1 Bowl for the third year running."

The first half of Frodon's season is all about getting him to Down Royal in November for a repeat bid in the Champion Chase.

Pic D'Orhy: careful placement looks to be key to the talented performer

Looking further ahead, Nicholls says: "Interestingly, the handicapper is tempting us to run in another big handicap at some point as he dropped us 6lb to 158 after his defeat in the Ultima at Cheltenham."

Nicholls could end up four-handed in the King George as he would love another crack at the race with last year's fourth **Saint Calvados**, who this season will be ridden by his new owner David Maxwell.

The stable's two-mile star **Greaneteen** is lethal round Sandown and it's no surprise to hear he will try to repeat last season's victories in the track's pair of Grade 1s over that trip, the Tingle Creek and Celebration Chase.

Hitman, another smart two-miler, didn't quite fulfil the high hopes his trainer entertained for him last season, but Nicholls says: "Despite not winning, he put up four top-class efforts and I still think he's a Grade 1 winner waiting to happen." After showing he gets 2m4f when runner-up at Aintree he may start off back there in the Old Roan Chase. Only six, he has time on his side.

Pic D'Orhy started to get his act together over fences last season and should gain further success at Grade 2 level, although his trainer warned: "There's a danger he could fall in between two stools, being high in the handicap but not quite up to Grade 1 level." Careful placement will be the key.

Clan Des Obeaux's likely appearance in the Coral Gold Cup off a rating of 172 will leave many of his rivals out of the handicap,

> There's a danger he could fall in between two stools, being high in the handicap but not quite up to Grade 1 level

but not so his stablemate **Threeunderthrufive** who would look very attractively weighted on 10st 5lb and is likely to end up a leading player. The talented seven-year-old's career record stands at 9-13 and could have been even more impressive had connections opted for the National Hunt Chase rather than the shorter Brown Advisory at Cheltenham. Nicholls says: "He's a smashing prospect for all the good staying handicaps but wouldn't want the ground too soft." He could prep for Newbury in a handicap hurdle to preserve his chase rating.

A five-year strike-rate of 38% at Plumpton translates to a profit of £15.86 for backers

Nicholls likes to lay one out for the Haldon Gold Cup and one possible candidate this November is **Il Ridoto**. He had a breathing operation in the summer and his trainer says: "He needs to be held up in a fast-run race over 2m and can go well in a big handicap when they go fast up front and he can come late." No wonder the Exeter Grade 2 is described as "ideal".

The trainer always relishes a challenge and he has set himself a tall order trying to get **Topofthegame** back on the track. The talented but fragile ten-year-old has been off for the last two seasons but Nicholls outlined tentative plans: "We're going to try to get him to the Grand National, with one run beforehand, possibly in the Cotswold Chase."

In no division does Nicholls look stronger than with his novice chasers, with at least seven inmates possessing Graded potential.

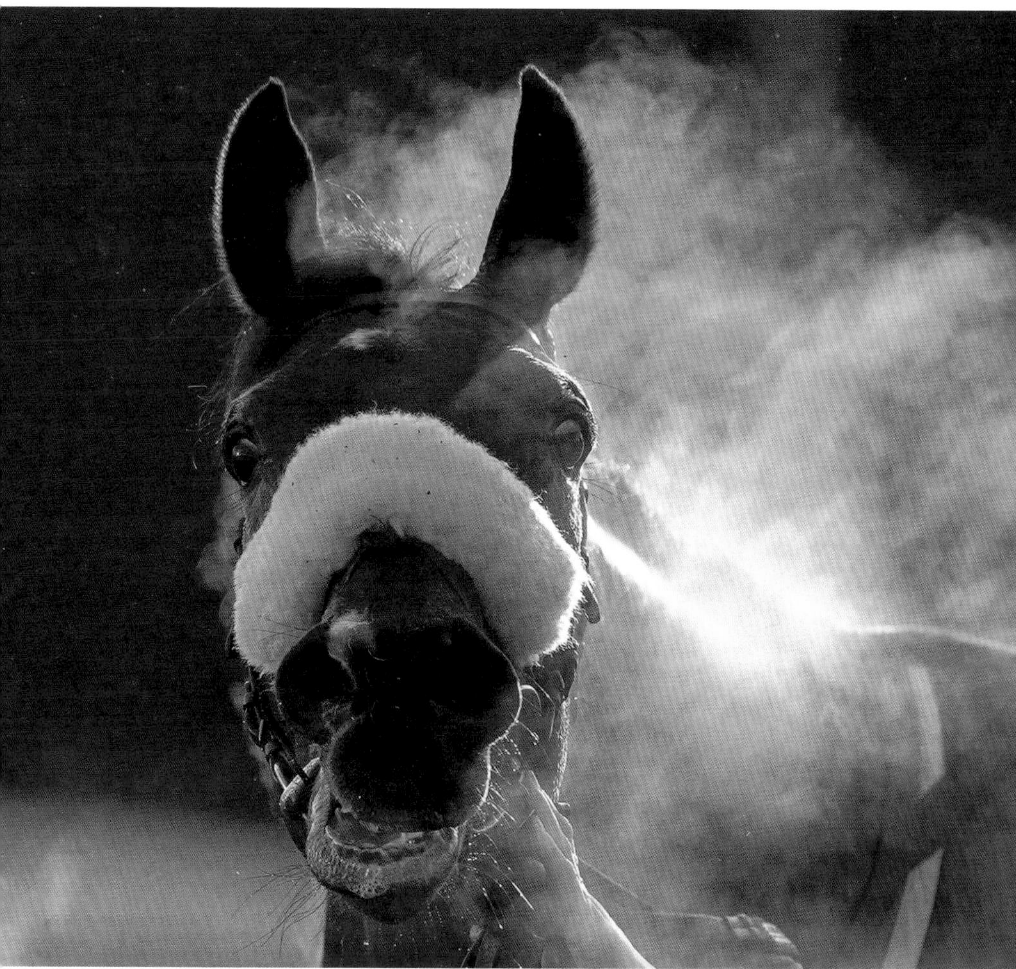

Gelino Bello is the one who makes his eyes light up. Described as being "a bit babyish" in the early part of last season, he matured with racing and his victory in the Grade 1 Sefton at Aintree marked him down as a fine prospect for staying novice chases. Nicholls says: "I can't wait to get him started and one of the Graded chases at Newbury in late November would be a target on the back of a run somewhere."

Monmiral looks made for fences and if the trainer had had his way the former top-class four-year-old would probably have gone chasing 12 months ago. But he stayed over hurdles in his second season when things didn't always go to plan. Nicholls says: "I'm itching to see him jump a fence and I hope he'll develop into one of our leading novices."

A chasing career for smart staying hurdler **McFabulous** was put on hold last autumn after he suffered a minor setback. There have in the past been doubts about how he would take to jumping fences, but the trainer was delighted by his improved hurdling last season, dispelling any jumping concerns. Given his preference for decent ground, expect to see him out fairly early. "In an ideal

PAUL NICHOLLS

DITCHEAT, SOMERSET

From top: Monmiral, Stage Star and Complete Unknown; (left) McFabulous

RECORD AROUND THE COURSES

	Total W-R	Per cent	Non-hcp Hdle	Non-hcp Chase	Hcp Hdle	Hcp Chase	N.H. Flat	£1 level stake
Market Rasen	39-198	19.7	18-70	1-2	14-81	2-26	4-19	-54.12
Fakenham	31-139	22.3	13-56	0-2	11-50	5-21	2-10	-17.62
Uttoxeter	21-106	19.8	11-43	1-3	5-38	1-13	3-9	-7.27
Southwell	18-105	17.1	11-37	1-3	3-42	3-13	0-10	-56.94
Huntingdon	15-57	26.3	6-23	0-0	2-16	1-6	6-12	-10.92
Stratford	15-108	13.9	8-44	0-0	2-40	3-14	2-10	-59.07
Fontwell	13-52	25.0	6-18	0-2	2-18	2-8	3-6	-3.72
Perth	13-55	23.6	5-17	0-1	6-23	1-12	1-2	+11.79
Newton Abbot	10-29	34.5	5-11	0-0	2-10	2-3	1-5	+20.05
Ayr	8-34	23.5	4-9	1-4	0-10	0-7	3-4	-9.65
Taunton	8-45	17.8	3-25	1-1	2-14	2-4	0-1	-24.84
Bangor	8-66	12.1	3-25	1-3	1-19	3-13	0-6	-44.64
Wincanton	7-31	22.6	4-16	0-0	0-7	1-6	2-2	-9.27
Leicester	6-19	31.6	5-11	1-1	0-3	0-4	0-0	+26.20
Sedgefield	6-24	25.0	2-6	0-1	1-5	0-6	3-6	-9.57
Warwick	6-81	7.4	4-37	0-4	0-16	0-9	2-15	-18.33
Musselburgh	5-11	45.5	1-2	0-0	1-2	2-5	1-2	+5.85
Newcastle	5-24	20.8	3-10	0-0	0-4	1-3	1-7	-8.66
Worcester	5-32	15.6	3-10	0-1	2-16	0-4	0-1	-16.55
Ludlow	5-45	11.1	4-18	0-3	1-15	0-5	0-4	-35.96
Carlisle	4-15	26.7	2-6	1-4	0-2	0-0	1-3	-4.06
Doncaster	4-19	21.1	1-7	1-2	1-5	0-3	1-2	+20.07
Plumpton	4-23	17.4	2-9	0-0	1-10	1-4	0-0	-5.76
Kelso	4-23	17.4	1-7	0-1	2-10	1-5	0-0	-10.21
Hereford	4-31	12.9	0-10	1-2	2-13	0-2	1-4	+7.00
Chepstow	4-33	12.1	1-13	1-3	1-7	0-6	1-4	-8.00
Lingfield	3-10	30.0	0-1	1-1	2-5	0-3	0-0	+14.00
Catterick	3-14	21.4	2-8	0-1	1-4	0-1	0-0	-4.13
Ffos Las	3-15	20.0	0-3	1-1	0-5	1-2	1-4	-0.63
Haydock	3-16	18.7	0-6	0-1	2-7	0-1	1-1	-3.83
Lingfield (AW)	2-13	15.4	0-0	0-0	0-0	0-0	2-13	-6.30
Ascot	2-14	14.3	0-5	0-2	2-5	0-1	0-1	+5.00
Aintree	2-30	6.7	0-8	0-1	2-11	0-8	0-2	-19.67
Cheltenham	2-42	4.8	1-12	0-3	1-20	0-4	0-3	-31.50
Exeter	1-7	14.3	0-2	0-1	0-1	0-1	1-2	-3.50
Hexham	1-7	14.3	0-2	1-3	0-2	0-0	0-0	-4.90
Sandown	1-15	6.7	0-5	1-2	0-6	0-1	0-1	-7.00
Cartmel	1-16	6.2	1-6	0-0	0-8	0-2	0-0	-13.25
Kempton	1-22	4.5	1-10	0-3	0-7	0-2	0-0	-18.50
Wetherby	1-35	2.9	0-18	0-4	0-7	1-3	0-3	-32.50
Newcastle (AW)	0-1	0.0	0-0	0-0	0-0	0-0	0-1	-1.00
Towcester	0-10	0.0	0-1	0-2	0-6	0-1	0-0	-10.00
Newbury	0-26	0.0	0-15	0-0	0-5	0-1	0-5	-26.00

world he'd have a run possibly at Chepstow's first meeting and then go to the Rising Stars at Wincanton; over 2m5f on good ground round a flat track, that race is made for him."

Challow winner **Stage Star**'s novice hurdle season ended in anti-climax with two non-completions at Cheltenham and Aintree. He had a breathing operation in early July and Nicholls says: "I hope that will help him recapture his smart form of early last season now he goes over fences."

Silent Revolution was another who failed to run up to his best at Cheltenham, but the trainer revealed: "He'd been held up after throwing a splint so we were forced to chuck him in at the deep end at the Festival." Still lightly raced, he is highly regarded.

Last year was a fill-in season for **Samarrive** but that didn't stop him taking his career record to 4-7. Nicholls predicts: "He can really come into his own now he switches to fences and I have high hopes for him."

Complete Unknown took time to get the hang of jumping hurdles last season but

Paul Nicholls has won the King George VI chase, Kempton's Boxing Day showpiece and Britain's second most prestigious race after the Cheltenham Gold Cup, a record 12 times with: See More Business (1997, 1999), Kauto Star (2006, 2007, 2008, 2009, 2011), Silviniaco Conti (2013, 2014), Clan Des Obeaux (2018, 2019), and Frodon (2020).

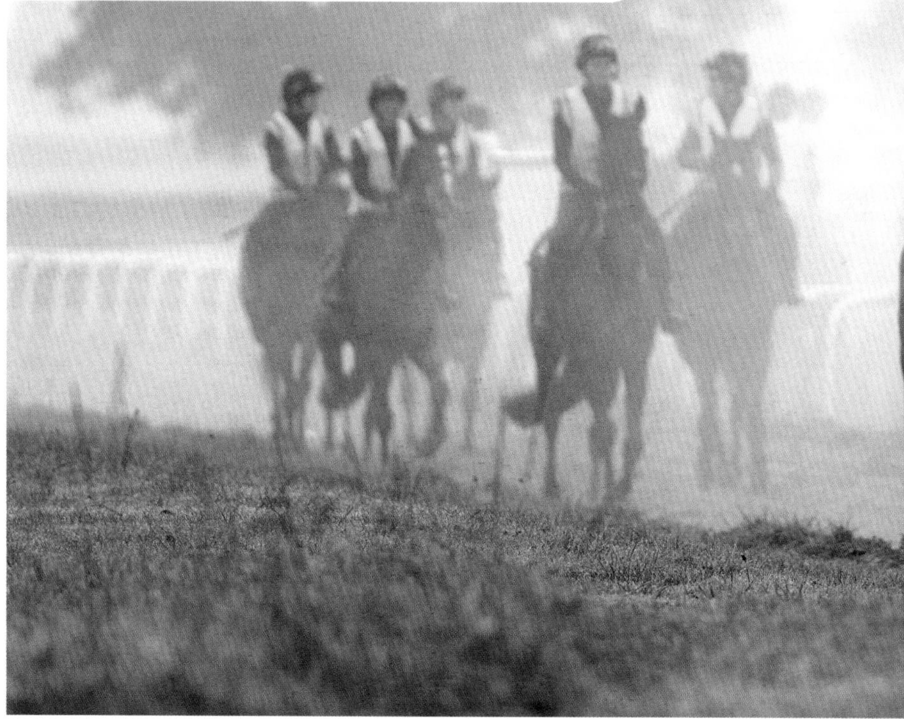

came good in the spring and is expected to continue his improvement over fences.

Considering he's well bred for the job and looks the part, **Flash Collonges** has so far been a shade disappointing over fences, but he was troubled with his breathing and that's been sorted out by a summer op. His trainer predicts: "He's a lot better than he's shown so far."

Nicholls' owners have shelled out small fortunes on young Irish point-to-pointers in the hope that not all the emerging new talent ends up with Messrs Mullins, Elliott or De Bromhead. It's early days, of course, but on pedigree, looks and racecourse performance, the undeniable promise is sufficient to put them in the 'could be anything' category.

At €360,000, **Jenny Wyse** was the most expensive. Gorgeous filly though she is, the daughter of Flemensfirth, who won her maiden point by 20 lengths in April, she is seen more as a long-term prospect and will be given plenty of time.

Expected to be more forward is **Stay Away Fay** (305,000gns), who showed immense promise when winning at Lingstown last December, the venue at which Bravemansgame first revealed his potential. He nearly ran for Nicholls in the spring and shouldn't be long in getting off the

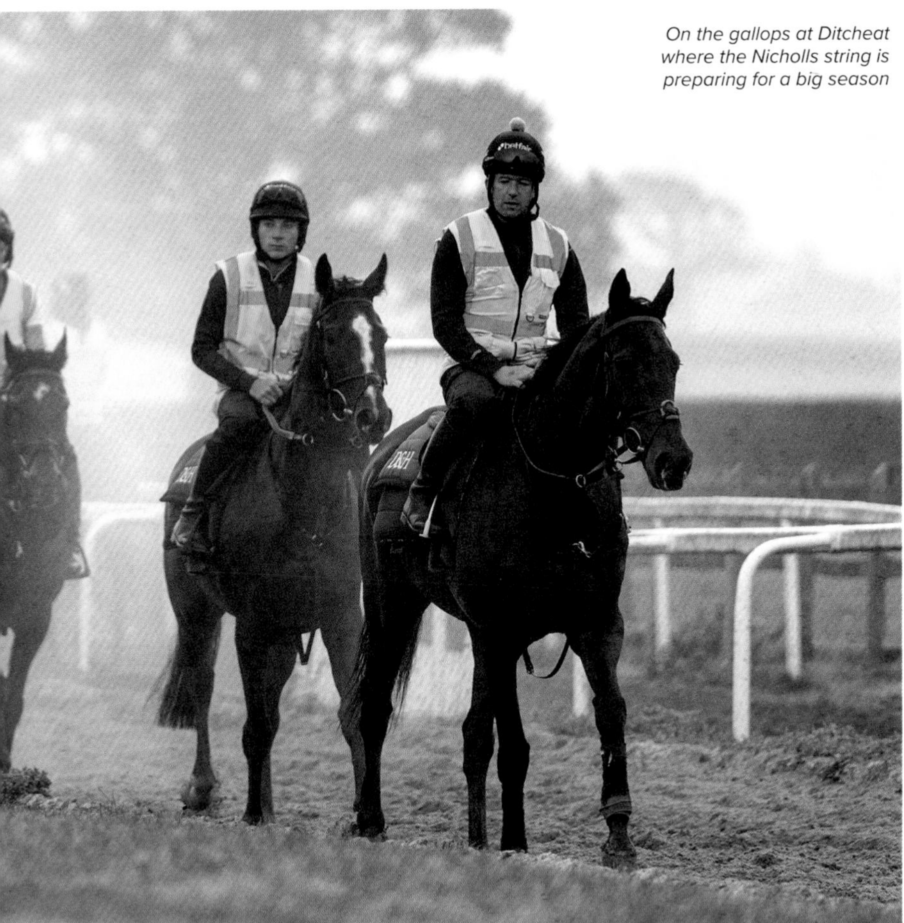

On the gallops at Ditcheat where the Nicholls string is preparing for a big season

mark in a bumper or novice hurdle.

Seeyouinmydreams (235,000gns) has everything going for her. She comes from a great family, was very impressive on her only start and could be a big force in mares' bumpers.

There are a pair of lovely prospects by Doyen: the athletic **Divilskin** (245,000gns) clocked a fast time when winning his only start in April, while **Captain Teague** likewise hacked up on his only start on soft ground. They shouldn't take long to show their potential over hurdles.

Castleward showed big improvement from his first run to his second and was another to leave clock watchers purring with delight.

The De La Heys are numerically the biggest owners at Ditcheat this season and they have a fine long-term prospect in **Wrappedupinmay**, who came home virtually alone on his debut at Dromahane.

Kirkistown winner **Hermes Allen** set his new owners back 350,000gns but he is not over-big and there may be others with more scope – like, for example **Byorderofthecourt**, a really impressive looker who has come via English point-to-points.

With Nicholls' preference for horses with sufficient scope for fences, there's always going to be a small number who stick to hurdlers long enough to progress through the ranks. **Knappers Hill** is one notable exception. Having spent the first part of last season thinking he was a Flat horse, he finally got the hang of jumping hurdles and finished on a high in a £50,000 handicap. His trainer sees him as an obvious contender for decent races like the Elite at Wincanton, the Greatwood at Cheltenham and the Gerry Feilden.

Those sorts of races could also be on the agenda for **Hacker Des Places**, whose performances at the backend, when he struck up a good partnership with Angus Cheleda, suggested he is improving fast.

Among the novice hurdlers, Nicholls is particularly sweet on **Henri The Second,** who can be excused his one defeat after he was struck into at Aintree passing the stands. He returned with quite a nasty injury but is fine now. Nicholls says: "He had to overcome greenness before registering his two wins and there's masses of improvement to come. With his high knee action, he'll always be suited by some cut."

We are advised to put a line through **Timeforatune**'s one bumper defeat at Newbury in February as the yard was not firing on all cylinders at the time. Nicholls added: "I liked the way he galloped all the way to the line for his two victories, suggesting he'll get further than 2m over hurdles."

Holetown Hero, still a maiden after three runs in bumpers, is seen in the mould of stablemate Kandoo Kid, who left his bumper form well behind when switching to hurdles. "He's had a breathing operation and I'm sure there's more to come."

Dancingontheedge is rated a decent prospect for mares' novice events. Harry Cobden had a job pulling her up when she won her only start in a Worcester bumper, which was a surprise as she hadn't shown much at home.

Iliade Allen is expected to step up markedly on her only run for the yard when down the field in the Grade 2 mares' bumper at Aintree, when she ran too free.

The team has been swelled by 24 unraced four-year-olds who did their pre-training in the spring at the nearby youth academy run in Ditcheat by top point-to-point rider Will Biddick. Three to have caught Nicholls' eye in their work this autumn are **Isaac Des Obeaux**, a three-parts brother to Clan Des Obeaux; **Hurricane Danny**, who is related to a stack of winners; and **Fire Flyer,** a son of Shantou who could be the most forward of the trio. All should make their presence felt in bumpers.

Of the new French imports, easily the most interesting is **Golden Son**. A leading

juvenile hurdler over there last winter, he chased home a future Grade 1 winner on his only run over fences in the spring but is expected to remain over hurdles and is set for a return to France in November for the very valuable Prix Renaud du Vivier, the French Champion Hurdle for four-year-olds.

Another to have been showing up well in his work is **Beau Balko**, a half-brother to Nicky Richards' useful hurdler Soft Risk and winner of his only start in a bumper at Moulins in the Provinces.

Ivaldi won his only start at Fontainebleau in March and could be one for the Persian War Novices' Hurdle at Chepstow.

Blueking D'Oroux, by the little-known but promising sire Jeu St Eloi, has twice run well at Auteuil behind Losange Bleu, probably the leading three-year-old over there, and is expected to be up to contesting some of the better juvenile events over here.

Iliko D'Olivate was beaten a whisker on his only hurdles start at Compiegne in March; he had some well-regarded types behind him and should turn out useful.

We are going to hear a lot more of **Grivetana,** who took time to adapt to British hurdles after coming from France before improving quickly in the spring. Nicholls says: "We are still learning about her but I really like her and predict there's a lot more to come as, off 121, she's on an attractive mark." He is keen to add the filly has progressed particularly well over the summer.

Flemenstide has taken an age to mature and, given his size, needs fences to be at his best. "That said," observes Nicholls, "he's better than a 122-rated hurdler in my book" so don't be surprised if he pops up in a handicap hurdle first.

Dual French Flat winner **Irish Hill** was forced to play second fiddle to a useful opponent at Warwick in May but Nicholls still reckons he's on a good mark and he's another to have progressed during the close season.

Taunton winner **Inca De Lafayette** "had run up a bit light and was over the top" when returning to the Somerset track in April and handicaps should come his way. And soft-ground lover **Sabrina** is "still improving and on a very workable handicap mark", a remark that also applies to **Huflower**. Nicholls says: "It has taken an age for this giant of a horse to get the hang of jumping, but I'm sure we'll see plenty of improvement."

Breathing issues have meant **Sonigino** hasn't really progressed since he came to Britain but Nicholls reports: "He's had a summer op and without doubt has the ability to win races over fences off his mark of 119."

Interview by Ben Newton

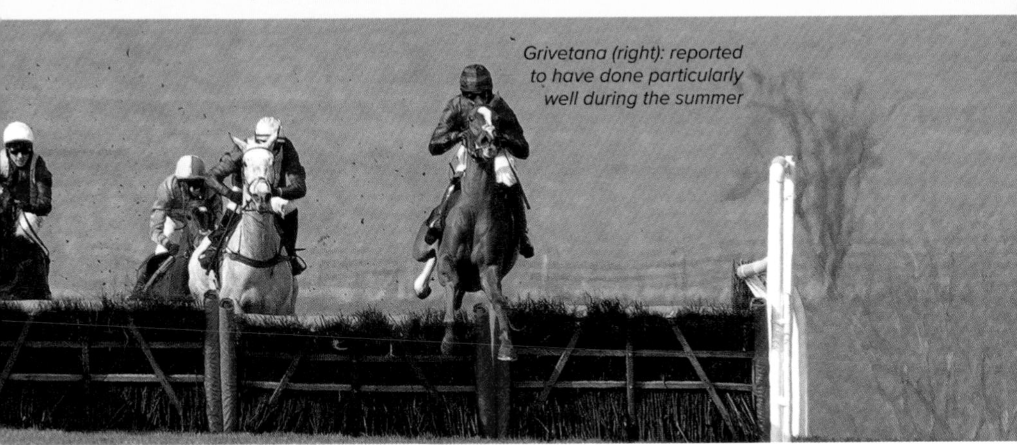

Grivetana (right): reported to have done particularly well during the summer

The future looks bright after quick start from new base

HALFWAY to equalling their record season and going rattlingly well. That's Ben Pauling's new Naunton Downs yard, set in 166 acres of rolling Cotswolds countryside.

By early September, Pauling had already sent out 25 winners this summer at a strike-rate of 31 per cent, as well as managing to have in excess of 70 per cent of runners reach the first three.

That is impressive by any standard, so has the move from rented stables at Bourton Hill Farm four miles away to bespoke premises brought about the transformation?

"Yes, I do believe that," says Pauling

Global Citizen: victorious in the Grand Annual at Cheltenham

WINNERS IN LAST FIVE SEASONS 44, 33, 18, 44, 36

emphatically. "They do seem to be a particularly healthy bunch of horses and I firmly believe it's because of the environment they're in.

"I put the success down to having healthy horses. If a horse is healthy, then the chance of having any respiratory problems is less.

"And if a horse is well, then it's easier to train, and if it's easier to train, then you normally get to the racecourse in better form than if you've had a stop-start preparation.

"It's been a fabulous start. When you move to a new yard you are always concerned that the horses might take time to settle in, while we take a while to see what works and doesn't work on the gallops.

"All in all, it's been pretty seamless to date and we're enjoying it very much, and we're very excited about what the future holds."

Building from scratch began in January 2021 and Pauling and his wife Sophie and their string of 85 moved in five months ago.

"In one day we rode every single horse across country in four lots. It was great fun," remembers Pauling.

And leading the team this season is **Global Citizen**, 28-1 winner of the Johnny Henderson Grand Annual at the Cheltenham Festival in March.

It was his first victory since landing a Grade 2 chase at Kempton in December 2019, although he had performed creditably in Graded races over hurdles and fences in the interim, including fourth in the 2020 Arkle.

"He did us proud, winning multiple

Grade 2s, but he's a very exuberant individual and I just feel he put himself to the sword a fair few times culminating in his fourth in the Arkle.

"We were thrilled with him but I felt it left its mark and it took us 18 months to build his confidence back.

"So it was a great day for everyone when he won the Grand Annual in such emphatic style in March.

"I did think his confidence was back and he'd run a good race, although the form boys wouldn't have him for toffee because he was a ten-year-old.

"He'll handle any ground except tacky conditions. He was out very early on September 12 in a two-mile chase at Worcester as a prep race for the American National at Far Hills on October 15 over two miles four.

"You could argue his best form is over two miles, although I firmly believe he'll be okay over two and a half."

It's a race Pauling knows well having saddled Jaleo to finish fifth in 2018.

"He seems to be in the form he finished last season in. He seems very well in himself and we couldn't be happier with him.

"Although he's ten rising 11, I'd like to think he could possibly mix it back in some decent handicaps, if not in some Graded or Listed races somewhere along the line. He's not had a hard life and I'd like to think he's got plenty left in the tank this season.

"He's rated 143 and realistically he's got to be rated north of 150 to be going into level-weights races, but we'll keep an open mind."

Next in line is **Shakem Up'Arry**, owned by former football manager Harry Redknapp, who ended the season with a third in the Red Rum Chase at Aintree.

"I don't think we've seen the best of him. I think he'll undoubtedly improve for having come to this yard, as lots of them have. He seems very well in himself.

"Everyone who rides him seems to think he wants two and a half miles, although over that distance he hasn't been seen at his best, but I quite fancy a stab at the Paddy Power Gold Cup at Cheltenham on November 12, which is over two and a half, first time out because he's very good fresh.

"I think he could do very well in that if I have him wound up and A1 first time out.

"He's a very nice horse and looks very well handicapped at the moment. He's an exceptional jumper and his forte is being able to go through heavy ground without even realising it. He's able to take horses out of their comfort zone early doors because he's just relentless."

Make a bold note of the seven-year-old **Slipway**, who won the Highland National at Perth at the backend of last season over 3m6½f, "jumping from fence to fence impeccably".

"In my eyes he's the perfect Grand National type. He's a lovely horse, a proper staying chaser, and an unbelievable jumper," says Pauling.

"He's made for the job. If ever I've trained a horse that was designed to jump those fences and go four and a half miles, it's him.

"And he's owned by the Embiricos family, who won the National with Aldaniti, so it wouldn't be off their radar either."

Slipway is rated 133 and will need to go up around a stone to get into the National, but Pauling is confident he can.

Pauling's only previous runner in the National was Kildisart in April, who blundered and unseated James Bowen at the Chair.

Bowtogreatness redeemed himself after falling three out when leading on debut over hurdles at Ffos Las by winning two novice hurdles very easily last season.

"I was going to chuck him in at the deep end at Cheltenham, but I didn't think he was quite ready," says Pauling, "so I took him to Aintree where I thought he'd need three miles in a Grade 1 novice hurdle.

"I did him an injustice; he has far more speed than I thought. He travelled far too well and didn't relax at any point.

"We'll drop him back to two and a half miles, if not two miles, over fences as a

BEN PAULING

NAUNTON, GLOUCESTERSHIRE

From top: Shakem Up'Arry, Slipway and Bowtogreatness

RECORD AROUND THE COURSES

	Total W-R	Per cent	Non-hcp Hdle	Non-hcp Chase	Hcp Hdle	Hcp Chase	N.H. Flat	£1 level stake
Huntingdon	23-137	16.8	6-45	5-10	7-44	3-23	2-15	+48.93
Southwell	22-120	18.3	5-25	1-2	9-59	3-15	4-19	+15.22
Doncaster	19-112	17.0	11-42	2-9	4-36	2-18	0-7	+50.52
Warwick	17-145	11.7	5-46	0-1	2-38	2-21	8-39	-62.50
Worcester	16-100	16.0	2-16	2-5	2-40	8-31	2-8	+20.19
Newbury	16-102	15.7	5-33	1-4	3-25	3-24	4-16	-17.90
Kempton	14-84	16.7	6-29	2-4	2-26	3-19	1-6	+16.44
Fontwell	13-83	15.7	1-15	0-3	5-30	6-27	1-8	-24.34
Market Rasen	12-81	14.8	4-16	0-1	4-36	3-21	1-7	-36.88
Ffos Las	11-38	28.9	6-11	1-2	2-8	2-10	0-7	+50.08
Stratford	11-48	22.9	1-9	0-2	5-14	4-19	1-4	+21.20
Uttoxeter	8-75	10.7	2-18	0-0	3-33	3-13	0-11	-37.88
Carlisle	7-27	25.9	2-7	1-3	3-9	0-2	1-6	+11.75
Bangor	7-64	10.9	0-9	1-4	3-25	2-15	1-11	-17.25
Ludlow	7-75	9.3	5-44	0-2	0-12	1-7	1-10	-37.05
Cheltenham	7-109	6.4	1-17	2-14	2-45	2-20	0-13	-23.00
Newton Abbot	5-28	17.9	1-6	0-0	3-15	1-6	0-1	-12.73
Ascot	5-52	9.6	2-12	1-3	1-17	0-13	1-7	+2.50
Plumpton	4-22	18.2	1-11	0-0	2-9	1-2	0-0	+18.00
Haydock	4-25	16.0	2-6	0-2	1-12	1-4	0-1	+0.70
Leicester	4-34	11.8	3-16	0-1	0-4	1-13	0-0	+0.37
Taunton	4-35	11.4	0-10	0-0	1-16	3-7	0-2	+25.58
Hereford	4-38	10.5	2-17	0-0	2-14	0-6	0-1	+25.50
Sandown	4-50	8.0	0-10	1-3	2-22	1-14	0-1	-20.25
Aintree	4-52	7.7	1-11	0-2	0-15	2-16	1-8	-22.00
Wincanton	3-37	8.1	0-13	0-1	2-11	0-7	1-5	-23.17
Exeter	3-47	6.4	1-15	0-3	1-12	0-9	1-8	-34.75
Lingfield	2-14	14.3	0-5	0-0	2-3	0-6	0-0	+39.25
Fakenham	2-14	14.3	0-3	0-1	1-7	1-2	0-1	-8.80
Kelso	2-17	11.8	0-6	0-3	0-2	2-6	0-0	-5.00
Sedgefield	2-22	9.1	1-4	0-0	0-8	1-8	0-2	-16.63
Wetherby	2-40	5.0	2-14	0-3	0-13	0-7	0-3	-33.27
Chepstow	2-43	4.7	1-17	0-0	0-6	0-10	1-10	-34.50
Wolverhampton (AW)	1-2	50.0	0-0	0-0	0-0	0-0	1-2	+27.00
Hexham	1-4	25.0	1-2	0-0	0-1	0-1	0-0	-1.13
Musselburgh	1-8	12.5	0-3	0-0	0-0	1-3	0-2	-1.50
Newcastle	1-9	11.1	1-6	0-0	0-1	0-0	0-2	-6.38
Perth	1-12	8.3	0-1	0-0	0-2	1-9	0-0	-1.00
Catterick	1-13	7.7	1-6	0-0	0-3	0-3	0-1	-11.67
Kempton (AW)	0-1	0.0	0-0	0-0	0-0	0-0	0-1	-1.00
Ayr	0-5	0.0	0-2	0-0	0-2	0-0	0-1	-5.00
Lingfield (AW)	0-5	0.0	0-0	0-0	0-0	0-0	0-5	-5.00

novice chaser. I think he could be well handicapped and I hope he can become a smart novice chaser. I think he's versatile on trip and will eventually stay three miles."

Del La Mar Rocket posted some good performances in bumpers and was expected to be a smart novice hurdler last season.

"He just didn't know how to get out of the way of the hurdles in his first two runs," says Pauling.

"Then his jumping got better and better and he won at Ffos Las. He'll start off in a handicap hurdle somewhere on soft ground and then go novice chasing. He's a staying type with a touch of class about him."

Densworth was highly regarded before his racecourse debut in a Uttoxeter bumper last November, but virtually pulled himself up.

"We were concerned that he just wasn't right at all, so we sent him off to the vets and he did a bone scan and found any amount of little issues, but nothing astronomic," says Pauling.

Time and patience paid off handsomely because he won a Worcester bumper on his next outing in June by 15 lengths.

"He's done a lot of schooling and is a fairly good jumper, so I think he could be a tidy little novice hurdler and is one to keep on the right side of."

Another for the notebook is **Fine Casting**, who won twice over hurdles, including a decent race at Newbury in January.

"I think he's very talented and the right side of the handicapper," says Pauling. "He'll probably run in a novice handicap hurdle first time out before going novice chasing.

"He took a little while to jump with fluency last season, so because of that I'm half thinking he could have a couple of runs in handicaps and could end up in some decent handicap hurdles before we chuck him into a fence."

Harper's Brook won an English point-to-point and ran in a Wetherby bumper, which he looked as though he was going to win until stopping suddenly in the last furlong, finishing third just under four lengths behind Hillcrest, who went on to win four more races and be rated 148.

"He scoped filthy dirty, so that showed me how useful he was," says Pauling. "He then went to Carlisle and won what turned out to be a useful novice hurdle very nicely."

He flopped in a Grade 2 at Sandown and fell at Cheltenham before running second at Exeter, then finished the season with an impressive victory under a penalty at Ffos Las.

"He's a big, gorgeous chasing type, so he'll go straight novice chasing and I think he'll need to be targeted at races rather than run willy-nilly. We have a nice bunch of novice chasers and I can see him figuring in some of the better novice chases from Christmas on."

Henry's Friend was very backward last season and didn't show much at home to excite Pauling. So his racecourse debut was delayed until May in a maiden hurdle at Aintree in which he was the outsider of four, but he sluiced in by 20 lengths and looks one to follow closely.

"I thought he'd run nicely but I didn't expect him to do what he did. He was very green but he went and won as he liked.

"I'm not sure the race was up to much but the way he did it, and as green as he was, I can only think he's got a big engine and a good attitude to the job. I think he'll go on to be a decent novice hurdler."

Nestor Park: might show significant improvement over long distances

Malinello didn't run last season after picking up a ligament injury in his foot, but before that he had shown decent form over hurdles, winning at Market Rasen and finishing second at Kempton and Wincanton.

"I think he's going to be better over a fence and if he returns with the ability previous to his little setback, I'm sure he's going to be a nice novice chaser as well. He'll be out early November time."

Trying to get a win over fences into **Nestor Park** has been "painful", according to Pauling, who has watched him finish second and third in the Mandarin Chase at Newbury,

I'm looking forward to stepping him up above three miles – maybe something like the Eider
MANSIONBET

as well as be placed in other good handicaps. Victory finally in February came at Newbury over 2m6½f.

"I think he's better over three miles. I actually think this season could be quite exciting for him because he hasn't tried the marathon trips and when he does I think he can come into his own.

"So I'm looking forward to stepping him up above three miles. Maybe something like the Eider could be right up his street because he's a relentless galloper that loves soft ground. I think we've hit the ceiling with the trip we're at, but I think with a step up in trip we'll see a vast improvement in the horse.

"Sadly, I don't think he's ever going to be a National horse. I just don't think he's brave enough but I'll probably campaign him as if he were, then avoid the big day itself."

Sending **One Touch** over fences two seasons ago "just did not work", but a return to hurdles has rekindled his fire and he has won his last two outings in handicaps this summer.

"There were a couple of races where he bled and he completely lost his confidence, and it's taken a year or so to get him back on track," says Pauling.

"He won by ten lengths at Bangor without coming off the bridle and looked quite good. I never doubted him. I always thought he had ability, he just needed to believe in himself, and I think he could progress quite nicely this season.

"He's not a summer horse. I just wanted to

Not At Present: multiple winner over hurdles and could develop into a useful novice chaser

run him in a few races where he was going to regain confidence. I think he could be seen in some competitive handicap hurdles."

Quinta Do Mar will go novice chasing this season after winning a couple of handicap hurdles last year and could be good enough to contest Listed races. "He's a tough individual with the right attitude," says Pauling.

"**Severance** is probably the unluckiest horse I've ever trained," says Pauling. "He was supersonically competitive last season, hitting the crossbar several times. He was second at Cheltenham, fourth at Kelso, second at Aintree and second in the Swinton Hurdle at Haydock.

"He's been tweaked physically and he'll be aimed at the Welsh Champion Hurdle. I'll be very surprised if he doesn't win one big pot this season. He wears his heart on his sleeve, so stepping him up in trip might improve him."

Watch out for when David Bass is in the saddle – backing him blind for the yard yields a profit of £51.37
Ben Pauling's bespoke new stable has been built in an estate of 166 acres which contains an 18-hole golf course and a tennis court.

Not At Present won four times and was second twice in seven outings over hurdles last season but the first time he was tried over fences at the end of July "he looked a bit gormless", according to his trainer.

"I got him out nice and early because he does appreciate better ground. He's a big horse who doesn't realise the ability he's got. I think over three miles novice chasing he could improve to become a really nice young chaser."

Pauling has "any amount" of what he regards as really smart prospects among some talented Irish point-to-pointers who he expects will make their mark, and has selected this quartet: **Amarillobymorning** (second in his only Irish outing); **Joe Dadancer** (fell at the last when poised to win on his only Irish outing); **No Questions Asked** (British winner of only race); and **Storminhome** (winner of one of his two Irish races).

Interview by Lawrie Kelsey

JAMIE SNOWDEN

Kiltealy Briggs heads to victory at Haydock last December, a win that saw him become his stable's leading earner

WINNERS IN LAST FIVE SEASONS 49, 23, 46, 31, 35

Kiltealy and co ready to add to impressive stats

IF OWNERS studied statistics before choosing a trainer, they'd surely be forming an orderly queue outside the gates of Jamie Snowden's Folly House stable in Lambourn.

Punters, too, should by now be dialled into Snowden's statistical strength having realised that following his runners is no blind folly.

Last season he finished 19th in the trainers'

BETVICTOR
3

From top: Hardy Du Seuil, Git Maker and Legends Ryde; (left) Pisgah Pike

JAMIE SNOWDEN

UPPER LAMBOURN, BERKSHIRE

RECORD AROUND THE COURSES

	Total W-R	Per cent	Non-hcp Hdle	Non-hcp Chase	Hcp Hdle	Hcp Chase	N.H. Flat	£1 level stake
Fontwell	33-176	18.7	10-51	2-4	8-46	8-39	5-36	-22.71
Ffos Las	15-64	23.4	6-20	0-2	4-21	4-14	1-7	-7.91
Worcester	15-112	13.4	3-36	3-7	1-27	8-35	0-7	-43.42
Stratford	14-75	18.7	5-24	1-5	3-12	3-28	2-6	-19.07
Newton Abbot	14-90	15.6	4-27	1-7	4-29	5-20	0-7	-37.92
Uttoxeter	14-112	12.5	4-29	0-6	3-36	6-31	1-10	-27.60
Southwell	11-79	13.9	4-21	0-0	5-27	2-20	0-11	-13.93
Catterick	10-22	45.5	3-7	2-2	0-5	3-5	2-3	+3.22
Haydock	9-27	33.3	1-5	2-4	2-6	4-10	0-2	+12.20
Exeter	9-53	17.0	3-19	0-5	2-15	3-12	1-2	-2.67
Ludlow	9-54	16.7	3-16	2-3	1-15	1-6	2-14	-11.30
Wincanton	9-77	11.7	2-27	1-5	1-23	4-18	1-4	-33.20
Market Rasen	9-80	11.2	3-29	1-3	1-20	2-17	2-11	-10.46
Wetherby	8-49	16.3	3-14	2-6	2-7	0-10	1-12	-8.84
Huntingdon	8-93	8.6	2-36	1-6	1-21	2-20	2-10	-61.64
Hexham	7-28	25.0	4-10	1-4	0-6	0-5	2-3	-11.55
Sedgefield	7-36	19.4	5-16	0-0	0-6	1-8	1-6	+6.90
Chepstow	7-56	12.5	2-19	0-0	2-17	2-11	1-9	-7.76
Plumpton	7-86	8.1	3-30	1-4	0-20	2-22	1-10	-51.34
Carlisle	6-19	31.6	2-3	1-3	1-4	0-4	2-5	+7.69
Fakenham	6-33	18.2	1-9	0-2	2-5	3-13	0-4	-4.40
Hereford	6-34	17.6	0-7	0-2	1-11	5-11	0-3	+0.32
Lingfield	6-34	17.6	6-20	0-0	0-2	0-12	0-0	-9.71
Bangor	6-54	11.1	2-10	0-7	0-14	2-18	2-5	-22.37
Cheltenham	6-70	8.6	1-18	1-6	1-19	3-19	0-8	-10.50
Taunton	5-53	9.4	3-18	1-2	0-18	0-7	1-8	-13.43
Kempton	4-29	13.8	1-7	0-3	1-11	2-8	0-0	-15.75
Kelso	3-8	37.5	2-3	0-1	1-1	0-3	0-0	-0.08
Doncaster	3-27	11.1	1-10	0-1	1-12	0-1	1-3	-11.00
Leicester	2-17	11.8	0-3	0-3	2-4	0-7	0-0	-7.00
Warwick	2-38	5.3	1-7	0-2	0-10	0-11	1-8	-31.47
Newbury	2-40	5.0	0-12	0-1	1-12	1-7	0-8	-18.00
Musselburgh	1-2	50.0	0-0	1-1	0-1	0-0	0-0	+1.25
Perth	1-3	33.3	1-2	0-0	0-0	0-1	0-0	-1.39
Newcastle	1-5	20.0	1-2	0-0	0-2	0-1	0-0	-3.60
Ayr	1-6	16.7	0-0	0-2	1-3	0-1	0-0	+11.00
Cartmel	1-15	6.7	0-3	0-1	0-4	1-7	0-0	-11.00
Ascot	1-18	5.6	0-5	0-2	1-4	0-4	0-3	-12.50
Aintree	1-28	3.6	0-5	0-2	0-7	1-11	0-3	-11.00
Sandown	1-29	3.4	1-6	0-9	0-8	0-4	0-2	-10.00
Southwell (AW)	0-1	0.0	0-0	0-0	0-0	0-0	0-1	-1.00
Kempton (AW)	0-2	0.0	0-0	0-0	0-0	0-0	0-2	-2.00
Lingfield (AW)	0-6	0.0	0-0	0-0	0-0	0-0	0-6	-6.00

table based on numbers of winners, with just three trainers above him having managed a better 46 per cent strike-rate of winners to individual runners.

In a record-breaking season of 49 winners, 37 per cent of his runners finished in the first two and a phenomenal 65 per cent of all runners were placed, bringing in £480,000 prize-money.

His biggest two earners were Kiltealy Briggs (£36,440) and Hardy Du Seuil (£32,425), both of whom won twice from seven outings.

Kiltealy Briggs was successful at Haydock and Musselburgh, and was placed at Aintree and Kempton before being pulled up in the Grade 3 Ultima Handicap at the Cheltenham Festival, then ending his season by being pulled up in a Grade 2 at Ayr.

"He was a second-season novice last year and probably reaped the benefit of that because his jumping was very good. He won twice and was placed in Graded company as well.

"He slightly disappointed at the back of the season when we stepped him up to three miles. We thought he was going to be a three-mile staying chaser but he looks to be better at just sub-three miles.

"So we're going to aim him at the Grand Sefton at Aintree in November over two miles five. We'll give him a prep race in October, maybe Chepstow or Market Rasen."

Hardy Du Seuil landed chases at Carlisle and Hereford, before ending the season with three seconds at Haydock, Kelso and Southwell.

"He had a very good season novice chasing last year as a four-year-old with a weight-for-age allowance. He won a couple of times and was second in a Grade 2 at Haydock.

Super Survivor scores in emphatic style at Carlisle

"His jumping was a little bit of a flaw and we felt he could have won both the Kelso and Southwell races.

"So we're going back over hurdles with him this season and going for the Welsh Champion Hurdle. He's got bags of speed, so we'll stick to two miles."

Git Maker will be a quiz question for the Folly House team in years to come as the horse who gave Snowden a full house of victories at all British courses when one of the three novice hurdles he landed from four starts last season came at Newcastle on April 9.

It followed Kiltealy Briggs' win two months earlier at Musselburgh as the first of the last two tracks Snowden needed.

Git Maker is "a proper staying chaser for the future", says Snowden, who adds: "He's going novice chasing this season but he wants soft ground, so he'll be out whenever it rains."

Ga Law was a very promising recruit from France in January 2020 where he won his only start over hurdles as a three-year-old in heavy ground.

That autumn he racked up a hat-trick of novice chases, including the Grade 2 Rising Stars at Wincanton, then ran a creditable third in the Grade 1 Henry VIII at Sandown. In February last year he finished second in the Grade 2 Pendil Novices' Chase at Kempton.

"We decided to skip Cheltenham and aim him at the two-and-a-half mile novice at Aintree, but unfortunately he developed a leg. So we decided to give him plenty of time off.

"He's fully recovered. He's been cantering away for over a month and is in great order.

Jamie Snowden used to ride out for Nigel Twiston-Davies while still at school and during his gap year before going to Newcastle University he worked as an assistant trainer for a Flat yard in New Zealand.

■ The stable has a five-year strike-rate of 27% at Wetherby and a profit of £9.41

"We'll look to get a run into him in October, then hopefully go for the Paddy Power at Cheltenham in November."

Not far behind Snowden's top two earners was **Legends Ryde**, who started her campaign with a win in a Ffos Las mares' novice handicap chase, and bookended the season with wins in two chases at Fontwell.

"She was a very good bumper horse but slightly lost her way when she went novice hurdling. She picked up where we thought she was all along when she went chasing and had a fabulous year last season. She won three and was second to L'Homme Presse at Ascot in a graduation chase.

"There's a Listed mares' chase at Market Rasen in November for her, although she might go to Hereford before that. But she doesn't have to stick to those mares' races. She can run against the boys.

"She's a lovely mare and could be one for staying handicap chases and perhaps those local Nationals."

Milldam was placed in three novice hurdles in France before arriving in Lambourn and his first taste of British racing came at the Cheltenham Festival in March when he was a creditable 13th of 21 in the Boodles Juvenile Hurdle.

"He reminds me very much of where Ga Law and Hardy Du Seuil were last season and the season before. So we're going to go novice handicap chasing with him this season. Hopefully, he can utilise that four-year-old weight-for-age allowance and be as good as the other two."

Park This One was a British point-to-point winner who quickly made his mark in bumpers, finishing second at Hereford in February before comfortably landing an Exeter bumper.

"He was pretty impressive when he won that bumper, so he could be quite exciting when he goes novice hurdling. He wants soft ground, so he'll be out whenever it starts raining."

Pisgah Pike won at Market Rasen in July and returns for a Listed race at the track in late September, while last season's progressive novice chaser **Soldier Of Destiny** will be aimed at the Grade 2 Old Roan Chase over two and a half miles at Aintree in late October.

"He'll have a prep race. He's still a novice over hurdles, so there's the option of that. He's a bold-jumping galloper and similar to Present View, who won for us at the festival [2014]," says Snowden.

Super Survivor, just touched off in an Irish point-to-point, won two of his three novice hurdles in the spring and was runner-up in the other.

"He was bought as a novice chaser and that's where we're going this season with him," says Snowden.

A trio for the notebook are: **Tallow For Coal**, who won a couple of chases last season and could be one for local Nationals; **You Wear It Well**, who won a mares' bumper and was second in another and will go mares' novice hurdling this season; and **Up For Parole**, winner of a decent handicap hurdle at Haydock and not disgraced in the Lanzarote at Kempton. "There should be a decent handicap in him," says the trainer.

Snowden, who has bought 20 acres of land for expansion in Upper Lambourn close to his present yard, is delighted with an intake of talent from the point-to-point field from whom he is hoping for big things this season.

They include **Colonel Harry**, who bolted up by six lengths in a point-to-point at Ballyvodock; **Bill Jack**, second in a point-to-point at Curraghmore; **Roger Pol** second in a Ballygarry point-to-point; easy Monksgrange winner **Regarde**; and **Doc McCoy**, a British winning pointer.

Also worth making a note of is **Passing Well**, runner-up in a well-contested Punchestown bumper at the end of April who could be "very good", and **Mollycoddled**, a three-year-old bred by Camilla, the Queen Consort.

Interview by Lawrie Kelsey

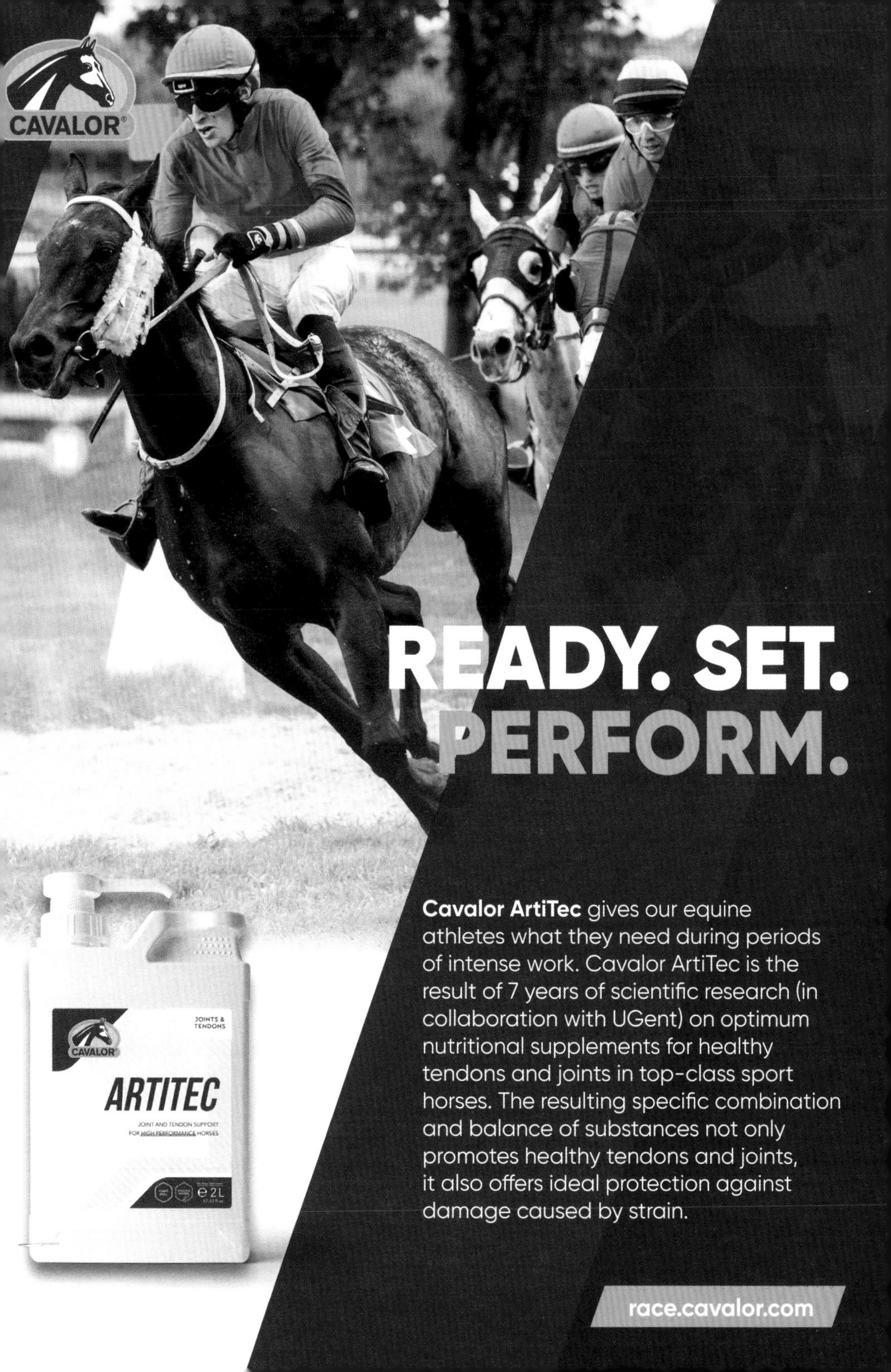

JOINTS & TENDONS
CAVALOR
ARTITEC
JOINT AND TENDON SUPPORT
FOR HIGH PERFORMANCE HORSES
℮ 2L

Secret National target

THE Grand National could be a major target for **Secret Reprieve** but he needs his season to have some rhythm running through it – a little Merseybeat perhaps.

So maybe Evan Williams and his team could adopt The Beatles song 'Rain' which was on the B-side of the group's 1966 hit single 'Paperback Writer' as they urge the heavens to open.

Because rain is exactly what the 2020 Welsh

WINNERS IN LAST FIVE SEASONS 53, 44, 49, 53, 52

Secret Reprieve: winner of the 2020 Welsh Grand National at Chepstow

Grand National winner needs so that he can run in races this side of Christmas as Williams maps out the eight-year-old's season.

"Last season was a write-off," says the Vale of Glamorgan trainer. "Things just didn't happen for him. He never got a chance to run before Christmas. It didn't rain last year and he needs to start off on the right ground. He went straight to the Welsh National and it was too much for him."

Secret Reprieve finished a respectable fifth at Chepstow before being pulled up in deep ground almost two months later in Haydock's Grand National Trial.

"I wouldn't judge him on last year; I still have belief in him. I still believe there's plenty left in the locker and that he could be a Grand National horse.

"He just needs to get his career back on track. It would be nice to get a bit of rhythm through his season. And it's not that he needs cut in the ground; he handles nice ground. These sorts of horses just need to start off on the right ground."

Despite his Haydock flop, Secret Reprieve

From top: Prime Venture: Bold Plan and Coole Cody; (left) Annsam

EVAN WILLIAMS

LLANCARFAN, VALE OF GLAMORGAN

RECORD AROUND THE COURSES

	Total W-R	Per cent	Non-hcp Hdle	Non-hcp Chase	Hcp Hdle	Hcp Chase	N.H. Flat	£1 level stake
Ffos Las	87-692	12.6	18-144	2-19	32-243	27-241	8-45	-157.57
Ludlow	57-454	12.6	15-119	3-15	12-111	23-180	4-29	-179.92
Chepstow	54-418	12.9	17-99	1-7	14-135	21-153	1-24	+22.21
Newton Abbot	33-235	14.0	5-46	4-19	13-87	11-78	0-5	-69.35
Exeter	27-149	18.1	3-33	5-22	13-48	6-42	0-4	+24.37
Taunton	27-227	11.9	3-56	0-2	14-91	9-71	1-7	-47.21
Uttoxeter	25-230	10.9	7-52	1-7	7-91	9-70	1-10	-25.18
Sedgefield	21-85	24.7	4-12	0-0	4-27	12-44	1-2	+17.15
Worcester	20-164	12.2	5-46	1-4	8-52	5-60	1-2	-43.15
Fontwell	15-107	14.0	3-19	0-1	5-44	7-38	0-5	-31.69
Warwick	13-102	12.7	3-25	1-6	4-37	5-25	0-9	-17.92
Stratford	13-136	9.6	4-27	0-3	2-31	7-65	0-10	-68.63
Haydock	12-122	9.8	1-18	0-7	10-48	1-47	0-2	+10.25
Cheltenham	12-158	7.6	2-28	1-9	2-58	7-60	0-3	-13.00
Hereford	12-168	7.1	1-43	3-5	3-61	5-54	0-5	-97.03
Southwell	11-144	7.6	6-42	0-4	2-59	1-33	2-6	-70.40
Bangor	10-131	7.6	2-37	0-6	3-39	5-40	0-9	-72.73
Carlisle	9-32	28.1	2-7	2-7	1-6	4-10	0-2	-2.22
Fakenham	8-47	17.0	2-9	1-3	1-12	4-22	0-1	-6.71
Market Rasen	8-64	12.5	1-8	0-4	4-31	3-20	0-1	-20.67
Wincanton	8-74	10.8	1-19	1-1	3-24	2-23	1-7	-17.26
Catterick	6-23	26.1	1-6	0-3	1-7	3-6	1-1	+7.24
Huntingdon	6-37	16.2	3-8	0-3	1-10	1-13	1-3	-13.47
Plumpton	6-42	14.3	0-6	0-0	3-18	3-15	0-3	-5.88
Aintree	6-70	8.6	2-13	0-2	1-20	3-30	0-5	-23.50
Sandown	6-84	7.1	1-13	1-5	1-33	3-32	0-1	-25.75
Ayr	5-11	45.5	2-2	0-0	1-3	2-6	0-0	+20.96
Leicester	5-36	13.9	0-9	0-0	1-9	4-18	0-0	-12.67
Ascot	5-69	7.2	0-12	0-3	1-25	4-27	0-2	-28.00
Lingfield	4-27	14.8	0-7	0-1	1-9	3-10	0-0	-9.00
Kempton	4-48	8.3	3-15	0-2	1-12	0-18	0-1	-27.25
Newbury	4-76	5.3	2-12	0-1	2-25	0-26	0-12	-40.01
Perth	3-15	20.0	1-1	1-2	1-3	0-9	0-0	+1.00
Doncaster	3-22	13.6	1-5	0-2	1-5	1-9	0-1	-6.25
Cartmel	3-26	11.5	0-0	0-3	1-11	2-12	0-0	-3.50
Wetherby	2-17	11.8	1-4	0-2	0-3	1-8	0-0	-5.33
Musselburgh	1-1	100.0	0-0	0-0	1-1	0-0	0-0	+3.50
Kelso	1-5	20.0	0-2	0-1	0-1	1-1	0-0	+0.00
Newcastle	1-12	8.3	0-4	0-1	0-3	1-4	0-0	-1.00
Hexham	0-3	0.0	0-1	0-0	0-1	0-1	0-0	-3.00
Lingfield (AW)	0-3	0.0	0-0	0-0	0-0	0-0	0-3	-3.00

was made as short as 12-1 for the Grand National in April, but he was rated too low to make the 40-runner line-up and failed to make the cut by two.

If anyone fancies getting in early, Secret Reprieve can be backed at 33-1 for this season's National.

Meanwhile, Williams is still trying to find a successor to the ill-fated Silver Streak, who lived up to his name when winning Kempton's Grade 1 Christmas Hurdle in December 2020 and died a year later after a routine canter injury.

About the same time the yard also lost the highly promising five-year-old hurdler Star Gate, winner of his first three races and rated 143, yet the yard recovered to win 53 races and £888,000 prize-money last season.

The mission this season for the team at Fingerpost Farm is to surpass both those figures without a recognised star to guide them. A rejuvenated Secret Reprieve would certainly help, but among the string of around 80 there is plenty of talent lower down the pecking order.

Coole Cody won two Grade 3 handicaps

last season, including the Plate at the Cheltenham Festival in March. He's 11 with limited upside but is still a talented performer on his day and Williams will aim to discover if the Coole fire still burns brightly.

"He had a quite remarkable season," says Williams, "and to win at the festival was fantastic. It was really above all of our expectations."

So what has Williams got planned for him this season?

"Nothing at all, really," is the instant reply. "I suppose Cheltenham is what suits him. He would be giving an awful lot of weight away in some of those handicaps but I suppose we could claim off him – that would be one option – or we could go down the conditions route. There are plenty of those.

"He's a horse who saves his best for Cheltenham, but I honestly don't know where we'll go. We'll just tip away quietly, see how we're looking, and take it from there.

"We could start him off over hurdles around Cheltenham with a claimer on. It'll

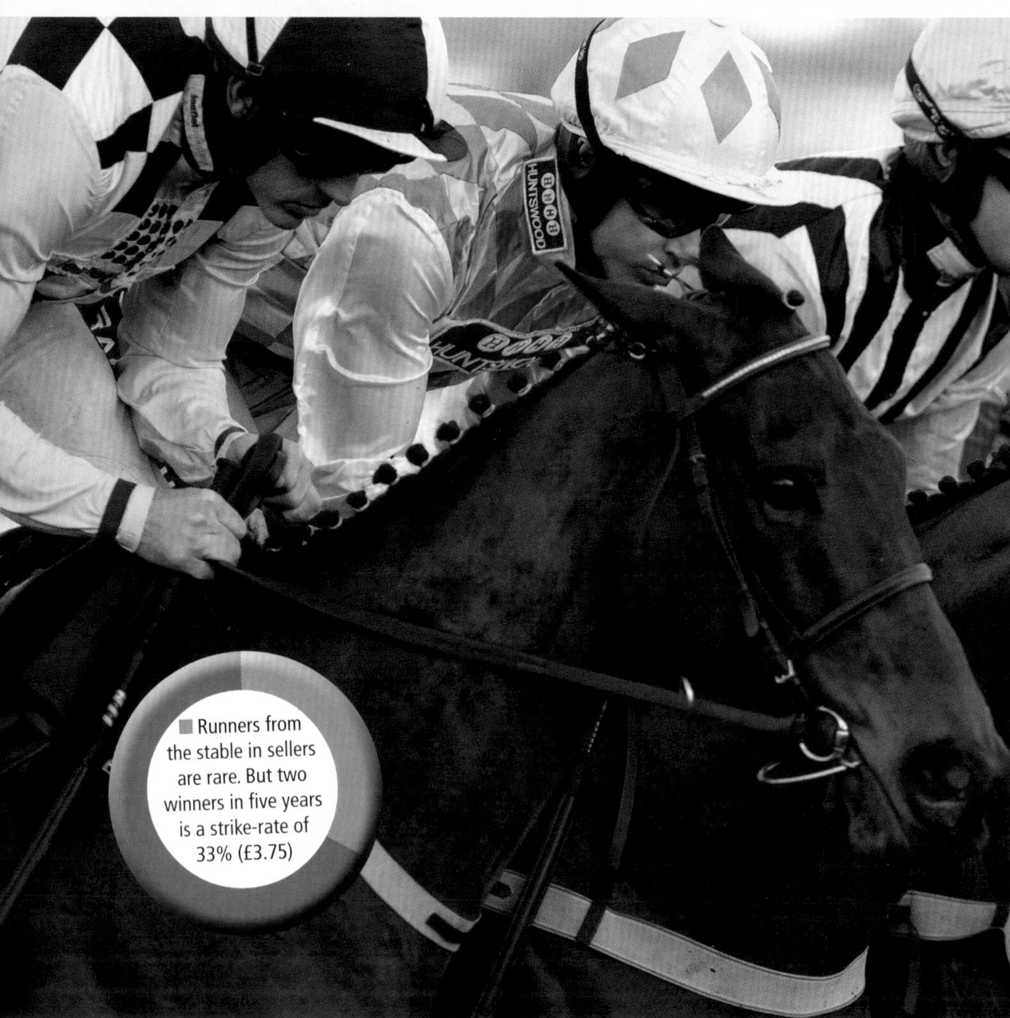

■ Runners from the stable in sellers are rare. But two winners in five years is a strike-rate of 33% (£3.75)

be a case of just enjoying the old boy, but if we don't think he can be competitive, we won't persevere."

Annsam switched between hurdles and fences last season, winning a Listed chase at Ascot and a Newton Abbot handicap hurdle, both over three miles.

"He's a very good jumper, although he's still very inexperienced, but I think he could be competitive in something like the Coral Gold Cup at Newbury in late November.

"He can make the odd mistake over fences, but that's purely because he hasn't really got the experience yet, but he definitely has plenty of ability.

"He's a horse with not a lot of mileage on the clock, so he could be an ideal horse for that race and sneak into it off a handy weight. The race is in November, so he'd have a run or two first. If we can get him there in some sort of form, it would be a nice place to go because I think he needs a flat track."

Dans Le Vent is nine and begins the season with a hurdles rating of 141 after

Dans Le Vent (orange diamonds): could be one for the Scottish National in the long term

The nosebanded Current Mood holds a slight advantage before going on to score at Chepstow

contesting Grade 2 and 3 handicaps, winning the Betfair Exchange Stayers' Hurdle at Haydock.

He was unplaced in the Coral Cup at the Cheltenham Festival and ended the season falling at the first in a Grade 3.

"He was very consistent but he fell at Aintree in his last race in April and had a little bit of an injury, so he didn't go out into the field until late.

"Because of that he probably won't start early and won't be seen until after Christmas. We might go over fences with him and he might be a horse for the Scottish National. On his day he has quite a bit of ability but I won't rush him."

The Last Day has been plagued by niggly leg injuries but always promised to win a good race one day – and that came at Aintree in April when he landed the Grade 3 Red Rum Handicap.

"He came out of the race very well, which was not something we could say about him very often.

"He's not a young horse but he's not got many miles on the clock and I think he's a horse who could slot into something like the Haldon Gold Cup [at Exeter in early November].

"He's needed luck. We've had rain when we wanted and we've been able to give him a holiday when we wanted. As long as we get a drop of rain, we'll get him ready for Exeter."

Current Mood, a seven-year-old mare, won three times last season and was considered good enough to contest the Imperial Cup at Sandown in March, although she jumped poorly and was never travelling before finishing well beaten.

"She was a good, progressive mare last year. I expected her to run better than she did at Sandown but maybe she'd had her season," says Williams.

"She's big and strong and I imagine she'll go jumping this season. I've nothing in mind but chasing will be the way forward for her. She'll be ready in October."

Bold Plan won his last three races over

hurdles in the spring to earn a rating of 131.

"He had a great end to his year. He's a funny little character at the best of times but when he's hot, he's hot. We might mix chasing with hurdling with him. He's more than capable over fences.

"He might be a horse for the Tote Silver Trophy at Chepstow in October, which we won with Court Minstrel in 2015 and 2017."

L'Astroboy is a fascinating character who could turn into a very useful recruit. Williams is hardly renowned for having bumper winners, particularly not first time out, so eyebrows were raised in more than one quarter when L'Astroboy obliged at 25-1 at Ffos Las on debut.

The five-year-old wore down the more fancied Tahmuras (won next time out) from the Paul Nicholls' stable in the last few strides to surprise even Williams.

"He's a nice horse but a raw horse. We have a lot of young horses and he's one who came through," he says. "We very seldom have bumper winners, so he did surprise me, but if any of our bumper horses win they surprise me because I don't often have bumper-type horses. Ours tend to be long-term prospects.

"He showed a good attitude and went about the old job well. He'll start off in a maiden hurdle somewhere and we'll go from there. He probably needs some cut in the ground because he handled the soft ground that day.

"We have no particular plans for him. He's cantering away at the moment and we'll probably start him off in a maiden hurdle somewhere and go from there."

Howdyalikemenow did very well for a novice last year, winning three small hurdle races as well as running with credit in a couple of deep handicaps.

"He's a horse who could do well in a Welsh Champion Hurdle if he got in. He's tough and genuine with plenty of ability and could definitely show improvement over fences.

"We'll see how he goes but he'll definitely

No wonder Evan Williams is a big fan of the Welsh Grand National – the 1965 winner Norther was ridden by his father Rhys in point-to-points, while dual winner Limonali was trained nearby. And just for good measure, Haydn Lewis who finished second on Billy Budd in 1956 has worked for Williams!

jump a fence at some stage this season."

Aeronisi is one for the notebook. A month after arriving from another stable the six-year-old pleased his new master with a brave half-length win in a small Fontwell chase with the rest well beaten.

The handicapper put him up 7lb to a mark of 103 but he looks capable of winning more races.

"He had only the one run for us and then the weather went dry, but the form of the race has worked out quite nicely," says Williams. "He's summered very well and could be a horse for some good sport in staying races around the country tracks.

"He could definitely be worth following in staying chases off lower weights at places like Chepstow and Exeter. He's a very nice little horse with a good attitude."

Another horse to have only one appearance for Williams after switching yards is **Libberty Hunter**.

After landing two bumpers for Brian Eckley, the six-year-old finished sixth, beaten just under seven lengths in a well-contested Listed bumper at Newbury in February.

"He's a nice horse and the form has worked out very, very well. You could see him being a bit of sport over hurdles. We'd start him off low key and he'd need a bit of cut in the ground, but he showed a good attitude and he could definitely be a bit of fun in maiden and novice hurdles somewhere down the line."

In a similar vein is **Bebraveforglory**, another six-year-old newcomer who arrived in February and promptly won over hurdles before switching to fences and finishing third at Southwell and Hereford.

At the other end of the age scale is 11-year-old **Prime Venture**, who won the final of the 2021 Veterans Chase Series at Sandown in January.

"People like to follow those old horses and those races are popular. It's a hundred-grand pot and we'll definitely be aiming him at it again."

Finally, take note of a quartet of former Irish point-to-pointers: **Doyen Star**, a Rathcannon winner in April who fetched £120,000 at Goffs UK sale four days later; **Loop Head**, a March winner at Nenagh who was bought for £80,000; **Hurricane Highway**, a ten-length winner in March at Liscarroll who cost £90,000; and **Puddles In The Park**, who was placed in Ireland.

"They are all very nice young horses who have been competitive in Irish points. Fingers crossed, they'll turn out well," says Williams.

Interview by Lawrie Kelsey

John Fitzgerald
ARTIST & SCULPTOR

Going for gold with Royale Pagaille and L'Homme Presse

WINNING the Cheltenham Gold Cup is the pinnacle of every trainer's ambition and alongside the Grand National they are the twin peaks of jump racing.

Venetia Williams scaled the Grand National summit when Mon Mome won the 2009 race at 100-1 and the same horse came closest to climbing the ultimate peak when third behind Imperial Commander and Denman in the 2010 Gold Cup.

Williams' Aramstone stables in

WINNERS IN LAST FIVE SEASONS 60, 53, 39, 42, 34

Herefordshire has produced nothing before or since Mon Mome capable of winning the Gold Cup until March this year when **Royale Pagaille** finished a gallant fifth in a thrilling race behind runaway winner A Plus Tard.

Only three lengths covered the next five home and with a little more luck the eight-year-old might have equalled Mon Mome's finishing position.

He is likely to be prepared for a third successive Gold Cup attempt, although his path to the festival is yet to be mapped out. As with all her horses, Williams will wait until the rain arrives before deciding which races and which tracks are suitable stepping stones.

He has summered "all right despite there being little grass" as has his exciting stablemate **L'Homme Presse**, who earned his 14-1 odds for next spring's finale after a thrilling victory in the festival's Grade 1 Brown Advisory Novices' Chase.

He justified 9-4 favouritism with some quick and slick jumping over three miles and half a furlong in very soft ground.

He never looked in danger and the manner of victory suggested going up another two furlongs would pose no problems.

But Williams was far from at ease watching his performance and said afterwards: "I'm going to need to watch it again to enjoy it properly. I haven't felt so sick watching a race, which is rare."

The man in a hurry, whose rating rose 36lb to 164 in a little over three months, was made favourite after four successive victories, including the Grade 2 Dipper Novices' Chase at Cheltenham and the Grade 1 Scilly Isles Novices' Chase at Sandown, by winning margins totalling 50 lengths.

This season the seven-year-old is unlikely to begin the long route to Cheltenham until November or December when the ground softens.

"He was very exciting in the novice division last year but it's a whole different ball game this season taking on all the top horses. It will be exciting to see how he fares," says Williams.

The two Gold Cup contenders are the vanguard of an elite Aramstone team, including Chambard and Didero Vallis, who finished first and third in the Kim Muir at the festival at odds of 40-1 and 66-1 respectively.

Plans are fluid for **Chambard**, who "really stepped up on everything last season at the extraordinary age of ten," says Williams.

His first run at the beginning of the year was an easy win in an Exeter chase, followed by a couple of seconds, then two more victories before his Cheltenham success.

"He got held up a bit in the autumn and didn't have his first run until the first of January, but he was a revelation after that," says Williams. "He'd had a wind op [last summer] which helped him."

Chambard has been given no targets as yet with Williams waiting for the ground to soften before making any decisions.

"He's rated 141, so we'll wait and see. There'll be plenty of nice handicaps he can contest."

Plans are also fluid for "Jekyll and Hyde" character **Didero Vallis**, who finished three and a half lengths behind Chambard in the Kim Muir.

"Nine days before Cheltenham he'd been tailed off in the Grand Military at Sandown, running absolutely appallingly, which he'd done a few times," says Williams.

Didero Vallis's last victory was at Catterick in February 2021 when, according to rider Charlie Deutsch, he jumped brilliantly. The winning time before that came at Haydock in December 2018, with 779 days between wins.

The strange case of Didero Vallis could be a page-turner for Williams this season.

Frero Banbou had been "knocking on the door" with a trio of third-place finishes before winning at Lingfield, and was then second at Sandown before his third in the

From top: Didero Vallis, Frero Banbou and Funambule Sivola

VENETIA WILLIAMS

KINGS CAPLE, HEREFORDSHIRE

RECORD AROUND THE COURSES

	Total W-R	Per cent	Non-hcp Hdle	Non-hcp Chase	Hcp Hdle	Hcp Chase	N.H. Flat	£1 level stake
Ludlow	38-234	16.2	2-55	1-10	10-53	23-112	2-4	-54.51
Chepstow	32-236	13.6	3-57	0-3	4-40	24-126	1-10	-62.21
Exeter	28-172	16.3	10-36	1-13	4-37	13-77	0-9	-22.77
Haydock	27-155	17.4	5-19	3-11	5-35	13-85	1-5	+60.47
Warwick	24-164	14.6	4-27	2-12	3-30	14-82	1-13	-51.82
Sandown	24-182	13.2	0-13	2-15	3-43	19-108	0-3	-64.95
Hereford	23-114	20.2	3-30	1-2	6-32	12-46	1-4	-1.29
Ascot	23-142	16.2	2-7	1-8	2-24	18-100	0-3	+29.05
Wincanton	22-162	13.6	3-26	1-5	4-28	13-101	1-2	-51.65
Bangor	22-166	13.3	2-42	3-5	1-27	16-81	0-11	-31.31
Leicester	20-75	26.7	3-13	4-6	2-15	11-41	0-0	-7.56
Newbury	20-139	14.4	1-14	2-10	0-21	17-93	0-1	+7.87
Ffos Las	19-99	19.2	1-17	1-1	4-17	11-56	2-8	+19.91
Uttoxeter	19-154	12.3	5-32	1-5	5-38	7-71	1-8	-76.78
Fontwell	18-77	23.4	2-9	2-6	2-18	11-41	1-3	+5.72
Taunton	18-94	19.1	4-19	1-4	8-32	5-37	0-2	-3.47
Huntingdon	18-97	18.6	4-20	2-12	3-23	9-40	0-2	-28.69
Carlisle	16-67	23.9	3-10	1-4	1-10	10-38	1-5	+12.34
Plumpton	16-81	19.8	7-26	1-3	3-24	4-26	1-2	-33.16
Lingfield	15-86	17.4	2-16	0-5	1-12	12-53	0-0	-31.25
Wetherby	14-62	22.6	2-6	0-3	2-7	10-42	0-4	+1.27
Cheltenham	14-239	5.9	0-10	2-29	1-50	11-147	0-3	-41.50
Southwell	11-45	24.4	2-6	1-1	1-8	6-28	1-2	-8.23
Market Rasen	11-68	16.2	3-10	1-2	2-17	5-35	0-4	-28.88
Catterick	7-32	21.9	3-7	0-2	1-5	3-16	0-2	-4.57
Doncaster	7-55	12.7	0-5	0-7	1-5	6-37	0-1	-21.80
Musselburgh	6-16	37.5	0-0	0-2	3-7	2-6	1-1	+10.00
Stratford	6-54	11.1	1-10	0-2	1-10	3-29	1-3	-15.50
Kempton	6-83	7.2	1-14	1-9	1-21	3-39	0-0	-39.50
Newton Abbot	4-52	7.7	2-13	1-3	0-12	1-22	0-2	-17.89
Kelso	3-23	13.0	0-1	0-4	1-5	2-13	0-0	-1.75
Worcester	3-23	13.0	0-1	2-8	1-5	0-8	0-1	-10.08
Aintree	3-94	3.2	0-10	0-16	0-13	3-55	0-0	-67.50
Newcastle	2-14	14.3	0-1	1-1	0-0	1-12	0-0	-1.80
Perth	2-26	7.7	1-3	0-2	0-6	1-15	0-0	-19.89
Cartmel	1-6	16.7	0-0	0-1	0-1	1-4	0-0	-2.75
Fakenham	1-15	6.7	0-1	0-2	0-2	0-9	1-1	-7.00
Kempton (AW)	0-2	0.0	0-0	0-0	0-0	0-0	0-2	-2.00
Hexham	0-4	0.0	0-2	0-0	0-0	0-2	0-0	-4.00
Sedgefield	0-7	0.0	0-1	0-0	0-1	0-5	0-0	-7.00
Ayr	0-15	0.0	0-0	0-2	0-3	0-10	0-0	-15.00

Grand Annual at the festival, all at around two miles.

He was staying on up the Cheltenham hill and, but for a bad mistake at the last, he might have been second.

"We have options of stepping him up in trip, which we might look into," says Williams.

"He won a nice race at Lingfield and ran consistently all season. As with the others, we haven't given him any targets yet, although hopefully he can win another nice race this season."

Funambule Sivola has been campaigned between two miles and two and a half, winning twice over two miles before outrunning his 40-1 odds to finish second to Energumene in the Queen Mother Champion Chase at the festival.

He had some top two-milers behind him that day, including Envoi Allen, Politologue and Put The Kettle On, which marked him out as a class act.

However, he has run well over two and a half miles too, as he did when finishing second in the Peterborough Chase at

Huntingdon in December with the likes of Eldorado Allen and Allmankind behind. So what is his best distance?

"We'll probably bring him back to two. All the evidence suggests two miles is the trip, although I'm not certain," says the trainer.

"But we have options [of going up to two and a half]. He has no ground preference but, like all ours, we don't want to run them on dry ground."

Williams has a host of other fine festival performers to look forward to this season, including Ryanair fourth **Fanion D'Estruval**.

"He's not a big horse and is slightly in no-man's land with his rating of 160. He's right at the top of the handicap and just not quite managing to nail it in the Gradeds. He's seven now and there's every reason to hope that he can step up again this season."

Bellatrixsa ended the season with victory on the Flat in the Chester Plate Handicap over 2m2½f, a race the stable won with Green Book the previous year, and that followed victories in mares' handicap hurdles at Ludlow and Hereford in February.

"She did very well when competing against her own in the novices last season," says Williams.

"She stays well, which she confirmed at Chester when she won the same race on the Flat we won with Green Book, the Chester Plate Handicap.

"We're probably going to take her chasing this season. She hasn't jumped fences yet and she's only five, but she's a big mare."

Green Book won three handicap hurdles before finishing fifth in the Albert Bartlett.

"We haven't run him on the Flat because he's had a busy time and we wanted to give him a rest. He stays three miles but equally he can be successful at shorter trips."

His first two runs over hurdles last season were over just short of two miles at Haydock, finishing second in one and winning the other. Then he won over 2m5f at Ludlow and a Grade 3 at Sandown over 2m7½f, which gives Williams various trip options.

Pink Legend performed well in several good races last season, winning at Ascot and a Listed mares' chase at Huntingdon before finishing a half-length second in the mares' chase at the festival.

"She's not always the most consistent," admits Williams, "but ran some nice races last year. She could go back for the same race at Cheltenham. That's what everybody with a nice mare would do in March. It would be nice to see her win that Huntingdon race as well."

Will she race against her own sex again? "Well, probably," says Williams. "There are some nice races. There's a great programme for fillies and mares now, but they need to be ready to run on the day and if not you have to look elsewhere."

Christopher Wood was a useful hurdler for Paul Nicholls before switching to Williams' care in February this year.

He finished second in a handicap hurdle at Ascot a couple of weeks after the change of scenery, then ran a creditable sixth at 40-1 in the Coral Cup at the festival the following month.

"We were very pleased with him," says Williams, who added, "we're going to go chasing with him. I know Paul Nicholls ran him once over fences [odds-on third at Sedgefield in May last year] and chose not to pursue that line, but I've schooled him and taken away some positives from that. So that's what we're going to do."

Brave Seasca is on the way back from injury after a crashing fall at the fourth fence in front of the stands in the Arkle, having earned his place in the line-up after two handicap chase victories at Warwick and one at Ascot.

"I'm not sure he's particularly well named," says Williams tongue-in-cheek. "He got very gobsmacked when coming up to the stands in the Arkle. He'd jumped the first couple of fences really well, then all of a sudden looked in awe at the stands and didn't concentrate on the obstacle in front of him – and fell.

"He had quite a battering. He fractured ribs and had other injuries and took a long time to recover. But he's recovered now and seems to be fine, but time will tell. Let's hope he has no memory of it."

Fontaine Collonges is another member of a strong group of mares at Aramstone, who proved her worth with wins in novice mares' chases over two and a half miles at Warwick and Lingfield, and is expected to do well again this season.

The 2022-23 campaign follows a record breaker last season when the stable sent out 60 winners (the best numerically for eight years) to top the £1.5 million prize-money mark for the first time.

Interview by Lawrie Kelsey

The stable has sent out 70 winners between 2m7f and 3m2½f in the last five years – an 18% strike-rate (+£56.18)

L'Homme Presse heads to festival victory

Venetia Williams rode the Peter Ransom-trained 200-1 outsider Marcolo in the 1988 Grand National but got only as far as Becher's Brook on the first circuit where she fell.

RACING POST
THE
EXPERTS

FESTIVAL FANCIES PAUL KEALY

Ten who should make it to big spring festivals

AHOY SENOR

When you're asked to nominate ten horses who might make it to the spring festivals you're going to struggle to come up with much in the way of originality and it's fair to say Ahoy Senor is not that original.

Leaving aside the established stars in the chase division, Ahoy Senor is surely one to be excited about this season, even if he has to prove that the undulations of Cheltenham are for him.

You can't argue he ran badly when second to L'Homme Presse in the Brown Advisory, but he wasn't always fluent and he was in the end well held.

So far the Lucinda Russell-trained eight-year-old has looked much more at home on flat, left-handed tracks, though, and if all he did was win another Grade 1 at Aintree in April you'd be a little disappointed. However, he remains a work in progress and will have plenty of time to try Cheltenham again.

His choice of early season options would be the Betfair Chase at Haydock and the now renamed Coral Gold Cup, and personally I hope he goes for the latter.

Newbury looked to be very much his bag when he sauntered home by 31 lengths to get off the mark over fences at the track last season and he has a little of Denman about him in the way he gallops, if not quite in the way he jumps as yet.

Denman famously won two Hennessys, as they were called then, and the first came off a mark of 161, which is what Ahoy Senor will have to defy if he takes his place. He doesn't have to win it by 11 lengths, though, and I think he'd be up to it.

BEAR GHYLLS

Putting a horse in the list who has missed a season for a small trainer may not prove a wise move, but Nicky Martin is fully capable and Bear Ghylls was one of the most exciting prospective novice chasers in Britain last year until he suffered a fetlock injury in October 2020.

It was only a minor injury by all accounts, though, and Martin said she could have run him in the second part of last season, but decided to preserve his novice status for another year. Hopefully that will prove a wise move as Bear Ghylls very much has the stamp of a chaser and his bumper and hurdles form suggests he can prove top class.

A wide-margin winner of his Warwick bumper in March 2020 at odds of 33-1, he proved that to be no fluke when winning his first three hurdles starts with a bit to spare, and he was particularly impressive at Exeter on his handicap debut. It was still a big ask for him to be sent into battle against Bob Olinger in the Ballymore at Cheltenham a couple of months later, but he ran a perfectly creditable race to finish fourth on his debut in top-flight company and he may well have been closer but for a ground-losing mistake three out.

Word from the Martin yard is that Bear Ghylls has been impressing everyone in his schooling and his work and hopefully we will get to see what he is made of this season.

CHAMP KIELY

Willie Mullins will, as usual, have a huge number of novices ready to go to war with over hurdles this season and it will take some time before we get to know who some of the real stars are. It would be fair to say he doesn't normally start his really good ones over hurdles as early as July (although the likes of Easy Game and the prolific Bachasson were out that early), but Champ Kiely looked well above average when winning at the Galway Festival, a meeting Easy Game won at in his novice season.

Having unseated three out when making ground on his point debut at Dromahane in December 2020, Champ Kiely made his debut for Mullins in a bumper the following May, getting home by half a length from the runner-up with the pair 16 lengths clear. It was still some way short of top-class bumper form, but just over a year later the six-year-old rocked up at Galway and turned a maiden hurdle into a procession, winning eased down by 21 lengths.

The runner-up was rated 116 and won next time out, while the third had been placed in Group company on the Flat, and Champ Kiely made them look like trees. He has clearly had his problems and there's no knowing how high he will rank in the yard, but there's certainly a big engine there.

CONSTITUTION HILL

Talking of big engines, there may be none bigger than Constitution Hill's when it comes to 2m hurdlers for the 2022-23 season. Beaten a head by the now Jonjo O'Neill-trained Anyharminasking in a Tipperary point-to-point in April last year, Constitution Hill looked special from the moment he set foot on a racecourse for Nicky Henderson last season.

He ran only three times, but left a deep impression on each occasion, starting with a 14-length success from Might I on his debut at Sandown in December and following up with a 12-length romp in the Grade 1 Tolworth Hurdle at the same track a month later.

Even that performance, in what looked a substandard race for the grade, could not prepare us for what was to follow in the Supreme Novices' Hurdle at Cheltenham. There Constitution Hill smashed the track record as he sauntered to a 22-length success from stablemate and subsequent Aintree Grade 1 winner Jonbon.

That wasn't all he smashed either, as he set a new record for being the highest-rated novice since horses were awarded ratings in Britain, and he also became the highest-rated novice in the history of Racing Post Ratings and Timeform. His official mark of 170 puts him 4lb ahead of dual Champion Hurdle winner Honeysuckle and, while that figure doubtless annoyed some of the latter's fans, the clock doesn't lie.

The Supreme's winning time was nearly six seconds faster than the Champion Hurdle and Constitution Hill was still faster than Honeysuckle after the last despite having already been around 20 lengths ahead on the clock when arriving at it.

There was much talk of a match with Honeysuckle at Punchestown, but nothing came of it, and there's very little chance of them meeting before Cheltenham if both get there. There's still a long way to go until Cheltenham in March, but Constitution Hill is going to be a very short price wherever he lines up on the way, and he's with the right man in eight-times Champion Hurdle winner Henderson.

FACILE VEGA

It should seem a bit ridiculous that a horse can be quoted at as short as 2-1 for a Grade 1 novice hurdle at Cheltenham before having even jumped a hurdle in public, but it's hard to argue with the bookmakers for

Champ Kiely: Galway winner could go on to bigger and better things this season

attempting to keep Facile Vega onside.

There was always going to be plenty of talk about him as he's the second foal of six-times Cheltenham Festival winner Quevega and, unlike the first, Princess Vega, he is living up to his pedigree.

Described as "even better than I thought he was" by Willie Mullins after winning the Grade 2 bumper at the Dublin Racing Festival by 12 lengths, Facile Vega lived up to that with a Grade 1 double at Cheltenham and Punchestown, readily beating the well-touted American Mike at the former venue and then having to work a bit harder but ultimately always being in control against Redemption Day at the latter.

We still don't know whether he can jump, but a peak RPR of 141 for both Grade 1 wins puts him in a select group and historically gives him excellent prospects of making the grade. Since 2009 just 12 other horses have achieved an RPR of 141 or higher in a bumper (excluding jumpers' bumpers) and nine of those went on to win at Grade 1 level over hurdles or fences.

Only one, Champagne Fever in 2013, won the Supreme Novices' Hurdle, the race which Facile Vega is so short for, but he was also one of very few to hit an RPR that high twice in bumpers and he did so by completing the same Cheltenham-Punchestown double.

FAROUK D'ALENE

It's always worth remembering that the best novices do not always go on to become the best in open company and that often there are horses from the same generation that improve past them. When Al Boum Photo lay winded on the floor after a tired fall two out in the 2018 RSA there will have been few who saw him as a potential Gold Cup winner, and he of course won it twice. Well, Farouk D'Alene had a far better chance of winning the same Cheltenham novice last March when coming down two out and there is a chance he is being underestimated in the ante-post Gold Cup market.

Farouk D'Alene's career has been one of steady improvement. He won both his bumpers (best RPR 128), two out of his three hurdles (146, when beating subsequent Albert Bartlett winner Vanillier at Limerick), and, last season, two of his five chases.

A winner on his debut, he was then a close second twice, including in the Grade 1 Faugheen Novice Chase at Limerick, before warming up for Cheltenham with a Grade 2 success from Beacon Edge at Navan. He had to work hard for that success and the bare form left him some way behind the main British protagonists for what is now the Brown Advisory Novices' Chase, but he was well supported, opening up at 15-2 before going off at 9-2.

Farouk D'Alene was going just as well as leader and winner L'Homme Presse approaching the second-last, and that was despite a less than fluent round of jumping, which finally caught up with him at that point. That effort proved he has a serious engine, though, and as with any novice, he is going to have the potential to improve in the jumping department.

GALOPIN DES CHAMPS

The horse most punters are expecting to serve it up to reigning Gold Cup winner A Plus Tard next spring is Galopin Des Champs, and it's easy enough to see why.

He wouldn't be the first top-class horse with whom Willie Mullins has won the Martin Pipe Conditional Jockeys' Handicap Hurdle at Cheltenham and, having already run to higher figures over fences than his previous winners Don Poli and Kilultagh Vic, Galopin Des Champs looks like being the best of the lot.

He followed his 2021 Cheltenham success with a runaway victory at Grade 1 level at Punchestown, and then wowed everyone on his first start over fences last season when jumping brilliantly and running out a 22-length winner at Leopardstown. He was equally impressive in landing the Grade 1

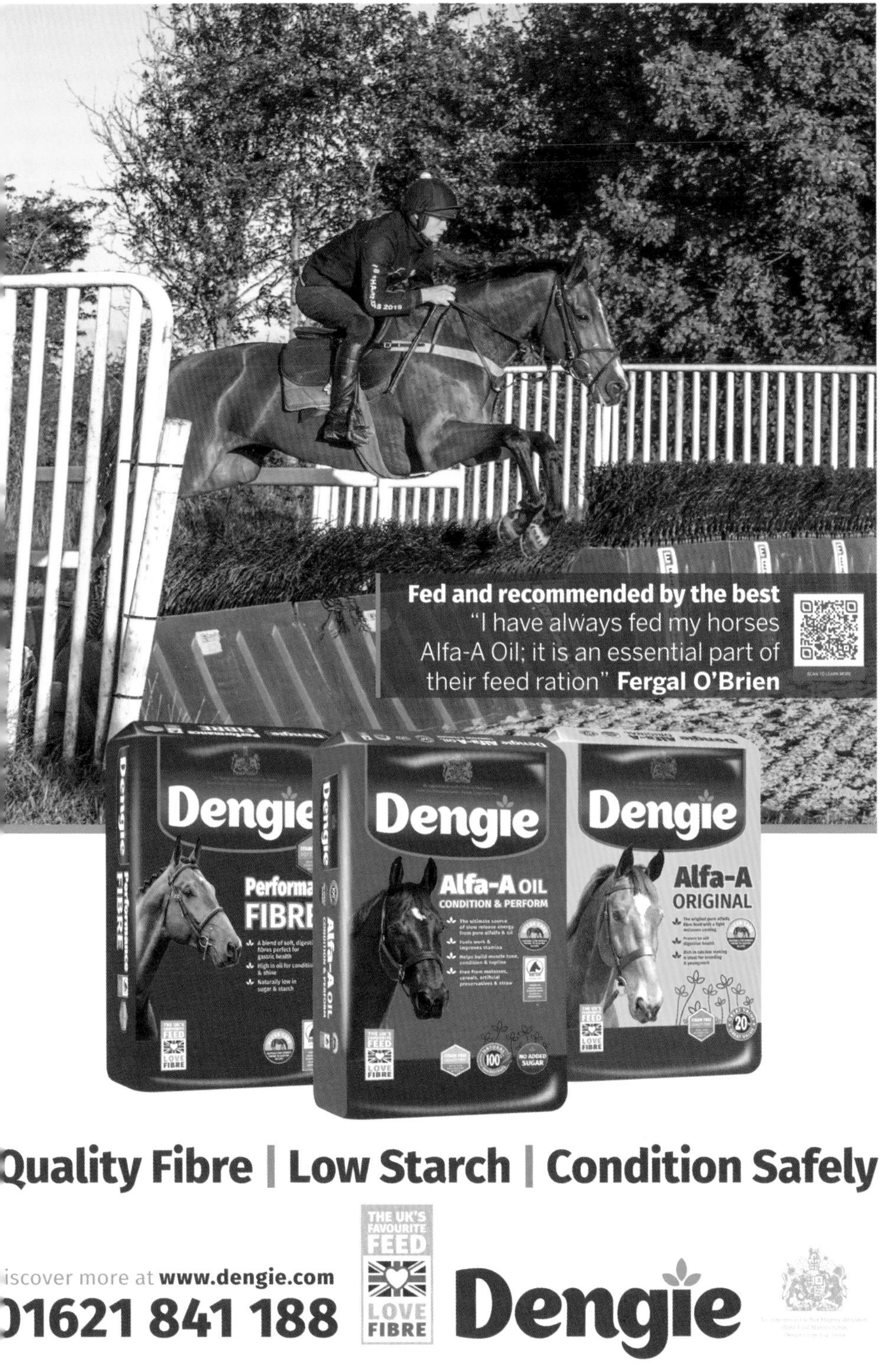

Ladbrokes Novice Chase at the same track at the Dublin Racing Festival, a run which made him slight favourite in what looked a match for the Turners Novices' Chase at Cheltenham. Unfortunately that's where it all went wrong as Galopin Des Champs fell at the last when cantering to what would have been a wide-margin victory over his big market rival Bob Olinger, who was admittedly well below form.

That fall did not affect him in the slightest, though, as he closed his season by running away with a Grade 1 at Fairyhouse, returning a peak RPR of 177, a figure just 7lb shy of A Plus Tard's Gold Cup-winning run.

All of his chase runs have been over 2m4-2m5½f but his hurdles Grade 1 came over 3m and it will be disappointing if the Gold Cup is not his main aim this season.

HITMAN

This one might be a surprise entry on the list as he seems to have been around for a while, but he's one of those Paul Nicholls-trained horses who started life over fences very early and he remains so young that it would be dangerous to think he has peaked.

Whether he turns into another Frodon for the yard remains to be seen, but Hitman, who is about to embark on his third season over fences, has achieved a pretty high level and his efforts last season suggest he was improving even though he didn't manage to win.

Sent straight over fences when first joining Nicholls in 2020, he ran second in the Grade 1 Henry VIII at Sandown and third in the Grade 1 Manifesto at Aintree, but he still has only two novice chase successes to his name. He shouldn't be knocked for that, though, as he continued to step up in terms of performance in defeat last season, starting with a second to Eldorado Allen in the Haldon Gold Cup and then finishing runner-up to stablemate and Sandown specialist Greaneteen in the Tingle Creek.

A slightly sub-par effort in the Game Spirit followed, but he then ran a career best when second to Fakir D'Oudaries in the Melling Chase at Aintree on his first run at 2m4f since his novice days.

Outpaced by the high-class winner between the last two, he nevertheless stayed on well, and his trainer is intending to step him further up in trip this season. Following that Aintree effort, which came still just over a week short of his actual sixth birthday, Nicholls described him as still a 'big, weak horse' and a work in progress, so don't be surprised if he takes his form to a new level this year.

JONBON

Being a bit of a cynic, I must admit it took me a while to take to Jonbon as he arrived with a massive price tag following his point win and was being talked of as a superstar before he'd achieved much at all.

As a brother to the brilliant if injury-prone Douvan, he was always going to be hyped up, but it's fair to say he almost lived up to it. A very comfortable winner of his first two novice hurdles last season in falsely run races (in the first they took nearly a minute just to set off), he had to work a lot harder to win the Rossington Main on soft ground at Haydock in January, but that was when I started to warm to him as he showed that he could dig deep as well as toy with average rivals.

> “Don’t be surprised if Hitman takes his form to a new level this season”

Jonbon did not, however, make much impression against brilliant stablemate Constitution Hill at Cheltenham, finishing a distant second to him in the Supreme, but he once again showed his battling qualities when gamely holding off El Fabiolo, who seemed to be travelling all over him at one point, in the Grade 1 Top Novice's at Aintree. Jonbon will tackle fences this season and he's at the head of a wide open market for both the 2m Arkle and 2m4f Turners and, while he has yet to try any further than two miles, it is for the latter that I've backed him.

To these eyes he looks to have more stamina than speed and if he is to go to the top over fences, I expect it will be at the intermediate trip as a novice.

THE NICE GUY

The Nice Guy must have had his share of problems as he didn't make the racetrack until late November last year, which was little more than a month short of his seventh birthday. The patience of trainer Willie Mullins and owner Malcolm Denmark was

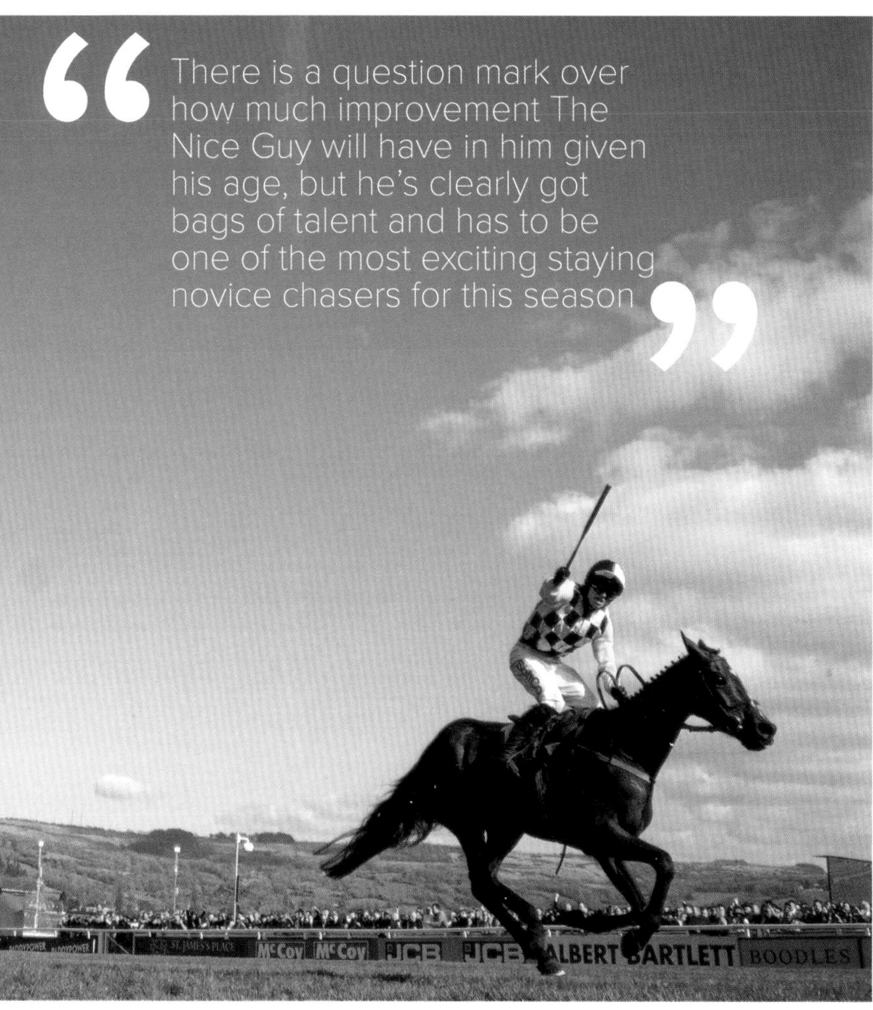
There is a question mark over how much improvement The Nice Guy will have in him given his age, but he's clearly got bags of talent and has to be one of the most exciting staying novice chasers for this season
McCoy
McCoy
JCB
ALBERT BARTLETT
BOODLES

fully rewarded, though, as by the end of the season he was a dual Grade 1 winner, having taken the Albert Bartlett at Cheltenham and followed up in the Punchestown equivalent.

In winning at Cheltenham he also joined a very select group. History has shown us that the Albert Bartlett is a really tough race and the key to success has more often than not been plenty of experience, whether in points, bumpers or hurdles.

In the 15 years before The Nice Guy's victory, only two Albert Bartlett winners had gone into the race with fewer than six outings under all codes to their names. They were Bobs Worth, who went on to win the RSA and Gold Cup and Minella Indo, who also won a Gold Cup. Bobs Worth had run five times and Minella Indo four, but The Nice Guy trumped the pair, having had only three outings and just one over hurdles.

There is a question mark over how much improvement he'll have in him given his age, but he's clearly got bags of talent and has to be one of the most exciting staying novice chasers for this season.

ANTE-POST ANALYSIS NICK WATTS

Vauban has long-range appeal for top honours

CHAMPION HURDLE

All things being equal, Constitution Hill will hose up in his prep races during the winter and line up as an odds-on favourite for the Champion Hurdle in March.

If you don't mind tying your money up for the winter months in the expectation of certain victory then there is no need to read on. However, if you like a bit more adventure then there are alternatives at better prices who shouldn't be discounted.

Chief among those is **Vauban**, who looked an atypical winner of the Triumph Hurdle last season – in short, a horse who should get better rather than one who suffers from difficult second-season syndrome.

Very well bred – so much so that he could be a star stayer on the Flat should connections so wish – Vauban enjoyed a near-perfect juvenile hurdles campaign, winning three Grade 1s in a row, with his only defeat coming through lack of experience on his debut.

For each of those wins he beat the same horse – Fil Dor – so if being hypercritical he has been operating in a small pool. But, on the positive side, all his wins came very easily, and at Cheltenham he overcame some novicey jumping – particularly at the last – to scoot home showing a hugely impressive turn of foot.

His jumping will improve with practice – and a turn of foot wins you races – so although he doesn't have a wide-margin win to his name like Constitution Hill, it would be unwise to view him as inferior at this stage – just different. A price of 8-1 with Coral is tempting.

Sir Gerhard would be interesting if connections confirmed him as staying over hurdles this season – but that is very much open to debate. I would ignore his Punchestown run as it seems clear he goes off the boil post-Cheltenhan, and if concentrating solely on his performances up to and including the festival it makes for very impressive reading.

The 20-1 is tempting, but with the lack of concrete news as to his forthcoming plans, it may be best to wait with him.

CHAMPION CHASE

After winning his first Champion Chase last season, Willie Mullins, trainer of Vauban, suddenly finds himself with a plethora of options in this division with Energumene, Ferny Hollow and Gentleman De Mee all viable winners.

Energumene is short enough at this stage, while Ferny Hollow is injury-prone, so the one for me is **Gentleman De Mee**, who makes plenty of appeal at around 12-1.

He has always been huge on ability but needed to become more tractable to be able to prove it. Fences seem to have done that, as he won his last three races of the season easily, culminating in an impressive defeat of Arkle winner Edwardstone in Grade 1 company at Aintree.

His jumping is pretty good, and now he is

Vauban: last season's Triumph Hurdle winner can continue climbing through the ranks

not over-exerting himself early in his races, he has become very dangerous and is up to a mark of 164.

That mark is still some 12lb shy of Shishkin and Energumene, but he has the promise of much more to come this season, and the Irish programme for two-mile chasers gives him ample opportunity to get his confidence sky-high before coming over to the festival. A race such as the Grade 2 Hilly Way Chase at Cork springs to mind as an ideal starting point.

STAYERS' HURDLE

The Stayers' Hurdle will see Flooring Porter bidding for a hat-trick and it's easy to see him doing it, so dominant has he been in the last two years.

However, if you take the view that **Bob Olinger** will go back to hurdles this season – perfectly plausible after his travails at the end of last season – he could be a big danger and is 16-1. When has he ever been that price?

His run at the Cheltenham Festival has been well documented – being pulverised by Galopin Des Champs until that rival fell at the last – and his subsequent effort at Punchestown to me looked like one of a horse who had lost confidence.

It is hard to see him as a Champion Hurdle prospect over two miles, but it's very easy to see him being a player in a race such as this with stamina unlikely to be an issue.

I can't see Henry de Bromhead persevering long over fences. Perhaps he will get one last try this autumn, but if he doesn't come up to scratch surely a return to hurdles will be in the offing?

It's risky, but Champ took the same route last season when his chasing career was shelved.

GOLD CUP

There is only one horse I want to be with for the Gold Cup and that is **Allaho**, who has surely earned himself a crack at the big prize after his stunning Punchestown Gold Cup win.

To annihilate the 2021 winner, Clan Des Obeaux, by 14 lengths was a performance of the highest order and he didn't look to be slowing down at the end of three miles on that occasion.

It's true that he will have further to go at Cheltenham, and will have a steep hill to get up, but his exuberant jumping will expose any flaws in his rivals, and if he can be contained sufficiently during the race, he could find himself making lengths over some frantically chasing rivals on the final circuit. It could get nervy from the last to the line, but he will be nine next year and should have enough experience to see out the distance.

At 10-1 I am willing to take the chance, especially when his shorter-price stablemate, Galopin Des Champs has exactly the same question marks to answer regarding stamina as he is yet to go three miles over fences.

GRAND NATIONAL

The Grand National is a long way off at this stage so it's not a race to take a firm view on just yet, but bearing in mind Willie Mullins sent **Gaillard Du Mesnil** to the Irish National as a novice last season, in which he finished a creditable third, the master trainer should have no qualms about aiming him at Aintree in 2023.

Seven-year-olds used to be a big no-no in this race, as did novices, but Noble Yeats threw both of those statistics out of the window with victory in April, and Gaillard Du Mesnil will have jumped enough fences by the time of the race to ensure he will be a novice in name only.

There is a possibility that he might have won the National Hunt Chase at Cheltenham a month before Aintree and, if that proves to be the case, he will be on a lot of radars for the marathon showpiece. He can be backed at 50-1 with bet365.

MY TEN FOR THE SEASON RICHARD BIRCH

The horses to keep on your side away from big stage

AERONISI

Aeronisi probably won't achieve a rating within 50lb of his close relative Minella Indo, the 2021 Cheltenham Gold Cup winner, but that doesn't mean he won't win a staying chase or two this term off a launch pad of 103.

The lightly raced six-year-old made a winning start for Evan Williams in a 3m2f Fontwell handicap chase in March, surviving a blunder at the third-last to beat Twenty Twenty by half a length.

That was Aeronisi's first run over fences and he looks a young stayer to follow around the gaff tracks.

BALLYCAMUS

There was lots to like about the way five-year-old Ballycamus ploughed through the Hereford mud under 11st 11lb to secure a 2m5f handicap hurdle in March.

As a son of Presenting, it's perfectly reasonable to anticipate an even better performer on good ground, and there ought to be plenty of opportunities away from the deep winter mud when he's sent chasing.

Winner of an Irish maiden point-to-point before joining Nigel Twiston-Davies, he shouldn't be hard to place off 108.

BLACK POPPY

Black Poppy *(left)* is one of those horses who tends to win in tight finishes, so the handicapper can't hit him too hard.

He showed a good cruising speed when landing handicap hurdles at Hereford and Newbury last term, and arguably would have won on a return visit to Berkshire if he'd jumped the final flight cleanly.

This six-year-old gives the impression

Just Toby (leading): looks to be well treated on a mark of 85 over fences

there is plenty more to come from him off a mark of 121, particularly when given good or good to soft ground.

FARMER'S GAMBLE

Farmer's Gamble has no pretensions to joining Dan Skelton's 'A Team', but this dual winner last season nonetheless makes considerable appeal as a young stayer to follow.

A big, backward six-year-old who is related to Bonanza Boy, it's no surprise he produced a career-best effort on just his fifth start when stepped up to 3m at Perth in April.

The chestnut stayed on relentlessly to beat World Trip by five lengths, and a 5lb rise for that success looks lenient.

He'll do even better when upped to 3m2f+ and sent chasing. Keep him firmly onside.

JUST TOBY

Just Toby may not develop into a 110+ horse this season, but a chase mark of 85 gives him ample scope to win staying handicap chases.

The six-year-old son of Tobougg produced a highly likeable display when landing a Wincanton 3m1f novices' handicap chase in March by a length and three-quarters from Maliboo.

That was only his second start over fences and he showed improvement for the longer trip and drier ground.

Firmly in command at the finish that day, Just Toby could enjoy profitable autumn/spring campaigns away from very soft ground.

KING ORRY

King Orry, a huge seven-year-old with stacks of physical scope, was heavily backed on several occasions over fences last season, but consistently let his supporters down with weak finishes.

A string of defeats means he starts the new campaign on a basement mark of 69, and there are reasons for believing he could take his form to another level after a summer break.

Common sense dictates he may still have been a raw, weak horse during 2021-22, and he also ran at times when his stable was uncharacteristically out of form.

Expect considerable improvement at the West Country tracks when he reappears in 3m handicap chases.

MOROZOV COCKTAIL

Morozov Cocktail's forte is bottomless stamina as demonstrated by his bold second to Dubai Devils in a Hexham 4m handicap chase in March.

The fact he was able to win over 2m7f at Newcastle the following month suggests he could continue on an upward curve well into the new season. Tim Easterby's six-year-old was equipped with blinkers for the first time at Hexham and they aided his concentration.

A rating of 106 means Morozov Cocktail will have to show considerable improvement to get into some of the regional Nationals or even the Eider Chase, but those sorts of races could well be likely destinations further down the line.

ON THE PLATFORM

John Groucott's runners tend to do particularly well at Bangor and Uttoxeter, and both those tracks appear ideal for On The Platform, an 87-rated six-year-old chaser who should do well during 2022-23.

He pulled nine lengths clear of the third when finishing a two-length second to Oceans Red in a 3m Bangor novices' handicap chase in March.

It was a particularly creditable performance in view of the fact he was conceding 17lb to the winner, who went in again two starts later.

On The Platform has raced just five times over fences, and this promises to be a big season for him.

STRINGTOYOURBOW

After massively catching the eye when a neck second to Shearer over 2m4f at Newbury in March, Stringtoyourbow explosively went one better upped to 3m at Ayr's Scottish Grand National meeting the following month.

Always in cruise control under Jack Tudor, the five-year-old son of Getaway barely needed shaking up to ease eight and a half lengths clear of Colonel Manderson.

The Punchestown festival was mentioned by Christian Williams as a possible target afterwards, but Stringtoyourbow wasn't seen out again.

A 14lb rise for that Ayr romp was by no means unexpected, and the best is very much to come from this highly promising young stayer.

WARRIORS STORY

It doesn't take a genius to work out that Warriors Story will embark upon the 2022-23 campaign as potentially a very well-handicapped hurdler.

After all, Johnson's Blue, the horse he obliterated by seven and a half lengths at Newcastle in April, duly progressed to land his next four starts, culminating in the quite valuable Cumbria Crystal Cup at Cartmel to earn himself an official mark of 120.

Warriors Story, who probably wasn't right when disappointing on his only subsequent outing at Perth, kicks off the new season with a rating of 92, something which will have given his excellent trainer Nick Alexander plenty of reason to smile over the summer.

Morozov Cocktail can continue to do well in staying handicap chases

BELOW THE RADAR ROBBIE WILDERS

Ten smart performers whose talent might have been underestimated

A DREAM TO SHARE

John Kiely is without a Graded winner since 2017 but that could change this season with A Dream To Share, who has looked a top prospect in bumpers. A Dream To Share travelled all over a Willie Mullins-trained odds-on favourite on his debut at Tipperary in May and put the race to bed in excellent style when asked. It was a similar story at Roscommon in June. A Dream To Share scored eased down when held up in a slowly run race under a highly confident ride. This twice-raced four-year-old has bags of ability and it will be fascinating to see how he fares over hurdles.

ESPOIR DE ROMAY

This eight-year-old has struggled since he took a crashing fall two out in the Grade 1 Mildmay Novices' Chase at the 2021 Aintree festival, but could bounce back this season. Espoir De Romay was poised to give Chantry House a real race that day before coming down and our handicappers agreed as the pair were each handed a Racing Post Rating of 167. Kim Bailey's talented chaser has disappointed in three starts since but has been handed a reprieve by the assessor, who has dropped him to a mark of 150. That could seriously underestimate him and the Coral Gold Cup at Newbury is a feasible early season target.

FLAME BEARER

Flame Bearer became Pat Doyle's first Grade 2 winner since 2004 with a pair of wins last season, and improved again when thrown into a Punchestown Grade 1 novice hurdle on his final start in the spring. Doyle's stable star showed a gritty attitude to snatch second that day after an awkward jump at the second-last and did well to pull clear of smart operators Three Stripe Life and Kilcruit, succumbing only to the top-class State Man. Flame Bearer has proved his worth in Ireland but may be lesser known to British racing fans and rates a smart proposition for novice chases this campaign. His ability to handle a range of ground conditions is also a plus.

GENTLEMANSGAME

This six-year-old entered many notebooks when second in the 2021 Nathaniel Lacy & Partners Solicitors Novices' Hurdle on just his second outing under rules, and again two starts later when finishing runner-up to Galopin Des Champs at Punchestown. This lightly raced type failed to click into gear last winter but advanced his form in the spring with a couple of career-best efforts, the latter a third to Klassical Dream on his first run in an open Grade 1 at Punchestown. He could reach a high level in staying novice chases for powerful owners Robcour, but probably does not want testing ground.

Flame Bearer: on the up and could spring a surprise in Britain this season

JUNGLE BOOGIE

It is unusual for an unbeaten Willie Mullins-trained horse to fly under the radar but Jungle Boogie could be doing just that. A stylish, wide-margin winner of a bumper, a maiden hurdle and a novice chase, Jungle Boogie is open to any amount of improvement after just three runs. He featured prominently in many of the ante-post Grade 1 novice chase markets at the Cheltenham and Punchestown festivals this year, but unfortunately we never saw this fragile eight-year-old at either of those flagship meetings. He has dazzled on the track and let's hope for a clear run this winter.

MAID O'MALLEY

This low-mileage nine-year-old got on a real roll at the beginning of the year and landed a couple of low-grade mares' handicaps before taking her form to a new level in the Mares' Chase at the Cheltenham Festival. While she fell two out that day, she was in the process of putting in a bold bid against much higher-rated rivals and belying odds of 100-1. Maid O'Malley disappointed at Haydock when last seen in April but I can forgive a horse a bad run after a fall, and the ground may have been too quick. She is worth keeping onside in mares' chases over intermediate trips.

MEET AND GREET

Oliver McKiernan tends to target his best horses at the Punchestown festival and Meet And Greet performed well above expectations when third to The Nice Guy and Minella Cocooner in the Irish Mirror Novice Hurdle. Considering the first two home fought out the finish of the Albert Bartlett the previous month, and Meet And Greet was running over three miles for the first time, it was a creditable effort. The fact this horse pulled 14 lengths clear of the fourth in a warm race was also impressive. He seems to have the pace for two miles and stamina for three, so should pay his way for the McKiernan yard once more.

NICKLE BACK

It is a concern we have not seen Nickle Back since he bolted up last October in a Fontwell novice hurdle, but he has the talent to take the Sarah Humphrey stable to new heights this year. A ready 30-length winner that day, Nickle Back recorded an eyecatching RPR of 143 there and proved his debut second at odds of 66-1 to the smart ill-fated hurdler Cadzand was no fluke. He gave the odds-on shot a real scare then. Nickle Back has just two runs to his name and it is likely there is plenty more in the locker.

SILVER HALLMARK

I'm convinced we are yet to see the best of the lightly raced Silver Hallmark, who caught the eye with a decent fourth to Fiddlerontheroof in the Listed Colin Parker on his return at Carlisle last October. He was unsuited by the conditions of the race and shaped really well. You can draw a line through his next run in the Rowland Meyrick as that was a gruelling contest and he doesn't want three miles. It was a bit more like it at Kelso in February, but the handicapper saw fit to drop him 3lb and there are handicaps to be won off a mark of 142 for this former Grade 2-winning novice.

SLIP OF THE TONGUE

Padraig Roche's stable flagbearer was a work in progress last season but can show the benefit of that with another year on his back. It can be tough for five-year-olds meeting more experienced older horses off level weights in Graded races, but Slip Of The Tongue still managed to reach a decent level. He ran a remarkable race at Punchestown in Listed company in February after getting the last all wrong and almost unshipping Mark Walsh, but dug in gamely to repel the useful Deploy The Getaway. He will continue to progress and should be followed whether he remains over hurdles or jumps a fence.

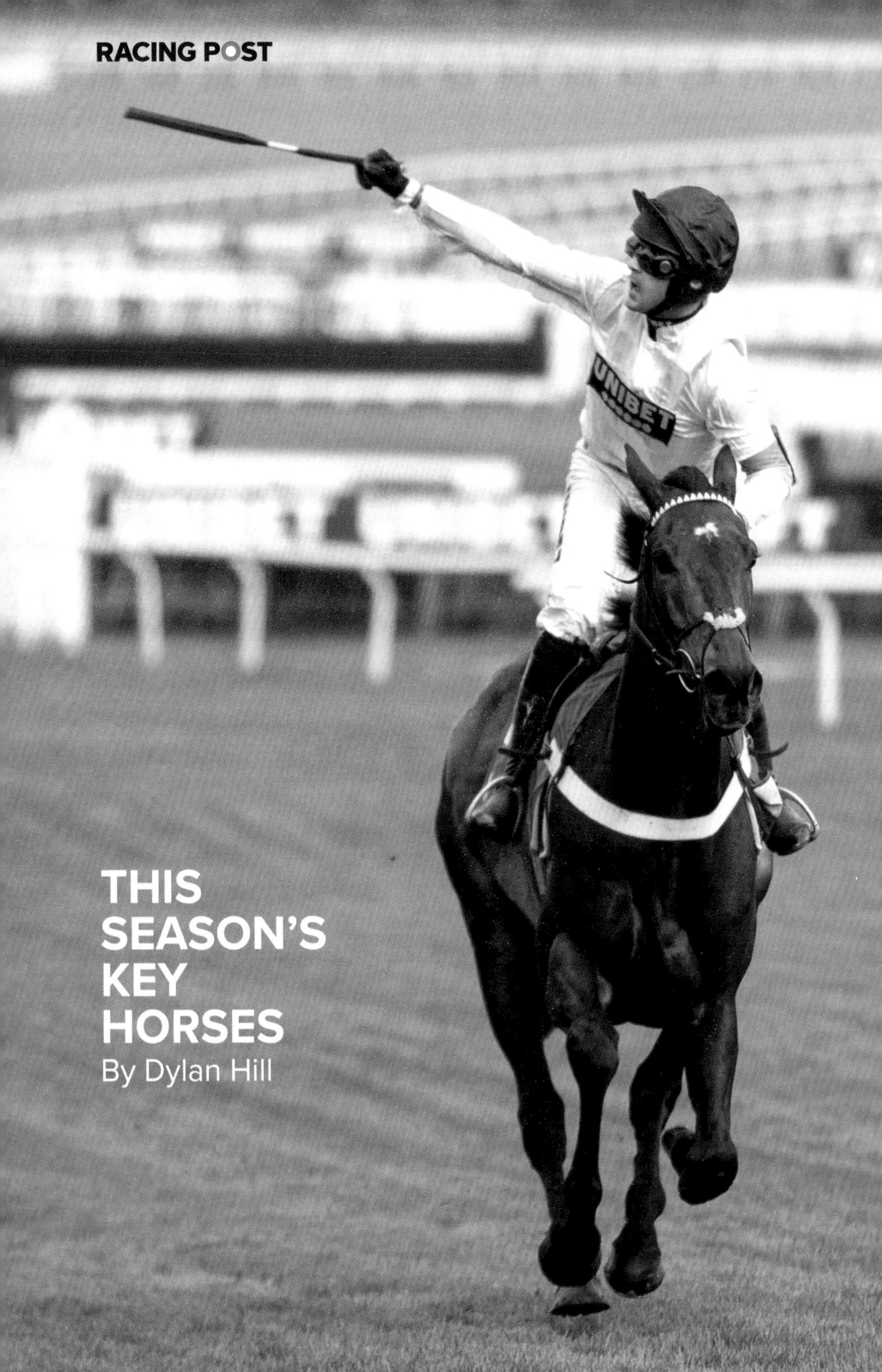

RACING POST

THIS SEASON'S KEY HORSES

By Dylan Hill

A Plus Tard (Fr)

8 b g Kapgarde - Turboka (Kahyasi)

Henry de Bromhead (Ire) — Cheveley Park Stud

PLACINGS: 1/2121/3213/212/121- — RPR **184+c**

Starts	1st	2nd	3rd	4th	Win & Pl
19	8	8	3	-	£922,600

	3/22	Chel	3m2½f Cls1 Gd1 Ch gd-sft	£351,688
	11/21	Hayd	3m1½f Cls1 Gd1 Ch gd-sft	£114,865
	12/20	Leop	3m Gd1 Ch yield	£75,000
	12/19	Leop	2m1f Gd1 Ch soft	£66,441
144	3/19	Chel	2m4f Cls1 Nov List 138-145 Ch Hcap soft	£39,389
	12/18	Naas	2m3f Ch yield	£7,904
0	4/18	Autl	2m2f List Hdl 4yo Hcap heavy	£39,823
	10/17	Sbri	2m2f Hdl 3yo gd-sft	£6,974

Sensational 15-length winner of last season's Cheltenham Gold Cup, comprehensively reversing 2021 form with runner-up Minella Indo; had also run away with the Betfair Chase at Haydock; has run only three times in each of the last three seasons.

A Wave Of The Sea (Ire)

6 b g Born To Sea - Je T'Adore (Montjeu)

Joseph O'Brien (Ire) — John P McManus

PLACINGS: 04137510/P5062F19-6F — RPR **150c**

Starts	1st	2nd	3rd	4th	Win & Pl
25	6	3	2	1	£232,493

142	2/22	Leop	2m1f 119-144 Ch Hcap yield	£49,580
133	2/21	Leop	2m1½f 125-141 Ch Hcap soft	£52,679
	9/20	Kbgn	2m4f Ch yield	£5,500
	2/20	Leop	2m Gd1 Hdl 4yo yield	£75,000
	11/19	DRoy	2m½f Hdl 3yo soft	£7,986
	10/19	Punc	2m Hdl 3yo gd-yld	£8,253

Has won the valuable 2m1f handicap chase at the Dublin Racing Festival for each of the last two seasons; ran almost exclusively over longer trips in between, doing best when second in the Munster National; only ninth in the Grand Annual on final run.

Abacadabras (Fr)

8 b g Davidoff - Cadoubelle Des As (Cadoudal)

Gordon Elliott (Ire) — Gigginstown House Stud

PLACINGS: 4/211212/2152F1/435- — RPR **152h**

Starts	1st	2nd	3rd	4th	Win & Pl
18	6	5	1	2	£356,867

4/21	Aint	2m4f Cls1 Gd1 Hdl gd-sft	£104,984
11/20	Punc	2m Gd1 Hdl heavy	£50,000
12/19	Leop	2m Nov Gd1 Hdl soft	£53,153
11/19	Navn	2m Nov Gd3 Hdl sft-hvy	£17,275
10/19	Gowr	2m Mdn Hdl gd-yld	£7,454
10/18	Gway	2m½f NHF 4yo yield	£5,451

Three-time Grade I winner, most recently when outclassing a modest field for the grade in the Aintree Hurdle in 2021; has just come up short in stronger Grade I races and disappointed in just two runs last season, including on first run over 3m behind Klassical Dream.

Constitution Hill wins last season's Supreme Novices' Hurdle

Absolute Notions (Ire)

4 b g Milan - Colleen Donnoige (Beneficial)

Gordon Elliott (Ire) — M Conaghan

PLACINGS: 1 — RPR **119+b**

Starts	1st	2nd	3rd	4th	Win & Pl
1	1	-	-	-	£49,579

4/22	Punc	2m½f NHF 4-5yo gd-yld	£49,580

Runaway winner of the valuable Goffs Land Rover Bumper at Punchestown on debut last season, looking a very useful prospect; out of a half-sister to smart staying chasers Macgeorge and Chief Dan George and should stay at least 2m4f over hurdles.

Adagio (Ger)

5 b g Wiener Walzer - Aspidistra (Hernando)

David Pipe — Bryan Drew & Friends / Prof C Tisdall

PLACINGS: 121122/228-5 — RPR **157h**

Starts	1st	2nd	3rd	4th	Win & Pl
10	3	5	-	-	£128,187

1/21	Chep	2m Cls1 Gd1 Hdl 4yo soft	£28,475
12/20	Chel	2m1f Cls2 Hdl 3yo soft	£12,512
11/20	Wwck	2m Cls4 Hdl 3yo good	£3,769

Hasn't won since landing a Grade I juvenile hurdle in 2020 but has run several fine races in defeat; finished second in the Triumph Hurdle that season as well as the Greatwood and Kingwell Hurdles last term; well beaten in two runs subsequently at Grade I level.

Adamantly Chosen (Ire)

5 b g Well Chosen - Sher's Adamant (Shernazar)

Willie Mullins (Ire) — Watch This Space Syndicate

PLACINGS: 12210-40 — RPR **140+h**

Starts	1st	2nd	3rd	4th	Win & Pl
7	2	2	-	1	£65,069

2/22	Thur	1m7½f Mdn Hdl yield	£4,958
4/21	Punc	2m½f NHF 4-5yo yield	£52,679

Still a work in progress but has shown plenty of promise; got off the mark at the third attempt last season by 27 lengths only to race too keenly when 11-2 for the Martin Pipe at Cheltenham; good fourth of 24 at Punchestown having got too far back only to disappoint when favourite for the Galway Hurdle.

Adrimel (Fr)

7 b/br g Tirwanako - Irise De Gene (Blushing Flame)

Tom Lacey — Lady Bamford & Alice Bamford

PLACINGS: 1/110/111PP/P119P- — RPR **145c**

Starts	1st	2nd	3rd	4th	Win & Pl
13	7	-	-	-	£46,576

139	2/22	Hayd	2m4f Cls3 Nov 123-139 Ch Hcap heavy	£8,169
	12/21	Hayd	2m½f Cls3 Nov Ch soft	£7,563
	1/21	Wwck	2m5f Cls1 Nov Gd2 Hdl heavy	£12,814
	12/20	Hayd	1m7½f Cls2 Hdl heavy	£9,583
	11/20	Sand	2m Cls4 Mdn Hdl soft	£3,899
	2/20	Donc	2m½f Cls5 NHF 4-6yo soft	£2,274
	12/19	Uttx	2m Cls5 NHF 4-6yo heavy	£2,274

Prolific gelding who has won seven out of eight

races under rules away from Cheltenham and Aintree, most notably a Grade 2 novice hurdle in 2021; yet to fire in stronger races, finishing ninth in the Plate at Cheltenham last season and pulled up at the Grand National meeting.

Ahorsewithnoname

7 b m Cacique - Sea Of Galilee (Galileo)

Nicky Henderson — D J Burke & P Alderson

PLACINGS: 431/26/2232- — RPR **133**h

Starts	1st	2nd	3rd	4th	Win & Pl
9	1	4	2	1	£41,754

	Date	Course	Race	Prize
	4/19	Sedg	2m1f Cls5 NHF 4-6yo good	£2,859

Remarkably finished second in the mares' novice hurdle last season despite going off at 50-1 having never won over hurdles; had still run well to be placed three times in Listed novices and confirmed upward curve by going from strength to strength on the Flat this summer.

Ahoy Senor (Ire)

7 b g Dylan Thomas - Dara Supreme (Darazari)

Lucinda Russell — Mrs C Wymer & PJS Russell

PLACINGS: U/1211/U12121- — RPR **166+**c

Starts	1st	2nd	3rd	4th	Win & Pl
9	5	3	-	-	£227,861

	Date	Course	Race	Prize
	4/22	Aint	3m1f Cls1 Nov Gd1 Ch gd-sft	£67,524
	2/22	Weth	3m Cls1 Nov Gd2 Ch good	£25,628
	11/21	Newb	2m7½f Cls1 Nov Gd2 Ch gd-sft	£28,475
	4/21	Aint	3m½f Cls1 Nov Gd1 Hdl gd-sft	£42,328
	3/21	Ayr	2m4½f Cls4 Mdn Hdl soft	£3,769

Classy and progressive staying novice chaser last season, peaking with a brilliant win at Aintree when winning a Grade 1 at the Grand National meeting for the second successive year; second behind Bravemansgame and L'Homme Presse in other Grade 1 races last season.

Al Dancer (Fr)

9 gr g Al Namix - Steel Dancer (Kaldounevees)

Sam Thomas — Walters Plant Hire

PLACINGS: 10/12425/139P/04532- — RPR **152**c

Starts	1st	2nd	3rd	4th	Win & Pl
23	7	4	3	3	£148,459

	Date	Course	Race	Prize
	10/20	NAbb	2m5f Cls2 Ch gd-sft	£14,076
	10/19	Chel	2m Cls2 Nov Ch gd-sft	£15,640
141	2/19	Asct	1m7½f Cls1 Gd3 125-145 Hdl Hcap gd-sft	£47,830
129	12/18	Chel	2m1f Cls3 116-137 Hdl Hcap good	£9,747
	11/18	Ffos	2m Cls4 Nov Hdl soft	£4,159
	10/18	Carl	2m1f Cls4 Nov Hdl gd-sft	£4,549
	3/18	Bang	2m½f Cls5 Mdn NHF 4-6yo soft	£2,395

Former Betfair Hurdle winner who has often been fancied to land a similar pot over fences and was third in the 2020 Paddy Power Gold Cup; flopped in that race last season and reverted to hurdles but got back on track when a neck second in a handicap chase at Newbury on final run.

Alaphilippe (Ire)

8 b g Morozov - Oscar Bird (Oscar)

Fergal O'Brien — Nic Brereton

PLACINGS: 2F4P1/111215/52- — RPR **144+**h

Starts	1st	2nd	3rd	4th	Win & Pl
8	4	2	-	-	£48,435

	Date	Course	Race	Prize
	2/21	Hayd	3m½f Cls1 Nov Gd2 Hdl soft	£12,814
	12/20	Sedg	2m4f Cls4 Nov Hdl soft	£3,769
	11/20	Ayr	2m4½f Cls4 Mdn Hdl soft	£3,769
	10/20	Ffos	2m Cls5 Mdn NHF 4-6yo heavy	£2,274

Agonisingly came up a neck short in last season's Pertemps Final at Cheltenham having been laid out for the race on just his second run out of novice company; had been much busier during novice campaign, winning four times and finishing fifth in the Albert Bartlett; likely chasing type.

Ahoy Senor: ended last season on a high with Aintree victory

Allaho (Fr)

8 b g No Risk At All - Idaho Falls (Turgeon)

Willie Mullins (Ire) — Cheveley Park Stud

PLACINGS: 413/2213/6411/2111-1 — RPR **181+c**

Starts	1st	2nd	3rd	4th	Win & Pl
17	8	4	2	2	£719,269

Date	Course	Race	Prize
4/22	Punc	3m Gd1 Ch gd-yld	£136,345
3/22	Chel	2m4½f Cls1 Gd1 Ch soft	£211,425
1/22	Thur	2m4½f Gd2 Ch gd-yld	£18,097
12/21	Punc	2m4½f Gd1 Ch yld-sft	£42,143
3/21	Chel	2m4½f Cls1 Gd1 Ch gd-sft	£150,350
1/21	Thur	2m4f Gd2 Ch sft-hvy	£18,438
1/20	Fair	2m5½f Ch yld-sft	£7,012
2/19	Clon	3m Nov Gd3 Hdl gd-yld	£21,261

Underlined status as arguably the best chaser around last season, winning four out of four; wide-margin winner of the Ryanair Chase for the second year in a row before a similar demolition job over 3m at Punchestown (first run over the trip since 2020).

Allart (Ire)

8 b g Shantou - The Adare Woman (Oscar)

Nicky Henderson — R A Bartlett

PLACINGS: 3/F115/1F/ — RPR **156c**

Starts	1st	2nd	3rd	4th	Win & Pl
7	3	-	1	-	£26,506

Date	Course	Race	Prize
12/20	Asct	2m3f Cls1 Nov Gd2 Ch soft	£14,807
2/20	Donc	2m½f Cls4 Nov Hdl soft	£3,769
1/20	Ludl	2m Cls4 Nov Hdl soft	£4,224

Smart but fragile youngster who hasn't run since a fall at Haydock in January 2021; had made a hugely impressive chase debut that season when beating Fiddlerontheroof in a Grade 2 at Ascot, looking a better chaser than hurdler (fifth in the 2020 Supreme).

Allegorie De Vassy (Fr)

5 b m No Risk At All - Autignac (Solon)

Willie Mullins (Ire) — Mrs S Ricci

PLACINGS: P52/311- — RPR **138+h**

Starts	1st	2nd	3rd	4th	Win & Pl
6	2	1	1	-	£39,142

Date	Course	Race	Prize
1/22	Fair	2m2½f Nov Gd3 Hdl gd-yld	£14,378
1/22	Fair	2m2½f Hdl yield	£6,693

Exciting mare who won both starts following move from France last season only to miss Cheltenham through injury; had been a leading player for the mares' novice hurdle after beating subsequent Grade 1 winner Brandy Love at Fairyhouse, albeit helped by rival's poor jumping.

Allmankind

6 b g Sea The Moon - Wemyss Bay (Sadler's Wells)

Dan Skelton — The Gredley Family

PLACINGS: 1113/311141/315P7- — RPR **165+c**

Starts	1st	2nd	3rd	4th	Win & Pl
15	8	-	3	1	£203,068

Rating	Date	Course	Race	Prize
160	10/21	Aint	2m4f Cls1 Gd2 140-160 Ch Hcap good	£50,793
	4/21	Ayr	2m4½f Cls1 Nov Gd2 Ch good	£14,288
	2/21	Wwck	2m Cls1 Nov Gd2 Ch soft	£14,238
	12/20	Sand	1m7½f Cls1 Nov Gd1 Ch soft	£25,929
	11/20	Wwck	2m Cls3 Nov Ch good	£7,121
	12/19	Chep	2m Cls1 Gd1 Hdl 3yo heavy	£37,018
	11/19	Chel	2m½f Cls1 Gd2 Hdl 3yo soft	£18,224
	11/19	Wwck	2m Cls4 Hdl 3yo gd-sft	£4,549

Looked a horse going places when making all

Allart (right): classy chaser on the comeback trail

in the Old Roan Chase at Aintree last season, making it five wins out of six over fences; bitterly disappointing in three subsequent runs and made a string of mistakes when switched to hold-up tactics on final run back at Aintree.

Amarillo Sky (Ire)

6 b g Westerner - Bag Of Tricks (Flemensfirth)

Joe Tizzard — J P Romans & Taylor, O'Dwyer

PLACINGS: 1/44710/16412F156- — RPR **149+c**

Starts	1st	2nd	3rd	4th	Win & Pl
14	4	1	-	3	£39,430

135	2/22	Newb	2m½f Cls2 Nov 116-137 Ch Hcap soft	£10,892
128	11/21	Winc	1m7½f Cls3 Nov 125-134 Ch Hcap good	£8,169
125	5/21	NAbb	2m1f Cls3 116-126 Hdl Hcap good	£5,146
115	3/21	Extr	2m1f Cls4 100-120 Hdl Hcap gd-sft	£3,769

Progressive novice chaser last season, winning twice including a ten-length handicap victory at Newbury; solid fifth when just 5-1 for the Grand Annual at Cheltenham but out of his depth in Grade 1 novice company when last of six at Aintree on final run.

American Mike (Ire)

5 b g Mahler - American Jennie (Lord Americo)

Gordon Elliott (Ire) — Bective Stud

PLACINGS: 1/112-3 — RPR **135b**

Starts	1st	2nd	3rd	4th	Win & Pl
4	2	1	1	-	£41,779

	12/21	Navn	2m List NHF 4-7yo gd-yld	£11,853
	10/21	DRoy	2m1f NHF 4-7yo soft	£5,268

Hyped up throughout last season, especially after storming to a 17-length win in a Listed bumper at Navan; didn't quite live up to that billing in the spring, though still a good second behind Facile Vega at Cheltenham before a disappointing third at Punchestown.

Andy Dufresne (Ire)

8 b g Doyen - Daytona Lily (Beneficial)

Gordon Elliott (Ire) — John P McManus

PLACINGS: 1/1/1213/113P/22-F — RPR **161c**

Starts	1st	2nd	3rd	4th	Win & Pl
12	5	3	2	-	£110,018

	12/20	Navn	2m1f Nov Gd3 Ch soft	£17,500
	10/20	Wxfd	2m Ch soft	£5,500
	1/20	Punc	2m½f Nov Gd2 Hdl soft	£22,250
	11/19	Navn	2m4f Mdn Hdl sft-hvy	£7,188
	1/19	DRoy	2m NHF 5-7yo yield	£5,550

Very highly rated in younger days (sent off favourite on first eight runs under rules, winning six times) but has just come up short in stronger company since then, failing to win since 2020; still ran a big race when second in last season's Grand Annual on handicap debut.

Annie Mc (Ire)

8 b m Mahler - Classic Mari (Classic Cliche)

Jonjo O'Neill — Coral Champions Club

PLACINGS: 324151/41119/7511/2- — RPR **143c**

Starts	1st	2nd	3rd	4th	Win & Pl
16	7	2	1	2	£104,363

	2/21	Wwck	2m4f Cls1 List Ch soft	£17,832
	12/20	Donc	2m4½f Cls1 List Ch heavy	£22,667
	2/20	Bang	2m4½f Cls4 Nov Ch soft	£5,718
	1/20	Weth	2m3½f Cls4 Nov Ch soft	£4,606
	12/19	Winc	2m4f Cls3 Nov Ch heavy	£9,097
127	3/19	Newb	2m4½f Cls1 Nov 107-127 Hdl Hcap gd-sft	£24,760
118	1/19	Chep	2m3½f Cls3 117-129 Hdl Hcap gd-sft	£6,238

Ran only once last season, missing the Mares' Chase at the Cheltenham Festival through injury for the second successive year, but has been prolific in the past; has won five out of six chases in mares' company, though no better than fifth when more highly tried in three others.

Annsam

7 b g Black Sam Bellamy - Bathwick Annie (Sula Bula)

Evan Williams — Wayne Clifford

PLACINGS: 3/16511/F21P/431P31- — RPR **143+c**

Starts	1st	2nd	3rd	4th	Win & Pl
17	6	1	3	1	£87,716

130	4/22	Newb	3m Cls2 124-141 Hdl Hcap gd-sft	£8,169
134	12/21	Asct	3m Cls1 List 130-150 Ch Hcap gd-sft	£39,865
	12/20	Ludl	2m4f Cls3 Ch soft	£7,389
118	1/20	Catt	2m3½f Cls3 115-130 Hdl Hcap soft	£6,563
113	12/19	Tntn	2m3f Cls3 109-129 Hdl Hcap soft	£8,382
	5/19	Winc	1m7½f Cls5 Mdn Hdl gd-fm	£3,249

Lightly raced chaser who ran out a decisive winner of last season's Silver Cup at Ascot; pulled up after a bad mistake in the Coral Trophy at Kempton but successfully reverted to hurdles, winning at Newbury last spring; strong stayer and seen as a National horse by his trainer.

Any Second Now (Ire)

10 b g Oscar - Pretty Neat (Topanoora)

Ted Walsh (Ire) — John P McManus

PLACINGS: 1F/62U31/99P13/9612- — RPR **170c**

Starts	1st	2nd	3rd	4th	Win & Pl
29	6	6	5	-	£460,573

	2/22	Fair	3m1½f Gd3 Ch soft	£14,130
	3/21	Navn	2m Gd2 Ch heavy	£18,438
	2/20	Naas	2m Gd3 Ch heavy	£23,250
143	3/19	Chel	3m2f Cls2 133-144 Am Ch Hcap gd-sft	£41,510
	1/17	Punc	2m Nov Gd2 Hdl soft	£22,440
	12/16	Navn	2m Mdn Hdl 4yo yld-sft	£5,426

Placed in the last two runnings of the Grand National, finishing an unlucky third in 2021 and second off a 7lb higher mark last season; has had virtually identical preparations both times, showing virtually nothing until winning his prep run after the publication of the weights.

Anyharminasking: progressive hurdler who won his final two starts last season

Anyharminasking (Ire)

5 b g Getaway - Collen Beag (Mountain High)

Jonjo O'Neill — Mrs Gay Smith

PLACINGS: 1/42211- — RPR **141+h**

Starts		1st	2nd	3rd	4th	Win & Pl
5		2	2	-	1	£16,605
127	1/22	Sedg	2m1f Cls3 113-132 Hdl Hcap good			£8,278
114	1/22	Catt	1m7½f Cls4 105-120 Hdl Hcap gd-sft			£4,030

Massive improver when sent handicapping last season, winning easily at Catterick and Sedgefield having been beaten three times in novice company; raised 23lb but capable of performing at much higher level on literal reading of point-to-point win over Constitution Hill.

Appreciate It (Ire)

8 b g Jeremy - Sainte Baronne (Saint Des Saints)

Willie Mullins (Ire) — Miss M A Masterson

PLACINGS: 31/3112/1111/7- — RPR **156h**

Starts		1st	2nd	3rd	4th	Win & Pl
9		6	1	1	-	£241,766
	3/21	Chel	2m½f Cls1 Nov Gd1 Hdl soft			£52,799
	2/21	Leop	2m Nov Gd1 Hdl sft-hvy			£65,848
	12/20	Leop	2m Nov Gd1 Hdl soft			£40,000
	11/20	Cork	2m Mdn Hdl heavy			£7,000
	2/20	Leop	2m Gd2 NHF 4-7yo yield			£50,000
	12/19	Leop	2m4f NHF 4-7yo soft			£6,389

Brilliant unbeaten novice hurdler two seasons ago, winning the Supreme by 24 lengths, but missed nearly all of last season after a setback; had plans for a chasing campaign shelved, instead heading straight to the Champion Hurdle, but was badly outpaced in seventh.

Ash Tree Meadow (Fr)

6 b g Bonbon Rose - Alzasca (Grape Tree Road)

Gordon Elliott (Ire) — Alymer Stud

PLACINGS: 61/33124-31114 — RPR **153+c**

Starts		1st	2nd	3rd	4th	Win & Pl
10		4	1	3	2	£44,031
	7/22	Klny	2m1f Nov Ch good			£7,933
136	6/22	Prth	2m4f Cls3 Nov 120-139 Ch Hcap good			£6,317
	6/22	Prth	2m Cls3 Nov Ch good			£7,624
	1/22	Navn	2m4f Mdn Hdl yield			£5,950

Progressive young chaser who quickly won three in a row over fences this summer having only started chasing in mid-May; fine fourth when stepped up in class for the Galway Plate; had also shown promise over hurdles last winter, including when fourth in a Grade 2 at Fairyhouse.

Ashdale Bob (Ire)

7 b g Shantou - Ceol Rua (Bob Back)

Jessica Harrington (Ire) — Diarmuid Horgan

PLACINGS: 435/11F91/2U37323-2 — RPR **158h**

Starts		1st	2nd	3rd	4th	Win & Pl
16		3	3	4	1	£126,272
	4/21	Fair	2m4f Nov Gd2 Hdl yield			£18,438
	12/20	Navn	2m4f Nov Gd2 Hdl sft-hvy			£17,500
	11/20	Navn	2m4f Mdn Hdl soft			£7,500

Struggled when sent novice chasing last season but flourished when reverting to hurdles despite

not winning; finished with a fine second behind Klassical Dream in a 3m Grade 1 at Punchestown and still unexposed as a stayer (second run over the trip over hurdles).

Ashroe Diamond (Ire)

5 b m Walk In The Park - Saine D'Esprit (Dom Alco)

Willie Mullins (Ire) — Blue Blood Racing Club

PLACINGS: 1241- — RPR **122+b**

Starts	1st	2nd	3rd	4th	Win & Pl
4	2	1	-	1	£39,326

	Date	Course	Race	Prize
	4/22	Aint	2m1f Cls1 Gd2 NHF 4-6yo gd-sft	£28,135
	5/21	Wxfd	2m NHF 4-7yo sft-hvy	£5,795

Easy six-length winner of a Grade 2 mares' bumper at Aintree last season, capping a progressive campaign punctuated by a winter break; had finished a half-length fourth at the same level at Leopardstown; likely to stick to 2m but bred to get further.

Ashtown Lad (Ire)

8 b g Flemensfirth - Blossom Trix (Saddlers' Hall)

Dan Skelton — Darren & Annaley Yates

PLACINGS: F3/217/2115P4/14235- — RPR **148c**

Starts	1st	2nd	3rd	4th	Win & Pl
12	3	2	1	2	£38,548

	Date	Course	Race	Prize
	10/21	Weth	3m Cls3 Nov Ch gd-sft	£7,080
123	11/20	Uttx	2m7½f Cls3 119-133 Hdl Hcap soft	£5,913
	10/20	Weth	2m3½f Cls4 Nov Hdl soft	£5,198

Very useful staying novice chaser last season despite failing to add to first-time-out win; ran best race when third behind Ahoy Senor at Wetherby and shaped much better than bare form when fifth on handicap chase debut in the Scottish Grand National, fading late over marathon trip.

Ballygrifincottage (left): multiple point-to-point winner could do well in novice chases this season

Asterion Forlonge (Fr)

8 gr g Coastal Path - Belle Du Brizais (Turgeon)

Willie Mullins (Ire) — Mrs J Donnelly

PLACINGS: 1/1114/1FF433/1UF47- RPR **168c**

Starts	1st	2nd	3rd	4th	Win & Pl
15	5	-	2	3	£181,005

152	4/21	Punc	2m5f Nov 131-152 Ch Hcap yield	£42,143
	11/20	Punc	2m3½f Ch sft-hvy	£6,250
	2/20	Leop	2m Nov Gd1 Hdl yield	£75,000
	1/20	Naas	2m Mdn Hdl gd-yld	£7,986
	11/19	Thur	2m NHF 5-7yo soft	£5,591

Hugely talented but enigmatic chaser who hasn't come close to fulfilling potential over fences; has failed to get round more often than he has won and let down at other times by tendency to hang right; would have finished second in last season's King George but for final-fence fall.

Authorised Speed (Fr)

5 b g Authorized - Tangaspeed (Vertical Speed)

Gary Moore — Gallagher Bloodstock

PLACINGS: 22145- RPR **128h**

Starts	1st	2nd	3rd	4th	Win & Pl
5	1	2	-	1	£10,481

	1/22	Newb	2m½f Cls5 NHF 4-6yo gd-sft	£1,906

Did best of the British-trained runners in the Champion Bumper at Cheltenham when an excellent fifth behind Facile Vega; put a poor run in a Listed bumper at Newbury behind him having gone into that race as 13-8 favourite after a 20-length win at that track.

Aye Right (Ire)

9 b g Yeats - Gaybric (Presenting)

Harriet Graham & Gary Rutherford — Geoff & Elspeth Adam

PLACINGS: 1/12U15/232230/5139- RPR **163+c**

Starts	1st	2nd	3rd	4th	Win & Pl
27	8	8	4	1	£198,455

151	11/21	Newc	2m7½f Cls1 List 132-151 Ch Hcap gd-sft	£39,865
	1/20	Newc	2m7½f Cls4 Nov Ch soft	£4,289
136	9/19	Kels	2m5f Cls2 124-136 Hdl Hcap good	£11,696
130	4/19	Ayr	3m½f Cls3 Nov 111-135 Hdl Hcap good	£10,007
122	1/19	Ayr	2m5½f Cls3 120-136 Hdl Hcap soft	£9,357
	10/18	Kels	2m5f Cls4 Nov Hdl good	£4,549
	9/18	Kels	2m5f Cls4 Nov Hdl gd-fm	£4,224
	11/17	Carl	2m1f Cls5 NHF 4-6yo soft	£2,274

Consistent in top staying handicap chases in the last two seasons and landed a big one when winning the Rehearsal Chase last term; then stepped up in grade, finishing third in the Cotswold Chase and ninth in the Cheltenham Gold Cup.

Balco Coastal (Fr)

6 b g Coastal Path - Fliugika (Roi De Rome)

Nicky Henderson — Mark Blandford

PLACINGS: 27/112P3- RPR **136h**

Starts	1st	2nd	3rd	4th	Win & Pl
6	2	1	1	-	£29,281

	12/21	Ludl	2m Cls4 Nov Hdl gd-sft	£4,901
	12/21	Hntg	2m Cls4 Nov Hdl good	£5,010
	2/21	Kemp	2m Cls5 NHF 4-6yo std-slw	£2,274

Useful novice hurdler last season; won first two races at Huntingdon and Ludlow before finishing second behind North Lodge in a Grade 2 at Cheltenham; unsuited by soft ground when a disappointing favourite in the Imperial Cup but bounced back with a good third at Aintree.

Ballyadam (Ire)

7 b g Fame And Glory - Grass Tips (Bob Back)

Henry de Bromhead (Ire) — Cheveley Park Stud

PLACINGS: 131/114224/F2505-0 RPR **145h**

Starts	1st	2nd	3rd	4th	Win & Pl
14	3	3	1	2	£102,653

	11/20	Fair	2m Nov Gd1 Hdl soft	£35,000
	10/20	DRoy	2m½f Mdn Hdl soft	£5,000
	3/20	Dpat	2m1½f NHF 4-7yo yield	£5,000

High-class novice hurdler two seasons ago, winning the Royal Bond and finishing second in two more Grade 1 races; disappointing last season, even when back over hurdles after finishing second in a beginners' chase, but showed more promise when fifth in the County Hurdle.

Ballygrifincottage (Ire)

7 b g Stowaway - Long Long Time (Dr Massini)

Dan Skelton — Friends From Insurance

PLACINGS: U/111314- RPR **142h**

Starts	1st	2nd	3rd	4th	Win & Pl
3	1	-	1	1	£28,603

	1/22	Ling	2m7f Cls2 Nov Hdl heavy	£15,843

Three-time point-to-point winner in Ireland who did well in the face of some stiff tasks over hurdles last season; finished third in a Grade 2 at Cheltenham on British debut and finished fourth in the Albert Bartlett either side of a good win at Lingfield; likely to go novice chasing.

Banbridge (Ire)

6 ch g Doyen - Old Carton Lass (Presenting)

Joseph O'Brien (Ire) — R A Bartlett

PLACINGS: P/328/11147110- RPR **140+h**

Starts	1st	2nd	3rd	4th	Win & Pl
9	5	-	-	1	£67,687

137	3/22	Chel	2m4½f Cls2 132-144 Cond Hdl Hcap gd-sft	£39,023
	1/22	Navn	2m Nov Hdl yield	£7,933
	7/21	Rosc	2m5f Nov Hdl soft	£8,429
	5/21	Punc	2m½f Mdn Hdl soft	£6,321
	5/21	Klny	2m1f NHF 5-8yo gd-yld	£5,268

Progressive novice hurdler last season, winning for the fourth time over hurdles in the Martin Pipe at Cheltenham; sent off favourite for a 3m Grade 1 at Aintree despite stepping up in class and trip but finished tailed off.

Bardenstown Lad

7 ch g Black Sam Bellamy - Pougatcheva (Epervier Bleu)

John McConnell (Ire) — Ms Caroline Ahearn

PLACINGS: 4/11/3113113-F — RPR **147h**

Starts	1st	2nd	3rd	4th	Win & Pl
9	5	-	3	-	£49,101

	Date	Course	Race	Prize
	2/22	Muss	3m Cls2 Nov Hdl good	£10,406
	10/21	Chel	3m Cls2 Nov Hdl good	£8,325
	8/21	Ctml	2m6f Cls4 Nov Hdl good	£4,085
	7/21	Wxfd	3m Mdn Hdl good	£5,268
	3/21	Tipp	2m3½f NHF 6-7yo soft	£4,214

Won four novice hurdles last season to add to point-to-point and bumper victories; coped well with sharp rise in class when third in the Albert Bartlett at Cheltenham only to fall early at Punchestown; likely to go novice chasing.

Bavington Bob (Ire)

7 br g Court Cave - Chocolate Silk (Sayarshan)

Ann Hamilton — Ian Hamilton

PLACINGS: 43PU4/511/15211113- — RPR **147+c**

Starts	1st	2nd	3rd	4th	Win & Pl
16	7	1	2	2	£47,197

	Date	Course	Race	Prize
130	4/22	Kels	2m7½f Cls3 116-132 Ch Hcap gd-sft	£7,407
125	2/22	Carl	3m½f Cls3 114-127 Ch Hcap heavy	£7,951
117	1/22	Newc	2m7½f Cls3 109-127 Ch Hcap soft	£8,169
116	12/21	Newc	2m7½f Cls4 Nov 90-116 Ch Hcap good	£3,594
113	10/21	Hexm	2m4f Cls3 113-128 Hdl Hcap good	£5,174
109	3/21	Hexm	2m4f Cls4 103-119 Hdl Hcap gd-sft	£3,268
105	3/21	Carl	2m3½f Cls5 79-105 Cond Hdl Hcap soft	£2,794

Hugely progressive novice chaser last season and rattled off a four-timer in the north, climbing 23lb in the handicap; yet to win above Class 3 level and a well-beaten third at Haydock when stepped up in grade, though clearly below par there just 12 days after latest win.

Beacon Edge (Ire)

8 b g Doyen - Laurel Gift (Presenting)

Noel Meade (Ire) — Gigginstown House Stud

PLACINGS: 3122/113314/F21F27-P — RPR **157c**

Starts	1st	2nd	3rd	4th	Win & Pl
19	6	4	3	2	£138,675

	Date	Course	Race	Prize
	11/21	Fair	2m4f Nov Gd1 Ch good	£36,875
	2/21	Navn	2m5f Gd2 Hdl heavy	£18,438
	10/20	Gway	2m4½f Gd3 Hdl soft	£13,750
	10/20	Dpat	2m3f Hdl yield	£5,750
	10/19	Punc	2m Mdn Hdl yield	£6,922
	10/18	Ayr	2m Cls5 NHF 4-6yo good	£2,274

Stayers' Hurdle fourth in 2021 who soon reached a similar level over fences last season, winning the Drinmore; proved equally effective at 3m with a close second to Farouk D'Alene at Navan only to run poorly at Cheltenham and Punchestown in the spring.

Beauport (Ire)

6 b g Califet - Byerley Beauty (Brian Boru)

Nigel Twiston-Davies — Bryan & Philippa Burrough

PLACINGS: 43131/22214- — RPR **147+h**

Starts	1st	2nd	3rd	4th	Win & Pl
10	3	3	2	2	£91,706

	Date	Course	Race	Prize
142	3/22	Uttx	2m4f Cls2 121-142 Hdl Hcap soft	£25,720
122	3/21	Sand	2m4f Cls1 Nov Gd3 117-132 Hdl 4-7yo Hcap soft	£28,230
	1/21	Font	2m5½f Cls4 Nov Hdl soft	£3,769

Runaway winner of the 2021 EBF Final who continued to progress in good handicap hurdles last season; finished second three times before winning at Uttoxeter and was unlucky in running when fourth at Aintree's Grand National meeting; has the look of a nice chaser.

Before Midnight

9 ch g Midnight Legend - Lady Samantha (Fraam)

Sam Thomas — Walters Plant Hire & Potter Group

PLACINGS: 2102/64/22321/11426- — RPR **154c**

Starts	1st	2nd	3rd	4th	Win & Pl
21	6	7	2	2	£125,153

	Date	Course	Race	Prize
144	11/21	Asct	2m1f Cls2 135-159 Ch Hcap good	£44,226
136	10/21	Chel	2m Cls2 133-159 Ch Hcap good	£31,218
129	4/21	Chep	2m Cls2 120-137 Ch Hcap good	£10,034
	2/21	Kemp	2m Cls4 NHF std-slw	£3,899
	1/19	Tntn	2m3f Cls4 Nov Hdl 4-7yo gd-sft	£5,133
	4/18	Fknm	2m Cls5 NHF 4-6yo gd-sft	£2,274
	1/18	Bang	2m½f Cls5 NHF 4-6yo heavy	£2,274

Hugely progressive in 2021 when winning three 2m handicap chases in a row, including valuable races at Cheltenham and Ascot; length second at Doncaster subsequently but below par on final run at Aintree; best on good ground.

Billaway (Ire)

10 b g Well Chosen - Taipans Girl (Taipan)

Willie Mullins (Ire) — The Turner Family

PLACINGS: 312/212/21125/2211-1 — RPR **144c**

Starts	1st	2nd	3rd	4th	Win & Pl
19	7	9	1	-	£102,812

	Date	Course	Race	Prize
	4/22	Punc	3m Hunt Ch gd-yld	£14,874
	3/22	Chel	3m2½f Cls2 Am Hunt Ch gd-sft	£24,445
	2/22	Naas	3m1f Hunt Ch sft-hvy	£6,693
	1/21	Naas	3m1f Hunt Ch heavy	£7,112
	12/20	DRoy	2m5½f Hunt Ch soft	£4,500
	1/20	Naas	3m Hunt Ch soft	£7,513
	3/19	Dpat	2m7½f Mdn Hunt Ch gd-yld	£5,550

Leading hunter chaser last season, pulling off the big Cheltenham/Punchestown double having been beaten in photo finishes in both races in 2021; thrives on racing and has five wins and four seconds from ten races across the last two seasons.

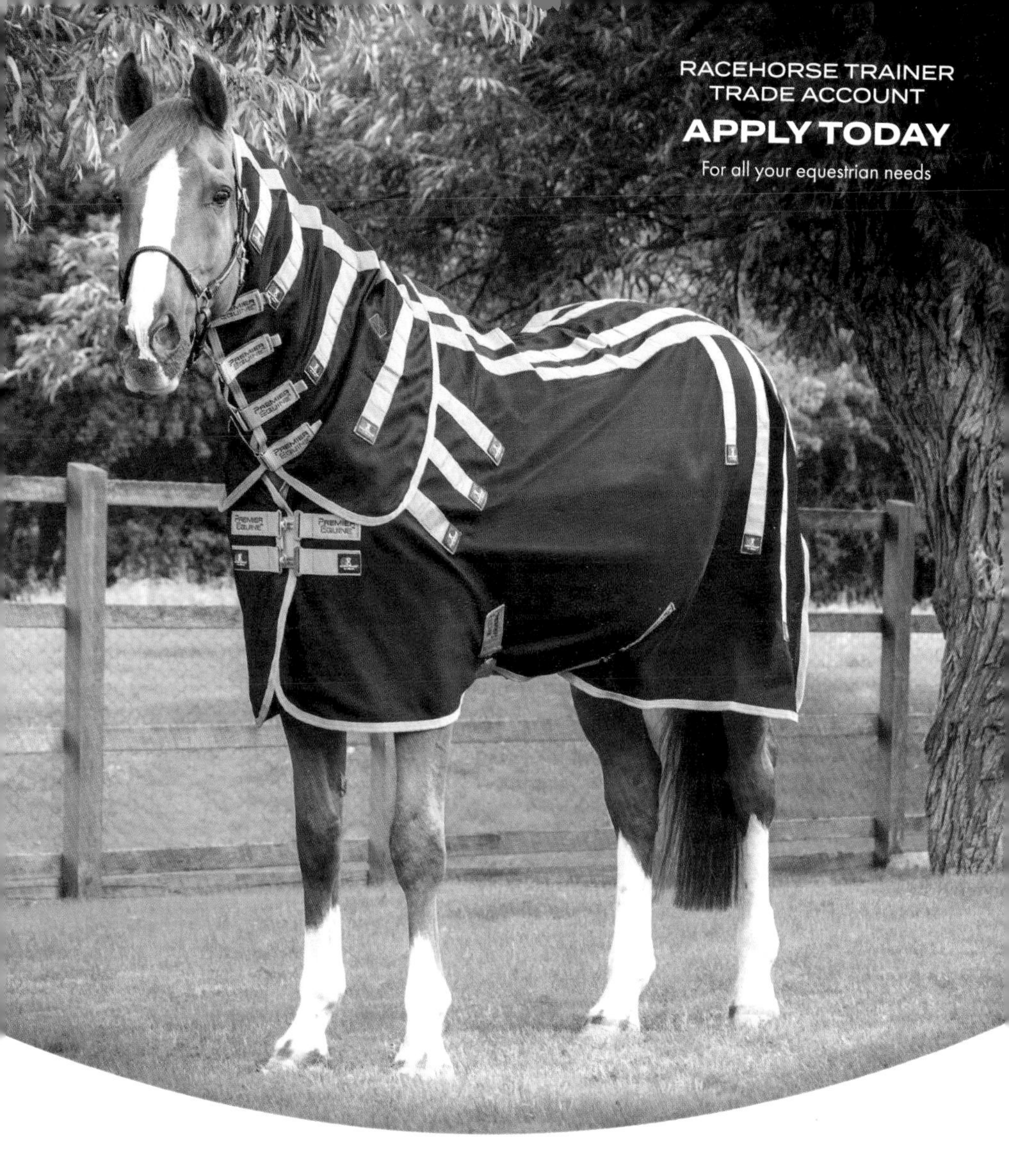
RACEHORSE TRAINER
TRADE ACCOUNT
APPLY TODAY
For all your equestrian needs

Blazing Khal (Ire)

6 b g Kalanisi - Blazing Sonnet (Oscar)

Charles Byrnes (Ire) — Byrnes Bloodstock

PLACINGS: 52/541/111- — RPR **150+h**

Starts	1st	2nd	3rd	4th	Win & Pl
8	4	1	-	1	£70,013

12/21	Chel	3m Cls1 Nov Gd2 Hdl gd-sft	£28,475
11/21	Chel	2m5f Cls1 Nov Gd2 Hdl good	£28,230
10/21	Gway	2m3f Mdn Hdl soft	£6,321
12/20	Limk	2m NHF 4-7yo heavy	£4,500

Won three out of three novice hurdles last season, most impressively when stepped up to 3m for a second Grade 2 win at Cheltenham over subsequent Grade I winner Gelino Bello; had been favourite for the Albert Bartlett until ruled out through injury.

Blue Lord (Fr)

7 b g Blue Bresil - Lorette (Cachet Noir)

Willie Mullins (Ire) — Simon Munir & Isaac Souede

PLACINGS: 123F/31113-1 — RPR **160+c**

Starts	1st	2nd	3rd	4th	Win & Pl
10	5	1	3	-	£209,836

4/22	Punc	2m Nov Gd1 Ch gd-yld	£61,975
2/22	Leop	2m1f Nov Gd1 Ch yield	£74,370
1/22	Naas	2m Nov Ch soft	£9,668
12/21	Fair	2m Ch yld-sft	£6,848
11/20	Punc	2m½f Mdn Hdl soft	£6,000

Dual Grade I winner last season, narrowly beating Riviere D'Etel at Leopardstown and Coeur Sublime at Punchestown; only third in the Arkle at Cheltenham behind Edwardstone, with Riviere D'Etel and Coeur Sublime further back to raise doubts over form of Grade I wins.

Blue Sari (Fr)

7 b g Saddex - Blue Aster (Astarabad)

Willie Mullins (Ire) — John P McManus

PLACINGS: 12/14P/PF/P2414-P — RPR **155+c**

Starts	1st	2nd	3rd	4th	Win & Pl
13	3	2	-	3	£45,070

2/22	Gowr	2m4f Ch heavy	£6,445
11/19	Punc	2m4f Mdn Hdl 4yo soft	£7,188
1/19	Gowr	2m NHF 4yo soft	£5,827

Talented but fragile gelding; went some way to getting career back on track last season having failed to get round in his previous four races, notably when hacking up in a beginners' chase at Gowran, but broke blood vessels again when pulled up at Punchestown on final run.

Bob Olinger (Ire)

7 b g Sholokhov - Zenaide (Zaffaran)

Henry de Bromhead (Ire) — Robcour

PLACINGS: 11/2111/111-P — RPR **162+c**

Starts	1st	2nd	3rd	4th	Win & Pl
9	7	1	-	-	£235,232

3/22	Chel	2m4f Cls1 Nov Gd1 Ch soft	£101,564
1/22	Punc	2m4f Nov Gd3 Ch soft	£17,353
11/21	Gowr	2m4f Ch soft	£8,165
3/21	Chel	2m5f Cls1 Nov Gd1 Hdl gd-sft	£52,753
1/21	Naas	2m4f Nov Gd1 Hdl heavy	£42,143
12/20	Navn	2m4f Mdn Hdl sft-hvy	£6,000
3/20	Gowr	2m2f NHF 4-7yo sft-hvy	£5,000

Long seen as a superstar in the making but reputation nosedived towards end of last season; still gained second Cheltenham Festival win but was a poor second until Galopin Des Champs' exit and then pulled up at Punchestown; plenty to prove but still a top-class prospect.

Bonttay (Ire)

5 b m Westerner - Ben's Turn (Saddlers' Hall)

Fergal O'Brien — C B Brookes & Fergal O'Brien

PLACINGS: 111- — RPR **110+b**

Starts	1st	2nd	3rd	4th	Win & Pl
3	3	-	-	-	£23,056

11/21	Chel	2m½f Cls1 List NHF 4-6yo good	£12,529
10/21	Chel	2m½f Cls2 NHF 4-6yo good	£7,805
8/21	MRas	2m½f Cls4 NHF 4-6yo good	£2,723

Unbeaten in three bumpers last season, including two at Cheltenham; beat subsequent Listed winner Top Dog in October and followed up at that level herself when back in mares' company at the November meeting; out of a dual hurdles winner so bred for jumping.

Botox Has (Fr)

6 b g Dream Well - Bournie (Kahyasi)

Gary Moore — John & Yvonne Stone

PLACINGS: 2/121/1406P/F8231- — RPR **148h**

Starts	1st	2nd	3rd	4th	Win & Pl
14	4	3	1	1	£121,488

2/22	Font	2m3f Cls1 Gd2 Hdl gd-sft	£51,496
10/20	Chel	2m½f Cls2 Hdl 4yo good	£20,019
12/19	Chel	2m1f Cls2 Hdl 3yo soft	£15,640
10/19	Font	2m1½f Cls4 Hdl 3yo good	£3,861

Narrow winner of last season's National Spirit Hurdle at Fontwell, ending a barren run stretching back to 2020; had been in better form last season since given a chance by the handicapper (twice placed in 3m handicaps at Cheltenham) and 6lb below peak mark even after Fontwell.

Braeside (Ire)

8 b g Presenting - The Kids Dante (Phardante)

Gordon Elliott (Ire) — KTDA Racing

PLACINGS: 33316F/435226/14P3P- — RPR **150+c**

Starts	1st	2nd	3rd	4th	Win & Pl
21	2	5	5	3	£53,464

133	10/21	Cork	3m4f 119-136 Ch Hcap heavy	£21,071
	1/20	Fair	2m6½f Mdn Hdl heavy	£5,509

Largely progressive staying chaser; got off the mark in his second campaign over fences when winning last year's Cork Grand National and ran another big race when fourth in the Paddy Power Chase; seemingly less effective in small-field novice chases.

Brandy Love (Ire)

6 b m Jet Away - Bambootcha (Saddlers' Hall)

Willie Mullins (Ire) — Claudio Michael Grech

PLACINGS: 1/13/121- — RPR **146h**

Starts	1st	2nd	3rd	4th	Win & Pl
5	3	1	1	-	£73,567

4/22	Fair	2m4f Nov Gd1 Hdl yield	£49,580
12/21	Naas	2m Mdn Hdl yield	£6,321
12/20	Fair	2m NHF 4yo sft-hvy	£5,000

Endured a frustrating campaign last term but proved herself top dog in the mares' novice hurdle division when thrashing Cheltenham winner Love Envoi by eight lengths at Fairyhouse; had hung badly when suffering sole defeat at that track before missing Cheltenham through injury.

Bob Olinger: lucky winner at the festival

Brave Seasca (Fr)

7 bl g Brave Mansonnien - Miss Laveron (Laveron)

Venetia Williams — Brooks & Taylor Families

PLACINGS: 9/4/41/61113F- — RPR **152c**

Starts	1st	2nd	3rd	4th	Win & Pl
10	4	-	1	2	£38,990

137	1/22	Wwck	2m Cls2 133-157 Ch Hcap soft	£16,338
128	12/21	Asct	2m1f Cls3 Nov 125-136 Ch Hcap gd-sft	£8,169
121	12/21	Wwck	2m Cls4 Nov 105-121 Ch Hcap soft	£4,357
	2/21	Hntg	2m Cls4 Nov Hdl soft	£3,769

Progressive novice chaser last season, completing a hat-trick of handicap wins with a decisive defeat of Sky Pirate; not quite up to top novices (third behind Edwardstone at Warwick before falling in the Arkle) but had been well fancied for the Grand Annual before taking Grade I route.

Bravemansgame (Fr)

7 b g Brave Mansonnien - Genifique (Nickname)

Paul Nicholls — John Dance & Bryan Drew

PLACINGS: 1/36/211132/11114- — RPR **165+c**

Starts	1st	2nd	3rd	4th	Win & Pl
13	7	2	2	1	£176,406

159	2/22	Newb	2m7½f Cls3 Nov 140-159 Ch Hcap gd-sft	£10,519
	12/21	Kemp	3m Cls1 Nov Gd1 Ch soft	£56,950
	11/21	Hayd	2m5½f Cls2 Ch gd-sft	£26,015
	10/21	NAbb	2m5f Cls2 Ch gd-sft	£12,155
	12/20	Newb	2m4½f Cls1 Nov Gd1 Hdl soft	£23,848
	11/20	Newb	2m4½f Cls3 Nov Hdl good	£6,498
	11/20	Extr	2m1f Cls3 Nov Hdl good	£5,913

Among last season's top staying novice chasers despite a frustrating spring; won first four races over fences, including a comprehensive defeat of Ahoy Senor in a 3m Grade I at Kempton; missed Cheltenham due to soft ground and suffered from ulcers when only fourth at Aintree.

Brazil (Ire)

4 b c Galileo - Dialafara (Anabaa)

Padraig Roche (Ire) — John P McManus

PLACINGS: 654113- — RPR **139+h**

Starts	1st	2nd	3rd	4th	Win & Pl
6	2	-	1	1	£65,846

137	3/22	Chel	2m½f Cls1 Gd3 122-137 Hdl 4yo Hcap gd-sft	£45,016
	2/22	Naas	1m7½f Nov Hdl 4yo soft	£8,181

Rapidly progressive juvenile hurdler last season who did brilliantly to concede 8lb to monster gamble Gaelic Warrior when winning the Fred Winter at Cheltenham; just 5-2 when stepped up to Grade I level at Aintree but slightly underwhelming when a well-beaten third.

Brewin'Upastorm (Ire)

9 b g Milan - Daraheen Diamond (Husyan)

Olly Murphy — Mrs Barbara Hester

PLACINGS: F42/11U/65115/1F12P- — RPR **160h**

Starts	1st	2nd	3rd	4th	Win & Pl
20	8	2	-	3	£192,319

	1/22	Ling	2m3½f Cls2 Hdl heavy	£52,030
	11/21	Aint	2m4f Cls2 Hdl gd-sft	£20,812
	2/21	Font	2m3f Cls1 Gd2 Hdl gd-sft	£28,609
148	1/21	Tntn	2m3f Cls2 122-148 Hdl Hcap soft	£9,495
	11/19	Tntn	2m2f Cls4 Nov Ch good	£6,590
	10/19	Carl	2m Cls3 Ch gd-sft	£7,473
	12/18	Hntg	2m Cls4 Nov Hdl gd-sft	£5,523
	1/18	Hrfd	2m Cls5 Am NHF 4-6yo soft	£2,599

Smart hurdler who won at Aintree and Lingfield last season and was unlucky not to score at Graded level, all at around 2m4f; fell at the last when holding every chance in the Relkeel Hurdle and was beaten a head when going for a second successive National Spirit Hurdle.

Bring On The Night

5 ch g Gleneagles - Brasileira (Dubai Destination)

Willie Mullins (Ire) — Mrs J Donnelly

PLACINGS: 14-5 — RPR **138h**

Starts	1st	2nd	3rd	4th	Win & Pl
3	1	-	-	1	£14,069

2/22	Naas	1m7½f Mdn Hdl soft	£5,950

Smart Flat stayer (second in the Ascot Stakes behind Coltrane this summer) who took well to hurdles last season; won well first time out at Naas and was very highly tried subsequently, finishing a respectable fourth in the Supreme at Cheltenham but only fifth at Punchestown.

Bristol De Mai (Fr)

11 gr g Saddler Maker - La Bole Night (April Night)

Nigel Twiston-Davies — Simon Munir & Isaac Souede

PLACINGS: 2/1F34/229/12P/P32P- — RPR **167c**

Starts	1st	2nd	3rd	4th	Win & Pl
40	11	12	6	2	£853,257

	11/20	Hayd	3m1½f Cls1 Gd1 Ch heavy	£90,032
	11/18	Hayd	3m1½f Cls1 Gd1 Ch good	£112,540
	11/17	Hayd	3m1½f Cls1 Gd1 Ch heavy	£113,072
	11/17	Weth	3m Cls1 Gd2 Ch soft	£57,218
154	1/17	Hayd	3m Cls1 Gd2 142-162 Ch Hcap soft	£28,475
	2/16	Sand	2m4f Cls1 Nov Gd1 Ch gd-sft	£25,628
	1/16	Hayd	2m4f Cls1 Nov Gd2 Ch heavy	£18,438
	12/15	Leic	2m4f Cls3 Nov Ch soft	£6,330
	11/15	Wwck	2m Cls3 Nov Ch 4-5yo gd-sft	£9,384
	12/14	Chep	2m Cls1 Gd1 Hdl 3yo heavy	£19,933
	9/14	Autl	2m2f Hdl 3yo v soft	£19,200

Five-time Grade I winner most famous for winning the Betfair Chase three times; hasn't won since the last of those victories but twice ran to a high level last season, including when second in the Grand National Trial at Haydock on first run in a conventional handicap since 2017.

Bristol De Mai: high-class 3m chaser who was winless last season but ran some fine races in defeat

Broken Halo

7 b g Kayf Tara - Miss Invincible (Invincible Spirit)

Paul Nicholls — Giraffa Racing

PLACINGS: 1/P13/P3141- — RPR **143+c**

Starts	1st	2nd	3rd	4th	Win & Pl
8	3	-	2	1	£24,910

	3/22	Font	2m5½f Cls3 Nov Ch gd-sft	£7,733
127	1/22	Extr	2m3f Cls3 Nov 117-136 Ch Hcap heavy	£7,951
	3/21	Winc	2m5½f Cls4 Nov Hdl gd-sft	£3,769

Progressive novice chaser last season, albeit in modest company; won easily at Fontwell and Exeter on contrasting ground, jumping well, having bled when disappointing at Lingfield in between (only run above Class 3 level).

Bronn (Ire)

5 b g Notnowcato - Cluain Easa (Accordion)

Willie Mullins (Ire) — Simon Munir & Isaac Souede

PLACINGS: 1/1521-4 — RPR **141+h**

Starts	1st	2nd	3rd	4th	Win & Pl
6	3	1	-	1	£41,797

4/22	Fair	2m4f Nov Gd2 Hdl yield	£19,832
1/22	Naas	2m Mdn Hdl soft	£6,941
4/21	Baln	2m1½f NHF 4yo yld-sft	£5,268

Useful novice hurdler last season; gained most notable win in a 2m4f Grade 2 at Fairyhouse, doing well to get up after being badly hampered, albeit in a weak race for the grade; twice well beaten at Grade 1 level, including when fourth stepping up to 3m at Punchestown.

Burrows Saint (Fr)

9 b g Saint Des Saints - La Bombonera (Mansonnien)

Willie Mullins (Ire) — Mrs S Ricci

PLACINGS: 4111/531/2624/323U-0 — RPR **157c**

Starts	1st	2nd	3rd	4th	Win & Pl
26	5	7	4	3	£433,161

	12/19	Punc	2m3½f Hdl gd-yld	£10,649
144	4/19	Fair	3m5f 135-157 Ch Hcap gd-yld	£243,243
	3/19	Limk	3m½f Nov Gd3 Ch good	£22,590
	3/19	Gowr	2m4f Ch soft	£8,047
	11/17	Punc	2m4f Mdn Hdl 4yo sft-hvy	£7,108

Hasn't hit the heights expected since winning the 2019 Irish Grand National as a novice, winning just once over hurdles in the interim; has had last two campaigns geared towards the Grand National, finishing fourth in 2021 but unseating at the Chair last season.

Buzz (Fr)

8 gr g Motivator - Tiysha (Araafa)

Nicky Henderson — Thurloe For Royal Marsden Cancer Charity

PLACINGS: 114/31252/1- — RPR **157+h**

Starts	1st	2nd	3rd	4th	Win & Pl
9	4	2	1	1	£129,514

	11/21	Asct	2m3½f Cls1 Gd2 Hdl good	£39,865
137	11/20	Asct	1m7½f Cls2 112-138 Hdl Hcap soft	£11,261
	2/20	Donc	2m½f Cls4 Nov Hdl good	£3,769
	1/20	Tntn	2m½f Cls4 Mdn Hdl soft	£5,133

Reportedly set to return having made good progress from a fractured pelvis suffered when set to run in last season's Long Walk Hurdle; had been making rapid progress at the time, following up a career-best win on the Flat in the Cesarewitch with victory in the Ascot Hurdle.

Camprond (Fr)

6 b g Lope De Vega - Bernieres (Montjeu)

Philip Hobbs — John P McManus

PLACINGS: 2312/31421144-1 — RPR **147+h**

Starts	1st	2nd	3rd	4th	Win & Pl
13	5	3	2	3	£137,918

137	4/22	Punc	2m3f 119-145 Hdl Hcap yield	£49,580
	10/21	Chel	2m4f Cls2 Nov Hdl good	£10,406
	10/21	Chep	2m3½f Cls1 Nov Gd2 Hdl good	£34,170
	6/21	MRas	2m½f Cls4 Nov Hdl good	£3,159
	3/21	Tntn	2m½f Cls4 Mdn Hdl good	£3,769

Progressive hurdler who won four times in novice company having been kept on the go through the summer, including the Persian War at Chepstow, and returned in top handicaps in the spring; followed a good fourth in the Coral Cup by winning at Punchestown; should stay 3m.

Cape Gentleman (Ire)

6 ch g Champs Elysees - Hawaiian Heat (Galileo)

Emmet Mullins (Ire) — Mrs Margaret O'Rourke

PLACINGS: 1P1/93112F-92 — RPR **152+c**

Starts	1st	2nd	3rd	4th	Win & Pl
11	4	2	1	-	£71,100

	10/21	Cork	2m4f Nov Gd3 Ch heavy	£17,121
	10/21	Punc	2m1f Ch good	£6,585
	2/21	Kemp	2m Cls1 Nov Gd2 Hdl good	£12,814
	12/20	Punc	2m4f Mdn Hdl 4yo heavy	£6,000

Showed signs of real promise when sent novice chasing early in the campaign, twice winning easily, but bubble has burst slightly since; going well when falling four out in the Drinmore but then missed the rest of the season and twice below par on return this summer.

Capodanno (Fr)

6 ch g Manduro - Day Gets Up (Muhtathir)

Willie Mullins (Ire) — John P McManus

PLACINGS: 2/3134/112U4-1 — RPR **160+c**

Starts	1st	2nd	3rd	4th	Win & Pl
11	4	2	2	2	£129,327

	4/22	Punc	3m½f Nov Gd1 Ch gd-yld	£61,975
	12/21	Naas	2m3f Ch yield	£6,585
132	4/21	Punc	3m 125-140 Hdl Hcap yield	£26,339
	1/21	Clon	2m Mdn Hdl heavy	£5,268

Smart and progressive novice chaser last season; only fourth when stepped up to 3m in the Brown Advisory at Cheltenham but flourished under a more positive ride at Punchestown, running away with a Grade I (ordinary race for the grade with Bob Olinger flopping).

Captain Guinness (Ire)

7 b g Arakan - Presenting D'Azy (Presenting)

Henry de Bromhead (Ire) — Declan Landy

PLACINGS: 12B/P12F3/U13316-4 — RPR **164+c**

Starts	1st	2nd	3rd	4th	Win & Pl
15	4	2	3	1	£107,426

	Date	Course	Race	Prize
	2/22	Naas	2m Gd3 Ch soft	£14,130
	11/21	Naas	2m Gd3 Ch gd-yld	£14,487
	12/20	Punc	2m Ch heavy	£6,250
	12/19	Navn	2m Mdn Hdl soft	£7,986

Smart 2m chaser who has been very highly tried, finishing no better than third in seven Grade 1 chases and perhaps doing best in last season's Tingle Creek; won two Grade 3 chases at Naas last season on only occasions when dropped below the top level.

Carefully Selected (Ire)

10 b g Well Chosen - Knockamullen Girl (Alderbrook)

Willie Mullins (Ire) — Miss M A Masterson

PLACINGS: 21/1123/1/3111U/ — RPR **154c**

Starts	1st	2nd	3rd	4th	Win & Pl
10	6	1	2	-	£104,189

	Date	Course	Race	Prize
	1/20	Naas	3m Nov Gd3 Ch soft	£22,500
	1/20	Punc	2m4f Nov Gd3 Ch soft	£21,250
	11/19	Fair	2m5f Ch soft	£7,720
	3/19	Limk	2m6f Mdn Hdl heavy	£7,214
	2/18	Naas	2m NHF 4-7yo soft	£7,087
	12/17	Leop	2m4f NHF 4-7yo soft	£6,318

Has missed last two seasons through injury but had looked to be developing into a very smart staying chaser prior to that; won first three chases but couldn't get away with continued jumping errors when odds-on for the National Hunt Chase (held in third when unseated at the last).

Caribean Boy (Fr)

8 gr g Myboycharlie - Caribena (Linamix)

Nicky Henderson — Simon Munir & Isaac Souede

PLACINGS: 15692/31/1347P/0F1P- — RPR **154+c**

Starts	1st	2nd	3rd	4th	Win & Pl
19	4	1	2	1	£87,966

	Date	Course	Race	Prize
145	1/22	Kemp	3m Cls2 128-145 Ch Hcap soft	£13,008
	11/20	Newb	2m4f Cls1 Nov Gd2 Ch good	£17,085
138	2/20	Hayd	2m4f Cls3 Nov 127-138 Ch Hcap heavy	£9,747
	10/17	Autl	2m1½f Hdl 3yo v soft	£19,692

Very patchy record during the last two seasons but has looked smart on occasions, winning a Grade 2 novice chase in 2020 and adding a 3m handicap chase at Kempton last season; regarded by his trainer as a live Grand National hope only to miss Aintree through injury.

Buzz: won sole start last season and is set to return to action

Celebre D'Allen (Fr)

10 ch g Network - Revoltee I (Grand Seigneur)

Philip Hobbs — Allan Stennett

PLACINGS: 15/4921113/272/1115- — RPR **148+c**

Starts	1st	2nd	3rd	4th	Win & Pl
18	7	3	3	1	£171,176

	Date	Course	Race	Prize
135	2/22	Wwck	2m4f Cls2 130-150 Ch Hcap gd-sft	£26,015
126	12/21	Hayd	2m3f Cls3 122-135 Hdl Hcap heavy	£8,169
120	12/21	Hayd	2m3f Cls3 115-131 Hdl Hcap heavy	£6,862
	11/18	Autl	2m2½f Ch heavy	£22,088
0	10/18	Autl	2m3½f List Hdl Hcap v soft	£39,823
	8/18	Diep	2m3½f Ch v soft	£8,920
	12/17	Ange	2m3f Hdl heavy	£8,615

French hurdle and chase winner who flourished during first campaign in Britain last season; won twice over hurdles before switching back to fences to complete a hat-trick at Warwick; just 4-1 for the Plate at Cheltenham but managed only fifth, finishing well having got too far back.

Chacun Pour Soi (Fr)

10 b g Policy Maker - Kruscyna (Ultimately Lucky)

Willie Mullins (Ire) — Mrs S Ricci

PLACINGS: 53/1/121/1113/151U-2 — RPR **176+c**

Starts	1st	2nd	3rd	4th	Win & Pl
17	9	3	2	-	£627,801

	Date	Course	Race	Prize
	2/22	Leop	2m1f Gd1 Ch yield	£74,370
	4/21	Punc	2m Gd1 Ch yield	£131,696
	2/21	Leop	2m1½f Gd1 Ch soft	£65,848
	12/20	Leop	2m1f Gd1 Ch yield	£50,000
	12/20	Cork	2m½f Gd2 Ch sft-hvy	£35,000
	2/20	Leop	2m1f Gd1 Ch yield	£75,000
	5/19	Punc	2m Nov Gd1 Ch yield	£61,126
	3/19	Naas	2m Ch yld-sft	£8,047
	8/15	Diep	2m1f Hdl 3yo v soft	£8,558

Became a six-time Grade 1 winner when easing to a third successive victory in the Dublin Chase at Leopardstown last season; unseated rider in the Champion Chase (beaten at odds-on on two other runs in Britain) before failing to match Energumene at Punchestown.

Chambard (Fr)

10 b g Gris De Gris - Regina Park (Cadoudal)

Venetia Williams — David & Carol Shaw

PLACINGS: 23/2225/P466/122111- — RPR **142+c**

Starts	1st	2nd	3rd	4th	Win & Pl
28	8	10	2	2	£135,661

	Date	Course	Race	Prize
134	3/22	Chel	3m2f Cls2 127-145 Am Ch Hcap soft	£36,668
129	3/22	Hntg	2m7½f Cls3 Nov 129-132 Ch Hcap soft	£8,169
122	2/22	Font	2m3½f Cls4 Nov 96-122 Ch Hcap soft	£7,624
110	1/22	Extr	2m3f Cls4 99-117 Ch Hcap heavy	£6,753
	1/19	Extr	2m1f Cls4 Mdn Hdl gd-sft	£4,094
	9/16	StCl	1m4½f Gd1 NHF 4-5yo good	£18,382
	7/16	Le L	1m3½f NHF 4yo good	£7,353
	9/15	Agtn	1m4½f NHF 3yo good	£6,202

Remarkably progressive at the age of ten last season and completed a hat-trick with a 40-1 success in the Kim Muir at Cheltenham in first chase beyond 3m; very lightly raced for his age over fences (had lost confidence earlier in career) and totally unexposed as a stayer.

Champ (Ire)

10 b g King's Theatre - China Sky (Definite Article)

Nicky Henderson — John P McManus

PLACINGS: 111121/11F1/2P/1243- — RPR **165+h**

Starts	1st	2nd	3rd	4th	Win & Pl
19	10	5	1	1	£404,345

	12/21	Asct	3m½f Cls1 Gd1 Hdl gd-sft	£59,798
	3/20	Chel	3m½f Cls1 Nov Gd1 Ch soft	£98,764
	11/19	Newb	2m4f Cls1 Nov Gd2 Ch gd-sft	£22,887
	11/19	Newb	2m6½f Cls3 Ch gd-sft	£7,018
	4/19	Aint	3m½f Cls1 Nov Gd1 Hdl soft	£56,130
	12/18	Newb	2m4½f Cls1 Nov Gd1 Hdl gd-sft	£25,628
139	12/18	Newb	2m4½f Cls2 120-145 Hdl Hcap soft	£25,992
	5/18	Wwck	2m5f Cls4 Nov Hdl gd-sft	£4,549
	5/18	Prth	2m4f Cls4 Mdn Hdl good	£4,224
	1/17	Sthl	1m7½f Cls6 Mdn NHF 4-6yo soft	£2,053

Former RSA Chase winner who was reinvented as a staying hurdler last season after flopping in the 2021 Cheltenham Gold Cup; brilliant winner of the Long Walk Hurdle first time out but didn't quite build on that, though still a highly creditable fourth in the Stayers' Hurdle.

Champ Kiely (Ire)

6 b g Ocovango - Cregg So (Moscow Society)

Willie Mullins (Ire) — Miss M A Masterson

PLACINGS: U/1-1 — RPR **138+h**

Starts	1st	2nd	3rd	4th	Win & Pl
2	2	-	-	-	£13,696

7/22	Gway	2m5f Mdn Hdl good	£8,429
5/21	Limk	2m NHF yld-sft	£5,268

Made a stunning return from a long absence when scoring by 21 lengths on hurdles debut at Galway in July; had also won sole bumper at Limerick in May 2021 only to miss the rest of last season; big horse who looks a likely improver in good staying novice hurdles.

Chantry House (Ire)

8 br g Yeats - The Last Bank (Phardante)

Nicky Henderson — John P McManus

PLACINGS: U11/113/13111/1P1P- — RPR **164+c**

Starts	1st	2nd	3rd	4th	Win & Pl
13	9	-	2	-	£252,127

1/22	Chel	3m1½f Cls1 Gd2 Ch good	£67,524
11/21	Sand	3m Cls1 List Ch gd-sft	£17,085
4/21	Aint	3m1f Cls1 Nov Gd1 Ch gd-sft	£44,690
3/21	Chel	2m4f Cls1 Nov Gd1 Ch gd-sft	£73,918
2/21	Weth	2m5½f Cls4 Nov Ch soft	£4,289
11/20	Asct	2m3f Cls3 Nov Ch soft	£10,463
2/20	Newb	2m½f Cls3 Nov Hdl good	£6,758
12/19	Chel	2m1f Cls3 Nov Hdl 4-6yo gd-sft	£9,384
3/19	Wwck	2m Cls5 NHF 4-6yo soft	£2,599

Has been prolific since going chasing, winning six out of nine races including a Grade 1 double as a novice in 2021, but struggled in top company last season; pulled up in the King George and Cheltenham Gold Cup and also got away with poor jumping when winning the Cotswold Chase.

Chatham Street Lad (Ire)

10 br g Beneficial - Hearts Delight (Broken Hearted)

Michael Winters (Ire) — Vivian Healy

PLACINGS: 471123/5/1511341/73- — RPR **140c**

Starts	1st	2nd	3rd	4th	Win & Pl
25	7	2	3	3	£173,194

	3/21	Limk	3m½f Nov Gd3 Ch heavy	£14,487
141	12/20	Chel	2m4½f Cls1 Gd3 138-157 Ch Hcap soft	£59,798
128	11/20	Cork	2m½f 117-138 Ch Hcap heavy	£10,500
118	10/20	Baln	2m1f 90-118 Ch Hcap soft	£5,500
127	1/19	Cork	2m4f 112-140 Hdl Hcap soft	£13,851
117	12/18	Cork	2m 95-123 Hdl Hcap sft-hvy	£8,722
	1/18	Cork	2m Nov Hdl heavy	£9,267

Runaway winner of the Caspian Caviar Gold Cup at Cheltenham as a novice in 2020; hasn't quite gone on from that run, though did win a Grade 3 novice chase at Limerick later that season; disappointing in just two runs last term before missing Cheltenham after a setback.

Cheddleton

7 br g Shirocco - Over Sixty (Overbury)

Jennie Candlish — P & Mrs G A Clarke

PLACINGS: 1/2113/4113/32243- — RPR **154c**

Starts	1st	2nd	3rd	4th	Win & Pl
14	5	3	4	2	£61,937

12/20	Hayd	2m½f Cls3 Nov Ch heavy	£6,882
11/20	Carl	2m Cls3 Ch soft	£7,018
1/20	Kels	2m Cls4 Nov Hdl heavy	£4,224
12/19	Bang	2m½f Cls4 Nov Hdl heavy	£4,094
3/19	Hayd	1m7½f Cls4 NHF 4-6yo soft	£3,899

Had a good strike-rate in novice company in younger days but couldn't quite get the job done last season despite continuing to progress; finished second in 2m handicap chases at Cheltenham and Wetherby and never beaten far in five runs; best with cut in the ground.

Chris's Dream (Ire)

10 b g Mahler - Janebailey (Silver Patriarch)

Henry de Bromhead (Ire) — Robcour

PLACINGS: 9/1215/P110/25PU/U0- — RPR **124c**

Starts	1st	2nd	3rd	4th	Win & Pl
21	6	3	-	-	£175,562

	2/20	Gowr	2m4f Gd2 Ch heavy	£30,000
146	11/19	Navn	3m 121-149 Ch Hcap soft	£53,153
	2/19	Navn	3m Nov Gd2 Ch yield	£23,919
	12/18	Navn	2m4f Ch yield	£7,904
	2/18	Clon	3m Nov Gd3 Hdl heavy	£20,409
	12/17	Limk	2m3f Mdn Hdl soft	£5,791

Developed into a top chaser in 2020, running well in the Gold Cup until looking a non-stayer and finishing a neck second in Down Royal's Champion Chase; disappointing since then, including back in handicaps, although shaped with promise in the Becher Chase until unseating.

Cheddleton: should prove useful in 2m handicap chases when the mud is flying

Ciel De Neige (Fr)

7 b g Authorized - In Caso Di Neve (Country Reel)

Willie Mullins (Ire) — John P McManus

PLACINGS: 220/5199/290121112-5 — RPR **158c**

Starts	1st	2nd	3rd	4th	Win & Pl
22	5	5	1	3	£121,534

2/22	Punc	2m Nov Ch heavy	£10,908
12/21	Navn	2m4f Nov Ch gd-yld	£11,063
11/21	Thur	2m2f Ch good	£5,795
10/21	Slig	2m1½f Hdl yield	£6,058
12/20	Limk	2m Mdn Hdl heavy	£6,000

Took well to fences last season, winning first three chases before a nose second up at Grade 3 level; had shown best hurdles form in major handicaps (second in the 2020 Betfair Hurdle) but managed only fifth on handicap chase debut when favourite at Punchestown.

Cilaos Emery (Fr)

10 b g Califet - Queissa (Saint Preuil)

Willie Mullins (Ire) — Luke McMahon

PLACINGS: 1/11F14/218/4214U62- — RPR **149c**

Starts	1st	2nd	3rd	4th	Win & Pl
23	9	5	-	4	£281,779

11/21	Thur	2m6f List Ch good	£11,853
2/21	Naas	2m Gd3 Ch soft	£14,487
2/20	Gowr	2m Gd3 Hdl heavy	£30,000
12/19	Cork	2m½f Gd2 Ch soft	£45,180
11/19	Naas	2m Gd3 Ch sft-hvy	£17,275
1/19	Gowr	2m Ch soft	£8,047
4/17	Punc	2m½f Nov Gd1 Hdl gd-yld	£50,427
12/16	Navn	2m Mdn Hdl sft-hvy	£6,331
4/16	Punc	2m NHF 4yo gd-yld	£5,426

Versatile and high-class performer at his best (five-time Graded winner and fourth in the 2020 Champion Hurdle) but failed to hit those heights last season; still won a Listed chase at Thurles first time out and finished second in a Grade 2 at Fairyhouse on final run.

City Chief (Ire)

5 b g Soldier Of Fortune - Galant Ferns (Bob Back)

Nicky Henderson — Mrs J Donnelly

PLACINGS: 12211-5 — RPR **137h**

Starts	1st	2nd	3rd	4th	Win & Pl
5	2	2	-	-	£19,677

127	4/22	Ayr	3m½f Cls3 Nov 105-127 Hdl Hcap gd-sft	£7,897
	3/22	Hrfd	3m1½f Cls4 Mdn Hdl soft	£5,446

Raw chasing type who was progressive in novice hurdles last season; finished second on first two runs before improving when stepped up to 3m, winning at Hereford and Ayr; fair fifth when favourite for a competitive handicap at Punchestown on final run.

Clan Des Obeaux (Fr)

10 b g Kapgarde - Nausicaa Des Obeaux (April Night)

Paul Nicholls — Mr & Mrs P K Barber, G Mason & Sir A Ferguson

PLACINGS: 1152/218/2321/1231-2 — RPR **176+c**

Starts	1st	2nd	3rd	4th	Win & Pl
31	11	10	3	3	£1,076,185

	Date	Course	Race	Prize
	4/22	Aint	3m1f Cls1 Gd1 Ch gd-sft	£140,525
	4/21	Punc	3m½f Gd1 Ch yield	£131,696
	4/21	Aint	3m1f Cls1 Gd1 Ch gd-sft	£84,963
	12/19	Kemp	3m Cls1 Gd1 Ch soft	£144,050
	2/19	Asct	3m Cls1 Gd2 Ch gd-sft	£28,475
	12/18	Kemp	3m Cls1 Gd1 Ch gd-sft	£142,375
	11/17	Hayd	2m5½f Cls2 Ch heavy	£32,490
	3/17	Extr	2m3f Cls3 Nov Ch gd-sft	£7,148
	11/16	Newb	2m4f Cls1 Nov Gd2 Ch gd-sft	£19,933
	12/15	Newb	2m½f Cls4 Hdl 3yo soft	£3,249
	4/15	Lrsy	1m4f NHF 3yo gd-sft	£3,876

Five-time Grade I winner who has thrived after skipping Cheltenham in the last two seasons; won a second successive Bowl at Aintree last season and got closest to Allaho when looking for a Punchestown Gold Cup repeat; had also finished second when going for a third King George.

Classic Getaway (Ire)

6 br g Getaway - Classic Magic (Classic Cliche)

Willie Mullins (Ire) — Cheveley Park Stud

PLACINGS: 1/121P-2d — RPR **141h**

Starts	1st	2nd	3rd	4th	Win & Pl
5	2	1	1	-	£14,566

	Date	Course	Race	Prize
	1/22	Punc	2m4½f Mdn Hdl yield	£5,950
	5/21	Tipp	2m4f NHF 4-7yo heavy	£5,268

Bought for £570,000 after impressing in sole point-to-point and also hacked up on sole bumper start only to prove slightly underwhelming over hurdles last season; won just once in four races (at 1-3) and pulled up in the Albert Bartlett at Cheltenham; could do better over fences.

Clondaw Castle (Ire)

10 b g Oscar - Lohort Castle (Presenting)

Tom George — J French, D McDermott, S Nelson & T Syder

PLACINGS: 21144/291/213212/34- — RPR **130c**

Starts	1st	2nd	3rd	4th	Win & Pl
23	8	5	3	3	£235,297

	Date	Course	Race	Prize
154	2/21	Kemp	3m Cls1 Gd3 132-158 Ch Hcap good	£42,713
151	11/20	Newb	2m4f Cls2 129-151 Ch Hcap good	£18,768
143	2/20	Wwck	2m4f Cls2 130-148 Ch Hcap gd-sft	£31,280
134	2/19	Hntg	2m½f Cls3 Nov 119-134 Ch Hcap good	£9,653
	1/19	Leic	2m Cls3 Nov Ch gd-fm	£8,058
	1/18	Kels	2m Cls4 Nov Hdl soft	£4,159
	11/17	Hntg	2m Cls4 Mdn Hdl gd-sft	£3,249
	3/17	Strf	2m½f Cls4 Mdn NHF 4-6yo soft	£3,249

Developed into a very smart chaser two seasons ago, winning a valuable handicap chase at Kempton on first run over 3m; hasn't quite built on that in stronger company since, including in just two runs last season when taking record at Grade I or Grade 2 level to 0-9.

Cloudy Glen (Ire)

9 b g Cloudings - Ribble (Supreme Leader)

Venetia Williams — Exors Of The Late Trevor Hemmings

PLACINGS: 42F102F6/150U2P/1P9- — RPR **154+c**

Starts	1st	2nd	3rd	4th	Win & Pl
27	6	4	1	1	£204,250

	Date	Course	Race	Prize
140	11/21	Newb	3m2f Cls1 Gd3 135-158 Ch Hcap gd-sft	£142,375
134	11/20	Font	3m3½f Cls3 118-137 Ch Hcap heavy	£10,222
	12/19	Hayd	2m4f Cls3 Ch soft	£9,747
	3/19	Carl	2m3½f Cls3 Nov Hdl heavy	£6,498
115	1/19	Chep	2m3½f Cls4 94-118 Hdl Hcap gd-sft	£4,094
115	12/18	Hayd	2m3f Cls4 99-119 Cond Hdl Hcap soft	£6,498

Narrow winner of the Ladbrokes Trophy at Newbury over Fiddlerontheroof (pair clear) on last season's reappearance, having also won first time out in 2020; has largely struggled otherwise and had breathing issues but did finish second in the 2021 Kim Muir.

Cobblers Dream (Ire)

6 br g Yeats - Miss Parkington (Bob Back)

Ben Case — Lady Jane Grosvenor

PLACINGS: P1/1321120- — RPR **138+h**

Starts	1st	2nd	3rd	4th	Win & Pl
8	4	2	1	-	£94,563

	Date	Course	Race	Prize
128	1/22	Kemp	2m5f Cls1 List 122-144 Hdl Hcap soft	£56,950
122	12/21	Donc	2m3½f Cls3 118-140 Hdl Hcap gd-sft	£4,956
	9/21	Wwck	2m Cls4 Nov Hdl good	£4,085
	4/21	Cork	2m3f NHF 4-6yo good	£5,268

Progressive novice hurdler last season, proving particularly effective when switched to handicaps; ran out an emphatic winner of the Lanzarote Hurdle at Kempton before a fine second in the Martin Pipe at Cheltenham; disappointed when joint favourite at Aintree.

Coeur Sublime (Ire)

7 b g Elusive Pimpernel - Love Knot (Lomitas)

Henry de Bromhead (Ire) — C Jones

PLACINGS: 12F423/130/47/2317-2 — RPR **156c**

Starts	1st	2nd	3rd	4th	Win & Pl
16	3	4	3	2	£124,220

	Date	Course	Race	Prize
	1/22	Gowr	2m Ch soft	£6,445
	11/19	DRoy	2m½f Gd2 Hdl yld-sft	£26,577
	11/18	DRoy	2m½f Hdl 3yo gd-yld	£8,177

Finished a head second behind Blue Lord in a Grade I novice chase at Punchestown on final run last term, underlining latent talent having been a Champion Hurdle dark horse three seasons ago; has won just once since then, though, with injuries punctuating a chequered career.

Horseboxes – Uprating and Downplating

...orating Horseboxes

...you may be aware, the DVSA is paying close attention to the horsebox industry and in particular, ...ightweight horseboxes which they suspect may be operating overweight.

...have seen cases of horseboxes being stopped, ...cked and impounded on the roadside, owing to running ...weight. The horses in transit have to be loaded into a ...erent box and taken away, and the resultant fines are ... increasing in size. Yet, there is an alternative.

...ech is keen to promote its uprating service for ...weight horseboxes (3500kg), whereby the horsebox ...gain an extra 200-300kg in payload. This provides ... payload capability when carrying an extra horse and/ ...ack and offers peace of mind for the owner.

...ech has carried out extensive work and testing on ...weight models and has covered uprates for most ...weight vehicles.

...worth noting that some uprates require modifications ...hanges to the vehicle's braking, tyres and/or ...pension, for which SvTech provides a simple purpose-built suspension assister kit. This will take between 1-2 hours for you to fit. Your horsebox will then go for a formal inspection to bring it into the 'Goods' category, and, depending on the vehicle's age, may also require fitment of a speed limiter, for which there are one or two options. Most importantly, vehicles registered after May 2002 must be fitted with manufacturer's ABS, if going above 3500kg.

If you're unsure, or don't believe that you need to uprate your lightweight horsebox, try taking it to a public weighbridge when you're fully loaded with your horse, tack, passenger, hay, etc. and weigh off each axle individually and the vehicle as a whole. There could be a distinct chance that you've overloaded one of the axles, even if you're within the GVW. If there is a problem, we can help. Call us to discuss your options.

...ownplating Horseboxes

...ou own a 10 - 12.5 tonnes horsebox and do you want ...-HGV licence holder to drive it? Your horsebox could be ...nplated to 7.5 tonnes so that any driver with a licence ...ed prior to 1st Jan 1997 could drive it.

...ou are paying too much Vehicle Excise Duty.

...ou want to escape the need for a tachograph.

...most important aspect when downplating is to leave ...rself suitable payload to carry your goods. The Ministry ...uires that for horseboxes of 7500kg there is a minimum ...load of 2000kg. Hence, when downplating to 7500kg, ...unladen weight must not exceed 5500kg. For 3500kg ...seboxes, you must ensure that you have a payload of ...east 1000kg, thus, when empty it cannot weigh more ...n 2500kg.

Due to recent changes at DVSA, we are no longer required to make a mechanical change to the vehicle and, once downrated, we will be supplying you with a revised set of Ministry plating certificates, or if exempt, plating and testing, a converter's plate and certificate at the lower weight.

Depending upon vehicle usage, it is at the discretion of DVSA as to whether they will require a formal inspection of your vehicle.

TO DISCOVER YOUR OPTIONS, PLEASE DOWNLOAD, FILL IN AND RETURN OUR ENQUIRY FORM – WWW.SVTECH.CO.UK

SvTech

Special Vehicle Technology

T +44 (0)1772 621800

E webenquiries@svtech.co.uk

Colonel Mustard (Fr)

7 ch g Makfi - Waldblume (Halling)

Lorna Fowler (Ire) — Mrs A Frost & P G Davies & R H Fowler

PLACINGS: 21243/212337- — RPR **144h**

Starts	1st	2nd	3rd	4th	Win & Pl
11	2	4	3	1	£67,434

	Date	Course	Race	Prize
	10/21	Gway	2m½f Mdn Hdl soft	£6,321
	9/20	Punc	2m½f NHF 4-7yo soft	£4,500

Has proved a smart performer across two seasons in novice hurdles despite winning only once; twice placed at Grade 1 level, notably behind the Ballymore one-two at Leopardstown in February, and came third in a red-hot County Hurdle at Cheltenham; likely to go novice chasing.

Commander Of Fleet (Ire)

8 b g Fame And Glory - Coonagh Cross (Saddlers' Hall)

Gordon Elliott (Ire) — Gigginstown House Stud

PLACINGS: /1412/P/001/5F1P831- — RPR **157h**

Starts	1st	2nd	3rd	4th	Win & Pl
16	6	1	1	1	£274,936

	Date	Course	Race	Prize
152	3/22	Chel	2m5f Cls1 Gd3 137-154 Hdl Hcap soft	£56,270
144	12/21	Navn	3m½f 118-144 Hdl Hcap yield	£52,679
	3/21	Thur	3m Hdl yield	£6,058
	2/19	Leop	2m6f Nov Gd1 Hdl gd-yld	£66,441
	11/18	Punc	2m4½f Mdn Hdl 4yo good	£7,359
	4/18	Punc	2m½f NHF 4-5yo yld-sft	£52,212

Shock 50-1 winner of last season's Coral Cup at Cheltenham, benefiting from return to handicap company having struggled in top staying races; still unlikely to fulfil potential of younger days when second in 2019 Albert Bartlett having proved fragile since then; best on soft ground.

Coole Cody: Cheltenham specialist who added two victories at the track to his CV last season

Commodore (Fr)

10 gr g Fragrant Mix - Morvandelle (Video Rock)

Venetia Williams — Mrs C Watson & Mrs S Graham

PLACINGS: 30/11/50P4P/2U9P/10- RPR **146+c**

Starts	1st	2nd	3rd	4th	Win & Pl
22	4	3	1	3	£81,708

133	12/21	Chel	3m2f Cls1 Gd3 133-159 Ch Hcap gd-sft	£34,331
122	3/19	Sand	3m Cls3 117-136 Ch Hcap soft	£12,512
109	12/18	Wwck	3m Cls4 101-122 Ch Hcap gd-sft	£6,498
	10/16	Lign	2m5½f Ch 4yo good	£4,235

Plagued by breathing problems during his career and has an extremely inconsistent profile but was revitalised by a second operation when hacking up in a 3m2f handicap chase at Cheltenham last season; ran just once more when never dangerous in the Grand National.

Complete Unknown (Ire)

6 b g Dylan Thomas - Silver Stream (Milan)

Paul Nicholls — C K Ong & I Warwick

PLACINGS: U/1/323212- RPR **138h**

Starts	1st	2nd	3rd	4th	Win & Pl
7	2	3	2	-	£62,335

126	3/22	Sand	2m4f Cls1 Nov Gd3 116-135 Hdl 4-7yo Hcap soft	£45,016
	3/21	Thur	2m NHF 5-7yo heavy	£5,268

Authoritative winner of last season's EBF Final at Sandown, conceding weight to all placed horses; relished strong stamina test at 2m4f and should appreciate 3m (good second when stepped up to that trip in Listed company at Perth on final run); likely to go novice chasing.

Conflated (Ire)

8 b g Yeats - Saucy Present (Presenting)

Gordon Elliott (Ire) — Gigginstown House Stud

PLACINGS: 31344/321314/U211F2- RPR **172c**

Starts	1st	2nd	3rd	4th	Win & Pl
23	6	4	4	4	£256,044

	2/22	Leop	3m½f Gd1 Ch yield	£117,647
145	12/21	Navn	2m4f 119-145 Ch Hcap yield	£21,071
	3/21	Naas	2m4½f Nov Gd3 Ch sft-hvy	£14,487
	12/20	Navn	2m4f Ch soft	£6,250
	11/19	Fair	2m Mdn Hdl soft	£6,922
	3/19	Clon	2m NHF 5-7yo good	£5,550

Massive improver last season, stepping out of handicap company to run away with the Irish Gold Cup from Minella Indo; looked set for a well-beaten second when falling two out in the Ryanair Chase before improving back up at 3m when second in the Bowl at Aintree.

Constitution Hill

5 b g Blue Bresil - Queen Of The Stage (King's Theatre)

Nicky Henderson — Michael Buckley

PLACINGS: 2/111- RPR **172+h**

Starts	1st	2nd	3rd	4th	Win & Pl
3	3	-	-	-	£124,450

3/22	Chel	2m½f Cls1 Nov Gd1 Hdl gd-sft	£76,594
1/22	Sand	2m Cls1 Nov Gd1 Hdl heavy	£40,053
12/21	Sand	2m Cls3 Nov Hdl gd-sft	£7,805

Highest-rated winner of a Cheltenham novice hurdle in Racing Post Ratings history on the strength of a sensational 22-length victory in last season's Supreme, storming home in a remarkably fast time; had also romped home on both previous hurdle runs at Sandown.

Coole Cody (Ire)

11 b g Dubai Destination - Run For Cover (Lafontaine I)

Evan Williams — Wayne Clifford

PLACINGS: 4P/12216344/2F18713- RPR **157+c**

Starts	1st	2nd	3rd	4th	Win & Pl
35	8	7	3	4	£301,893

145	3/22	Chel	2m4½f Cls1 Gd3 132-155 Ch Hcap soft	£67,524
143	12/21	Chel	2m4½f Cls1 Gd3 131-157 Ch Hcap gd-sft	£74,035
137	11/20	Chel	2m4f Cls1 Gd3 134-158 Ch Hcap soft	£74,035
	8/20	NAbb	2m5f Cls3 Nov Ch good	£6,303
136	11/17	Chel	2m5f Cls3 111-137 Hdl Hcap soft	£12,512
	9/17	NAbb	2m5½f Cls4 Nov Hdl gd-sft	£3,899
	9/17	NAbb	2m2½f Cls4 Nov Hdl gd-sft	£6,498
	3/17	Winc	2m4f Cls5 Mdn Hdl heavy	£2,599

Has a brilliant record in big Cheltenham handicap chases and won the Racing Post Gold Cup and the Plate last season to add to 2020 Paddy Power Gold Cup victory; up to clear career-high mark after latest win and a well-beaten third back at Cheltenham on only subsequent run.

Copperless

7 b g Kayf Tara - Presenting Copper (Presenting)

Olly Murphy — Aiden Murphy & Alan Peterson

PLACINGS: 211F/1- RPR **139h**

Starts	1st	2nd	3rd	4th	Win & Pl
5	3	1	-	-	£65,594

126	5/21	Hayd	1m7½f Cls1 Gd3 122-144 Hdl Hcap soft	£56,950
117	3/21	Tntn	2m½f Cls4 104-117 Hdl Hcap good	£3,769
	10/20	MRas	2m½f Cls4 Mdn Hdl good	£3,769

Lightly raced and progressive hurdler who was going from strength to strength when last seen in May 2021; had been going well when falling two out at Aintree's Grand National meeting but made up with a runaway win in the Swinton; 15lb higher but still a likely type for top handicaps.

Corach Rambler (Ire)

8 b g Jeremy - Heart N Hope (Fourstars Allstar)

Lucinda Russell — The Ramblers

PLACINGS: PP5/21161/3114U1- RPR **151+c**

Starts	1st	2nd	3rd	4th	Win & Pl
9	5	-	1	1	£101,774

140	3/22	Chel	3m1f Cls1 Gd3 138-164 Ch Hcap gd-sft	£70,338
134	12/21	Chel	3m1½f Cls3 Nov 132-143 Ch Hcap gd-sft	£8,169
127	10/21	Aint	3m1f Cls3 Nov 123-134 Ch Hcap good	£8,714
	3/21	Carl	3m1f Cls4 Nov Hdl soft	£3,769
	1/21	Ayr	3m½f Cls4 Nov Hdl heavy	£3,769

Crowned a tremendous novice season over fences when winning the Ultima Handicap Chase for a third chase win, including two at Cheltenham; stayed on strongly from the rear that day and should get further despite managing only a tame fourth over 3m5f in the Classic Chase.

Dancing On My Own (Ire)

8 b g Milan - Morning Supreme (Supreme Leader)

Henry de Bromhead (Ire) — Sean & Bernardine Mulryan

PLACINGS: 5234P/416/13F02- — RPR **149c**

Starts	1st	2nd	3rd	4th	Win & Pl
13	2	2	2	2	£43,480

10/21	Klny	2m1f Ch yld-sft	£5,795
10/19	Wxfd	2m½f Mdn Hdl heavy	£5,857

Took a long time to build on impressive chase debut win last season but ran a cracker when second in the Red Rum at Aintree, apparently relishing quicker ground; had shown rich promise over hurdles as a youngster only to miss two years with injury; still quite lightly raced.

Darasso (Fr)

9 br g Konig Turf - Nassora (Assessor)

Joseph O'Brien (Ire) — John P McManus

PLACINGS: 4330/11258214121-372 — RPR **162+h**

Starts	1st	2nd	3rd	4th	Win & Pl
36	11	10	4	4	£435,735

	4/22	Fair	2m4f Gd2 Hdl yield	£29,748
	1/22	Naas	1m7½f Gd3 Hdl gd-yld	£14,130
	11/21	Navn	2m4f Gd2 Hdl good	£18,438
	6/21	List	2m3f Ch good	£8,955
	5/21	Klny	2m4f Hdl gd-yld	£8,165
	3/19	Navn	2m Gd2 Ch soft	£23,919
	2/19	Gowr	2m Gd3 Hdl yield	£31,892
	3/18	Comp	2m3½f Ch 5yo heavy	£20,389
	3/18	Comp	2m3½f Ch 5yo heavy	£22,088
0	11/17	Autl	2m3½f List Hdl 4yo Hcap v soft	£40,385
0	10/17	Autl	2m2f List Hdl 4yo Hcap v soft	£40,385

Smart and versatile performer who won three

Graded races over hurdles last season, though came up short at the top level; has proved equally effective over fences despite being more lightly raced, running a cracker when second in the Galway Plate this summer.

Dark Raven (Ire)

5 br g Malinas - Mary Wilkie (Oscar)

Willie Mullins (Ire) — Simon Munir & Isaac Souede

PLACINGS: 11/ — RPR **130b**

Starts		1st	2nd	3rd	4th	Win & Pl
2		2	-	-	-	£57,946
	4/21	Fair	2m NHF 4-5yo yield			£52,679
	3/21	Leop	2m NHF 4yo yield			£5,268

Missed last season through injury but had looked a smart prospect in early 2021; won both bumpers at Leopardstown and Fairyhouse by wide margins, hacking up by 11 lengths at the big Easter festival in a valuable sales race.

Darver Star (Ire)

10 b g Kalanisi - Maggies Oscar (Oscar)

Gavin Cromwell (Ire) — SSP Number Twentytwo Syndicate

PLACINGS: /13277/66F2P1257-211 — RPR **157+h**

Starts		1st	2nd	3rd	4th	Win & Pl
31		9	5	4	1	£249,239
	9/22	Gway	2m5½f Hdl good			£8,676
	8/22	Kbgn	3m1f Hdl good			£5,950
	12/21	Punc	2m3f Hdl heavy			£8,955
	10/20	Punc	2m1f Ch yield			£6,250
	10/19	Limk	2m5f Nov List Hdl heavy			£18,072
	9/19	List	2m4f Nov Hdl yield			£11,959
133	8/19	Klny	2m1f 109-137 Hdl Hcap yld-sft			£26,577
	8/19	Dpat	2m3f Hdl gd-yld			£10,649
106	4/19	Wxfd	2m4f 105-123 Hdl Hcap yield			£9,157

Not far off the best hurdlers at his peak (third in the 2020 Champion Hurdle) and close to that level again this summer according to Racing Post Ratings when hacking up at Galway; had lost his way over fences in the interim before showing mixed form back over hurdles last term.

Dashel Drasher

9 b g Passing Glance - So Long (Nomadic Way)

Jeremy Scott — Mrs B Tully & R Lock

PLACINGS: 41111/2U1/3111/312P- — RPR **167c**

Starts		1st	2nd	3rd	4th	Win & Pl
21		10	2	4	1	£229,137
149	12/21	Newb	2m4½f Cls2 123-149 Hdl Hcap soft			£10,406
	2/21	Asct	2m5f Cls1 Gd1 Ch soft			£59,620
152	1/21	Asct	2m5f Cls2 132-154 Ch Hcap soft			£32,844
	12/20	Asct	2m5f Cls2 Ch heavy			£18,768
	12/19	Hayd	2m5½f Cls2 Nov Ch soft			£12,996
	4/19	Chel	2m4½f Cls2 Nov Hdl good			£12,380
	3/19	Newb	2m4½f Cls3 Nov Hdl gd-sft			£6,238
	2/19	Asct	2m3½f Cls2 Nov Hdl gd-sft			£15,857
	1/19	Chep	2m3½f Cls4 Nov Hdl gd-sft			£4,094
	2/18	Winc	1m7½f Cls5 NHF 4-6yo heavy			£2,274

Had his finest hour when winning the Ascot Chase in 2021, completing a remarkable Ascot hat-trick; disappointed twice at that track last season but twice ran well in between, winning over hurdles at Newbury and finishing a short-head second at Lingfield's new Winter Million card.

Dinoblue: impressive on her debut and could yet prove a force in mares' hurdle races

Delta Work (Fr)

9 br g Network - Robbe (Video Rock)

Gordon Elliott (Ire) — Gigginstown House Stud

PLACINGS: 113/14115/5U3/46613- — RPR **166+c**

Starts		1st	2nd	3rd	4th	Win & Pl
26		9	3	6	3	£678,333
	3/22	Chel	3m6f Cls2 Ch heavy			£39,023
	2/20	Leop	3m Gd1 Ch yield			£118,856
	12/19	Leop	3m Gd1 Ch yield			£93,018
	4/19	Punc	3m½f Nov Gd1 Ch yld-sft			£53,153
	12/18	Leop	3m Nov Gd1 Ch good			£52,212
	12/18	Fair	2m4f Nov Gd1 Ch good			£46,991
	11/18	DRoy	2m3½f Ch good			£8,177
139	3/18	Chel	3m Cls1 Gd3 135-155 Hdl Hcap soft			£56,950
	5/17	Punc	2m½f Mdn Hdl good			£6,844

Prolific Grade 1 winner in his youth but hasn't finished first or second over regulation fences since landing the Irish Gold Cup in February 2020; bounced back to winning ways in the Cross Country Chase at last season's Cheltenham Festival before finishing third in the Grand National.

Dingo Dollar (Ire)

10 ch g Golden Lariat - Social Society (Moscow Society)

Sandy Thomson — M Warren, J Holmes, R Kidner & J Wright

PLACINGS: 362P/355U/0P12/435U- — RPR **153c**

Starts		1st	2nd	3rd	4th	Win & Pl
27		5	4	3	3	£137,799
137	3/21	Newc	2m7½f Cls3 120-142 Ch Hcap gd-sft			£7,018
	2/18	Donc	3m Cls4 Nov Ch gd-sft			£4,494
130	12/17	Newb	2m7½f Cls3 Nov 125-137 Ch Hcap soft			£6,498
	4/17	Font	3m1½f Cls4 Nov Hdl good			£3,249
	1/17	Bang	2m7f Cls4 Mdn Hdl gd-sft			£3,249

Has run well in several major staying handicap chases in recent years, including when second in the Scottish National in 2021; dropped back to the same mark after struggling slightly last term, doing best when third in the Rehearsal Chase.

Dinoblue (Fr)

5 ch m Doctor Dino - Blue Aster (Astarabad)

Willie Mullins (Ire) — John P McManus

PLACINGS: 194-4 — RPR **136h**

Starts		1st	2nd	3rd	4th	Win & Pl
4		1	-	-	2	£9,327
	1/22	Clon	2m½f Mdn Hdl heavy			£4,958

Held in very high regard last season and sent off just 11-8 for the mares' novice hurdle at the Cheltenham Festival after a 15-length debut win, though ultimately disappointing; finished ninth at Cheltenham before doing only slightly better when fourth at Fairyhouse and Punchestown.

Diol Ker (Fr)

8 b g Martaline - Stiren Bleue (Pistolet Bleu)

Noel Meade (Ire) — Gigginstown House Stud

PLACINGS: 2/1/F34129/6F592410- — RPR **149+c**

Starts	1st	2nd	3rd	4th	Win & Pl
18	3	3	2	2	£81,527

137	3/22	Naas	3m½f 132-158 Ch Hcap heavy	£49,580
	12/20	Limk	2m4f Hdl heavy	£6,750
	11/19	Fair	2m4f Mdn Hdl heavy	£5,857

Smart staying hurdler who failed to get close to that level initially last season over fences before suddenly flourishing in handicaps; finished a good fourth in the Thyestes before winning the Leinster National; suffered a rough passage when tenth in the Irish Grand National.

Do Your Job (Ire)

8 b g Fame And Glory - Full Of Birds (Epervier Bleu)

Michael Scudamore — Mark Dunphy

PLACINGS: 152/112422/1F2211- — RPR **151+c**

Starts	1st	2nd	3rd	4th	Win & Pl
14	5	6	-	1	£102,922

	4/22	Ayr	2m4½f Cls1 Nov Gd2 Ch gd-sft	£26,283
140	2/22	Newc	2m4f Cls3 117-140 Ch Hcap gd-sft	£6,535
	11/21	Wwck	2m Cls3 Nov Ch gd-sft	£9,516
	10/20	Ayr	2m Cls4 Nov Hdl 4-6yo soft	£3,769
	10/20	Ffos	2m Cls4 Nov Hdl 4-6yo heavy	£3,769

Progressive chaser who did particularly well towards the end of last season when making a successful handicap debut at Newcastle and easily following up in a soft Grade 2 novice at Ayr; travelled notably strongly at 2m4f both times and should prove equally effective back at 2m.

Doctor Parnassus (Ire)

4 b g Make Believe - We'Ll Go Walking (Authorized)

Dan Skelton — D W Fox

PLACINGS: 1178- — RPR **132h**

Starts	1st	2nd	3rd	4th	Win & Pl
4	2	-	-	-	£12,915

	2/22	Tntn	2m3f Cls4 Nov Hdl gd-sft	£4,956
	1/22	Asct	1m7½f Cls3 Hdl 4yo soft	£6,699

Failed to win on the Flat but instantly proved a much better hurdler last season, winning by ten lengths at Ascot first time out before going on to finish seventh in the Triumph Hurdle; future in handicaps but disappointing eighth on handicap debut at Sandown (lost two front shoes).

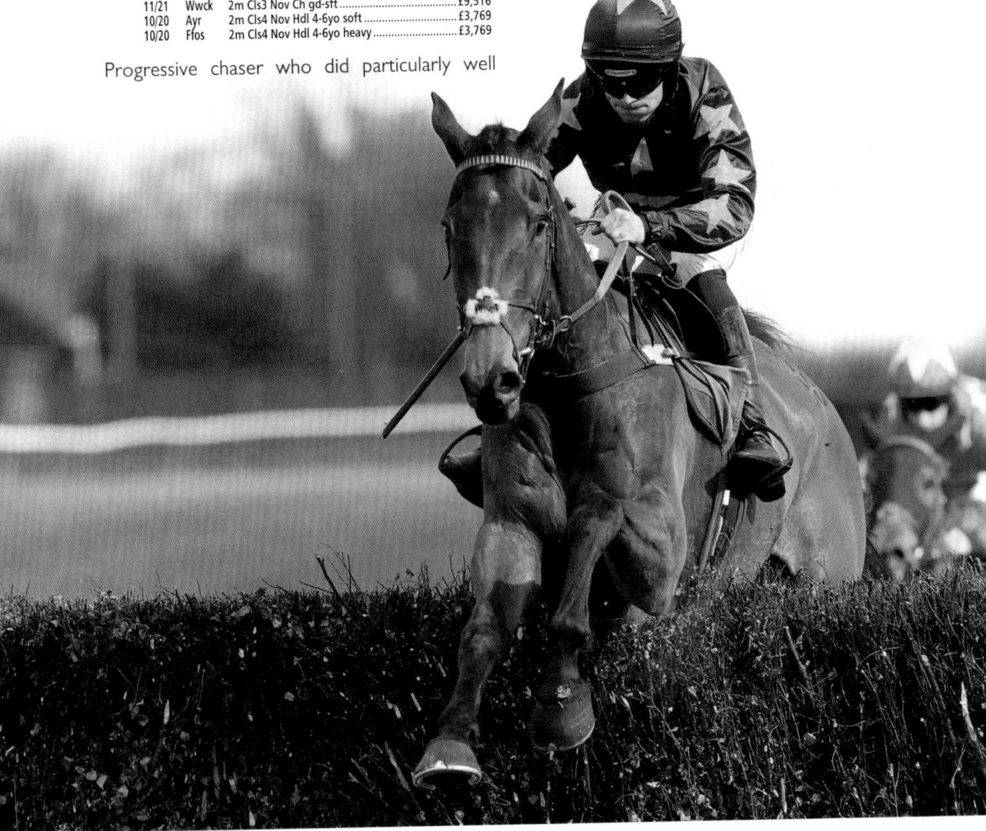

Doddiethegreat (Ire)

6 b g Fame And Glory - Asturienne (Sleeping Car)

Nicky Henderson — Kenneth Alexander

PLACINGS: 11/1- — RPR **137+h**

Starts	1st	2nd	3rd	4th	Win & Pl
3	3	-	-	-	£8,958

	11/21	Kemp	2m5f Cls4 Nov Hdl good	£4,085
	3/21	Hntg	2m Cls5 NHF 4-6yo gd-sft	£2,274
	11/20	Ludl	2m Cls5 NHF 3-5yo good	£2,599

Unbeaten gelding who looked an exciting prospect when making a winning debut over hurdles at Kempton last season only to miss the rest of the campaign through injury; hacked up by 22 lengths that day when stepping up to 2m5f after two bumper wins.

Does He Know

7 b g Alkaased - Diavoleria (Slip Anchor)

Kim Bailey — Yes He Does Syndicate

PLACINGS: 1/22/111085/11210- — RPR **158+c**

Starts	1st	2nd	3rd	4th	Win & Pl
13	6	3	-	-	£98,532

	2/22	Asct	3m Cls1 Nov Gd2 Ch soft	£29,753
	10/21	Chel	3m½f Cls2 Nov Ch good	£13,008
	10/21	Chep	2m7½f Cls2 Nov Ch good	£10,892
	11/20	Chel	2m5f Cls1 Nov Gd2 Hdl gd-sft	£14,807
	10/20	Chel	2m5f Cls2 Nov Hdl good	£10,047
	10/20	Ludl	2m5f Cls4 Nov Hdl gd-fm	£3,899

Smart staying novice chaser last season, winning three times including the Reynoldstown at Ascot by 14 lengths; proved himself on soft ground that day having previously been felt to want good ground; disappointed on handicap debut when well fancied for the Ultima at Cheltenham.

Dolos (Fr)

9 b g Kapgarde - Redowa (Trempolino)

Paul Nicholls — Mrs Johnny De La Hey

PLACINGS: /12714/44267/87817-2 — RPR **155+c**

Starts	1st	2nd	3rd	4th	Win & Pl
37	7	10	6	3	£217,551

143	2/22	Sand	1m7½f Cls2 127-147 Ch Hcap gd-sft	£15,609
157	2/20	Sand	1m7½f Cls2 140-157 Ch Hcap soft	£19,577
154	5/19	Kemp	2m2f Cls2 128-154 Ch Hcap good	£14,389
149	2/19	Sand	1m7½f Cls2 128-154 Ch Hcap soft	£18,768
	11/17	Asct	2m3f Cls3 Ch gd-sft	£9,986
	4/17	Chep	2m Cls4 Nov Hdl good	£3,899
	10/16	Chep	2m Cls4 Hdl 3yo good	£3,899

Very useful chaser at his best but out of sorts for some time until making most of handicapper's generosity to win at Sandown last term after rapid fall in weights; still 10lb below highest winning mark, though beaten twice more subsequently.

Do Your Job: last season's form suggests he could do well in handicaps now

Dubrovnik Harry (Ire)

6 b g Yeats - Kashmir Lady (Rock Of Gibraltar)

Harry Fry — Manhole Covers

PLACINGS: 3123- — RPR **135+h**

Starts	1st	2nd	3rd	4th	Win & Pl
4	1	1	2	-	£16,774

	1/22	Extr	2m2½f Cls4 Mdn Hdl heavy	£4,085

Lightly raced hurdler who ran a fine race when third in last season's EBF Final at Sandown (least experienced in the field and best of those held up); had looked particularly effective on heavy ground when winning by 25 lengths at Exeter.

Dunvegan (Fr)

9 gr g Le Havre - Or Des Joncs (Turgeon)

Pat Fahy (Ire) — George Turner & Clipper Logistics Group

PLACINGS: 0P/3132/4PP36/39112- — RPR **164c**

Starts	1st	2nd	3rd	4th	Win & Pl
23	6	5	4	1	£149,143

146	1/22	Fair	2m1f 130-158 Ch Hcap soft	£42,143
139	11/21	Fair	2m½f 122-148 Ch Hcap good	£21,071
	12/19	Punc	2m Ch soft	£7,454
	12/18	Fair	2m4f Mdn Hdl gd-yld	£6,269
	4/18	Punc	2m NHF 4-7yo yld-sft	£9,540
	1/18	Fair	2m NHF 5-7yo heavy	£5,451

Massive improver last season, flourishing back at 2m after a disappointing campaign over further; won two valuable handicap chases at Fairyhouse and acquitted herself well when stepped up to the top level to finish second behind Chacun Pour Soi at Leopardstown.

Dusart (Ire)

7 b g Flemensfirth - Dusty Too (Terimon)

Nicky Henderson — R A Bartlett

PLACINGS: 13/1151- — RPR **155+c**

Starts	1st	2nd	3rd	4th	Win & Pl
6	4	-	1	-	£58,363

147	4/22	Ayr	3m Cls2 Nov 126-147 Ch Hcap gd-sft	£26,015
	2/22	Extr	3m Cls3 Nov Ch gd-sft	£7,951
	1/22	Leic	2m6½f Cls3 Nov Ch gd-sft	£7,895
	11/20	Newb	2m½f Cls4 Nov Hdl good	£3,769

Very lightly raced gelding who still looked a work in progress last season and did well to defy top weight in a novice handicap at Ayr on final run; had jumped markedly left in winning first two races over fences before a battling fifth on ground softer than ideal in the Brown Advisory.

Dysart Dynamo (Ire)

6 b g Westerner - Dysart Dancer (Accordion)

Willie Mullins (Ire) — Ms Eleanor Manning

PLACINGS: 1/111F-5 — RPR **153+h**

Starts	1st	2nd	3rd	4th	Win & Pl
6	4	-	-	-	£37,581

	1/22	Punc	2m Nov Gd2 Hdl soft	£18,097
	12/21	Cork	2m Mdn Hdl soft	£6,321
	4/21	Punc	2m NHF 4-7yo yield	£5,795
	3/21	Clon	2m2½f NHF 5-7yo soft	£5,268

Talented, free-going front-runner who won first

four races by wide margins, including a Grade 2 novice hurdle by 19 lengths last season; still going easily when falling three out in the Supreme but suffered a heart fibrillation when flopping at Punchestown; likely to go novice chasing.

Early Doors (Fr)

9 b g Soldier Of Fortune - Ymlaen (Desert Prince)

Joseph O'Brien (Ire) — John P McManus

PLACINGS: 0/521/2262/01/5655-8 — RPR **154c**

Starts	1st	2nd	3rd	4th	Win & Pl
22	5	5	2	-	£237,840

139	7/20	Gway	2m6½f 135-158 Ch Hcap gd-yld	£100,000
145	3/19	Chel	2m4½f Cls2 126-145 Cond Hdl Hcap gd-sft	£43,330
	11/17	Naas	2m Gd3 Hdl 4yo sft-hvy	£17,083
	10/17	Wxfd	2m Mdn Hdl 4yo soft	£6,055
	2/17	Punc	2m½f NHF 4yo heavy	£5,265

Has a good record in top handicaps, winning the 2019 Martin Pipe at Cheltenham and 2020 Galway Plate; missed nearly 18 months after that and largely out of sorts since, though ran a big race when fifth in the Irish National on only his second run beyond 3m.

Easy Game (Fr)

8 b g Barastraight - Rule Of The Game (Lavirco)

Willie Mullins (Ire) — Nicholas Peacock

PLACINGS: 01127U1/5P21U31-1110 — RPR **165+c**

Starts	1st	2nd	3rd	4th	Win & Pl
32	13	5	3	1	£327,643

7/22	Tram	2m6f Ch good	£7,933
6/22	List	2m3f Ch sft-hvy	£8,676
5/22	Klny	2m4f Gd3 Ch good	£14,130
4/22	Fair	2m4f Gd2 Ch yield	£49,580
9/21	List	2m4f Ch gd-yld	£11,063
4/21	Fair	2m4f Gd2 Ch yield	£42,143
10/20	Gowr	2m4f Gd2 Ch good	£17,500
8/20	Tram	2m5½f Ch good	£6,250
12/19	Leop	2m5f Ch yield	£9,318
12/18	Navn	2m4f Nov Gd2 Hdl yield	£22,190
11/18	Navn	2m4f Nov Gd3 Hdl good	£22,190
7/18	Gway	2m½f Nov Hdl 4yo good	£10,903
7/18	Klny	2m4½f Mdn Hdl good	£6,269

Smart chaser who landed a fourth Grade 2 victory when making it back-to-back wins in Fairyhouse's 2m4f Easter chase last season following a winter break; went on to win three more times through the summer but disappointed in the Galway Plate (had been second in 2021).

Easysland (Fr)

8 b/br g Gentlewave - Island Du Frene (Useful)

Jonjo O'Neill — John P McManus

PLACINGS: FF011/11111/42/PPP-P — RPR **171c**

Starts	1st	2nd	3rd	4th	Win & Pl
23	9	1	1	1	£182,778

	3/20	Chel	3m6f Cls2 Ch soft	£40,235
	2/20	Pau	3m7½f List Ch v soft	£30,508
139	12/19	Chel	3m6f Cls2 122-148 Ch Hcap gd-sft	£21,896
	11/19	Comp	3m3f List Ch heavy	£20,757
	10/19	Comp	2m7½f Ch heavy	£9,081
	2/19	Pau	2m4½f Ch 5-6yo heavy	£11,243
	1/19	Pau	2m4½f Ch 5-6yo v soft	£12,108
	11/18	Drtl	2m5f Ch 4-5yo soft	£6,372
	2/18	Pau	2m1½f Hdl 4yo heavy	£13,593

Brilliant cross-country chaser when trained in France as a youngster, winning twice at Cheltenham three seasons ago; switched to Jonjo O'Neill but proved hugely disappointing when pulled up on all four runs in a mix of disciplines, though handicap mark has plummeted in that time.

Echoes In Rain (Fr)

6 b m Authorized - Amarantine (King's Best)

Willie Mullins (Ire) — Barnane Stud

PLACINGS: 5/1411/13435-2 — RPR **156h**

Starts	1st	2nd	3rd	4th	Win & Pl
11	4	1	2	2	£194,121

4/21	Punc	2m½f Nov Gd1 Hdl yield	£52,679
4/21	Fair	2m Nov Gd2 Hdl yield	£18,438
2/21	Naas	1m7½f Nov Gd2 Hdl soft	£18,438
12/20	Naas	2m Mdn Hdl 4yo heavy	£6,000

High-class mare who ran exclusively in Grade 1 company and did well in the face of some very stiff tasks, even giving Honeysuckle a race at Punchestown; disappointing in the Mares' Hurdle at Cheltenham when running beyond 2m for the first time (keen in rear and given plenty to do).

Editeur Du Gite (Fr)

8 b g Saddex - Malaga De St Sulpice (Saint Cyrien)

Gary Moore — The Preston Family, Friends & T Jacobs

PLACINGS: 2/1/P6/252P11/U114P- — RPR **156c**

Starts	1st	2nd	3rd	4th	Win & Pl
15	5	3	-	1	£123,173

147	12/21	Chel	2m½f Cls2 129-152 Ch Hcap gd-sft	£15,609
140	11/21	Chel	2m Cls2 132-152 Ch Hcap good	£23,234
132	4/21	Aint	2m Cls1 Gd3 123-149 Ch Hcap gd-sft	£42,203
125	3/21	Newb	2m½f Cls3 115-129 Ch Hcap good	£7,018
	5/18	Comp	2m2f Hdl 4yo heavy	£19,115

Tremendously progressive chaser who won two 2m Cheltenham handicaps last season, making it four wins in his last five races at the time; fine fourth in the Grand Annual back there on unsuitably heavy ground but pulled up when raised in class and trip at Aintree.

Edwardstone

8 b g Kayf Tara - Nothingtoloose (Luso)

Alan King — Robert Abrey & Ian Thurtle

PLACINGS: 1126/5U1353/B111112- — RPR **164+c**

Starts	1st	2nd	3rd	4th	Win & Pl
20	8	5	2	-	£297,754

	3/22	Chel	2m Cls1 Nov Gd1 Ch gd-sft	£102,482
	2/22	Wwck	2m Cls1 Nov Gd2 Ch gd-sft	£29,614
	12/21	Kemp	2m Cls1 Nov Gd2 Ch soft	£29,614
	12/21	Sand	1m7½f Cls1 Nov Gd1 Ch gd-sft	£42,914
	11/21	Wwck	2m Cls3 Nov Ch gd-sft	£10,565
141	1/21	MRas	2m½f Cls2 123-141 Hdl Hcap heavy	£9,384
	12/19	Aint	2m1f Cls3 Nov Hdl gd-sft	£7,798
	11/19	Winc	1m7½f Cls3 Nov Hdl 4-6yo good	£6,238

Britain's outstanding 2m novice chaser last season, completing a five-race winning streak in the Arkle at Cheltenham; had also excelled at right-handed Kempton and Sandown plus much sharper Warwick; not quite at his best when second to Gentleman De Mee at Aintree.

Eklat De Rire (Fr)

8 b g Saddex - Rochdale (Video Rock)

Henry de Bromhead (Ire) P Davies

PLACINGS: 121/11U/1P0- RPR **161+c**

Starts	1st	2nd	3rd	4th	Win & Pl
8	4	1	-	-	£41,843

	10/21	Wxfd	2m7f List Ch heavy	£11,853
	1/21	Naas	3m1f Nov Gd3 Ch heavy	£14,487
	12/20	Punc	3m1½f Ch heavy	£6,250
	3/20	Thur	2m7f Mdn Hdl sft-hvy	£7,000

Very lightly raced gelding who has looked set for big things when winning three of his six chases, even beating Conflated first time out last term, but hasn't yet delivered on a bigger stage; no better than tenth when favourite for the Ladbrokes Trophy and the Thyestes.

El Barra (Fr)

8 br g Racinger - Oasaka (Robin Des Champs)

Willie Mullins (Ire) Mrs S Ricci

PLACINGS: 2/10421/12313-13 RPR **155c**

Starts	1st	2nd	3rd	4th	Win & Pl
12	5	2	3	1	£125,484

140	4/22	Punc	2m5f Nov 129-152 Ch Hcap gd-yld	£49,580
	3/22	Limk	2m1½f Ch sft-hvy	£6,445
	4/21	Punc	2m Nov Hdl yield	£10,536
	4/21	Fair	2m Mdn Hdl yield	£6,321
	11/20	Thur	2m NHF 5-7yo soft	£4,500

Steadily progressive gelding who has peaked at the Punchestown festival in each of the last two seasons, winning there for the second year in a row in a novice handicap chase in April; fine third in the Galway Plate next time; bled at Cheltenham on only run in Graded company.

El Fabiolo (Fr)

5 b g Spanish Moon - Sainte Mante (Saint Des Saints)

Willie Mullins (Ire) Simon Munir & Isaac Souede

PLACINGS: 3/12-1 RPR **155+h**

Starts	1st	2nd	3rd	4th	Win & Pl
4	2	1	1	-	£41,982

	4/22	Punc	2m Nov Hdl gd-yld	£9,916
	1/22	Tram	2m Mdn Hdl heavy	£5,206

Very lightly raced gelding who ran a huge race for one so inexperienced when a neck second behind Jonbon in a 2m Grade 1 at Aintree on just his third run over hurdles (second for current connections); won easily down in grade at Punchestown; likely to go novice chasing.

Eldorado Allen (Fr)

8 gr g Khalkevi - Hesmeralda (Royal Charter)

Joe Tizzard J P Romans & Terry Warner

PLACINGS: U/230/114225/132137- RPR **168c**

Starts	1st	2nd	3rd	4th	Win & Pl
19	5	5	4	1	£228,023

	2/22	Newb	2m7½f Cls1 Gd2 Ch gd-sft	£34,572
151	11/21	Extr	2m1½f Cls1 Gd2 148-168 Ch Hcap gd-sft	£40,411
	11/20	Chel	2m Cls1 Nov Gd2 Ch gd-sft	£17,387
	10/20	NAbb	2m½f Cls3 Nov Ch gd-sft	£8,058
	11/18	Sand	2m Cls4 Mdn Hdl heavy	£6,498

Smart and consistent chaser who won the Denman Chase and Haldon Gold Cup last season to make it three Grade 2 victories; Denman win opened up new doors at around 3m, though dropped back to 2m4f for two subsequent runs, including when third in the Ryanair.

Elimay (Fr)

8 gr m Montmartre - Hyde (Poliglote)

Willie Mullins (Ire) John P McManus

PLACINGS: 26/1111/22121/3211-2 RPR **150c**

Starts	1st	2nd	3rd	4th	Win & Pl
22	9	9	2	1	£341,079

	3/22	Chel	2m4½f Cls1 Gd2 Ch gd-sft	£67,582
	2/22	Naas	2m List Ch sft-hvy	£12,395
	4/21	Fair	2m5f List Ch yield	£11,853
	2/21	Naas	2m List Ch soft	£11,853
	1/20	Thur	2m4½f Nov Gd2 Ch yield	£28,750
	12/19	Cork	2m½f Nov Gd3 Ch soft	£21,261
	5/19	Klny	2m1f List Hdl good	£16,622
	5/19	Punc	2m4f Hdl yield	£13,851
	5/17	Autl	2m1½f Hdl 3yo v soft	£19,692

High-class mare who made amends for a narrow defeat in the 2021 Mares' Chase at Cheltenham with a thrilling last-gasp victory in last season's renewal; slightly disappointing otherwise last season, suffering a third defeat as favourite when well beaten at Punchestown.

Elixir De Nutz (Fr)

8 gr g Al Namix - Nutz (Turgeon)

Joe Tizzard Terry Warner

PLACINGS: 6/F2111/77/2/4211PP- RPR **145+c**

Starts	1st	2nd	3rd	4th	Win & Pl
16	6	3	-	1	£91,361

135	2/22	Kemp	2m2f Cls3 Nov 123-135 Ch Hcap good	£8,169
	1/22	Plum	2m3½f Cls3 Nov Ch soft	£7,407
	1/19	Sand	2m Cls1 Nov Gd1 Hdl soft	£28,475
	12/18	Chel	2m1f Cls3 Nov Hdl 4-6yo good	£9,285
	11/18	Chel	2m½f Cls1 Nov Gd2 Hdl good	£18,006
	10/17	Agtn	1m6f NHF 3yo gd-sft	£6,838

Formerly high-class novice hurdler who won the Tolworth Hurdle in 2019; ran just three times across the following two seasons but back on track when winning twice over fences last term; pulled up when back up in class for the Grand Annual and the Red Rum.

En Beton (Fr)

8 br g Network - Nee A Saint Voir (Pistolet Bleu)

Willie Mullins (Ire) Cheveley Park Stud

PLACINGS: 2/52/31/15- RPR **147+c**

Starts	1st	2nd	3rd	4th	Win & Pl
7	2	2	1	-	£25,768

	12/21	Punc	2m7f Ch heavy	£6,585
	4/21	Tram	2m4½f Mdn Hdl good	£6,321

Giant chasing type who has been very lightly raced but proved a revelation on first run over fences last season, jumping superbly to win a beginners' chase by 21 lengths; ran only once more when disappointing at Naas; remains an interesting staying prospect.

Energumene (Fr)

8 br g Denham Red - Olinight (April Night)

Willie Mullins (Ire) — Tony Bloom

PLACINGS: 1/311/111/1121-1 — RPR **179+c**

Starts	1st	2nd	3rd	4th	Win & Pl
11	9	1	1	-	£588,975

	Date	Course	Race	Prize
	4/22	Punc	2m Gd1 Ch gd-yld	£136,345
	3/22	Chel	2m Cls1 Gd1 Ch soft	£226,672
	12/21	Cork	2m½f Gd2 Ch soft	£36,875
	4/21	Punc	2m Nov Gd1 Ch yield	£60,580
	2/21	Leop	2m1½f Nov Gd1 Ch soft	£65,848
	1/21	Naas	2m Nov Ch heavy	£10,272
	11/20	Gowr	2m4f Ch heavy	£7,750
	3/20	Gowr	2m Nov Mdn Hdl sft-hvy	£6,750
	1/20	Thur	2m NHF 4-7yo yield	£5,008

Brilliant 2m chaser who took record to seven wins out of eight over fences with Grade I wins at Cheltenham and Punchestown last season; had suffered sole chase defeat in a thriller against Shishkin at Ascot before capitalising on that rival's flop in the Champion Chase.

Enjoy D'Allen (Fr)

8 b/br g Network - Triple Star (Dom Alco)

Ciaran Murphy (Ire) — John P McManus

PLACINGS: /255322211223/735U9- — RPR **153c**

Starts	1st	2nd	3rd	4th	Win & Pl
22	2	6	3	1	£95,332

	Date	Course	Race	Prize
127	1/21	Thur	2m5½f 116-132 Ch Hcap sft-hvy	£8,429
	1/21	Fair	2m5f Nov Ch heavy	£9,746

Very useful staying chaser who has run well in big handicaps in Ireland, finishing third in the Irish Grand National and Paddy Power Chase in 2021; bought by JP McManus ahead of last season's Grand National but exited at the first and managed only ninth in the Irish version.

Enniskerry (Ire)

8 b g Jeremy - Princess Gaia (King's Theatre)

Barry Connell (Ire) — Barry Connell

PLACINGS: 224P/1128-01 — RPR **143+c**

Starts	1st	2nd	3rd	4th	Win & Pl
10	3	3	-	1	£28,882

	Date	Course	Race	Prize
	7/22	Gway	2m2f Ch good	£8,429
	6/21	Rosc	2m4f Nov Hdl good	£8,429
	5/21	Dpat	2m3f Mdn Hdl good	£5,268

Lightly raced gelding who made an eyecatching start over fences at Galway in July when running away with a strong beginners' chase, prompting trainer to nominate Grade I targets; had also looked useful over hurdles last summer but yet to win on ground softer than good.

Enrilo (Fr)

8 bl g Buck's Boum - Rock Treasure (Video Rock)

Paul Nicholls — Martin Broughton & Friends

PLACINGS: 141/1513/21P11d/FP4P- — RPR **147c**

Starts	1st	2nd	3rd	4th	Win & Pl
16	6	1	2	2	£75,688

	Date	Course	Race	Prize
138	2/21	Newb	2m7½f Cls3 Nov 128-141 Ch Hcap gd-sft	£7,018
	11/20	Extr	3m Cls2 Nov Ch good	£12,021
	12/19	Sand	2m4f Cls1 Nov Gd2 Hdl soft	£17,085
	10/19	Winc	2m4f Cls4 Nov Hdl good	£5,198
	2/19	Kemp	2m Cls5 NHF 4-6yo good	£3,119
	10/18	Worc	2m Cls5 NHF 4-6yo good	£2,274

First past the post in the bet365 Gold Cup as a novice in 2021 only to be demoted to third; well fancied for several similar staying handicaps last season but was pulled up twice and fell in the Ladbrokes Trophy, completing just once when fourth in the Coral Trophy at Kempton.

Envoi Allen (Fr)

8 b g Muhtathir - Reaction (Saint Des Saints)

Henry de Bromhead (Ire) — Cheveley Park Stud

PLACINGS: 11/1111/111F/P1613-3 — RPR **166c**

Starts	1st	2nd	3rd	4th	Win & Pl
18	13	-	2	-	£499,798

	Date	Course	Race	Prize
	12/21	Leop	2m1f Gd1 Ch gd-yld	£65,848
	10/21	DRoy	2m3½f Gd2 Ch soft	£26,339
	1/21	Punc	2m4f Nov Gd3 Ch heavy	£18,438
	11/20	Fair	2m4f Nov Gd1 Ch soft	£35,000
	10/20	DRoy	2m3½f Ch yield	£5,500
	3/20	Chel	2m5f Cls1 Nov Gd1 Hdl soft	£70,338
	1/20	Naas	2m4f Nov Gd1 Hdl gd-yld	£47,838
	12/19	Fair	2m Nov Gd1 Hdl yld-sft	£47,838
	11/19	DRoy	2m½f Mdn Hdl soft	£7,986
	3/19	Chel	2m½f Cls1 Gd1 NHF 4-6yo soft	£42,203
	2/19	Leop	2m Gd2 NHF 4-7yo gd-yld	£46,509
	12/18	Navn	2m List NHF 4-7yo yield	£14,967
	12/18	Fair	2m NHF 4yo good	£5,451

Dual Cheltenham Festival winner who had the world at his feet at one stage but has largely struggled in the last 18 months; did win a Grade I last season but in a poor three-runner race and looked to find that 2m trip too sharp in subsequent runs at Cheltenham and Punchestown.

Epatante (Fr)

8 b m No Risk At All - Kadjara (Silver Rainbow)

Nicky Henderson — John P McManus

PLACINGS: /119/111/123/31121-3 — RPR **159+h**

Starts	1st	2nd	3rd	4th	Win & Pl
18	11	3	3	-	£898,372

	Date	Course	Race	Prize
	4/22	Aint	2m4f Cls1 Gd1 Hdl gd-sft	£143,231
	12/21	Kemp	2m Cls1 Gd1 Hdl soft	£74,035
	11/21	Newc	2m Cls1 Gd1 Hdl gd-sft	£44,545
	11/20	Newc	2m Cls1 Gd1 Hdl good	£45,814
	3/20	Chel	2m½f Cls1 Gd1 Hdl soft	£264,610
	12/19	Kemp	2m Cls1 Gd1 Hdl soft	£74,035
137	11/19	Newb	2m½f Cls1 List 122-141 Hdl Hcap gd-sft	£28,475
	2/19	Extr	2m1f Cls4 Nov Hdl gd-sft	£4,549
	11/18	Kemp	2m Cls4 Nov Hdl good	£4,094
	11/17	StCl	1m4½f Gd1 NHF 3yo heavy	£21,368
	9/17	Le L	1m4f NHF 3yo v soft	£7,692

Former Champion Hurdle winner who won three times last season to take Grade I tally to six; most impressive when stepped up to 2m4f in the Aintree Hurdle, following Champion Hurdle

second behind Honeysuckle, though only third when odds-on at Punchestown on final run.

Erne River (Ire)

7 b g Califet - Lusty Beg (Old Vic)

Nick Kent — Crossed Fingers Partnership

PLACINGS: 321/31/111F3- RPR **154+c**

Starts	1st	2nd	3rd	4th	Win & Pl
7	4	-	2	-	£35,012

	2/22	Weth	2m5½f Cls3 Nov Ch soft	£7,679
127	1/22	Donc	2m4½f Cls3 Nov 122-134 Ch Hcap gd-sft	£11,273
	5/21	Wwck	2m3f Cls4 Nov Hdl soft	£3,159
	3/21	Donc	2m3½f Cls4 Nov Hdl good	£3,769

Lightly raced gelding who won his last two novice hurdles in 2021 before hacking up twice more when switched to fences last season; fell (still in contention) when stepped up to Grade 1 company at Aintree and a well-beaten third in an open Grade 2 at Sandown.

Escaria Ten (Fr)

8 b g Maresca Sorrento - Spartes Eria (Ballingarry)

Gordon Elliott (Ire) — McNeill Family

PLACINGS: 1/23110/5123P/829- RPR **159c**

Starts	1st	2nd	3rd	4th	Win & Pl
13	3	3	2	-	£50,989

	12/20	Thur	3m1f Ch soft	£7,000
	1/20	Ayr	3m½f Cls4 Nov Hdl heavy	£4,289
	1/20	Cork	3m Mdn Hdl soft	£7,188

Smart and lightly raced staying chaser who finished third in the 2021 National Hunt Chase behind Galvin (sent off favourite) and was a nose second in last season's Bobbyjo Chase; failed to stay when ninth in the Grand National having looked a threat turning for home.

Espoir De Guye (Fr)

8 b g Khalkevi - Penelope De Guye (Dom Alco)

Venetia Williams — Mrs J Hitchings

PLACINGS: 5172/211P/1842/16P- RPR **154+c**

Starts	1st	2nd	3rd	4th	Win & Pl
15	5	3	-	1	£83,834

145	2/22	Wwck	2m4f Cls2 131-145 Ch Hcap heavy	£15,609
144	11/20	Asct	2m5f Cls2 123-144 Ch Hcap soft	£15,640
130	12/19	Asct	2m3f Cls2 123-145 Ch Hcap heavy	£21,896
121	12/19	Extr	2m3f Cls3 121-142 Ch Hcap soft	£10,267
	6/18	Sabl	2m3f Hdl 4yo gd-sft	£8,496

Has struggled with his breathing but has won first time out in each of the last two seasons after wind surgery; hacked up at Warwick last season on first run since finishing second in same race a year earlier but disappointed subsequently and pulled up at Cheltenham on final run.

Espoir De Romay (Fr)

8 b g Kap Rock - Miss Du Seuil (Lavirco)

Kim Bailey — The Midgelets

PLACINGS: 3/1310/121F/33P- RPR **150c**

Starts	1st	2nd	3rd	4th	Win & Pl
12	4	1	4	-	£40,477

140	3/21	Leic	2m4f Cls3 130-140 Ch Hcap heavy	£7,018
	11/20	Hntg	2m4f Cls3 Nov Ch good	£7,310
132	1/20	Winc	2m4f Cls3 112-132 Cond Am Hdl Hcap soft	£7,148
	11/19	Wwck	2m3f Cls4 Nov Hdl gd-sft	£4,549

High-class novice chaser two seasons ago and might well have won a Grade 1 at Aintree but for falling two out; bitterly disappointing in just three runs last season, though, and pulled up on final run back at Aintree when jumping poorly; dropped 10lb for last two runs.

Facile Vega (Ire)

5 b g Walk In The Park - Quevega (Robin Des Champs)

Willie Mullins (Ire) — Hammer & Trowel Syndicate

PLACINGS: 111-1 RPR **141+b**

Starts	1st	2nd	3rd	4th	Win & Pl
4	4	-	-	-	£149,987

	4/22	Punc	2m½f Gd1 NHF 4-7yo gd-yld	£49,580
	3/22	Chel	2m½f Cls1 Gd1 NHF 4-6yo heavy	£45,560
	2/22	Leop	2m Gd2 NHF 4-7yo yield	£49,580
	12/21	Leop	2m NHF 4yo soft	£5,268

Brilliant bumper performer last season, winning all four races including the big Grade 1 double at Cheltenham and Punchestown; most impressive on quicker ground when showing a stunning turn of foot at Leopardstown but also ploughed through heavy when winning well at Cheltenham.

Fakir D'Oudairies (Fr)

7 b g Kapgarde - Niagaria Du Bois (Grand Tresor)

Joseph O'Brien (Ire) — John P McManus

PLACINGS: 21122/2P221/314211-5 RPR **171+c**

Starts	1st	2nd	3rd	4th	Win & Pl
26	8	9	1	4	£679,626

	4/22	Aint	2m4f Cls1 Gd1 Ch gd-sft	£140,561
	2/22	Asct	2m5f Cls1 Gd1 Ch soft	£86,933
	11/21	Clon	2m4½f Gd2 Ch soft	£26,339
	4/21	Aint	2m4f Cls1 Gd1 Ch gd-sft	£104,963
	12/19	Fair	2m4f Nov Gd1 Ch soft	£47,838
	11/19	Navn	2m1f Ch sft-hvy	£9,051
	1/19	Chel	2m1f Cls1 Gd2 Hdl 4yo gd-sft	£18,006
	1/19	Cork	2m Mdn Hdl 4-5yo soft	£7,492

Three-time Grade 1 winner who has been very well placed to exploit Britain's shortage of top talent in the last two seasons; easily landed a second successive Melling Chase at Aintree last term to add to Ascot Chase victory; 0-5 at the top level in Ireland outside novice company.

Facile Vega: superstar performer last season with four wins from four starts in bumpers

Fanion D'Estruval (Fr)

7 b g Enrique - Urfe D'Estruval (Martaline)

Venetia Williams — David Wilson

PLACINGS: 7/11115/2F445/41234- RPR **165+c**

Starts	1st	2nd	3rd	4th	Win & Pl
17	6	2	1	4	£182,440

151	11/21	Newb	2m4f Cls2 131-151 Ch Hcap gd-sft	£26,015
137	11/19	Newb	2m½f Cls3 Nov 124-142 Ch Hcap soft	£12,449
	7/19	Autl	2m1½f Ch 4yo v soft	£22,486
	6/19	Toul	2m1½f Ch 4yo gd-sft	£9,081
	5/19	Comp	2m2f Hdl 4yo v soft	£19,459
	4/19	Angl	2m3f Hdl 4-5yo gd-sft	£5,622

Did well in good handicap chases last season, winning at Newbury before finishing second in a more valuable race at Ascot; forced back into top company subsequently and came third in the Ascot Chase but yet to finish better than that in eight runs at Grade 1 or Grade 2 level.

Fantastikas (Fr)

7 b g Davidoff - Negresse De Cuta (Baroud D'Honneur)

Nigel Twiston-Davies — Imperial Racing Partnership 2016

PLACINGS: 272/22213/12317P- RPR **149+c**

Starts	1st	2nd	3rd	4th	Win & Pl
14	3	6	2	-	£60,786

	1/22	Ling	2m7½f Cls2 Nov Ch heavy	£26,575
128	11/21	Ling	2m7½f Cls3 112-129 Ch Hcap gd-sft	£5,882
	2/21	Font	2m3f Cls4 Nov Hdl gd-sft	£3,769

Very useful novice chaser last season, winning twice and running well in top company in between; fair seventh when well fancied for the Ultima at Cheltenham on handicap debut; expected to be suited by marathon trips but pulled up in the Scottish Grand National.

Farclas (Fr)

8 gr g Jukebox Jury - Floriana (Seattle Dancer)

Gordon Elliott (Ire) — Gigginstown House Stud

PLACINGS: 6F55P/111/53425/U2F- RPR **153c**

Starts	1st	2nd	3rd	4th	Win & Pl
20	4	4	1	1	£206,740

6/19	Rosc	2m Nov Ch good	£8,324
5/19	Punc	2m Nov Ch good	£11,099
5/19	DRoy	2m3½f Ch good	£6,659
3/18	Chel	2m1f Cls1 Gd1 Hdl 4yo soft	£71,188

Knocking on the door in major staying handicaps over the last two seasons; finished second in last season's Troytown, having filled the same spot in the 2021 Plate at Cheltenham; fifth in the Grand National that year but missed that race last season to run in the Irish version (fell).

Fastorslow (Fr)

6 b g Saint Des Saints - Popova (Kahyasi)

Martin Brassil (Ire) — Sean & Bernardine Mulryan

PLACINGS: 121/2002-2 RPR **150+h**

Starts	1st	2nd	3rd	4th	Win & Pl
8	2	4	-	-	£79,045

9/19	Autl	2m1½f Ch 3yo v soft	£23,784
6/19	Chat	2m1f Hdl 3yo v soft	£8,216

French hurdle and chase winner who excelled in big handicap hurdles last spring; went desperately close to winning the Coral Cup when pipped by Commander Of Fleet and proved equally effective on quicker ground when second at Punchestown; could go back over fences.

Ferny Hollow (Ire)

7 b/br g Westerner - Mirazur (Good Thyne)

Willie Mullins (Ire) — Cheveley Park Stud

PLACINGS: 1/2211/1/11- — RPR **168+c**

Starts	1st	2nd	3rd	4th	Win & Pl
7	5	2	-	-	£117,251

12/21	Leop	2m1f Nov Gd1 Ch soft	£52,679
12/21	Punc	2m1f Ch yld-sft	£6,585
11/20	Gowr	2m Mdn Hdl heavy	£7,000
3/20	Chel	2m½f Cls1 Gd1 NHF 4-6yo soft	£42,203
2/20	Fair	2m NHF 5-7yo heavy	£5,000

Immensely promising but fragile gelding who has won his last five races but has run just three times since landing the 2020 Champion Bumper; won a Grade 1 novice chase at Leopardstown to become hot favourite for the Arkle only to miss out with a ligament injury.

Fiddlerontheroof (Ire)

8 b g Stowaway - Inquisitive Look (Montjeu)

Joe Tizzard — Taylor, Burley & O'Dwyer

PLACINGS: /22110/2122223/1225- — RPR **164c**

Starts	1st	2nd	3rd	4th	Win & Pl
19	5	10	2	-	£247,030

10/21	Carl	2m4f Cls1 List Ch soft	£17,165
11/20	Extr	2m3f Cls3 Ch gd-sft	£7,018
1/20	Sand	2m Cls1 Nov Gd1 Hdl soft	£28,475
12/19	Sand	2m Cls3 Nov Hdl heavy	£6,256
3/19	Navn	2m NHF 5-7yo soft	£5,827

Smart and consistent staying chaser who has been very much a nearly horse in the last two seasons, winning just twice but finished second seven times; ran well in top handicaps last season, notably when second behind Cloudy Glen in the Ladbrokes Trophy.

Fighter Allen (Fr)

7 b g Vision D'Etat - Reaction (Saint Des Saints)

Willie Mullins (Ire) — C Jones

PLACINGS: 17/1P330/7241-F — RPR **148+c**

Starts	1st	2nd	3rd	4th	Win & Pl
12	3	1	2	1	£29,053

4/22	Tram	2m5½f Ch yield	£6,445
11/20	Punc	2m5½f Mdn Hdl heavy	£7,000
5/19	Le L	1m4f NHF 4yo soft	£5,405

Big horse who was a massive improver when sent chasing last season; impressed when landing a beginners' chase at Tramore having earlier finished second behind Stattler; sent off just 4-1 for the novice handicap at Punchestown only to fall at the first.

Fil Dor (Fr)

4 gr g Doctor Dino - La Turbale (Ange Gabriel)

Gordon Elliott (Ire) — Caldwell Construction

PLACINGS: 11122-2 — RPR **141h**

Starts	1st	2nd	3rd	4th	Win & Pl
6	3	3	-	-	£112,785

12/21	Leop	2m Gd2 Hdl 3yo soft	£23,705
11/21	Fair	2m Gd3 Hdl 3yo good	£14,487
10/21	DRoy	2m1f Hdl 3yo soft	£6,058

High-class juvenile hurdler last season when beaten only by Vauban, finishing second three times behind that rival after three victories; came

closest in the Triumph Hurdle at Cheltenham when staying on well and could benefit from step up in trip; has the size and scope for fences.

Fire Attack (Ire)

7 b g Westerner - Seesea (Dr Massini)

Joseph O'Brien (Ire) Gigginstown House Stud

PLACINGS: 12/26F2P/51U2-1F RPR **146c**

Starts	1st	2nd	3rd	4th	Win & Pl
13	3	4	-	-	£39,576

137	5/22	Punc	2m5f 114-138 Ch Hcap good	£11,403
	10/21	Wxfd	2m4f Ch heavy	£6,848
	12/19	Limk	2m2f NHF 4-7yo heavy	£5,591

Very lightly raced chaser who ran just three times as a novice last season (sole win on chase debut at Wexford) but quickly flourished in handicap company; won well at Punchestown in May and in front, albeit challenged, when falling five out in the Galway Plate.

First Flow (Ire)

10 b g Primary - Clonroche Wells (Pierre)

Kim Bailey A N Solomons

PLACINGS: 5/22132111/1116/613- RPR **168+c**

Starts	1st	2nd	3rd	4th	Win & Pl
22	11	3	2	2	£225,337

	12/21	Hntg	2m4f Cls1 Gd2 Ch good	£42,914
	1/21	Asct	2m1f Cls1 Gd1 Ch soft	£59,513
154	12/20	Weth	1m7f Cls2 133-154 Ch Hcap heavy	£12,021
148	11/20	Asct	2m1f Cls2 138-159 Ch Hcap soft	£15,640
	3/20	Carl	2m Cls3 Nov Ch heavy	£9,747
	2/20	Donc	2m½f Cls4 Nov Ch heavy	£4,289
141	2/20	Leic	2m Cls3 Nov 125-141 Ch Hcap heavy	£6,498
	12/19	Hrfd	2m Cls3 Nov Ch soft	£8,769
	1/18	Hayd	1m7½f Cls1 Nov Gd2 Hdl heavy	£17,085
	12/17	Newb	2m½f Cls4 Hdl heavy	£4,549
	11/17	Ling	2m Cls4 Nov Hdl soft	£5,198

High-class 2m chaser who had won six in a row when landing the Clarence House Chase at Ascot in 2021; back to winning ways last season in the Peterborough Chase but no match for Shishkin and Energumene on only subsequent run back at Ascot.

First Street

5 b g Golden Horn - Ladys First (Dutch Art)

Nicky Henderson Lady Bamford & Alice Bamford

PLACINGS: 221151325- RPR **147+h**

Starts	1st	2nd	3rd	4th	Win & Pl
9	3	3	1	-	£58,095

132	1/22	Kemp	2m Cls3 113-132 Hdl Hcap soft	£6,208
	9/21	Wwck	2m5f Cls4 Nov Hdl good	£4,085
	8/21	Bang	2m3½f Cls4 Nov Hdl good	£4,085

Flat-bred gelding who was a rapid improver last season, flourishing in top handicap hurdles having begun in bumpers only last May; finished third in the Betfair Hurdle before an even better run when beating all bar State Man in the County Hurdle.

Flame Bearer (Ire)

7 b g Fame And Glory - Banba (Docksider)

Pat Doyle (Ire) Linda Mulcahy & Mary Wolridge

PLACINGS: 2/11/53111-2 RPR **149+h**

Starts	1st	2nd	3rd	4th	Win & Pl
8	5	1	1	-	£75,125

	4/22	Fair	2m Nov Gd2 Hdl yield	£19,832
	2/22	Naas	1m7½f Nov Gd2 Hdl soft	£18,097
	1/22	Fair	2m Mdn Hdl gd-yld	£6,197
	3/21	Limk	2m NHF 5-7yo heavy	£5,268
	12/20	Thur	2m NHF 4-7yo soft	£4,500

Smart and progressive novice hurdler last season; won three times including two 2m Grade 2 races, doing well to overcome a troubled passage under a penalty at Fairyhouse; good second behind State Man at Punchestown when stepped up in trip; likely to go novice chasing.

Flegmatik (Fr)

7 ch g Fuisse - Crack D'Emble (Poliglote)

Dan Skelton N W Lake

PLACINGS: 13/203/15P445/4311P- RPR **146+c**

Starts	1st	2nd	3rd	4th	Win & Pl
17	4	1	3	3	£50,342

130	2/22	Kemp	2m4½f Cls3 118-130 Ch Hcap gd-sft	£10,892
123	2/22	Kemp	3m Cls3 120-139 Ch Hcap good	£10,892
126	10/20	Carl	2m Cls3 Nov 116-135 Ch Hcap good	£7,018
	12/18	Weth	2m Cls4 Hdl 3yo gd-sft	£4,614

Progressive chaser last season when seemingly improved by wind surgery; hacked up in two handicap chases at Kempton but shaped like a non-stayer on final run in the bet365 Gold Cup at Sandown (hadn't previously run beyond 3m).

Flooring Porter (Ire)

7 b g Yeats - Lillymile (Revoque)

Gavin Cromwell (Ire) Flooring Porter Syndicate

PLACINGS: 714162/132111/PF212- RPR **169+h**

Starts	1st	2nd	3rd	4th	Win & Pl
20	7	4	1	1	£514,875

	3/22	Chel	3m Cls1 Gd1 Hdl soft	£182,878
	3/21	Chel	3m Cls1 Gd1 Hdl gd-sft	£135,048
	12/20	Leop	3m Gd1 Hdl soft	£50,000
136	12/20	Navn	3m½f 128-154 Hdl Hcap soft	£45,000
122	7/20	Gowr	3m½f 107-122 Hdl Hcap good	£7,250
105	10/19	Cork	3m 80-107 Hdl Hcap yield	£6,655
	8/19	Bell	2m½f Mdn Hdl good	£6,123

Dual winner of the Stayers' Hurdle at Cheltenham, comfortably retaining his crown last season; failed to win in between but was unlucky when second behind Klassical Dream at Leopardstown (lost ground at the start) and was a solid second again behind Sire Du Berlais at Aintree.

First Flow: last season's Peterborough Chase winner is a high-class operator at around 2m

Floueur (Fr)

7 b g Legolas - Saraska D'Airy (Ungaro)

Gordon Elliott (Ire) — Claudio Michael Grech

PLACINGS: 31113/6663/P33130P- — RPR **148+c**

Starts	1st	2nd	3rd	4th	Win & Pl
16	4	-	6	-	£62,405

	Date	Course	Race	Prize
	1/22	Fair	2m5½f Ch gd-yld	£6,445
	1/20	Navn	2m2f Nov Hdl sft-hvy	£9,266
	11/19	Autl	2m2f Hdl 4yo heavy	£19,459
	10/19	Nant	2m1½f Hdl 4yo heavy	£9,081

Slow learner over fences but got off the mark at Fairyhouse last January before a fine third on handicap chase debut at Punchestown on heavy ground (bad mistake at the last); disappointing favourite in the Ultima at Cheltenham and pulled up in the Irish Grand National.

Fortescue

8 b g Shirocco - Last Of Her Line (Silver Patriarch)

Henry Daly — T F F Nixon

PLACINGS: 4/1211/92911/37231U- — RPR **151+c**

Starts	1st	2nd	3rd	4th	Win & Pl
22	6	3	4	1	£109,961

	Date	Course	Race	Prize
143	2/22	Asct	3m Cls1 List 135-155 Ch Hcap soft	£48,408
134	4/21	Prth	3m Cls3 127-141 Ch Hcap gd-sft	£6,317
128	3/21	Sand	3m Cls3 120-137 Ch Hcap soft	£7,538
121	3/20	Extr	3m Cls3 Nov 120-132 Ch Hcap soft	£9,097
117	1/20	Uttx	3m Cls4 Nov 100-120 Ch Hcap heavy	£4,289
112	10/19	Sthl	3m Cls4 Nov 108-122 Ch Hcap soft	£4,289

Got better and better in good staying handicap chases last season and showed great reserves of stamina when seeing off Fiddlerontheroof at Ascot; likely to be suited by marathon trips, though never a factor in the Grand National on first run beyond 3m2f.

Franco De Port: talented and unexposed chaser

Franco De Port (Fr)

7 b g Coastal Path - Ruth (Agent Bleu)

Willie Mullins (Ire) — Bruton Street V

PLACINGS: /172P/11252/F77240-3 — RPR **163c**

Starts	1st	2nd	3rd	4th	Win & Pl
17	4	4	1	1	£225,862

	Date	Course	Race	Prize
	12/20	Leop	2m1f Nov Gd1 Ch yield	£40,000
	11/20	Thur	2m2f Ch soft	£5,500
	11/19	Gowr	2m Nov Hdl 4yo heavy	£8,253
	3/19	Autl	2m1½f Hdl 4yo heavy	£19,459

Without a win since his finest hour in December 2020 when landing a Grade 1 novice chase but came close when second in last season's Thyestes; had been beaten in six successive races at the top level before switching to handicaps; still fairly unexposed over staying trips.

French Dynamite (Fr)

7 b g Kentucky Dynamite - Matnie (Laveron)

Mouse Morris (Ire) — Robcour

PLACINGS: 11514/2512/45161-3 — RPR **152+c**

Starts	1st	2nd	3rd	4th	Win & Pl
14	5	2	1	2	£82,732

	Date	Course	Race	Prize
	3/22	Thur	2m2f Nov Gd3 Ch good	£14,874
	11/21	Punc	2m3½f Ch yield	£6,585
	3/21	Leop	2m2½f Hdl yield	£8,955
	2/20	Thur	2m4½f Nov Hdl gd-yld	£9,000
	11/19	Thur	2m Mdn Hdl 4yo soft	£5,857

Dual winner as a novice chaser last season, scoring easily at Punchestown and narrowly adding a Grade 3 at Thurles; has gone 0-6 at a higher level but shaped with promise on handicap debut when third in a hot race at Punchestown behind El Barra (sent off favourite).

Frero Banbou (Fr)

7 b g Apsis - Lady Banbou (Useful)

Venetia Williams — P Davies

PLACINGS: 24711/73314/3331239- — RPR **147+c**

Starts	1st	2nd	3rd	4th	Win & Pl
17	4	2	6	2	£120,211

	Date	Course	Race	Prize
134	1/22	Ling	2m Cls2 115-141 Ch Hcap heavy	£26,015
124	3/21	Sand	1m7½f Cls3 113-126 Ch Hcap gd-sft	£7,018
	4/19	Autl	2m1½f Ch 4yo v soft	£21,622
	3/19	Le L	2m1f Ch 4yo v soft	£8,649

Dual French chase winner who has become

a standing dish in top 2m handicap chases in Britain; gained a second win for Venetia Williams at Lingfield last season and was placed in five other races, most notably when a fine third in the Grand Annual at Cheltenham.

Frodon (Fr)

10 b g Nickname - Miss Country (Country Reel)

Paul Nicholls — P J Vogt

PLACINGS: 111/3314/14151/1470- **RPR 171c**

Starts	1st	2nd	3rd	4th	Win & Pl
44	18	3	7	4	£1,051,682

	10/21	DRoy	3m Gd1 Ch soft	£65,848
	4/21	Sand	2m6½f Cls1 Gd2 Ch good	£23,919
	12/20	Kemp	3m Cls1 Gd1 Ch gd-sft	£116,178
164	10/20	Chel	3m1f Cls2 138-164 Ch Hcap good	£30,140
	1/20	Kemp	2m4½f Cls1 Gd2 Ch gd-sft	£34,170
	3/19	Chel	2m4½f Cls1 Gd1 Ch gd-sft	£196,945
	1/19	Chel	3m1½f Cls1 Gd2 Ch gd-sft	£56,536
164	12/18	Chel	2m4½f Cls1 Gd3 138-164 Ch Hcap good	£74,035
158	10/18	Aint	2m4f Cls1 Gd2 138-158 Ch Hcap good	£45,016
154	1/18	Chel	2m5f Cls1 Gd3 131-154 Ch Hcap heavy	£42,713
	2/17	Kemp	2m4½f Cls1 Nov Gd2 Ch good	£18,793
	2/17	Muss	2m4f Cls3 Nov Ch good	£7,798
149	12/16	Chel	2m5f Cls1 Gd3 132-158 Ch Hcap soft	£56,950
	11/16	Winc	2m4f Cls1 Nov Gd2 Ch good	£28,486
	9/16	Font	2m5f Cls4 Nov Ch good	£5,198
	9/16	NAbb	2m½f Cls3 Nov Ch good	£7,187
	2/16	Hayd	1m7½f Cls2 Hdl 4yo heavy	£9,747
	4/15	Autl	1m7f Hdl 3yo heavy	£20,465

Fairytale winner of the 2020 King George who added another Grade 1 win in the Champion Chase at Down Royal only to disappoint in three subsequent runs; since dropped to lowest mark since 2018 and has a fine record in major Cheltenham handicaps.

Frontal Assault (Ire)

7 b g Presenting - The Folkes Choice (King's Theatre)

Gordon Elliott (Ire) — Gigginstown House Stud

PLACINGS: 4/235/2421018/342P2- **RPR 149+c**

Starts	1st	2nd	3rd	4th	Win & Pl
15	2	5	2	2	£112,839

	2/21	Navn	3m Nov Gd3 Hdl heavy	£14,487
	12/20	Thur	2m7½f Nov Hdl soft	£7,250

Developed into a very useful staying novice chaser last season despite failing to win in five races; twice narrowly beaten in novice races and put sole flop on handicap chase debut in the Kim Muir behind him when a terrific second in the Irish Grand National.

Fuji Flight (Fr)

7 b g Day Flight - Silverlea (Shaanmer)

Venetia Williams — George & Drury

PLACINGS: 4/24F4632/3P/354115- **RPR 138+c**

Starts	1st	2nd	3rd	4th	Win & Pl
23	4	5	4	4	£114,012

127	3/22	Newb	2m7½f Cls3 Nov 127-135 Ch Hcap soft	£6,535
120	2/22	Hrfd	3m1f Cls4 Nov 118-122 Ch Hcap soft	£5,773
	9/18	Angl	1m5f NHF 3yo v soft	£4,425
	9/18	Leto	2m1½f Hdl 3yo good	£6,796

Developed into a very useful staying novice chaser last season having taken a long time to match form in France; won a hot novice handicap at Newbury to follow up breakthrough win at Hereford; run off his feet when favourite at Uttoxeter and looks an out-and-out stayer.

Funambule Sivola (Fr)

7 b g Noroit - Little Memories (Montjeu)

Venetia Williams — My Racing Manager Friends

PLACINGS: 0F55/1512112/29112P- **RPR 166c**

Starts	1st	2nd	3rd	4th	Win & Pl
19	6	6	-	-	£223,614

	2/22	Newb	2m½f Cls1 Gd2 Ch gd-sft	£34,170
152	1/22	Donc	2m½f Cls2 128-152 Ch Hcap good	£20,812
141	3/21	Asct	2m1f Cls2 Nov 129-141 Ch Hcap good	£16,243
133	2/21	Chep	2m Cls2 126-145 Ch Hcap soft	£11,930
124	12/20	Newb	2m½f Cls3 113-125 Ch Hcap soft	£7,018
112	11/20	Weth	1m7f Cls4 Nov 112-120 Ch Hcap gd-sft	£4,289

Developed into a very smart 2m chaser last season, with two wins including the Game Spirit Chase at Newbury before a well-beaten second in the Champion Chase; failed to convince at around 2m4f on three other runs despite second in the Peterborough Chase.

Fury Road (Ire)

8 b g Stowaway - Molly Duffy (Oscar)

Gordon Elliott (Ire) — Gigginstown House Stud

PLACINGS: 311143/142P/P23152-3 **RPR 159c**

Starts	1st	2nd	3rd	4th	Win & Pl
19	6	3	4	2	£233,451

	12/21	Leop	3m Nov Gd1 Ch yield	£52,679
	11/20	Punc	2m5½f Gd2 Hdl heavy	£30,000
	12/19	Limk	2m7f Nov Gd2 Hdl heavy	£39,865
	11/19	Navn	2m4f Nov Gd3 Hdl soft	£22,590
	11/19	DRoy	2m6f Mdn Hdl yld-sft	£7,986
	2/19	Fair	2m NHF 5-7yo gd-yld	£5,550

Very inconsistent but proved himself a very smart stayer on his day last season, winning a Grade 1 novice chase at Leopardstown and chasing home Ahoy Senor at Aintree; has won on heavy ground but has avoided testing conditions more recently (non-runner at Cheltenham).

Fusil Raffles (Fr)

7 b g Saint Des Saints - Tali Des Obeaux (Panoramic I)

Nicky Henderson — Simon Munir & Isaac Souede

PLACINGS: 1/11P0/11P12P/21453- **RPR 156c**

Starts	1st	2nd	3rd	4th	Win & Pl
18	8	3	1	1	£253,731

	10/21	Weth	3m Cls1 Gd2 Ch gd-sft	£57,218
	12/20	Chel	2m4½f Cls2 Nov Ch soft	£12,820
	10/20	Chel	2m Cls2 Nov Ch good	£12,512
	9/20	Uttx	2m Cls4 Nov Ch good	£4,289
	11/19	Winc	1m7½f Cls1 Gd2 Hdl gd-sft	£34,572
	5/19	Punc	2m Gd1 Hdl 4yo gd-yld	£53,153
	2/19	Kemp	2m Cls1 Gd2 Hdl 4yo good	£17,085
	7/18	Seno	2m2f Hdl 3yo soft	£5,947

Found life much tougher last season after a fruitful novice campaign and was lucky to gain sole victory in the Charlie Hall Chase after Shan Blue's fall; finished fourth and fifth when favourite for big handicaps at Cheltenham and Doncaster; fell 9lb in the weights through the campaign.

Ga Law (Fr)

6 b g Sinndar - Law (Lute Antique)

Jamie Snowden — The Footie Partnership

PLACINGS: 16/11132/ — RPR **151c**

Starts	1st	2nd	3rd	4th	Win & Pl
7	4	1	1	-	£42,912

	11/20	Winc	2m4f Cls1 Nov Gd2 Ch good	£15,217
128	10/20	Extr	2m3f Cls3 110-130 Ch Hcap gd-fm	£7,018
	9/20	Font	2m3½f Cls4 Ch good	£4,029
	10/19	Agtn	2m2f Hdl 3yo heavy	£6,054

Took really well to fences two seasons ago and won first three chases, though perhaps flattered having received big four-year-old allowances; ran two solid races in stronger company, including when second in a Grade 2 at Kempton; missed last season through injury.

Gaelic Warrior (Ger)

4 b g Maxios - Game Of Legs (Hernando)

Willie Mullins (Ire) — Mrs S Ricci

PLACINGS: 6/332- — RPR **132+h**

Starts	1st	2nd	3rd	4th	Win & Pl
4	-	1	2	-	£28,335

Monster gamble for last season's Fred Winter at Cheltenham, going off just 13-8 with connections sure he was much better than mark of 129 after three runs in France, but just got pipped by Brazil; still ran a fine race in defeat and retains novice status.

Gaillard Du Mesnil (Fr)

6 gr g Saint Des Saints - Athena Du Mesnil (Al Namix)

Willie Mullins (Ire) — Mrs J Donnelly

PLACINGS: 621222/2112/133333- — RPR **161c**

Starts	1st	2nd	3rd	4th	Win & Pl
16	4	6	5	-	£243,067

4/21	Punc	2m4f Nov Gd1 Hdl yield	£52,679
2/21	Leop	2m6f Nov Gd1 Hdl sft-hvy	£65,848
12/20	Leop	2m4f Mdn Hdl 4yo soft	£6,000
8/19	Sjdm	1m5f NHF 3yo gd-sft	£4,279

Dual Grade 1 winner as a novice hurdler two seasons ago but took time to get even close to a similar level over fences last term; penny dropped in the spring when third in the Brown Advisory Chase and the Irish Grand National (sent off favourite); retains novice status.

Galopin Des Champs (Fr)

6 bl g Timos - Manon Des Champs (Marchand De Sable)

Willie Mullins (Ire) — Mrs Audrey Turley

PLACINGS: 12P61/111F1- — RPR **177+c**

Starts	1st	2nd	3rd	4th	Win & Pl
10	6	1	-	-	£238,108

	4/22	Fair	2m4f Nov Gd1 Ch yield	£49,580
	2/22	Leop	2m5½f Nov Gd1 Ch yield	£74,370
	12/21	Leop	2m5f Ch yield	£9,219
	4/21	Punc	3m Nov Gd1 Hdl yield	£52,679
142	3/21	Chel	2m4½f Cls2 132-143 Cond Hdl Hcap gd-sft	£32,498
	5/20	Autl	2m2f Hdl 4yo v soft	£16,475

Best novice chaser for several years on Racing Post Ratings after a stunning campaign last season; became arguably most well known for an agonising final-fence spill when thrashing Bob Olinger at Cheltenham but bounced back with a third easy win from three completed chases at Fairyhouse.

Galvin (Ire)

8 b g Gold Well - Burren Moonshine (Moonax)

Gordon Elliott (Ire) — R A Bartlett

PLACINGS: 62/F422/11111/1214-6 — RPR **171+c**

Starts	1st	2nd	3rd	4th	Win & Pl
21	12	4	-	2	£308,332

12/21	Leop	3m Gd1 Ch yield	£92,188
10/21	Punc	3m Gd3 Ch good	£14,487
3/21	Chel	3m6f Cls1 Nov Gd2 Ch gd-sft	£52,753
10/20	Chel	3m½f Cls2 Nov Ch good	£12,558
10/20	Tipp	2m4f Nov Gd3 Ch good	£13,750
8/20	Klny	2m5f Nov Ch yield	£6,250
7/20	Klny	2m5f Ch yield	£6,250
2/19	Ayr	2m Cls4 Nov Hdl soft	£4,094
1/19	Navn	2m Nov Hdl yield	£8,879
8/18	Prth	2m Cls4 Mdn Hdl good	£4,549
7/18	Limk	2m NHF 4-7yo gd-yld	£5,996
7/18	Rosc	2m NHF 4-7yo good	£5,451

High-class staying chaser who progressed into a proper Grade 1 horse last season and even beat A Plus Tard to land the Savills Chase; only fourth behind that rival in the Cheltenham Gold Cup and no match for another superstar, Allaho, when sixth at Punchestown.

Gatsby Grey (Fr)

6 b g Waldpark - Rochepaille (Rochesson)

Oliver McKiernan (Ire) — Keep The Faith Syndicate

PLACINGS: 1/17471-2 — RPR **145+h**

Starts	1st	2nd	3rd	4th	Win & Pl
7	3	1	-	1	£40,488

3/22	Naas	2m Nov Hdl gd-yld	£7,933
12/21	Limk	2m Mdn Hdl heavy	£6,321
3/21	Navn	2m NHF 5-7yo sft-hvy	£5,268

Highly tried in novice hurdles last season but justified connections' boldness by finishing second at 100-1 behind Mighty Potter in a Grade 1 at Punchestown on final run; had previously won his only two runs below Graded level impressively; has the build of a chaser.

Gelino Bello (Fr)

6 b g Saint Des Saints - Parade (Robin Des Champs)

Paul Nicholls — Mr And Mrs J D Cotton

PLACINGS: 13/122411- — RPR **143+h**

Starts	1st	2nd	3rd	4th	Win & Pl
8	4	2	1	1	£97,256

4/22	Aint	3m½f Cls1 Nov Gd1 Hdl gd-sft	£56,270
3/22	Newb	2m4½f Cls4 Nov Hdl soft	£4,738
10/21	Aint	2m4f Cls4 Mdn Hdl good	£5,174
12/20	Plum	2m1½f Cls5 NHF 4-5yo soft	£2,274

Very useful staying novice hurdler last season and won the Sefton at Aintree on final run; no doubt that was a weak Grade 1 but had produced solid form all year, twice when second behind Blazing

Khal in Grade 2 races at Cheltenham; likely to go novice chasing.

Gentleman At Arms (Ire)

5 gr g Reliable Man - Sworn Sold (Soldier Hollow)

Stuart Edmunds — D & B Partnership

PLACINGS: 512212- — RPR **139h**

Starts	1st	2nd	3rd	4th	Win & Pl
6	2	3	-	-	£47,266

	Date	Course	Race	Prize
	3/22	Hntg	2m4½f Cls4 Nov Hdl good	£4,085
	12/21	Hntg	2m3½f Cls4 Nov Hdl soft	£4,085

Useful and progressive novice hurdler last season; won twice at Huntingdon and finished second three times in stronger company, most notably behind Gelino Bello when stepped up to 3m in a Grade 1 at Aintree on final run.

Gentleman De Mee (Fr)

6 b g Saint Des Saints - Koeur De Mee (Video Rock)

Willie Mullins (Ire) — John P McManus

PLACINGS: 22/10/752111- — RPR **167+c**

Starts	1st	2nd	3rd	4th	Win & Pl
10	4	3	-	-	£113,160

	Date	Course	Race	Prize
	4/22	Aint	2m Cls1 Nov Gd1 Ch gd-sft	£67,524
	3/22	Navn	2m Nov Gd3 Ch yield	£18,097
	2/22	Thur	2m½f Ch good	£5,702
	2/21	Naas	1m7½f Mdn Hdl soft	£6,321

Produced arguably the best performance by a 2m novice chaser all last season when beating Arkle hero Edwardstone at Aintree; had won just one of first seven races under rules but improved massively as last season went on, following up odds-on wins at Thurles and Navan.

Gentlemansgame

6 gr g Gentlewave - Grainne Ni Maille (Terimon)

Mouse Morris (Ire) — Robcour

PLACINGS: 1123/2071-3 — RPR **156h**

Starts	1st	2nd	3rd	4th	Win & Pl
8	2	2	2	-	£74,051

	Date	Course	Race	Prize
	3/22	Thur	2m7f Hdl good	£5,950
	1/21	Cork	2m Mdn Hdl 4-5yo sft-hvy	£6,321

Smart staying hurdler who bounced back to form last season when winning easily at Thurles and then finishing third behind Klassical Dream at Punchestown; had also been placed twice more at Grade 1 level as a novice in 2021; likely to go novice chasing.

Gericault Roque (Fr)

6 b g Montmartre - Nijinska Delaroque (Lute Antique)

David Pipe — Prof Caroline Tisdall And Bryan Drew

PLACINGS: 4/2131/32222- — RPR **144c**

Starts	1st	2nd	3rd	4th	Win & Pl
9	2	5	2	-	£66,302

	Date	Course	Race	Prize
117	3/21	Sand	2m Cls4 100-117 Cond Hdl Hcap gd-sft	£3,769
	1/21	Plum	2m Cls4 Mdn Hdl soft	£3,769

Very useful staying novice chaser last season despite failing to win in five races; beaten favourite three times but did little wrong in coming second four times, including in the Classic Chase at Warwick and the Ultima at Cheltenham from 5lb out of the handicap.

Gin Coco (Fr)

6 b g Cokoriko - Qlementine (Video Rock)

Harry Fry — David's Partnership

PLACINGS: 22/1-2 — RPR **133+h**

Starts	1st	2nd	3rd	4th	Win & Pl
4	1	3	-	-	£18,364

	Date	Course	Race	Prize
	3/22	Font	2m1½f Cls4 Mdn Hdl good	£5,827

Very lightly raced hurdler who did well last spring when returning from more than a year out; got off the mark in a maiden hurdle at Fontwell and then finished a fine second of 25 at Punchestown on handicap debut; open to significant improvement.

Global Citizen (Ire)

10 b g Alkaadhem - Lady Willmurt (Mandalus)

Ben Pauling — The Megsons

PLACINGS: 1417/414/PPP/920231- — RPR **146c**

Starts	1st	2nd	3rd	4th	Win & Pl
23	7	4	1	3	£244,207

	Date	Course	Race	Prize
136	3/22	Chel	2m Cls1 Gd3 136-156 Ch Hcap heavy	£70,338
	12/19	Kemp	2m Cls1 Nov Gd2 Ch soft	£22,780
	1/19	Hayd	1m7½f Cls1 Gd2 Hdl gd-sft	£42,713
146	12/18	Newb	2m½f Cls1 List 126-146 Hdl Hcap soft	£28,475
	2/18	Kemp	2m Cls1 Nov Gd2 Hdl good	£17,085
	2/18	Sthl	1m7½f Cls4 Nov Hdl soft	£4,094
	10/17	Worc	2m Cls6 NHF 4-6yo gd-fm	£1,689

Remarkable winner of the Grand Annual at Cheltenham last season on first run over fences since 2020; had been largely disappointing over hurdles but improved after a second wind operation last term, finishing second in Haydock's Champion Hurdle Trial.

Glory And Fortune (Ire)

7 b g Fame And Glory - Night Heron (St Jovite)

Tom Lacey — J Hinds

PLACINGS: 352/84025/211642154- — RPR **158h**

Starts	1st	2nd	3rd	4th	Win & Pl
19	5	4	1	3	£209,259

	Date	Course	Race	Prize
143	2/22	Newb	2m½f Cls1 Gd3 123-147 Hdl Hcap gd-sft	£87,219
134	10/21	Ffos	2m Cls2 132-151 Hdl Hcap good	£26,015
130	9/21	Plum	2m Cls3 108-130 Hdl Hcap good	£7,951
	10/19	Hntg	2m Cls4 Nov Hdl good	£4,224
	1/19	Chel	1m6f Cls1 List NHF 4yo gd-sft	£14,068

Smart and progressive hurdler who landed a third handicap of last season when defying a big weight to edge home by a short head in the Betfair Hurdle; had also finished second in the Christmas Hurdle and was second of the British runners when fifth in the Champion Hurdle.

Go Dante

6 b g Kayf Tara - Whoops A Daisy (Definite Article)

Olly Murphy — Mrs Barbara Hester

PLACINGS: 1/124- — RPR **133+h**

Starts	1st	2nd	3rd	4th	Win & Pl
4	2	1	-	1	£14,577

	10/21	Bang	2m½f Cls4 Nov Hdl gd-sft	£4,085
	3/21	Winc	1m7½f Cls5 Mdn NHF 4-6yo soft	£2,274

Won sole bumper and made an impressive start to hurdles career with an 18-length win at Bangor last season; beaten at 2-7 at Ascot next time but did better when a staying-on fourth in the Challow Hurdle despite again jumping poorly and being badly hampered.

Good Boy Bobby (Ire)

9 b g Flemensfirth - Princess Gaia (King's Theatre)

Nigel Twiston-Davies — Simon Munir & Isaac Souede

PLACINGS: 2125/1245432/31217P- — RPR **156+c**

Starts	1st	2nd	3rd	4th	Win & Pl
25	10	5	4	2	£113,912

146	12/21	Weth	3m Cls1 Gd3 141-150 Ch Hcap soft	£23,182
138	10/21	Weth	2m3½f Cls1 List 128-154 Ch Hcap gd-sft	£15,661
	10/20	Bang	2m1½f Cls4 Ch soft	£4,289
	11/19	Weth	1m7f Cls4 Nov Ch soft	£4,938
	4/19	Ffos	2m4f Cls4 Nov Hdl soft	£4,094
	3/19	Sthl	1m7½f Cls4 Nov Hdl good	£3,249
	10/18	Carl	2m1f Cls4 Nov Hdl gd-sft	£4,549
	3/18	Weth	2m Cls5 NHF 4-6yo heavy	£2,599
	1/18	Chep	2m Cls5 NHF 5-7yo heavy	£2,599
	11/17	Chep	2m Cls6 NHF 4-6yo soft	£1,949

Progressive handicap chaser early last season, winning twice at Wetherby, including the Rowland Meyrick, either side of a head second in the Rehearsal Chase; failed to land a blow under new hold-up tactics at Kempton before being pulled up in the Grand National.

Good Risk At All (Fr)

6 ch g No Risk At All - Sissi Land (Grey Risk)

Sam Thomas — Walters Plant Hire

PLACINGS: 211/22216- — RPR **138+h**

Starts	1st	2nd	3rd	4th	Win & Pl
8	3	4	-	-	£59,641

127	2/22	Asct	2m3½f Cls2 121-144 Hdl Hcap soft	£26,164
	2/21	Newb	2m½f Cls1 List NHF 4-6yo gd-sft	£11,390
	11/20	Chel	2m½f Cls1 List NHF 4-6yo soft	£10,251

Dual Listed bumper winner who again suggested big potential with a stunning nine-length win in a valuable 2m3f handicap hurdle at Ascot last season; slightly disappointing otherwise, though probably needed further when twice a beaten favourite over 2m.

Good Time Jonny (Ire)

7 b g Shirocco - Shaylejon (Old Vic)

Tony Martin (Ire) — A Shiels & Donal Gavigan & Niall Reilly

PLACINGS: 2319/64/95F316119-P — RPR **144+h**

Starts	1st	2nd	3rd	4th	Win & Pl
16	4	1	2	1	£79,873

129	2/22	Leop	3m 116-142 Hdl Hcap yield	£49,580
120	12/21	Leop	2m4f Nov 105-126 Hdl Hcap yld-sft	£13,170
111	10/21	Gowr	2m4f 107-128 Hdl Hcap good	£8,429
	1/20	Muss	1m7½f Cls4 NHF 4-6yo gd-sft	£3,249

Hugely progressive hurdler last season, winning three times including a valuable handicap at the

Good Boy Bobby: Wetherby specialist

Dublin Racing Festival; eschewed handicap targets (favourite for the Coral Cup at one point) to step into Grade 1 novice company but no better than ninth at Cheltenham and Punchestown.

Goshen (Fr)

6 b g Authorized - Hyde (Poliglote)

Gary Moore — Steven Packham

PLACINGS: 111U/018/547311- — RPR **163+h**

Starts	1st	2nd	3rd	4th	Win & Pl
13	6	-	1	1	£123,504

	Date	Course	Race	Prize
	2/22	Winc	1m7f Cls1 Gd2 Hdl soft	£39,865
	2/22	Sand	2m Cls1 List Hdl gd-sft	£17,085
	2/21	Winc	1m7½f Cls1 Gd2 Hdl heavy	£21,628
	1/20	Asct	1m7½f Cls3 Hdl 4yo heavy	£7,018
	12/19	Sand	2m Cls2 Hdl 3yo soft	£12,512
	11/19	Font	2m1½f Cls4 Hdl 3yo soft	£4,094

Largely disappointing since a remarkable performance in the 2020 Triumph Hurdle (well clear when unseating at the last) but got back on track when winning at Sandown and Wincanton at the end of last season; needs to go right-handed; exciting prospect for novice chases.

Gowel Road (Ire)

6 b/br g Flemensfirth - Hollygrove Samba (Accordion)

Nigel Twiston-Davies — Options O Syndicate

PLACINGS: 24110/61327- — RPR **145h**

Starts	1st	2nd	3rd	4th	Win & Pl
10	3	2	1	1	£55,182

	Date	Course	Race	Prize
134	11/21	Chel	2m5f Cls3 113-136 Hdl Hcap good	£13,070
	2/21	Newb	2m½f Cls3 Nov Hdl gd-sft	£5,913
122	1/21	Newb	2m½f Cls4 110-122 Hdl Hcap heavy	£3,769

Useful and progressive hurdler last season; won a 2m5f handicap at Cheltenham before running well in more valuable races over shorter trips at Newbury and Lingfield; likely to go novice chasing.

Grand Paradis (Fr)

6 gr g Martaline - Outre Mer (Sleeping Car)

Gordon Elliott (Ire) — Caldwell Construction

PLACINGS: 1411/FP322P1- — RPR **143c**

Starts	1st	2nd	3rd	4th	Win & Pl
11	4	2	1	1	£38,118

	Date	Course	Race	Prize
	4/22	Cork	2m4f Ch heavy	£7,685
	2/21	Thur	2m5f Nov Gd3 Hdl heavy	£14,487
	2/21	Fair	2m Mdn Hdl heavy	£6,321
	11/20	Fair	2m NHF 4yo soft	£4,500

Very smart novice hurdler (earned RPR of 150 for winning a Grade 3 by 13 lengths) who didn't hit the same heights over fences last season; still went off just 11-2 when pulled up in the Plate at Cheltenham after progressing in beginners' chase before getting off the mark at Cork.

Grand Roi (Fr)

6 b g Spanish Moon - Ultra D'Anjou (Nononito)

Gordon Elliott (Ire) — Bective Stud

PLACINGS: 6/31411/3120/344P3- — RPR **156+h**

Starts	1st	2nd	3rd	4th	Win & Pl
15	4	1	4	3	£53,221

	Date	Course	Race	Prize
	12/20	Limk	2m Gd2 Hdl 4yo heavy	£17,500
	2/20	Wwck	2m Cls4 Hdl 4yo heavy	£4,549
	1/20	Fknm	2m Cls3 Mdn Hdl gd-sft	£6,628
	12/19	Winc	1m7½f Cls5 NHF 3yo gd-sft	£2,274

Had a big reputation when winning three of first four races in Britain for Nicky Henderson but has been largely disappointing for Gordon Elliott; ran no race when well fancied for the last two

runnings of the Coral Cup and has just come up short in Graded races in Ireland otherwise.

Grangeclare West (Ire)

6 b g Presenting - Hayabusa (Sir Harry Lewis)

Willie Mullins (Ire) — Cheveley Park Stud

PLACINGS: 1/1- — RPR **115b**

Starts	1st	2nd	3rd	4th	Win & Pl
1	1	-	-	-	£5,267

	Date	Course	Race	Prize
	5/21	Punc	2m½f NHF 4-7yo soft	£5,268

Bought for £430,000 after winning sole point-to-point last season and made a winning start under rules at Punchestown last May, hacking up by nine lengths; missed the rest of the season through injury; bred to be a staying chaser and should flourish when stepped up in trip.

Greaneteen (Fr)

8 b g Great Pretender - Manson Teene (Mansonnien)

Paul Nicholls — Chris Giles

PLACINGS: 1/01114/12341/41251- — RPR **171+c**

Starts	1st	2nd	3rd	4th	Win & Pl
19	9	2	2	3	£399,213

	Date	Course	Race	Prize
	4/22	Sand	1m7½f Cls1 Gd1 Ch good	£92,192
	12/21	Sand	1m7½f Cls1 Gd1 Ch gd-sft	£85,425
	4/21	Sand	1m7½f Cls1 Gd1 Ch good	£65,493
151	11/20	Extr	2m1½f Cls1 Gd2 138-158 Ch Hcap good	£32,329
	2/20	Fknm	2m½f Cls3 Nov Ch soft	£8,058
138	2/20	Muss	2m Cls3 124-140 Ch Hcap gd-sft	£13,256
132	12/19	Asct	2m1f Cls3 Nov 119-132 Ch Hcap heavy	£10,007
	1/19	Font	2m1½f Cls4 Nov Hdl gd-sft	£4,094
	1/19	Extr	2m2½f Cls4 Mdn Hdl gd-sft	£4,549

Three-time Grade 1 winner, all at Sandown, winning the last two runnings of the Celebration Chase either side of a fairytale Tingle Creek victory; unlucky fourth in the 2021 Champion Chase but missed that race last season after a below-par run at Leopardstown.

Green Book (Fr)

5 b g Authorized - Mantissa (Oratorio)

Venetia Williams — Lady Price, C Shaw, C Boylan & I Tagg

PLACINGS: 2/211U1459- — RPR **140h**

Starts	1st	2nd	3rd	4th	Win & Pl
9	3	2	-	1	£80,345

	Date	Course	Race	Prize
130	2/22	Sand	2m7½f Cls1 Gd3 128-150 Hdl Hcap gd-sft	£56,270
122	12/21	Ludl	2m5f Cls4 102-122 Am Hdl Hcap gd-sft	£4,414
122	12/21	Hayd	1m7½f Cls3 107-129 Cond Hdl Hcap soft	£6,808

Very useful staying novice hurdler last season, climbing the ranks in handicaps and landing a

Greaneteen: last three wins have all been at Sandown

valuable payday when winning at Sandown in February; couldn't land a blow back in top novice company, though still a fair fifth in the Albert Bartlett at Cheltenham.

Grumpy Charley

7 gr g Shirocco - Whisky Rose (Old Vic)

Chris Honour G Thompson

PLACINGS: 13/69/251116/513P7- RPR **145+c**

Starts	1st	2nd	3rd	4th	Win & Pl
14	4	1	2	-	£31,061

137	12/21	Newb	2m6½f Cls3 Nov 131-142 Ch Hcap soft	£7,407
132	2/21	Chep	2m Cls3 117-132 Hdl Hcap soft	£5,913
	2/21	Chep	2m Cls4 Nov Hdl 4-7yo heavy	£4,419
	1/21	Chep	2m Cls4 Nov Hdl heavy	£3,769

Three-time winner as a novice hurdler (all on soft/heavy ground) and proved equally adept over fences when winning at Newbury on soft last season; disappointing in the spring and yet to make a mark above Class 3 level but never got preferred conditions again.

Guard Your Dreams

6 b g Fame And Glory - Native Sunrise (Definite Article)

Nigel Twiston-Davies Graham & Alison Jelley

PLACINGS: 2/1411673/131323U- RPR **150h**

Starts	1st	2nd	3rd	4th	Win & Pl
15	5	2	4	1	£148,863

	12/21	Chel	2m1f Cls1 Gd2 Hdl gd-sft	£79,730
140	10/21	Chel	2m4f Cls3 114-140 Hdl Hcap good	£8,169
128	1/21	Sand	2m Cls2 119-145 Hdl Hcap heavy	£10,010
	11/20	Bang	2m½f Cls4 Nov Hdl soft	£3,769
	9/20	Bang	2m½f Cls4 Mdn Hdl gd-sft	£4,029

Won twice at Cheltenham last season, landing a 2m4f handicap hurdle first time out before narrowly adding the International Hurdle; finished second or third four times in further Grade 2 races but limitations seemingly exposed as just below the very best.

Guard Your Dreams (right): talented hurdler has two wins on his CV at Cheltenham

Guily Billy (Fr)

6 gr g Coastal Path - Ukie (Dom Alco)

Henry de Bromhead (Ire) — Cheveley Park Stud

PLACINGS: P/1/21P- — RPR **133+h**

Starts		1st	2nd	3rd	4th	Win & Pl
3		1	1	-	-	£6,964
	12/21	Tram	2m Mdn Hdl soft			£5,268

Bought for £310,000 after winning an Irish point-to-point in 2020 and made a promising start over hurdles last season, landing a maiden at Tramore by 25 lengths; injured when pulled up on only subsequent run in a Grade 2 at Punchestown; remains a fine prospect.

Gunsight Ridge

7 b g Midnight Legend - Grandma Griffiths (Eagle Eyed)

Olly Murphy — Mrs Diana L Whateley

PLACINGS: 14/21232/3213P- — RPR **141+c**

Starts		1st	2nd	3rd	4th	Win & Pl
11		2	4	3	1	£35,511
130	1/22	Sand	1m7½f Cls2 130-141 Ch Hcap heavy			£15,945
	11/20	Donc	2m½f Cls4 Nov Hdl good			£3,769

Consistent and progressive chaser who won at Sandown last season but nonetheless hasn't quite lived up to expectations yet otherwise; beaten favourite in six of last seven races but had been placed every time until picking up a knock when pulled up in the Red Rum at Aintree.

Ha D'Or (Fr)

5 b g Nidor - Rosewort (Network)

Willie Mullins (Ire) — Mrs S Ricci

PLACINGS: 135/2132-2 — RPR **144h**

Starts		1st	2nd	3rd	4th	Win & Pl
8		2	3	2	-	£30,009
	1/22	Fair	2m Mdn Hdl gd-yld			£6,197
	7/20	Seno	1m3½f NHF 3yo soft			£4,534

Promising youngster who has won only one of seven races over hurdles but has been highly tried and ran well in strong company last term; finished a neck second to Flame Bearer in a Grade 2 at Fairyhouse and filled the same spot behind El Fabiolo at Punchestown.

Hacker Des Places (Fr)

5 gr g Great Pretender - Plaisance (Le Havre)

Paul Nicholls — Owners Group 068

PLACINGS: 3121/64131- — RPR **137h**

Starts		1st	2nd	3rd	4th	Win & Pl
9		4	1	2	1	£67,624
133	4/22	Aint	2m½f Cls2 122-143 Am Hdl Hcap gd-sft			£25,720
129	2/22	Chep	2m Cls3 105-129 Hdl Hcap heavy			£6,753
	12/20	Weth	2m Cls4 Hdl 3yo heavy			£3,769
	6/20	Dax	2m1½f Hdl 3yo soft			£8,258

Hugely progressive handicap hurdler who won at Aintree's Grand National meeting last season; relished quicker ground that day but has also won twice on heavy; looks a long-term chasing prospect but likely to have bigger handicap hurdles on his agenda first.

Happygolucky (Ire)

8 br g Jeremy - Mydadsabishop (Bishop Of Cashel)

Kim Bailey — Lady Dulverton

PLACINGS: 2/1334/12121/ — RPR **154c**

Starts		1st	2nd	3rd	4th	Win & Pl
9		4	2	2	1	£83,245
149	4/21	Aint	3m1f Cls1 Gd3 128-154 Ch Hcap gd-sft			£31,538
	12/20	Chel	3m1½f Cls2 Nov Ch gd-sft			£12,974
	10/20	Strf	2m5f Cls4 Ch gd-sft			£4,289
	10/19	Strf	2m6f Cls4 Mdn Hdl soft			£4,549

Missed last season through injury but had looked a smart and progressive staying chaser prior to that; won two of his three races in novice company in 2020-21, most notably at Cheltenham, and continued to flourish in handicaps, finishing second in the Ultima before winning at Aintree.

Harbour Lake (Ire)

6 br g Shantou - Aibrean (Winged Love)

Alan King — Exors Of The Late Trevor Hemmings

PLACINGS: 11B1- — RPR **132+h**

Starts		1st	2nd	3rd	4th	Win & Pl
4		3	-	-	-	£15,738
126	3/22	Bang	2m3½f Cls3 116-126 Hdl Hcap soft			£5,664
	12/21	Weth	2m Cls4 Nov Hdl soft			£4,085
	10/21	Weth	2m Cls3 Nov Hdl gd-sft			£5,991

Useful novice hurdler last season, winning three out of four races; set to finish a close fourth in a Listed race at Huntingdon when brought down at the last before bouncing back to score on handicap debut at Bangor; missed intended Grade 1 target at Aintree through injury.

Haut En Couleurs (Fr)

5 b g Saint Des Saints - Sanouva (Muhtathir)

Willie Mullins (Ire) — Mrs J Donnelly

PLACINGS: 13/31F6-5 — RPR **155+c**

Starts		1st	2nd	3rd	4th	Win & Pl
7		2	-	2	-	£50,029
	12/21	Leop	2m1f Ch gd-yld			£9,219
	10/20	Autl	2m2f Hdl 3yo heavy			£18,305

Very highly tried since joining Willie Mullins, competing at Grade 1 level in all but one of his six races despite managing no better than third; beat subsequent Grade 1 winner Gentleman De Mee in a beginners' chase last season but form tailed off subsequently.

Haute Estime (Ire)

5 b m Walk In The Park - Terre Haute (Oscar)

Lucinda Russell — Brahms & Liszt

PLACINGS: 24/314143- — RPR **127h**

Starts		1st	2nd	3rd	4th	Win & Pl
8		2	1	2	3	£31,818
	12/21	Hayd	2m3f Cls1 Nov List Hdl soft			£11,390
	10/21	Kels	2m Cls4 Nov Hdl good			£4,357

Useful and progressive mare last season; gained biggest win in a Listed mares' novice hurdle at Haydock and improved again when stepped up in class and trip for a 3m Grade 1 at Aintree, belying 100-1 odds to finish third behind Gelino Bello.

Henri The Second (Fr)

5 b g Saddler Maker - Rock Treasure (Video Rock)

Paul Nicholls — Martin Broughton & Friends

PLACINGS: 11P- — RPR **110+b**

Starts		1st	2nd	3rd	4th	Win & Pl
3		2	-	-	-	£13,865
	12/21	Asct	1m7½f Cls1 List NHF 4-6yo gd-sft			£11,960
	10/21	Chep	2m Cls5 Am NHF 4-6yo good			£1,906

Won first two bumpers last season, notably what proved a strong Listed race at Ascot (subsequent Champion Bumper fifth in second and Listed winner in third); appeared to be struck into when pulled up on final run at Aintree.

Hewick (Ire)

7 b g Virtual - Ballyburn Rose (Oscar)

Shark Hanlon (Ire) — T J McDonald

PLACINGS: 0011P2/124P2121P1-21 — RPR **166+c**

Starts	1st	2nd	3rd	4th	Win & Pl
27	7	6	-	2	£281,776

155	7/22	Gway	2m6½f 143-160 Ch Hcap good	£133,866
149	4/22	Sand	3m5f Cls1 Gd3 128-154 Ch Hcap good	£90,299
142	10/21	Sedg	3m5f Cls2 116-142 Ch Hcap good	£14,308
118	9/21	List	3m 107-132 Hdl Hcap good	£8,429
	6/21	Clon	2m7f Ch good	£5,795
102	9/20	Navn	2m6f 80-102 Hdl Hcap good	£5,000
94	9/20	Kbgn	3m1f 80-95 Hdl Hcap yield	£4,500

Sharply progressive chaser who has already landed two big staying prizes this year, landing the bet365 Gold Cup at Sandown and the Galway Plate; won that race off 155 and likely to be forced into Grade 1 company, though has hitherto been kept away from winter ground.

Hillcrest (Ire)

7 br g Stowaway - Shop Dj (Dushyantor)

Henry Daly — Exors Of The Late Trevor Hemmings

PLACINGS: 21/111U1P- — RPR **151+h**

Starts	1st	2nd	3rd	4th	Win & Pl
8	5	1	-	-	£55,741

2/22	Hayd	3m½f Cls1 Nov Gd2 Hdl heavy	£28,978
1/22	Chel	2m4½f Cls1 Nov List Hdl soft	£14,238
12/21	Weth	2m5½f Cls4 Nov Hdl gd-sft	£4,411
11/21	Aint	2m4f Cls4 Nov Hdl 4-6yo gd-sft	£5,174
3/21	Weth	2m Cls5 NHF 4-6yo gd-sft	£2,274

Giant chasing type who made a big impact in novice hurdles last season and won four times, most impressively in a Grade 2 at Haydock on heavy ground; favourite for the Albert Bartlett after that but was always in rear and pulled up; should make a fine novice chaser.

Hitman (Fr)

6 b g Falco - Tercah Girl (Martaline)

Paul Nicholls — Mason, Hogarth, Ferguson & Done

PLACINGS: 201/12F13/2232- — RPR **165c**

Starts	1st	2nd	3rd	4th	Win & Pl
12	3	5	2	-	£159,539

3/21	Newb	2m4f Cls3 Nov Ch good	£7,798
11/20	Ffos	2m Cls3 Ch soft	£7,791
1/20	Pau	2m½f Hdl 4yo v soft	£12,203

Smart and consistent chaser who ran well in defeat in all four runs last season; twice finished second at Grade 1 level, chasing home Greaneteen in the Tingle Creek and Fakir D'Oudairies in the Melling Chase; still a work in progress according to his trainer and set to step up in trip.

Hillcrest: smart novice hurdler can be expected to take high rank over fences

Hollow Games (Ire)

6 b g Beat Hollow - I'm Grand (Raise A Grand)

Gordon Elliott (Ire) — Bective Stud

PLACINGS: 1/11/11333-5 — RPR **145h**

Starts	1st	2nd	3rd	4th	Win & Pl
8	4	-	3	-	£60,178

11/21	Navn	2m4f Nov Gd3 Hdl good	£14,487
10/21	DRoy	2m6½f Mdn Hdl soft	£6,848
12/20	Leop	2m NHF 4-7yo soft	£5,000
11/20	Punc	2m NHF 4yo heavy	£5,000

Smart novice hurdler last season despite not quite living up to expectations after Grade 3 win; twice third in Grade 1 novices, including when favourite stepping up to 2m6f, and filled the same spot in the Martin Pipe; bred to make a chaser (out of the granddam of Remittance Man).

Home By The Lee (Ire)

7 b g Fame And Glory - Going For Home (Presenting)

Joseph O'Brien (Ire) — Sean O'Driscoll

PLACINGS: 1218U/113P10/0P226-0 — RPR **157h**

Starts	1st	2nd	3rd	4th	Win & Pl
18	6	3	1	-	£85,929

139	2/21	Naas	2m4½f Nov 118-139 Ch Hcap soft	£21,071
	11/20	Cork	2m4f Nov Gd3 Ch soft	£17,500
	10/20	Limk	2m6f Ch soft	£7,750
	1/20	Fair	2m4f Mdn Hdl yield	£6,511
	6/19	Rosc	2m NHF 4yo good	£6,659
	5/19	Klny	2m1f NHF 4yo good	£5,827

Has spent much of the last two seasons over fences, largely without success, but quickly proved much better when reverting to hurdles late last term; finished second in the Galmoy Hurdle at 80-1 and sixth in the Stayers' Hurdle at Cheltenham at 66-1.

Honeysuckle

8 b m Sulamani - First Royal (Lando)

Henry de Bromhead (Ire) — Kenneth Alexander

PLACINGS: 1111/1111/111/1111-1 — RPR **161+h**

Starts	1st	2nd	3rd	4th	Win & Pl
16	16	-	-	-	£1,317,181

4/22	Punc	2m Gd1 Hdl gd-yld	£136,134
3/22	Chel	2m½f Cls1 Gd1 Hdl gd-sft	£253,215
2/22	Leop	2m Gd1 Hdl yield	£94,118
11/21	Fair	2m4f Gd1 Hdl good	£52,679
4/21	Punc	2m Gd1 Hdl yield	£131,696
3/21	Chel	2m½f Cls1 Gd1 Hdl soft	£189,911
2/21	Leop	2m Gd1 Hdl sft-hvy	£75,000
11/20	Fair	2m4f Gd1 Hdl soft	£50,000
3/20	Chel	2m4f Cls1 Gd1 Hdl soft	£67,524
2/20	Leop	2m Gd1 Hdl yield	£94,915
12/19	Fair	2m4f Gd1 Hdl yld-sft	£66,441
11/19	Fair	2m4f Hdl heavy	£9,318
4/19	Fair	2m4f Nov Gd1 Hdl gd-yld	£53,153
1/19	Fair	2m2f Nov Gd3 Hdl yield	£19,392
12/18	Thur	2m Nov List Hdl good	£17,688
11/18	Fair	2m4f Mdn Hdl good	£5,996

Prolific mare who has won an astonishing 16 out of 16 under rules, including the last two runnings of the Champion Hurdle among 12 Grade 1 victories; probably dominating a weak division but has been vastly superior (narrowest margin of victory was three lengths last term).

Hors Piste (Fr)

5 b m Kapgarde - Valgardena (Dom Alco)

Willie Mullins (Ire) | Mrs J Donnelly

PLACINGS: 52/2183-12 | RPR **145+h**

Starts	1st	2nd	3rd	4th	Win & Pl
8	2	3	1	-	£31,628

5/22	Kbgn	2m3f Nov Hdl good	£5,950
2/22	Clon	2m3f Mdn Hdl heavy	£4,958

Useful and progressive mare who finished a fine third in a Grade I novice hurdle at Fairyhouse last season; put a disappointing run at Cheltenham behind her and confirmed upwardly mobile profile with a runaway win at Kilbeggan in May before a close second at Galway.

Hunters Yarn (Ire)

5 b g Fame And Glory - Full Of Birds (Epervier Bleu)

Willie Mullins (Ire) | Simon Munir & Isaac Souede

PLACINGS: 31/411- | RPR **124+b**

Starts	1st	2nd	3rd	4th	Win & Pl
5	3	-	1	1	£22,155

4/22	Fair	2m NHF 4-7yo yield	£9,916
3/22	Limk	2m NHF 5-7yo sft-hvy	£5,454
3/21	Thur	2m½f NHF 4yo yield	£5,268

Three-time bumper winner who did particularly well to defy a double penalty at Fairyhouse's Easter meeting last season; had earlier disappointed on hurdles debut when fourth at odds-on at Punchestown but remains a fine prospect to go back into that sphere.

I Like To Move It

5 b g Trans Island - Nobratinetta (Celtic Swing)

Nigel Twiston-Davies | Anne-Marie & Jamie Shepperd

PLACINGS: 1129/111520- | RPR **145h**

Starts	1st	2nd	3rd	4th	Win & Pl
10	5	2	-	-	£100,328

11/21	Chel	2m½f Cls1 Nov Gd2 Hdl good	£30,890
10/21	Chel	2m½f Cls2 Hdl 4yo good	£20,812
10/21	Worc	2m Cls4 Nov Hdl 4-6yo gd-sft	£4,629
12/20	Winc	1m7½f Cls5 NHF 3yo soft	£2,274
11/20	Aint	2m1f Cls4 NHF 3yo gd-sft	£3,249

Very useful novice hurdler last season; won three times early in the season, twice at Cheltenham including a soft Grade 2; switched to handicaps later in the campaign and finished a short-head second in the Betfair Hurdle before disappointing in the County.

Iberique Du Seuil (Fr)

4 b g Spanish Moon - Tulipe Du Seuil (Equerry)

Gordon Elliott (Ire) | Bective Stud

PLACINGS: 2221371- | RPR **134+h**

Starts	1st	2nd	3rd	4th	Win & Pl
7	2	3	1	-	£35,708

4/22	Fair	2m Gd2 Hdl 4yo yield	£19,832
12/21	Cork	2m Mdn Hdl 3yo soft	£6,321

Took a long time to justify initial expectations following arrival from France last season but

I Like To Move It: won three races last season, including two at Cheltenham

finally delivered when a surprise winner of a Grade 2 juvenile hurdle at Fairyhouse on final run; had been a beaten favourite in first two races, with only win in first five coming at odds-on.

Icare Allen (Fr)

4 b g Cokoriko - Coeur D'Allen (Network)

Willie Mullins (Ire) John P McManus

PLACINGS: 115143- RPR **137+h**

Starts	1st	2nd	3rd	4th	Win & Pl
6	3	-	1	1	£40,513

	2/22	Fair	2m½f Gd3 Hdl 4yo soft	£13,634
	12/21	Leop	2m Mdn Hdl 3yo yld-sft	£7,902
	8/21	Mlns	1m4f NHF 3yo soft	£6,696

Very useful juvenile hurdler last season; won twice and performed creditably in Grade 1 company, notably when fourth in the Triumph Hurdle (rallied strongly to suggest longer trips might help); disappointing third when 4-11 for a Grade 2 at Fairyhouse on final run.

Il Etait Temps (Fr)

4 gr g Jukebox Jury - Une Des Sources (Dom Alco)

Willie Mullins (Ire) Barnane Stud

PLACINGS: 5/235-4 RPR **140+h**

Starts	1st	2nd	3rd	4th	Win & Pl
5	-	1	1	1	£20,639

Thrown in at the deep end after arrival from France last season, with all three runs at Grade 1 level, and showed glimpses of real promise; stayed on well into third behind Vauban at Leopardstown and travelled strongly before fading into fifth in the Triumph Hurdle; still a novice.

Imperial Alcazar (Ire)

8 b g Vinnie Roe - Maddy's Supreme (Supreme Leader)

Fergal O'Brien Imperial Racing Partnership 2016

PLACINGS: 423/1221/910/2212- RPR **160+c**

Starts	1st	2nd	3rd	4th	Win & Pl
14	4	6	1	1	£87,694

144	1/22	Chel	2m4½f Cls2 Nov 124-144 Ch Hcap good	£15,609
139	1/21	Wwck	3m1f Cls2 123-149 Hdl Hcap heavy	£10,010
	1/20	Leic	2m4½f Cls3 Nov Hdl 4-7yo heavy	£8,058
	10/19	Aint	2m4f Cls4 Mdn Hdl soft	£5,198

Progressive novice chaser last season who flourished when switched to handicaps; hacked up in a novice handicap at Cheltenham in January and finished a solid second when favourite for the Plate at the festival; likely player in many similar valuable handicaps at Cheltenham.

Imperial Aura (Ire)

9 b g Kalanisi - Missindependence (Executive Perk)

Kim Bailey Imperial Racing Partnership 2016

PLACINGS: 1/11/31221/11UP/FPP- RPR **164c**

Starts	1st	2nd	3rd	4th	Win & Pl
16	7	2	2	-	£123,689

	11/20	Asct	2m5f Cls1 Gd2 Ch soft	£26,427
	11/20	Carl	2m4f Cls1 List Ch heavy	£13,668
143	3/20	Chel	2m4f Cls1 Nov List 138-145 Ch Hcap soft	£39,389
	11/19	Fknm	3m Cls3 Ch good	£13,666
	2/19	Newc	2m4½f Cls3 Nov Hdl gd-sft	£5,718
	10/18	Carl	2m3½f Cls4 Nov Hdl good	£4,874
	4/18	Ludl	2m Cls4 NHF 4-6yo soft	£3,899

Looked set for the top two seasons ago, following up a victory at the 2020 Cheltenham Festival by winning his first two races in that campaign, but has been a bitter disappointment since; has failed to complete in his last five races, including when pulled up the last twice.

Impulsive Dancer (Ire)

4 br g Dragon Pulse - Viennese Whirl (Montjeu)

Willie Mullins (Ire) Simon Munir & Isaac Souede

PLACINGS: 11- RPR **120+b**

Starts	1st	2nd	3rd	4th	Win & Pl
2	2	-	-	-	£22,558

	3/22	Limk	2m List NHF 4yo gd-yld	£17,353
	1/22	Naas	2m NHF 4yo soft	£5,206

Won both bumpers last season, hacking up by eight lengths on debut at Naas before following up in a Listed race at Limerick; appreciated much quicker ground that day but has already proved effective on soft.

Indefatigable (Ire)

9 b m Schiaparelli - Spin The Wheel (Kalanisi)

Paul Webber Philip Rocher

PLACINGS: 522311/36472/1623F2- RPR **147h**

Starts	1st	2nd	3rd	4th	Win & Pl
25	6	7	4	1	£183,641

	10/21	Weth	3m Cls1 Gd2 Hdl gd-sft	£28,475
145	3/20	Chel	2m4½f Cls2 136-145 Cond Hdl Hcap soft	£43,330
	2/20	Wwck	2m5f Cls1 List Hdl gd-sft	£14,238
	4/19	Chel	2m4½f Cls1 Nov List Hdl good	£14,068
	11/18	Uttx	2m Cls4 Nov Hdl gd-sft	£4,094
	4/18	Sthl	1m7½f Cls5 NHF 4-6yo good	£1,471

Smart mare whose finest hours came when winning last season's West Yorkshire Hurdle and the 2020 Martin Pipe; fell two out when going well in the Mares' Hurdle back at Cheltenham last term before finishing second in the Select Hurdle at Sandown for the second successive year.

Itchy Feet (Fr)

8 b g Cima De Triomphe - Maeva Candas (Brier Creek)

Olly Murphy — Kate & Andrew Brooks

PLACINGS: 34/411U/32253/224PP- — RPR **159c**

Starts	1st	2nd	3rd	4th	Win & Pl
21	5	6	3	3	£171,295

	Date	Course	Race	Prize
	2/20	Sand	2m4f Cls1 Nov Gd1 Ch soft	£31,323
	12/19	Leic	2m4f Cls3 Nov Ch soft	£8,382
	10/18	Kemp	2m Cls1 Nov List Hdl good	£11,390
	10/18	Sthl	1m7½f Cls4 Nov Hdl good	£4,094
	9/18	Strf	2m½f Cls5 NHF 4-6yo good	£2,599

Grade I winner as a novice chaser three seasons ago but has failed to win since; has finished second four times in that period, including when running well behind Bravemansgame and Allmankind last term, but was pulled up on final two runs.

Iwilldoit

9 b g Flying Legend - Lyricist's Dream (Dreams End)

Sam Thomas — Diamond Racing

PLACINGS: /3861612/91/6273/11- — RPR **152+c**

Starts	1st	2nd	3rd	4th	Win & Pl
17	5	2	2	-	£125,370

	Date	Course	Race	Prize
140	12/21	Chep	3m6½f Cls1 Gd3 140-166 Ch Hcap soft	£85,827
130	12/21	Chep	2m7½f Cls2 124-150 Ch Hcap gd-sft	£13,008
126	12/19	Kels	2m6½f Cls3 Nov 105-126 Ch Hcap soft	£11,826
113	3/19	Catt	3m1½f Cls4 107-122 Hdl Hcap soft	£4,159
103	1/19	Bang	2m7f Cls4 101-111 Hdl Hcap gd-sft	£4,094

Runaway winner of last season's Welsh Grand National, storming home by nine lengths to make it three wins in just four races over fences; missed the rest of the season but unlikely to be one for big spring targets anyway, with trainer describing him as a "mudlark".

James Du Berlais (Fr)

6 ch g Muhtathir - King's Daughter (King's Theatre)

Willie Mullins (Ire) — Simon Munir & Isaac Souede

PLACINGS: F996212/1212129/2- — RPR **158h**

Starts	1st	2nd	3rd	4th	Win & Pl
15	4	6	-	-	£322,070

	Date	Course	Race	Prize
	10/20	Autl	2m3½f Gd3 Hdl 4yo heavy	£36,038
	7/20	Autl	2m3½f Gd3 Hdl 4yo v soft	£36,038
0	5/20	Autl	2m2f List Hdl 4yo Hcap v soft	£34,322
0	11/19	Autl	2m2f List Hdl 3yo Hcap heavy	£47,027

High-class French recruit who was thrown in at the deep end by new connections in 2021, finishing ninth in the Champion Hurdle on stable debut and second in a 3m Grade I at Punchestown (third runner-up finish at the top level); missed last season through injury.

James's Gate (Ire)

5 b g Shantou - Annie May (Anshan)

Willie Mullins (Ire) — Sean & Bernardine Mulryan

PLACINGS: 13-4 — RPR **133b**

Starts	1st	2nd	3rd	4th	Win & Pl
3	1	-	1	1	£14,354

	Date	Course	Race	Prize
	2/22	Punc	2m NHF 5-7yo heavy	£5,206

Among last season's leading bumper performers, finishing third in the Champion Bumper at Cheltenham on just his second run after an eight-length win at Punchestown; well below par when fourth at 4-9 in an ordinary bumper back at Punchestown on final run.

Janidil (Fr)

8 b g Indian Daffodil - Janidouce (Kaldounevees)

Willie Mullins (Ire) — John P McManus

PLACINGS: 2/1115/13F1/22532F-P — RPR **166c**

Starts	1st	2nd	3rd	4th	Win & Pl
19	5	5	2	1	£302,615

	Date	Course	Race	Prize
	4/21	Fair	2m4f Nov Gd1 Ch yield	£42,143
	11/20	Naas	2m3f Ch sft-hvy	£6,250
135	12/19	Fair	2m 118-144 Hdl Hcap yld-sft	£53,153
125	11/19	DRoy	2m½f 116-139 Hdl Hcap soft	£26,577
	10/19	Tipp	2m Mdn Hdl yield	£5,857

Failed to win last season but was very highly tried and then fell at Fairyhouse when dropped below Grade I for the only time; had twice finished second behind Allaho, including in the Ryanair Chase at Cheltenham, but seemingly not quite as effective over 3m (third in the Irish Gold Cup).

Jason The Militant (Ire)

8 b g Sans Frontieres - Rock Angel (Desert King)

Henry de Bromhead (Ire) — Peter Michael Racing

PLACINGS: 3/2151/331U/73- — RPR **158h**

Starts	1st	2nd	3rd	4th	Win & Pl
11	3	1	4	-	£65,180

	Date	Course	Race	Prize
	2/21	Fair	2m Gd3 Hdl soft	£14,487
	2/20	Naas	2m Nov Gd2 Hdl sft-hvy	£23,250
	12/19	Limk	2m Mdn Hdl heavy	£7,188

Very smart dual-purpose performer who added a Listed win on the Flat last October to two Graded wins over hurdles; missed nearly all of last season but had finished a half-length second in the Hatton's Grace and unseated when favourite for the Aintree Hurdle in the campaign prior.

Jeff Kidder (Ire)

5 b g Hallowed Crown - Alpine (Rail Link)

Noel Meade (Ire) — Albert Dravins & Eamonn Scanlon

PLACINGS: 221711/13- — RPR **133h**

Starts	1st	2nd	3rd	4th	Win & Pl
8	4	2	1	-	£115,630

	Date	Course	Race	Prize
	5/21	Punc	2m Gd1 Hdl 4yo gd-yld	£52,679
	4/21	Fair	2m Gd2 Hdl 4yo yield	£18,438
125	3/21	Chel	2m½f Cls1 Gd3 123-141 Hdl 4yo Hcap gd-sft	£33,762
	11/20	Fair	2m Mdn Hdl 3yo soft	£5,000

Missed nearly all of last season but had progressed into a high-class juvenile hurdler two seasons ago; returned from a break to land the Fred Winter at Cheltenham at 80-1 and again defied market expectations when beating Zanahiyr in a Grade I at Punchestown at 22-1.

Jon Snow (Fr)

7 br g Le Havre - Saroushka (Westerner)

Willie Mullins (Ire) Mrs S Ricci

PLACINGS: 3321/11/8-31 RPR **139+c**

Starts	1st	2nd	3rd	4th	Win & Pl
9	4	1	3	-	£36,887

	Date	Course	Race	Prize
	8/22	Klny	2m7f Ch gd-yld	£5,702
	8/20	Klny	2m7f Nov Hdl soft	£8,750
	7/20	Gway	2m4½f Nov Hdl yield	£10,000
	3/20	Leop	2m2f Mdn Hdl soft	£6,750

Missed most of last season just as the penny seemed to have dropped in 2020 with wins at Leopardstown, Galway and Killarney; had long had a big reputation but was beaten in three maiden hurdles before finding his feet; made a promising start over fences this summer.

Jonbon (Fr)

6 b g Walk In The Park - Star Face (Saint Des Saints)

Nicky Henderson John P McManus

PLACINGS: 11/11121- RPR **155+h**

Starts	1st	2nd	3rd	4th	Win & Pl
6	5	1	-	-	£153,028

	Date	Course	Race	Prize
	4/22	Aint	2m½f Cls1 Nov Gd1 Hdl gd-sft	£56,319
	1/22	Hayd	1m7½f Cls1 Nov Gd2 Hdl soft	£28,475
	12/21	Asct	1m7½f Cls1 Nov Gd2 Hdl gd-sft	£28,475
	11/21	Newb	2m½f Cls3 Mdn Hdl gd-sft	£5,991
	3/21	Newb	2m½f Cls3 NHF 4-6yo gd-sft	£4,520

Full brother to Douvan who justified high expectations last season, winning four out of five including a battling success over El Fabiolo in a Grade 1 at Aintree; suffered sole defeat when second to Constitution Hill in the Supreme; should make a fine novice chaser.

Journey With Me (Ire)

6 ch g Mahler - Kilbarry Demon (Bob's Return)

Henry de Bromhead (Ire) Robcour

PLACINGS: 11/11F-7 RPR **142+h**

Starts	1st	2nd	3rd	4th	Win & Pl
5	3	-	-	-	£23,085

	Date	Course	Race	Prize
	2/22	Naas	2m3f Nov Hdl soft	£9,916
	12/21	Leop	2m4f Mdn Hdl yld-sft	£7,902
	3/21	Gowr	2m2f NHF 4-7yo heavy	£5,268

Wide-margin winner of sole point-to-point and bumper before impressively adding first two races over hurdles last season to his tally; took a tired fall at the last in the Ballymore (likely to finish third) and disappointed subsequently at Punchestown; likely to go novice chasing.

JPR One (Ire)

5 b g Court Cave - Lady Knightess (Presenting)

Joe Tizzard J P Romans

PLACINGS: 12105- RPR **131+h**

Starts	1st	2nd	3rd	4th	Win & Pl
5	2	1	-	-	£16,848

	Date	Course	Race	Prize
	1/22	Tntn	2m3f Cls4 Nov Hdl soft	£4,956
	11/21	Extr	2m½f Cls4 Nov Hdl gd-sft	£4,085

Looked a very promising novice hurdler early last season, winning twice either side of a neck defeat at Cheltenham; sent off second favourite for the Betfair Hurdle on handicap debut but beat only one home and then out of his depth in the Supreme at Cheltenham.

Jungle Boogie (Ire)

8 b g Gold Well - A Better Excuse (Moscow Society)

Willie Mullins (Ire) Malcolm C Denmark

PLACINGS: 11/1- RPR **147+c**

Starts	1st	2nd	3rd	4th	Win & Pl
3	3	-	-	-	£17,514

	Date	Course	Race	Prize
	1/22	Fair	2m5½f Ch yield	£6,693
	2/21	Punc	2m4f Mdn Hdl soft	£6,321
	11/20	Clon	2m½f NHF 5-7yo heavy	£4,500

Hugely exciting but fragile gelding who has had just three runs coming up to nine years old but has won them all; thrashed subsequent Leinster National winner Diol Ker by 12 lengths on sole chase run at Fairyhouse last January only to suffer a minor stress fracture.

Kalashnikov (Ire)

9 br g Kalanisi - Fairy Lane (Old Vic)

Amy Murphy Paul Murphy

PLACINGS: 12/1122U1/2285/7234/ RPR **164c**

Starts	1st	2nd	3rd	4th	Win & Pl
20	7	7	1	1	£282,718

	Date	Course	Race	Prize
	4/19	Aint	2m4f Cls1 Nov Gd1 Ch gd-sft	£56,394
	12/18	Plum	2m1f Cls3 Nov Ch soft	£7,343
	11/18	Wwck	2m Cls3 Nov Ch good	£9,495
141	2/18	Newb	2m½f Cls1 Gd3 129-148 Hdl Hcap soft	£88,273
	12/17	Donc	2m½f Cls4 Nov Hdl 4-6yo gd-sft	£3,899
	11/17	Weth	2m Cls3 Nov Hdl soft	£5,523
	3/17	Weth	2m Cls5 NHF 4-6yo gd-sft	£2,599

Missed last season through injury and now without a win since a Grade 1 novice chase in 2019, though has run well enough to go off favourite in four of eight subsequent races; second in the 2020 Peterborough Chase and ran to a similar level when fourth in the Ryanair on latest run.

Kemboy (Fr)

10 b g Voix Du Nord - Vitora (Victory Note)

Willie Mullins (Ire) Kemboy, Brett Graham & Ken Sharp Syndicate

PLACINGS: 1/1427/2219/48353-46 RPR **168+c**

Starts	1st	2nd	3rd	4th	Win & Pl
29	9	5	2	4	£748,751

	Date	Course	Race	Prize
	2/21	Leop	3m½f Gd1 Ch soft	£100,000
	5/19	Punc	3m½f Gd1 Ch yld-sft	£159,459
	4/19	Aint	3m1f Cls1 Gd1 Ch gd-sft	£112,260
	12/18	Leop	3m Gd1 Ch good	£91,372
	11/18	Clon	2m4f Gd2 Ch good	£26,106
147	4/18	Punc	2m5f Nov 126-147 Ch Hcap soft	£52,212
	4/18	Limk	3m Nov Gd3 Ch heavy	£22,190
	1/18	Fair	2m5½f Ch heavy	£7,632
	12/16	Limk	2m3f Mdn Hdl yield	£4,522

High-class staying chaser for several seasons but has found it increasingly hard to win and managed no better than third in five runs last term; had notched three Grade 1 victories four seasons ago but has won only one of 14 subsequent races, all but one at the top level.

Kilcruit (Ire)

7 b g Stowaway - Not Broke Yet (Broken Hearted)

Willie Mullins (Ire) — Miss M A Masterson

PLACINGS: 2/112/12313-4 — RPR **147h**

Starts	1st	2nd	3rd	4th	Win & Pl
10	4	3	2	1	£151,821

	Date	Course	Race	Prize
	1/22	Punc	2m Mdn Hdl yield	£5,950
	4/21	Punc	2m½f Gd1 NHF 4-7yo yield	£52,679
	2/21	Leop	2m Gd2 NHF 4-7yo sft-hvy	£52,679
	12/20	Navn	2m NHF 4-7yo soft	£4,500

Top-class bumper performer two seasons ago but disappointing over hurdles last term; won at the third attempt after two odds-on defeats and twice well beaten in Grade 1 company, jumping poorly at Punchestown when back up to a more suitable 2m4f; likely to go novice chasing.

Killer Clown (Ire)

8 b g Getaway - Our Soiree (Milan)

Emma Lavelle — Tim Syder

PLACINGS: /2553/U63123/661P10- — RPR **153+c**

Starts	1st	2nd	3rd	4th	Win & Pl
16	3	2	3	-	£69,460

	Date	Course	Race	Prize
140	3/22	Kemp	2m4½f Cls2 128-152 Ch Hcap good	£31,218
135	1/22	Winc	2m4f Cls2 126-145 Ch Hcap soft	£10,466
123	12/20	Kemp	2m4½f Cls3 Nov 123-140 Ch Hcap gd-sft	£10,722

Produced career-best performances to win 2m4f handicap chases at Wincanton and Kempton by wide margins last season; disappointing at other times and well beaten in the Topham at Aintree after being raised 8lb for latest win.

Kitty's Light

6 b g Nathaniel - Daraiyna (Refuse To Bend)

Christian Williams — R J Bedford & All Stars Sports Racing

PLACINGS: 5312113712/22P47223- — RPR **150c**

Starts	1st	2nd	3rd	4th	Win & Pl
20	4	6	3	1	£185,725

	Date	Course	Race	Prize
135	3/21	Kels	3m2f Cls2 125-142 Ch Hcap gd-sft	£18,159
123	10/20	Extr	3m Cls3 119-132 Ch Hcap gd-fm	£9,747
117	9/20	Wwck	3m Cls4 Nov 97-117 Ch Hcap good	£4,289
109	8/20	Sthl	2m4½f Cls4 Nov 97-118 Ch Hcap good	£3,964

Unlucky not to land a major staying handicap in the last 18 months; has finished second and third in the last two runnings of the bet365 Gold Cup as well as second in the Coral Trophy at Kempton and the Scottish Grand National.

Klassical Dream (Fr)

8 b g Dream Well - Klassical Way (Septieme Ciel)

Willie Mullins (Ire) — Mrs Joanne Coleman

PLACINGS: 324P/111/135/1145-12 — RPR **168+h**

Starts	1st	2nd	3rd	4th	Win & Pl
17	7	2	2	2	£640,125

	Date	Course	Race	Prize
	4/22	Punc	2m7½f Gd1 Hdl gd-yld	£136,345
	12/21	Leop	3m Gd1 Hdl soft	£52,679
	4/21	Punc	3m Gd1 Hdl yield	£131,696
	4/19	Punc	2m½f Nov Gd1 Hdl yield	£53,153
	3/19	Chel	2m½f Cls1 Nov Gd1 Hdl soft	£70,338
	2/19	Leop	2m Nov Gd1 Hdl good	£66,441
	12/18	Leop	2m Mdn Hdl 4yo gd-yld	£8,177

Reinvented as a top staying hurdler since returning from a long injury layoff in April 2021 and has won three Grade 1 races in that time, including at Leopardstown and Punchestown last season; below-par fifth when favourite for the Stayers' Hurdle at Cheltenham.

Knappers Hill (Ire)

6 b g Valirann - Brogella (King's Theatre)

Paul Nicholls — P K Barber & P J Vogt

PLACINGS: 111/1136011- — RPR **141+h**

Starts	1st	2nd	3rd	4th	Win & Pl
10	7	-	1	-	£107,197

	Date	Course	Race	Prize
134	4/22	Sand	2m Cls2 Nov 108-136 Hdl Hcap good	£51,440
	4/22	NAbb	2m1f Cls4 Nov Hdl good	£5,010
	11/21	Winc	1m7f Cls3 Nov Hdl 4-6yo good	£6,535
	10/21	Chep	2m Cls4 Nov Hdl good	£4,738
	4/21	Aint	2m1f Cls1 Gd2 NHF 4-6yo gd-sft	£19,132
	12/20	Asct	1m7½f Cls1 List NHF 4-6yo soft	£9,682
	10/20	Chep	2m Cls4 NHF 4-6yo good	£3,249

Four-time winner as a novice hurdler last season, most notably in a valuable novice handicap at Sandown; had also won three times in bumpers, including a Grade 2 at Aintree, but came up short in all three runs in Graded runs over hurdles, arguably doing best when sixth in the Betfair Hurdle.

Knight Salute

4 b g Sir Percy - Shadow Dancing (Unfuwain)

Milton Harris — Four Candles Partnership

PLACINGS: 1111191- — RPR **141+h**

Starts	1st	2nd	3rd	4th	Win & Pl
7	6	-	-	-	£168,383

	Date	Course	Race	Prize
	4/22	Aint	2m1f Cls1 Gd1 Hdl 4yo gd-sft	£62,080
	2/22	Kemp	2m Cls1 Gd2 Hdl 4yo gd-sft	£34,170
	12/21	Donc	2m½f Cls1 Gd2 Hdl 3yo gd-sft	£33,828
	11/21	Chel	2m½f Cls1 Gd2 Hdl 3yo good	£28,230
	10/21	Kemp	2m Cls3 Hdl 3yo good	£5,991
	9/21	Sedg	2m1f Cls4 Mdn Hdl 3yo good	£4,085

Last season's leading British juvenile hurdler, winning six out of seven races; completed a hat-trick of Grade 2 wins in the Adonis at Kempton and bounced back from sole blip in the Triumph Hurdle to land the Anniversary Hurdle at Aintree (Pied Piper demoted after dead-heat).

L'Homme Presse (Fr)

7 b g Diamond Boy - Romance Turgot (Bateau Rouge)

Venetia Williams — DFA Racing (Pink & Edwards)

PLACINGS: 52/16/111113- — RPR **166+c**

Starts	1st	2nd	3rd	4th	Win & Pl
10	6	1	1	-	£227,166

	Date	Course	Race	Prize
	3/22	Chel	3m½f Cls1 Nov Gd1 Ch soft	£98,558
	2/22	Sand	2m4f Cls1 Nov Gd1 Ch gd-sft	£46,096
	1/22	Chel	2m4½f Cls1 Nov Gd2 Ch soft	£31,323
	12/21	Asct	2m5f Cls2 Ch gd-sft	£20,812
128	12/21	Extr	2m3f Cls3 119-138 Ch Hcap gd-sft	£8,605
	4/21	Chep	2m Cls4 Nov Hdl good	£3,159

Crowned a memorable first season over fences with a hugely impressive win over Ahoy Senor in the Brown Advisory at Cheltenham in March; possibly over the top when a distant third behind the same rival at Aintree, though not felt to appreciate a greater test of speed by connections.

Langer Dan (Ire)

6 b g Ocovango - What A Fashion (Milan)

Dan Skelton — Colm Donlon

PLACINGS: 11226/95412/6B1- — RPR **148+h**

Starts	1st	2nd	3rd	4th	Win & Pl
13	4	3	-	1	£107,771

137	4/22	Aint	2m4f Cls1 Gd3 130-148 Hdl Hcap gd-sft	£42,203
130	3/21	Sand	2m Cls1 Gd3 121-146 Hdl Hcap soft	£28,230
	11/19	Weth	2m Cls1 List Hdl 3yo soft	£14,238
	10/19	Ludl	2m Cls4 Mdn Hdl 3yo good	£5,263

Has a fine record in big handicap hurdles and won at last season's Grand National meeting at Aintree to add to 2021 Imperial Cup; brought down when favourite for the Martin Pipe after bumping into Galopin Des Champs in that race in 2021; set to step up in class in staying hurdles.

Life In The Park (Ire)

5 b g Walk In The Park - Jeanquiri (Mansonnien)

Henry de Bromhead (Ire) — Barry Maloney

PLACINGS: F/361-1 — RPR **132+h**

Starts	1st	2nd	3rd	4th	Win & Pl
4	2	-	1	-	£22,068

119	4/22	Punc	2m4f 109-123 Hdl Hcap gd-yld	£14,874
	4/22	Tram	2m4½f Mdn Hdl yield	£5,454

Lightly raced hurdler who flourished last spring; got off the mark at the third attempt when hacking up in a maiden hurdle at Tramore by 17 lengths and followed up on handicap debut in a 24-runner race at Punchestown; remains unexposed.

Lifetime Ambition (Ire)

7 br g Kapgarde - Jeanquiri (Mansonnien)

Jessica Harrington (Ire) — Linda Mulcahy & Mary Wolridge

PLACINGS: 44/2243421/1142721-2 — RPR **149c**

Starts	1st	2nd	3rd	4th	Win & Pl
17	4	6	1	5	£76,665

3/22	Limk	3m½f Nov Gd3 Ch gd-yld	£14,130
10/21	DRoy	2m3½f Ch soft	£5,795
4/21	Punc	2m4½f Hdl yield	£10,536
3/21	Limk	2m3f Mdn Hdl heavy	£7,375

Very useful novice chaser last season and notably progressive in the spring when stepped up in trip on quicker ground; won a Grade 3 at Limerick and finished second behind Capodanno in a Grade 1 at Punchestown; regarded by connections as a Grand National horse.

Lisnagar Oscar (Ire)

9 b g Oscar - Asta Belle (Astarabad)

Rebecca Curtis — Racing For Fun

PLACINGS: 239F31/472F8/35P3PP- — RPR **148h**

Starts	1st	2nd	3rd	4th	Win & Pl
24	3	4	6	1	£259,386

3/20	Chel	3m Cls1 Gd1 Hdl soft	£182,878
2/19	Hayd	3m½f Cls1 Nov Gd2 Hdl good	£16,938
1/19	Chep	2m3½f Cls4 Nov Hdl gd-sft	£4,094

Shock winner of the 2020 Stayers' Hurdle at

Langer Dan wins at Aintree last season

Cheltenham but has shown only glimpses of that form since then, failing to win; finished third in last season's Cleeve Hurdle but pulled up in three runs either side of that; switched to handicaps for final run and dropped 20lb below peak mark.

Longhouse Poet (Ire)

8 b g Yeats - Moscow Madame (Moscow Society)

Martin Brassil (Ire) Sean & Bernardine Mulryan

PLACINGS: 1/121338/6231/7176- RPR **156c**

Starts	1st	2nd	3rd	4th	Win & Pl
14	4	2	3	-	£125,899

145	1/22	Gowr	3m1f 135-162 Ch Hcap soft	£49,580
	12/20	Punc	3m1f Ch heavy	£6,250
	12/19	Navn	2m4f Mdn Hdl soft	£7,188
	5/19	Punc	2m2f NHF 5-7yo gd-yld	£8,324

Lightly raced staying chaser who made up into a classy handicapper last season and quickened smartly to win the Thyestes; finished an eyecatching sixth when failing to stay the trip in the Grand National having travelled strongly and disputed the lead two out.

Lookaway (Ire)

5 ch g Ask - Barrack's Choice (Westerner)

Neil King Peter Beadles

PLACINGS: 111- RPR **127+b**

Starts	1st	2nd	3rd	4th	Win & Pl
2	2	-	-	-	£30,858

4/22	Aint	2m1f Cls1 Gd2 NHF 4-6yo gd-sft	£28,135
2/22	Newb	2m½f Cls4 NHF 4-6yo soft	£2,723

Top-class prospect who won both bumper races last season having been bought for £170,000 after landing sole point-to-point in Ireland; travelled strongly and kept on well when winning in Grade 2 company at Aintree and should reach a similar level over hurdles.

Lord Du Mesnil (Fr)

9 b g Saint Des Saints - Ladies Choice (Turgeon)

Richard Hobson — Paul Porter

PLACINGS: 11122/4991P/UP26P4-P — RPR **156c**

Starts	1st	2nd	3rd	4th	Win & Pl
40	4	7	6	5	£211,441

149	2/21	Hayd	3m4½f Cls1 Gd3 132-152 Ch Hcap soft	£42,713
137	12/19	Hayd	3m4½f Cls2 132-140 Ch Hcap soft	£16,314
127	12/19	Hayd	3m1½f Cls2 127-146 Ch Hcap heavy	£31,280
122	11/19	Newc	2m7½f Cls3 Nov 118-129 Ch Hcap heavy	£7,083

Stout stayer who won Haydock's Grand National Trial in 2021 having finished second in that race and won two other handicaps at that track the previous season; generally out of sorts last season, though still a fine second under top weight in the Rowland Meyrick.

Lord Lariat (Ire)

7 b g Golden Lariat - Johnny's Pride (Mister Lord)

Dermot McLoughlin (Ire) — P Blake

PLACINGS: 1173212/5F972611651- — RPR **154+c**

Starts	1st	2nd	3rd	4th	Win & Pl
24	6	3	1	-	£268,386

137	4/22	Fair	3m5f 137-158 Ch Hcap yield	£226,891
128	12/21	Punc	2m7f 109-128 Ch Hcap heavy	£7,638
124	11/21	Fair	2m5f 97-125 Ch Hcap good	£7,638
105	10/20	Fair	2m5f 86-116 Ch Hcap yield	£7,000
98	7/20	Tipp	3m 80-98 Hdl Hcap yield	£4,500
93	6/20	Tipp	2m4f 80-95 Hdl Hcap gd-yld	£4,500

Surprise 40-1 winner of last season's Irish Grand National when leaving previous form behind on first run beyond 3m; had been progressive at a much lower level earlier in the season, winning handicap chases at Fairyhouse and Punchestown; acts on any going.

Lossiemouth

7 b g Makfi - First Bloom (Fusaichi Pegasus)

Tom Lacey — Lady Cobham

PLACINGS: 011/522/1115- — RPR **146+h**

Starts	1st	2nd	3rd	4th	Win & Pl
10	5	2	-	-	£46,623

	12/21	Sand	2m4f Cls1 Nov Gd2 Hdl gd-sft	£28,475
123	11/21	Ffos	2m6f Cls3 99-127 Hdl Hcap soft	£4,735
117	10/21	Asct	2m3½f Cls4 Nov 100-118 Cond Hdl Hcap soft	£4,520
	2/19	Carl	2m1f Cls5 NHF 4-6yo gd-sft	£2,599
	12/18	Newc	1m6½f Cls5 NHF 3yo soft	£2,274

Sharply progressive during a second season as a novice hurdler last term, winning three times including a Grade 2 at Sandown by 14 lengths; disappointed when stepped up in class again for the Challow Hurdle, jumping poorly in fifth; has the size and scope for fences.

Lostintranslation (Ire)

10 b g Flemensfirth - Falika (Hero's Honor)

Joe Tizzard — Taylor & O'Dwyer

PLACINGS: 221/11P3/3P5P/15P80- — RPR **162+c**

Starts	1st	2nd	3rd	4th	Win & Pl
25	6	6	3	-	£420,984

	11/21	Asct	2m5f Cls1 Gd2 Ch good	£40,569
	11/19	Hayd	3m1½f Cls1 Gd1 Ch gd-sft	£112,540
	11/19	Carl	2m4f Cls1 List Ch soft	£17,085
	4/19	Aint	3m1f Cls1 Nov Gd1 Ch soft	£56,394
	1/19	Chel	2m4½f Cls1 Nov Gd2 Ch gd-sft	£19,695
	12/17	Newb	2m½f Cls3 Mdn Hdl soft	£6,498

Top-class staying chaser three seasons ago (won the Betfair Chase and third in the Cheltenham Gold Cup) but in decline since then; won a 2m5f Grade 2 at Ascot first time out last season but out of sorts again subsequently; handicaps likely now rated 23lb below peak mark.

Love Envoi (Ire)

6 b m Westerner - Love Divided (King's Ride)

Harry Fry — Noel Fehily Racing Syndicates

PLACINGS: 1/111112- — RPR **138h**

Starts	1st	2nd	3rd	4th	Win & Pl
7	6	1	-	-	£132,061

	3/22	Chel	2m1f Cls1 Nov Gd2 Hdl soft	£59,084
	2/22	Sand	2m4f Cls1 Nov Gd2 Hdl heavy	£28,475
	1/22	Ling	2m Cls2 Nov Hdl heavy	£15,609
	12/21	Wwck	2m5f Cls4 Nov Hdl heavy	£4,629
	12/21	Leic	2m4½f Cls4 Mdn Hdl gd-sft	£4,085
	3/21	Wxfd	2m4f NHF 5yo yield	£4,214

Prolific mare who won her first six races under rules, with five wins over hurdles last season (up to 2m5f) including the mares' novice at the Cheltenham Festival; put in her place by festival absentee Brandy Love when an eight-length second at Fairyhouse.

Mac Tottie

9 b g Midnight Legend - Tot Of The Knar (Kayf Tara)

Peter Bowen — Steve & Jackie Fleetham

PLACINGS: 8/P/8P12P12/41FP631- — RPR **147+c**

Starts	1st	2nd	3rd	4th	Win & Pl
27	8	6	2	2	£177,357

135	4/22	Aint	2m5f Cls1 Gd3 135-161 Ch Hcap gd-sft	£84,195
135	11/21	Aint	2m5f Cls2 120-146 Ch Hcap gd-sft	£41,152
127	3/21	Newb	2m7½f Cls3 Nov 122-135 Ch Hcap gd-sft	£7,018
118	12/20	MRas	2m5½f Cls3 Nov 117-127 Ch Hcap soft	£7,018
	10/18	Hexm	2m7½f Cls4 Nov Hdl good	£4,464
	8/18	Ctml	2m6f Cls4 Nov Hdl soft	£4,094
	7/18	Ctml	2m6f Cls4 Nov Hdl good	£4,549
	6/18	Worc	2m4f Cls5 Nov Mdn Hdl good	£3,119

Won twice over the Grand National fences last season, recovering from early setbacks to add the Topham Chase to the Grand Sefton; largely disappointing over regulation fences in between; yet to win beyond 3m but bred to stay and trainer eyeing a Grand National bid.

Lookaway: caps an unbeaten season with victory at Aintree and is highly likely to be a smart recruit to novice hurdles this season

Mackenberg (Ger)

7 b g Jukebox Jury - Mountain Melody (Refuse To Bend)

Donald McCain — T G Leslie

PLACINGS: UF/14/123421/37111P- — RPR **144+c**

Starts	1st	2nd	3rd	4th	Win & Pl
14	6	2	2	2	£40,522

	3/22	Catt	2m3f Cls3 Nov Ch soft	£7,733
127	2/22	Carl	2m Cls3 Nov 127-145 Ch Hcap soft	£7,951
123	1/22	Muss	2m4½f Cls3 Nov 118-127 Ch Hcap soft	£6,108
	4/21	Kemp	2m5f Cls4 Nov Hdl good	£3,522
	2/21	Newc	2m½f Cls5 NHF std-slw	£2,859
	10/20	Carl	2m1f Cls4 Nov Hdl good	£3,769
	12/19	Carl	2m1f Cls5 NHF 4-6yo soft	£2,274

Unbeaten in three races over fences, proving a much better chaser last term in between modest efforts over hurdles; easily won novice handicaps at Musselburgh and Carlisle before stepping up again to complete a hat-trick at Catterick; could jump better but has a big engine.

Madmansgame

5 bl g Blue Bresil - Grainne Ni Maille (Terimon)

Willie Mullins (Ire) — Dr S P Fitzgerald

PLACINGS: 110-5 — RPR **117+b**

Starts	1st	2nd	3rd	4th	Win & Pl
3	1	-	-	-	£6,638

	2/22	Navn	2m NHF 5-7yo heavy	£4,958

Beautiful chasing type who was bought for 250,000gns after winning sole point-to-point in Ireland and overcame greenness to make a successful start under rules at Navan; too keen when well beaten at Cheltenham and Punchestown; looks a proper stayer.

Magic Daze (Ire)

6 b m Doyen - Magic Maze (Gamut)

Henry de Bromhead (Ire) — Robcour

PLACINGS: 1312/43138-1 — RPR **145+c**

Starts	1st	2nd	3rd	4th	Win & Pl
9	3	1	3	1	£59,558

135	4/22	Punc	2m 117-143 Ch Hcap gd-yld	£24,790
	11/21	Cork	2m½f Ch soft	£8,165
	1/21	Clon	2m Mdn Hdl heavy	£5,268

Exciting front-running mare who won a valuable 2m handicap chase at Punchestown in April; had done well in novice chases earlier in the season only to disappoint in the Arkle at the Cheltenham Festival (second in the mares' novice hurdle at that meeting in 2021).

Mahler Mission (Ire)

6 b g Mahler - Finnow Turkle (Turtle Island)

John McConnell (Ire) — Colm Herron & Rockview Racing Syndicate

PLACINGS: 2/321171- — RPR **141+h**

Starts	1st	2nd	3rd	4th	Win & Pl
6	3	1	1	-	£41,899

	4/22	Prth	3m Cls1 Nov List Hdl gd-sft	£13,160
	1/22	Donc	3m½f Cls1 Nov Gd2 Hdl good	£17,165
	1/22	Sedg	2m4f Cls4 Mdn Hdl gd-sft	£5,651

Progressive staying novice hurdler last season; gained biggest win in a 3m Grade 2 at Doncaster, relishing good ground; far from disgraced when seventh in the Albert Bartlett and won again back in calmer waters at Perth; looks a future chaser.

Main Fact (USA)

9 b g Blame - Reflections (Sadler's Wells)

David Pipe — Munrowd's Partnership

PLACINGS: 4071P14/311111/174P/ — RPR **154h**

Starts	1st	2nd	3rd	4th	Win & Pl
17	8	-	1	3	£104,905

147	11/20	Hayd	3m½f Cls1 Gd3 133-155 Hdl Hcap soft	£45,560
132	3/20	Uttx	2m4f Cls2 127-144 Hdl Hcap heavy	£30,950
123	3/20	Weth	2m Cls3 123-135 Hdl Hcap heavy	£6,758
111	1/20	Ffos	2m Cls4 83-111 Hdl Hcap soft	£3,769
111	1/20	Uttx	2m Cls4 92-111 Cond Hdl Hcap heavy	£3,769
104	1/20	Wwck	2m Cls4 97-111 Hdl Hcap soft	£4,549
97	3/18	Weth	2m3½f Cls5 Nov 72-97 Hdl Hcap heavy	£3,509
89	11/17	Sedg	2m1f Cls4 80-104 Hdl Hcap soft	£3,249

Huge success story in 2020, winning nine races in a row across Flat and jumps, notably when stepped up to 3m to land a valuable handicap at Haydock; couldn't bridge the gap to Graded company and hasn't run since being pulled up in the 2021 Stayers' Hurdle at Cheltenham.

Major Dundee (Ire)

7 b g Scorpion - Be My Granny (Needle Gun)

Alan King — Exors Of The Late Trevor Hemmings

PLACINGS: 10F6/22810/1123- — RPR **141+c**

Starts	1st	2nd	3rd	4th	Win & Pl
13	4	3	1	-	£41,065

126	12/21	Bang	3m Cls3 115-127 Ch Hcap soft	£5,936
123	11/21	Fknm	2m5f Cls3 Nov 123-131 Ch Hcap good	£7,407
	3/21	Chep	2m7½f Cls4 Nov Hdl good	£3,769
	5/19	Sthl	1m7½f Cls5 Mdn NHF 4-6yo good	£2,274

Progressive and lightly raced stayer who was a big improver when switched to fences last season, winning handicaps at Fakenham and Bangor before a good second at Newbury; ran another cracker when third in the Scottish Grand National stepping up in class and trip.

Make Me A Believer (Ire)

7 br g Presenting - Kiltiernan Robin (Robin Des Champs)

David Pipe — Prof C Tisdall & Jane Gerard-Pearse

PLACINGS: F/1/213/ — RPR **138h**

Starts	1st	2nd	3rd	4th	Win & Pl
4	2	1	1	-	£13,367

	12/20	Chel	2m1f Cls3 Nov Hdl 4-6yo gd-sft	£6,279
	10/19	Chep	2m Cls4 NHF 4-6yo soft	£3,574

Hasn't run since January 2021 but had looked a progressive novice hurdler at that point; gained sole win over Any News at Cheltenham and finished a half-length third behind Adrimel in a 2m5f Grade 2 at Warwick.

Mackenberg: three out of three over fences and could continue to be a force in handicaps

Marie's Rock (Ire)

7 b/br m Milan - By The Hour (Flemensfirth)

Nicky Henderson — Middleham Park Racing

PLACINGS: 111/73/371P11-1 — RPR **153+h**

Starts	1st	2nd	3rd	4th	Win & Pl
12	7	-	2	-	£192,022

	Date	Course	Race	Prize
	4/22	Punc	2m3f Gd1 Hdl good	£61,975
	3/22	Chel	2m4f Cls1 Gd1 Hdl gd-sft	£67,524
	2/22	Wwck	2m5f Cls1 List Hdl gd-sft	£17,085
131	12/21	Kemp	2m5f Cls3 122-139 Hdl Hcap soft	£10,892
	12/19	Tntn	2m½f Cls1 Nov List Hdl soft	£12,529
	12/19	Hayd	1m7½f Cls2 Hdl soft	£12,660
	5/19	Ffos	2m Cls5 NHF 4-6yo good	£2,599

High-class mare who achieved a Grade I double at Cheltenham and Punchestown last spring, winning at double-figure prices both times; had been lightly raced prior to last term and improved rapidly to win four of her last five races, benefiting from step up in trip.

Martello Sky

6 gr m Martaline - Kentucky Sky (Cloudings)

Lucy Wadham — The Sky Partnership

PLACINGS: 12/151181/14117- — RPR **143+h**

Starts	1st	2nd	3rd	4th	Win & Pl
13	8	1	-	1	£71,555

	Date	Course	Race	Prize
	1/22	Sand	2m4f Cls1 List Hdl heavy	£14,238
140	12/21	Chel	2m4½f Cls2 119-145 Hdl Hcap gd-sft	£15,609
132	10/21	MRas	2m4½f Cls3 125-132 Hdl Hcap good	£10,892
	4/21	Chel	2m4½f Cls1 Nov List Hdl good	£8,970
	2/21	MRas	2m½f Cls3 Nov Hdl soft	£6,563
	12/20	Fknm	2m Cls4 Mdn Hdl gd-sft	£5,198
	10/20	Fknm	2m Cls5 NHF 4-6yo good	£2,274
	2/20	Fknm	2m Cls5 Mdn NHF 4-6yo soft	£3,248

Prolific and progressive mare who has won six out of nine races over hurdles; added three more victories last term, including a second Listed win at Sandown; seventh when stepped up to Graded company for the first time in the Mares' Hurdle at Cheltenham.

Master McShee

8 b g Malinas - Oscar Annie (Oscar)

Paddy Corkery (Ire) — Mrs D Corkery

PLACINGS: 6/21175/P31222- — RPR **159+c**

Starts	1st	2nd	3rd	4th	Win & Pl
12	3	4	1	-	£119,310

	Date	Course	Race	Prize
	12/21	Limk	2m3½f Nov Gd1 Ch heavy	£52,857
132	12/20	Leop	2m 116-135 Hdl Hcap soft	£10,500
	12/20	Cork	2m Mdn Hdl sft-hvy	£6,000

Fairytale Grade I winner for his small yard in a 2m4f novice chase at Limerick last Christmas; backed up that form with three excellent seconds subsequently, twice chasing home Galopin Des Champs and pushing Sizing Pottsie close in an open 2m Grade 2 at Navan.

McFabulous (Ire)

8 b g Milan - Rossavon (Beneficial)

Paul Nicholls — Giraffa Racing

PLACINGS: 711/2411/13128/2431- — RPR **155+h**

Starts	1st	2nd	3rd	4th	Win & Pl
17	8	3	2	2	£226,070

	Date	Course	Race	Prize
	4/22	Sand	2m5½f Cls1 Gd2 Hdl good	£45,560
	1/21	Kemp	2m5f Cls1 Gd2 Hdl soft	£17,085
	10/20	Chep	2m3½f Cls1 Nov Gd2 Hdl good	£17,085
132	3/20	Kemp	2m5f Cls1 Nov Gd3 123-134 Hdl 4-7yo Hcap gd-sft	£39,389
	2/20	MRas	2m4½f Cls3 Nov Hdl 4-7yo gd-sft	£6,498
	4/19	Aint	2m1f Cls1 Gd2 NHF 4-6yo soft	£25,322
	3/19	Newb	2m½f Cls5 NHF 4-6yo gd-sft	£2,599
	10/18	Chep	2m Cls4 NHF 4-6yo gd-sft	£3,899

Three-time Grade 2 winner, most recently in

last season's Select Hurdle at Sandown after a hitherto underwhelming campaign; limitations seemingly exposed in stronger company but could make a better chaser; yet to convince with his stamina in two runs over 3m.

Meet And Greet (Ire)

6 b g Mustameet - Lady Conn (Whitmore's Conn)

Oliver McKiernan (Ire) Keep The Faith Syndicate

PLACINGS: 294215/8312-3 RPR **149h**

Starts	1st	2nd	3rd	4th	Win & Pl
11	2	3	2	1	£31,376

	Date	Course	Race	Prize
	2/22	Naas	1m7½f Mdn Hdl soft	£6,197
	3/21	Leop	2m NHF 5-7yo gd-yld	£5,268

Very useful and progressive novice hurdler last season; won a 2m maiden hurdle at Naas before returning to finish second over course and distance in a Grade 2; took another big step forward on final run when third in a Grade 1 at Punchestown over 3m.

Metier (Ire)

6 b g Mastercraftsman - We'Ll Go Walking (Authorized)

Harry Fry G C Stevens

PLACINGS: 1117/P417- RPR **146+h**

Starts	1st	2nd	3rd	4th	Win & Pl
8	4	-	-	1	£94,428

	Date	Course	Race	Prize
139	1/22	Ling	2m Cls2 117-141 Hdl Hcap heavy	£52,030
	1/21	Sand	2m Cls1 Nov Gd1 Hdl heavy	£19,933
	11/20	Asct	1m7½f Cls2 Hdl soft	£11,696
	10/20	NAbb	2m2½f Cls4 Nov Hdl heavy	£3,769

Runaway winner of the Tolworth Hurdle in 2021 but hasn't built on that since then; produced much his best run when back on heavy ground at Lingfield last term to win a valuable 2m handicap hurdle only to disappoint again when seventh at Kelso on final run.

Metier: in and out last season but scored at Lingfield with ideal testing conditions

Might I (Ire)

6 b g Fame And Glory - Our Honey (Old Vic)

Harry Fry — Brian & Sandy Lambert

PLACINGS: 15/1232- — RPR **141h**

Starts	1st	2nd	3rd	4th	Win & Pl
6	2	2	1	-	£37,081

	10/21	NAbb	2m2½f Cls4 Nov Hdl heavy	£4,085
	12/20	Wwck	2m Cls5 NHF 4-6yo soft	£2,274

Highly promising novice hurdler last season despite winning only once, running well in the face of several stiff tasks; bumped into Constitution Hill on second run and finished second again in a 2m4f Grade I at Aintree on final run behind Three Stripe Life; likely to stick to hurdles.

Mighty Potter (Fr)

5 b g Martaline - Matnie (Laveron)

Gordon Elliott (Ire) — Caldwell Construction

PLACINGS: 1/131P-1 — RPR **151+h**

Starts	1st	2nd	3rd	4th	Win & Pl
6	4	-	1	-	£130,814

	4/22	Punc	2m½f Nov Gd1 Hdl gd-yld	£61,975
	12/21	Leop	2m Nov Gd1 Hdl yld-sft	£52,679
	10/21	DRoy	2m1f Mdn Hdl soft	£5,268
	3/21	Punc	2m NHF 4yo soft	£5,268

High-class novice hurdler last season, winning two Grade I races; beat Three Stripe Life at Leopardstown and bounced back from a poor run at Cheltenham (pulled up in the Supreme) with a dominant success at Punchestown; likely to go novice chasing.

Mighty Thunder

9 b g Malinas - Cool Island (Turtle Island)

Lucinda Russell — Allson Sparkle

PLACINGS: 18142/9116121/4PPP-0 — RPR **122c**

Starts	1st	2nd	3rd	4th	Win & Pl
31	8	5	4	2	£180,289

144	4/21	Ayr	4m Cls1 Gd3 129-155 Ch Hcap good	£84,405
129	2/21	Muss	4m1f Cls2 117-140 Ch Hcap soft	£19,028
	11/20	Hexm	3m Cls4 Nov Ch soft	£4,549
	10/20	Hexm	2m4f Cls4 Nov Ch soft	£4,394
120	12/19	Muss	3m Cls3 105-132 Hdl Hcap gd-sft	£6,888
115	9/19	Prth	3m Cls3 114-128 Hdl Hcap gd-sft	£9,487
	12/18	Kels	2m6½f Cls4 Mdn Hdl good	£4,224
	6/17	Prth	2m Cls5 NHF 4-6yo good	£2,599

Capped an outstanding first campaign over fences when running down Dingo Dollar close home in the 2021 Scottish National for a fourth chase win; endured a miserable campaign last term and was pulled up for the third race in a row in the Grand National.

Millers Bank

8 b g Passing Glance - It Doesn't Matter (Karinga Bay)

Alex Hales — Millers Bank Partnership

PLACINGS: 5/211/98113/1UU21-5 — RPR **159+c**

Starts	1st	2nd	3rd	4th	Win & Pl
15	6	2	1	-	£134,941

	4/22	Aint	2m4f Cls1 Nov Gd1 Ch gd-sft	£68,721
	10/21	Hntg	2m4f Cls3 Nov Ch good	£8,169
137	3/21	Newb	2m½f Cls3 122-140 Hdl Hcap good	£7,507
133	1/21	Kemp	2m Cls3 120-141 Hdl Hcap soft	£5,913
	12/19	MRas	2m½f Cls4 Nov Hdl gd-sft	£4,549
	11/19	Bang	2m½f Cls4 Nov Hdl heavy	£4,094

Fairytale Grade I winner for his small yard at Aintree last season, storming home by ten

lengths in an admittedly weak race for the grade after a mixed first season over fences; had been expected to appreciate step up to 3m but faded into a distant fifth over that trip at Punchestown.

Minella Cocooner (Ire)

6 b g Flemensfirth - Askanna (Old Vic)

Willie Mullins (Ire) — David Bobbett

PLACINGS: 2/12112-2 — RPR **154h**

Starts	1st	2nd	3rd	4th	Win & Pl
6	3	3	-	-	£137,934

	Date	Course	Race	Prize
	2/22	Leop	2m6f Gd1 Hdl yield	£74,370
	12/21	Navn	2m4f Mdn Hdl gd-yld	£6,321
	6/21	Kbgn	2m NHF 4-7yo good	£5,268

High-class staying novice hurdler last season; won a 2m6f Grade 1 at Leopardstown and then finished second behind The Nice Guy at Cheltenham and Punchestown, getting much closer on the latter occasion than he had in the Albert Bartlett; likely to go novice chasing.

Minella Crooner (Ire)

6 b g Shantou - Laren (Monsun)

Gordon Elliott (Ire) — David Barnard

PLACINGS: 1/11212-P — RPR **148+h**

Starts	1st	2nd	3rd	4th	Win & Pl
6	3	2	-	-	£43,754

	Date	Course	Race	Prize
	1/22	Punc	3m Mdn Hdl soft	£6,197
	11/21	Punc	2m NHF 4-7yo yield	£5,795
	10/21	Slig	2m2f NHF 4-7yo yield	£5,268

Progressive for much of last season and chased home Minella Cocooner in a 2m6f Grade 1 at Leopardstown; suffered a frustrating spring when missing Cheltenham through injury and pulled up at Punchestown; likely to go novice chasing and looks an out-and-out stayer.

Minella Drama (Ire)

7 b g Flemensfirth - Midsummer Drama (King's Theatre)

Donald McCain — Green Day Racing

PLACINGS: 22/211212/125142- — RPR **150c**

Starts	1st	2nd	3rd	4th	Win & Pl
12	5	5	-	1	£103,234

	Date	Course	Race	Prize
	1/22	Hayd	2m4f Cls1 Nov Gd2 Ch soft	£30,137
143	10/21	Uttx	2m Cls3 Nov 132-143 Ch Hcap gd-sft	£5,882
	2/21	MRas	2m4½f Cls1 Nov List Hdl soft	£10,402
	12/20	Bang	2m½f Cls4 Nov Hdl heavy	£3,769
	11/20	Sedg	2m1f Cls4 Nov Hdl good	£3,769

Useful and consistent novice chaser last season, winning twice including a 2m4f Grade 2 at Haydock; twice beaten under a penalty in the same grade but did well to finish second behind Do Your Job at Ayr after a notable blunder; acts on any going.

Minella Trump: emphatic winner who landed the Perth Gold Cup during the summer

Minella Indo (Ire)

9 b g Beat Hollow - Carrigeen Lily (Supreme Leader)

Henry de Bromhead (Ire) — Barry Maloney

PLACINGS: 21/1212/11F41/3P22-P — RPR **172c**

Starts	1st	2nd	3rd	4th	Win & Pl
18	6	5	3	1	£680,498

	Date	Course	Race	Prize
	3/21	Chel	3m2½f Cls1 Gd1 Ch gd-sft	£263,766
	11/20	Navn	3m Gd2 Ch soft	£30,000
	10/20	Wxfd	2m7f Gd3 Ch soft	£13,750
	1/20	Navn	3m Ch sft-hvy	£7,262
	5/19	Punc	3m Nov Gd1 Hdl yield	£53,153
	3/19	Chel	3m Cls1 Nov Gd1 Hdl gd-sft	£73,506

Lost Gold Cup crown to A Plus Tard last season but ran another fine race in second to extend Cheltenham Festival record to two wins and two seconds; generally less effective away from Cheltenham, with second in last season's Irish Gold Cup his best effort otherwise.

Minella Trump (Ire)

8 b g Shantou - One Theatre (King's Theatre)

Donald McCain — T G Leslie

PLACINGS: 1d4/35332/111111121-1 — RPR **149+c**

Starts	1st	2nd	3rd	4th	Win & Pl
20	11	4	3	1	£90,866

	Date	Course	Race	Prize
145	6/22	Prth	3m Cls2 129-147 Ch Hcap good	£14,514
140	4/22	Prth	3m Cls3 125-140 Ch Hcap gd-sft	£7,407
	11/21	Catt	2m3f Cls3 Nov Ch good	£7,895
135	11/21	Sand	2m4f Cls3 Nov 126-135 Ch Hcap gd-sft	£8,169
135	10/21	Sedg	2m3½f Cls3 Nov 124-135 Ch Hcap good	£5,882
130	9/21	Prth	2m4f Cls3 Nov 123-140 Ch Hcap gd-sft	£6,317
127	9/21	Prth	3m Cls3 Nov 118-137 Ch Hcap good	£6,317
125	8/21	Prth	2m4f Cls3 Nov 123-125 Ch Hcap good	£6,317
123	5/21	Prth	2m4f Cls3 103-127 Hdl Hcap soft	£5,773
	12/19	Sedg	2m4f Cls4 Nov Hdl soft	£4,094
	11/19	Sedg	2m1f Cls4 Nov Hdl soft	£4,094

Prolific chaser who won eight times last season, the last seven after switching back to fences, and maintained progress by adding the Perth Gold Cup in June; best on good ground and has done most of his winning in summer months; yet to tackle a field bigger than seven over fences.

Mister Coffey (Fr)

7 b g Authorized - Mamitador (Anabaa)

Nicky Henderson — Lady Bamford & Alice Bamford

PLACINGS: 1/12/1374/32220- — RPR **144+c**

Starts	1st	2nd	3rd	4th	Win & Pl
12	3	4	2	1	£69,655

	Date	Course	Race	Prize
128	11/20	Sand	2m Cls3 117-130 Hdl Hcap soft	£9,747
	12/19	Newb	2m½f Cls4 Hdl soft	£4,484
	4/19	Hntg	2m Cls5 NHF 4-6yo good	£2,274

Failed to win in five runs as a novice chaser last season but finished second three times, notably when favourite in the Kim Muir at Cheltenham; benefited from stepping up to 3m2f having otherwise run over shorter and returning to left-handed track.

Mister Fisher (Ire)

8 b g Jeremy - That's Amazing (Marignan)

Nicky Henderson — James & Jean Potter

PLACINGS: 8/72114/P1PU2/P14P2- — RPR **166+c**

Starts	1st	2nd	3rd	4th	Win & Pl
21	7	4	-	2	£184,325

	1/22	Kemp	2m4½f Cls1 Gd2 Ch soft	£45,560
	12/20	Chel	2m4f Cls1 Gd2 Ch soft	£21,356
	1/20	Donc	2m½f Cls1 Nov Gd2 Ch gd-sft	£19,933
	12/19	Chel	2m4½f Cls2 Nov Ch soft	£15,698
	1/19	Hayd	1m7½f Cls1 Nov Gd2 Hdl gd-sft	£17,085
	12/18	Kemp	2m Cls2 Nov Hdl gd-sft	£12,512
	3/18	Kemp	2m Cls5 Mdn NHF 4-6yo soft	£3,119

Smart chaser who has won Grade 2 chases at around 2m4f in each of the last two seasons, most recently in the Silviniaco Conti at Kempton; has failed to finish better than fourth in seven runs at Grade 1 level.

Mister Malarky

9 ch g Malinas - Priscilla (Teenoso)

Richard J Bandey — Wendy & Malcolm Hezel

PLACINGS: /06P1P/6U173P/05022- — RPR **154c**

Starts	1st	2nd	3rd	4th	Win & Pl
32	6	4	5	1	£197,434

150	12/20	Asct	3m Cls1 List 137-157 Ch Hcap heavy	£34,170
147	2/20	Kemp	3m Cls1 Gd3 133-159 Ch Hcap gd-sft	£56,950
	2/19	Asct	3m Cls1 Nov Gd2 Ch gd-sft	£22,780
130	1/19	Newb	2m7½f Cls3 120-130 Ch Hcap good	£7,343
126	11/18	Plum	2m3½f Cls3 Nov 126-136 Ch Hcap good	£7,522
	11/17	Kemp	2m Cls4 Nov Hdl 4-6yo gd-sft	£3,899

Rejuvenated last spring after a change of trainer and wind surgery, finishing second at Doncaster and Cheltenham; had been aiming to win a valuable staying handicap for a third successive season after victories at Kempton and Ascot in 2020.

Molly Ollys Wishes

8 b m Black Sam Bellamy - September Moon (Bustino)

Dan Skelton — Dean Pugh

PLACINGS: P24212/371113/151P8- — RPR **147+h**

Starts	1st	2nd	3rd	4th	Win & Pl
19	6	3	3	2	£89,584

	1/22	Asct	2m7½f Cls1 Gd2 Hdl soft	£34,170
	10/21	Weth	2m Cls1 List Hdl gd-sft	£12,529
	2/21	Wwck	2m5f Cls1 List Hdl heavy	£9,441
130	12/20	Kemp	3m½f Cls2 120-135 Hdl Hcap soft	£10,010
124	11/20	Hrfd	2m3½f Cls3 106-124 Hdl Hcap soft	£5,913
	1/20	Wwck	2m5f Cls4 Nov Hdl soft	£4,549

Smart mare who won a Grade 2 hurdle at Ascot last season to add to Listed victories at Warwick and Wetherby in 2021; pulled up when sent off favourite against geldings in the Rendlesham and again disappointed in a Grade 1 at Aintree.

Monalee (Ire)

11 b g Milan - Tempest Belle (Glacial Storm)

Henry de Bromhead (Ire) — Barry Maloney

PLACINGS: 4/1F12F/3214/P324/3/ — RPR **170c**

Starts	1st	2nd	3rd	4th	Win & Pl
21	5	7	3	3	£317,220

	2/19	Gowr	2m4f Gd2 Ch yld-sft	£31,892
	2/18	Leop	2m5f Nov Gd1 Ch soft	£52,212
	11/17	Punc	2m4f Ch sft-hvy	£7,371
	2/17	Clon	3m Nov Gd3 Hdl heavy	£19,712
	11/16	Punc	2m6f Mdn Hdl soft	£6,331

High-class staying chaser who finished fourth in the Cheltenham Gold Cup in 2020 (beaten less than two lengths) but hasn't run since picking up an injury after just one run the following season; tends to come up just short at top level, winning just once outside novice company.

Monmiral (Fr)

5 bl g Saint Des Saints - Achere (Mont Basile)

Paul Nicholls — Sir A Ferguson, G Mason, J Hales & L Hales

PLACINGS: 1/1111/542- RPR **152h**

Starts	1st	2nd	3rd	4th	Win & Pl
8	5	1	-	1	£169,116

	Date	Course	Race	Prize
	4/21	Aint	2m1f Cls1 Gd1 Hdl 4yo gd-sft	£42,203
	2/21	Hayd	1m7½f Cls2 Hdl 4yo soft	£9,747
	12/20	Donc	2m½f Cls1 Gd2 Hdl 3yo gd-sft	£28,468
	11/20	Extr	2m1f Cls4 Hdl 3yo soft	£3,769
	3/20	Autl	1m7f Hdl 3yo heavy	£21,153

Brilliant unbeaten juvenile two seasons ago but failed to make the step up to Champion Hurdle level last season, failing to land a blow in three runs; did best when second in the Aintree Hurdle having also won a Grade 1 at the track in 2021; built for fences and set to go chasing.

Mount Ida (Ire)

8 b m Yeats - Jolivia (Dernier Empereur)

Gordon Elliott (Ire) — Ktda Racing

PLACINGS: 21/1230/31213/117UU- RPR **154+c**

Starts	1st	2nd	3rd	4th	Win & Pl
16	6	3	3	-	£114,360

	Date	Course	Race	Prize
	1/22	Fair	2m5½f Gd3 Ch yield	£16,113
	11/21	Clon	2m4½f List Ch soft	£14,487
142	3/21	Chel	3m2f Cls2 132-142 Ch Hcap gd-sft	£32,498
	12/20	Cork	2m½f Nov Gd3 Ch sft-hvy	£17,500
	10/19	Gway	2m Mdn Hdl soft	£7,454
	4/19	Wxfd	2m NHF 4-7yo yield	£6,105

Very smart mare who won Grade 3 and Listed chases last season to add to her most notable success when a well-backed favourite in the 2021 Kim Muir; out of luck last spring but was going well when unseating in the Irish Grand National.

Mrs Milner (Ire)

7 b m Flemensfirth - Thegirlonthehill (Oscar)

Paul Nolan (Ire) — Softco

PLACINGS: 5/51702/1324F1/143-6 RPR **145+h**

Starts	1st	2nd	3rd	4th	Win & Pl
16	4	2	2	2	£106,369

	Date	Course	Race	Prize
	10/21	Limk	2m6½f List Hdl soft	£14,487
134	3/21	Chel	3m Cls1 Gd3 126-151 Hdl Hcap gd-sft	£42,203
116	7/20	Gway	2m½f 99-125 Hdl Hcap good	£15,000
	11/19	Thur	2m Mdn Hdl yld-sft	£5,857

Won the Pertemps Final in 2021 and again ran her best race last season at the Cheltenham Festival when a staying-on third in the Mares' Hurdle (hampered two out); had earlier won a 2m6f Listed hurdle but unsuited by shorter trip on good ground when sixth at Punchestown.

Mt Leinster (Ire)

8 b g Beat Hollow - Sixhills (Sabrehill)

Willie Mullins (Ire) — Roaringwater Syndicate

PLACINGS: 352/72134/6/323411-2 RPR **149+c**

Starts	1st	2nd	3rd	4th	Win & Pl
18	4	5	4	2	£87,840

	Date	Course	Race	Prize
136	4/22	Fair	2m½f Nov 117-140 Ch Hcap yield	£24,790
	3/22	Leop	2m1f Ch yield	£7,685
	12/19	Leop	2m Mdn Hdl soft	£7,986
	9/18	Baln	2m½f NHF 4yo sft-hvy	£5,724

Slow learner over fences last season but flourished into a smart 2m handicapper during the spring; needed five attempts to break chase duck but then followed up in a novice handicap at Fairyhouse and finished a fine second behind Magic Daze at Punchestown.

Musical Slave (Ire)

9 b g Getaway - Inghwung (Kayf Tara)

Philip Hobbs — John P McManus

PLACINGS: /158132/5U39/933112- RPR **141+c**

Starts	1st	2nd	3rd	4th	Win & Pl
22	6	2	4	-	£130,757

	Date	Course	Race	Prize
130	4/22	Hayd	3m1½f Cls2 114-140 Ch Hcap gd-sft	£25,782
128	3/22	Sand	3m Cls3 128-135 Ch Hcap gd-sft	£11,311
128	1/20	Extr	2m3f Cls3 Nov 125-136 Ch Hcap soft	£10,722
121	5/19	Punc	2m5f 110-123 Hdl Hcap yield	£16,622
117	3/19	Ludl	2m Cls3 111-129 Hdl Hcap gd-sft	£7,538
110	3/19	MRas	2m½f Cls4 109-117 Hdl Hcap gd-sft	£4,159

Useful staying chaser who bounced back to form last spring, winning handicaps at Sandown and Haydock before a fine second in the bet365 Gold Cup; raised 7lb for that run but had been competitive off similar mark in 2020 before losing his way.

My Drogo

7 b g Milan - My Petra (Midnight Legend)

Dan Skelton — Mr & Mrs R Kelvin-Hughes

PLACINGS: 21111/F1- RPR **154+c**

Starts	1st	2nd	3rd	4th	Win & Pl
7	5	1	-	-	£101,416

	Date	Course	Race	Prize
	12/21	Chel	2m4½f Cls2 Nov Ch gd-sft	£13,008
	4/21	Aint	2m4f Cls1 Nov Gd1 Hdl gd-sft	£42,239
	3/21	Kels	2m2f Cls1 Nov Gd2 Hdl gd-sft	£22,780
	12/20	Asct	1m7½f Cls1 Nov Gd2 Hdl soft	£14,305
	11/20	Newb	2m½f Cls3 Mdn Hdl good	£6,498

Britain's leading novice hurdler two seasons ago and looked to be heading to similar heights as a novice chaser last season until suffering a tendon injury likely to keep him off until the spring; had fallen two out on chase debut but won easily back at Cheltenham in December.

Molly Ollys Wishes: ended the season with two below-par efforts but had earlier scored in Grade 2 company at Ascot

My Mate Mozzie (Ire)

6 b g Born To Sea - Leo's Spirit (Fantastic Light)

Gavin Cromwell (Ire) — Alymer Stud

PLACINGS: 1/111248-0 — RPR **144h**

Starts	1st	2nd	3rd	4th	Win & Pl
7	3	1	-	1	£43,332

	11/21	Navn	2m Nov Gd3 Hdl good	£14,487
	10/21	Punc	2m Mdn Hdl good	£6,321
	4/21	Punc	2m2f NHF 5-7yo yield	£5,268

Smart novice hurdler early last season, twice winning easily and finishing a short-head second to Statuaire in the Royal Bond; kept away from winter ground and disappointing since then, finishing eighth in the County Hurdle and 12th in the Galway Hurdle.

Nassalam (Fr)

5 ch g Dream Well - Ramina (Shirocco)

Gary Moore — John & Yvonne Stone

PLACINGS: 211220/11221- — RPR **142+c**

Starts	1st	2nd	3rd	4th	Win & Pl
11	5	5	-	-	£79,710

144	2/22	Font	2m3½f Cls3 Nov 121-144 Ch Hcap soft	£6,535
	11/21	Newb	2m4f Cls1 Nov Gd2 Ch gd-sft	£32,483
140	10/21	Asct	2m3f Cls3 Nov 130-140 Ch Hcap soft	£6,535
	12/20	Font	2m1½f Cls4 Hdl 3yo soft	£3,769
	11/20	Font	2m1½f Cls4 Hdl 3yo heavy	£3,861

Useful novice chaser last season when winning three times, albeit flattered by Grade 2 victory at Newbury (third best on merit but saw two rivals depart in the straight); beaten favourite twice subsequently but signed off by winning at Fontwell.

Nells Son

7 b g Trans Island - Miss Nellie (Presenting)

Nicky Richards — Langdale Bloodstock

PLACINGS: 2/11/12414- — RPR **138+h**

Starts	1st	2nd	3rd	4th	Win & Pl
8	4	2	-	2	£49,018

	3/22	Kels	2m2f Cls1 Nov Gd2 Hdl soft	£28,475
	10/21	Kels	2m Cls4 Mdn Hdl good	£4,357
	3/21	Ayr	2m Cls4 NHF 4-6yo heavy	£3,249
	12/20	Ayr	2m Cls5 Mdn NHF 4-6yo heavy	£2,274

Useful novice hurdler last season; pulled off a surprise win when pipping North Lodge by a short head in a 2m2f Grade 2 at Kelso; twice well beaten in stronger races, though far from disgraced when fourth in a 2m4f Grade 1 at Aintree; likely to go novice chasing.

No Ordinary Joe (Ire)

6 b g Getaway - Shadow Dearg (Beneficial)

Nicky Henderson — John P McManus

PLACINGS: 14/113P- — RPR **138+h**

Starts	1st	2nd	3rd	4th	Win & Pl
6	3	-	1	1	£21,575

	5/21	Worc	2m4f Cls4 Nov Hdl gd-sft	£3,159
	5/21	Sthl	2m4½f Cls4 Nov Hdl good	£3,159
	11/20	Sand	2m Cls4 NHF 4-6yo soft	£3,249

Lightly raced hurdler who showed plenty of promise early last season; won two novice hurdles in May before returning from a break to finish a fine third on handicap debut in the Greatwood; warm favourite for another valuable handicap at Ascot only to be pulled up after racing keenly.

Noble Yeats (Ire)

7 b g Yeats - That's Moyne (Flemensfirth)

Emmet Mullins (Ire) — Robert Waley-Cohen

PLACINGS: 2/3161/1469P291- — RPR **160+c**

Starts	1st	2nd	3rd	4th	Win & Pl
12	4	1	1	1	£530,718

147	4/22	Aint	4m2½f Cls1 Gd3 142-161 Ch Hcap gd-sft	£500,000
	10/21	Gway	2m2½f Ch soft	£6,585
	3/21	Navn	2m6f Mdn Hdl yld-sft	£6,321
	1/21	Thur	2m3½f NHF 5-7yo sft-hvy	£5,268

Remarkably managed to win last season's Grand National as a novice last season, having been running in bumpers little over a year earlier; had won just one out of seven races over fences prior to that, with best run coming when second to Ahoy Senor in a Grade 2 at Wetherby.

North Lodge (Ire)

5 b g Presenting - Saddleeruppat (Saddlers' Hall)

Alan King — McNeill Family & Niall Farrell

PLACINGS: 1123- — RPR **142+h**

Starts	1st	2nd	3rd	4th	Win & Pl
4	2	1	1	-	£56,692

	1/22	Chel	2m4½f Cls1 Nov Gd2 Hdl good	£28,978
	12/21	Aint	2m1f Cls3 Nov Hdl soft	£6,372

Very useful novice hurdler last season; won a Grade 2 at Cheltenham on just his second run and twice ran well in defeat subsequently, failing by a short head under a 5lb penalty before finishing third behind Three Stripe Life in a Grade 1 at Aintree; one for good handicap hurdles.

Not So Sleepy

10 ch g Beat Hollow - Papillon De Bronze (Marju)

Hughie Morrison — Lady Blyth

PLACINGS: 415/110P/U157/156- — RPR **160h**

Starts	1st	2nd	3rd	4th	Win & Pl
14	5	-	-	1	£230,301

	11/21	Newc	2m Cls1 Gd1 Hdl gd-sft	£44,545
142	12/20	Asct	1m7½f Cls1 Gd3 128-148 Hdl Hcap heavy	£56,950
127	12/19	Asct	1m7½f Cls1 Gd3 127-150 Hdl Hcap heavy	£85,425
122	11/19	Asct	1m7½f Cls2 122-143 Hdl Hcap soft	£18,768
	2/19	Winc	1m7½f Cls4 Nov Hdl good	£4,224

Smart dual-purpose performer who has been very highly tried over hurdles (last five runs at Grade 1 level) but justified connections' bold approach when dead-heating in last season's Fighting Fifth Hurdle; has come fifth and sixth in the last two runnings of the Champion Hurdle.

Nube Negra (Spa)

8 br g Dink - Manly Dream (Highest Honor)

Dan Skelton | T Spraggett

PLACINGS: 5/8B36/1122/12/3143- | RPR **168+c**

Starts	1st	2nd	3rd	4th	Win & Pl
19	6	4	4	1	£258,140

	Date	Course	Race	Prize
	11/21	Chel	2m Cls1 Gd2 Ch good	£42,203
	12/20	Kemp	2m Cls1 Gd2 Ch soft	£46,364
	10/19	Fknm	2m½f Cls3 Nov Ch good	£8,058
	10/19	Wwck	2m Cls4 Ch good	£5,198
	1/18	Donc	2m½f Cls4 Nov Hdl soft	£4,094
	11/17	MRas	2m½f Cls4 Hdl 3yo gd-sft	£3,899

Seen as best when fresh and has won first time out in last three seasons as well as going close in the 2021 Champion Chase after a break; purposely lightly raced again last season but failed to build on Shloer Chase win and missed the Champion Chase due to soft ground.

Nuts Well

11 b g Dylan Thomas - Renada (Sinndar)

Ann Hamilton | Ian Hamilton

PLACINGS: 441113/1126/153P164- | RPR **160c**

Starts	1st	2nd	3rd	4th	Win & Pl
47	13	9	4	8	£284,597

	Date	Course	Race	Prize
	3/22	Kels	2m7½f Cls1 List Ch soft	£28,609
157	10/21	Kels	2m1f Cls2 134-160 Ch Hcap good	£20,931
155	10/20	Aint	2m4f Cls1 Gd2 138-155 Ch Hcap soft	£36,013
152	10/20	Kels	2m1f Cls2 135-157 Ch Hcap gd-sft	£15,698
146	2/20	Weth	2m3½f Cls2 123-148 Ch Hcap soft	£11,574
140	1/20	Muss	2m4½f Cls2 114-140 Ch Hcap gd-sft	£18,768
130	12/19	Weth	1m7f Cls3 118-140 Ch Hcap soft	£7,538
136	10/18	Kels	2m1f Cls2 132-158 Ch Hcap good	£24,760
	11/17	Carl	2m Cls2 Ch soft	£12,820
131	4/17	Newc	2m Cls3 118-131 Hdl Hcap good	£5,393
129	4/16	Newc	2m Cls3 120-136 Hdl Hcap soft	£7,148
122	3/16	Newc	2m Cls3 115-130 Hdl Hcap heavy	£9,747
	11/15	Hexm	2m Cls5 Mdn Hdl gd-sft	£3,080

Very smart chaser at his peak, winning the Old Roan Chase and finishing second in the Melling Chase two seasons ago; generally below his best last term, though did bounce back with a Listed win at Kelso when stepped up to around 3m only to disappoint twice subsequently.

Off Your Rocco (Ire)

6 b g Shirocco - Takeyourcapoff (King's Theatre)

Gordon Elliott (Ire) | Pioneer Racing

PLACINGS: 1/17114- | RPR **140+h**

Starts	1st	2nd	3rd	4th	Win & Pl
6	4	-	-	1	£33,230

Date	Course	Race	Prize
10/21	Limk	2m5f Nov List Hdl soft	£11,853
9/21	List	2m Nov Hdl good	£8,955
5/21	Klny	2m1f Mdn Hdl yield	£5,268
9/20	Dpat	2m2f NHF 4-7yo good	£4,500

Missed nearly all of the core jumps season last term but made a mark through the summer, making it four wins in five races under rules in a Listed novice hurdle at Limerick; below-par fourth on only subsequent run when favourite for a 2m5f Grade 2 at Cheltenham.

One For The Team

8 b g Shirocco - One Gulp (Hernando)

Nick Williams | Forty Winks Syndicate 2 & Partner

PLACINGS: 1/44/2231/3U2555/ | RPR **147c**

Starts	1st	2nd	3rd	4th	Win & Pl
13	2	3	2	2	£41,274

	Date	Course	Race	Prize
130	2/20	Newb	3m Cls2 124-138 Hdl Hcap good	£12,512
	3/18	Winc	1m7½f Cls5 Mdn NHF 4-6yo soft	£2,274

Hasn't won since February 2020 (and 0-5 over fences) but had shown plenty of promise in defeat when sent chasing before missing last season through injury; ran well in good novices and stayed on particularly well to finish fifth in the Ultima at Cheltenham after several jumping errors.

Nells Son; two out of five over hurdles last season and could do well in novice chases

Onemorefortheroad

7 b g Yorgunnabelucky - Vinomore (Grape Tree Road)

Neil King — Rupert Dubai Racing

PLACINGS: 6/3/13311/4111243- RPR **138h**

Starts	1st	2nd	3rd	4th	Win & Pl
13	6	1	4	2	£91,489

133	11/21	Newb	2m½f Cls1 List 131-149 Hdl Hcap gd-sft	£28,475
127	11/21	Hntg	2m Cls3 124-135 Hdl Hcap good	£10,892
	10/21	Strf	2m½f Cls3 Nov Hdl 4-6yo good	£5,991
120	3/21	Donc	2m3½f Cls4 96-120 Hdl Hcap good	£3,769
113	3/21	Hntg	2m Cls4 87-113 Hdl Hcap gd-sft	£3,769
	10/20	NAbb	2m1f Cls5 NHF 4-6yo gd-sft	£2,395

Won five times over hurdles during 2021 and has performed with huge credit in big 2m handicaps since then; made the frame in three valuable contests, including twice in the spring when fourth in the Imperial Cup and third in the Scottish Champion Hurdle.

Oscar Elite (Ire)

7 b g Oscar - Lady Elite (Lord Americo)

Joe Tizzard — Mrs Mary-Ann Middleton

PLACINGS: 581/119323/F3453P- RPR **145c**

Starts	1st	2nd	3rd	4th	Win & Pl
12	2	1	4	1	£57,360

	12/20	Chep	2m7½f Cls4 Nov Hdl heavy	£3,769
	11/20	Chep	2m3½f Cls4 Mdn Hdl heavy	£3,769

Placed in Grade 1 novice hurdles at Cheltenham and Aintree in 2021 but took a long time to show similar form over fences last season, failing to win at all; did much better when stepped up in trip at Cheltenham to finish third in the Ultima, though then pulled up at Aintree.

Paint The Dream

8 b g Brian Boru - Vineuil (Muhtathir)

Fergal O'Brien — David Brace

PLACINGS: 8U2250/22313/104414- RPR **164+c**

Starts	1st	2nd	3rd	4th	Win & Pl
23	4	5	3	4	£105,231

147	3/22	Newb	2m4f Cls1 Gd3 128-148 Ch Hcap soft	£28,475
147	10/21	Chep	2m3½f Cls2 133-158 Ch Hcap good	£20,812
137	12/20	Newb	2m6½f Cls3 Nov 131-148 Ch Hcap soft	£10,267
120	4/19	Prth	2m4f Cls4 Nov 102-120 Hdl Hcap good	£4,265

Remarkably easy winner of the Greatwood Gold Cup at Newbury last spring, hacking up by 15 lengths; raised 10lb for that victory and had struggled off higher marks previously but suggested he could hold his own at a higher level when fourth in the Melling Chase.

Paisley Park (Ire)

10 b g Oscar - Presenting Shares (Presenting)

Emma Lavelle — Andrew Gemmell

PLACINGS: 111/117/213P/33313-5 RPR **163+h**

Starts	1st	2nd	3rd	4th	Win & Pl
23	10	4	5	-	£609,489

	1/22	Chel	3m Cls1 Gd2 Hdl good	£39,389
	12/20	Asct	3m½f Cls1 Gd1 Hdl heavy	£45,560
	1/20	Chel	3m Cls1 Gd2 Hdl soft	£33,762
	11/19	Newb	3m Cls1 Gd2 Hdl gd-sft	£28,810
	3/19	Chel	3m Cls1 Gd1 Hdl gd-sft	£182,878
	1/19	Chel	3m Cls1 Gd2 Hdl gd-sft	£33,762
	12/18	Asct	3m½f Cls1 Gd1 Hdl soft	£56,950
147	11/18	Hayd	3m½f Cls1 Gd3 125-147 Hdl Hcap good	£56,950
140	10/18	Aint	2m4f Cls2 116-140 Hdl Hcap good	£17,204
	12/17	Hrfd	2m3½f Cls4 Nov Hdl soft	£4,549

Veteran staying hurdler who landed a seventh win at Grade 1 or Grade 2 level in last season's Cleeve Hurdle at Cheltenham; otherwise came up just short in a busy campaign last term, though still a solid third in the Long Walk at Ascot and Stayers' Hurdle at Cheltenham.

Party Business (Ire)

6 b g Shantou - Marias Dream (Desert Sun)

Ian Williams — Eventmasters Racing

PLACINGS: 32/81F551-4 RPR **141+h**

Starts	1st	2nd	3rd	4th	Win & Pl
9	2	1	1	1	£56,467

132	4/22	Aint	3m½f Cls1 Gd3 128-148 Hdl Hcap gd-sft	£42,203
	12/21	Asct	2m5½f Cls3 Mdn Hdl gd-sft	£6,481

Useful staying novice hurdler last season; did particularly well when sent handicapping in the spring, winning at Aintree's Grand National meeting after a solid fifth in the Martin Pipe; finished lame when only fourth at Haydock (sent off favourite) on following run.

Party Central (Ire)

6 b m Yeats - Itsalark (Definite Article)

Gordon Elliott (Ire) — Bective Stud

PLACINGS: 1221/14117-1 RPR **144+h**

Starts	1st	2nd	3rd	4th	Win & Pl
10	6	2	-	1	£128,938

	4/22	Punc	2m½f Nov List Hdl gd-yld	£14,874
121	2/22	Leop	2m1½f 109-135 Hdl Hcap yield	£49,580
	12/21	Punc	2m3½f Nov List Hdl yield	£11,853
	9/21	List	2m4f Mdn Hdl gd-yld	£7,375
	4/21	Fair	2m List NHF 4-7yo yield	£15,804
	10/20	Tipp	2m NHF 4yo good	£5,000

Smart novice hurdler last season, winning four times in mares' company including two Listed novices and a valuable handicap at Leopardstown; beaten twice on soft ground, including when seventh at the Cheltenham Festival, and did all her winning on quicker; likely to go novice chasing.

Pats Fancy (Ire)

7 b g Oscar - Pat's Darling (Supreme Leader)

Rebecca Curtis — Hydes, McDermott, Spencer, Frobisher & Lee

PLACINGS: 242/2612P06/41125- RPR **149+c**

Starts	1st	2nd	3rd	4th	Win & Pl
12	3	3	-	1	£33,667

135	12/21	Chep	2m7½f Cls3 Nov 135-146 Ch Hcap soft	£6,786
125	12/21	Chep	2m7½f Cls3 Nov 116-136 Ch Hcap gd-sft	£5,882
	11/20	Ffos	2m4f Cls4 Mdn Hdl heavy	£3,769

Useful staying novice chaser last season, winning twice at around 3m at Chepstow; shortest-priced British runner in the National Hunt Chase at Cheltenham at 11-1 but raced too keenly to get home and finished a weary fifth.

Pay The Piper (Ire)

7 b g Court Cave - Regal Holly (Gildoran)

Ann Hamilton — Ian Hamilton

PLACINGS: 23/U311112/21231224- RPR **149c**

Starts	1st	2nd	3rd	4th	Win & Pl
12	5	5	1	1	£56,060

140	12/21	Newc	2m½f Cls3 Nov 134-145 Ch Hcap gd-sft	£5,882
	10/21	Weth	1m7f Cls3 Nov Ch good	£10,342
129	3/21	Weth	2m Cls3 113-137 Hdl Hcap gd-sft	£5,913
	2/21	Carl	2m1f Cls4 Nov Hdl heavy	£3,769
	12/20	Sedg	2m1f Cls4 Mdn Hdl soft	£3,769

Consistent in a busy novice chase campaign last season, albeit kept to small-field races in the north; gained a second win at Newcastle over 2m before stepping back up in trip for two close seconds at Musselburgh and Wetherby, both when favourite.

Pentland Hills (Ire)

7 b g Motivator - Elle Galante (Galileo)

Nicky Henderson — Owners Group 031

PLACINGS: 111/529/ RPR **157h**

Starts	1st	2nd	3rd	4th	Win & Pl
6	3	1	-	-	£150,337

4/19	Aint	2m1f Cls1 Gd1 Hdl 4yo gd-sft	£56,155
3/19	Chel	2m1f Cls1 Gd1 Hdl 4yo gd-sft	£70,338
2/19	Plum	2m Cls4 Mdn Hdl good	£4,094

Outstanding juvenile hurdler in early days, winning the Triumph Hurdle in 2019 and following up at Aintree, but hasn't run since slightly disappointing during the following campaign; best run when a close second in the Champion Hurdle Trial at Haydock, still looking a work in progress.

Petit Tonnerre (Fr)

4 b g Waldpark - Perpette (Le Triton)

Jonjo O'Neill — John P McManus

PLACINGS: 111P- RPR **130+h**

Starts	1st	2nd	3rd	4th	Win & Pl
4	3	-	-	-	£39,413

135	2/22	MRas	2m½f Cls3 108-135 Hdl Hcap soft	£11,110
	9/21	Comp	2m1f Hdl 3yo v soft	£19,304
	8/21	Diep	2m1f Hdl 3yo soft	£9,000

Dual French hurdles winner who completed a hat-trick on first run for powerful connections when beating older horses in a handicap at Market Rasen; missed intended run in the Fred Winter at Cheltenham and pulled up when stepped up to Grade 1 level at Aintree.

Pic D'Orhy (Fr)

7 b g Turgeon - Rose Candy (Roli Abi)

Paul Nicholls — Mrs Johnny De La Hey

PLACINGS: 20/F61/2F424/1F131P- RPR **158+c**

Starts	1st	2nd	3rd	4th	Win & Pl
22	7	5	1	2	£353,936

	2/22	Kemp	2m4½f Cls1 Nov Gd2 Ch gd-sft	£34,170
	12/21	Asct	2m3f Cls1 Nov Gd2 Ch gd-sft	£29,614
147	10/21	Ffos	2m5f Cls3 Nov 132-147 Ch Hcap good	£9,581
146	2/20	Newb	2m½f Cls1 Gd3 130-153 Hdl Hcap good	£87,219
	9/18	Autl	2m2f Hdl 3yo v soft	£25,487
	4/18	Autl	1m7f Hdl 3yo v soft	£23,363
	3/18	Autl	1m7f Hdl 3yo heavy	£22,088

Did better as a second-season novice chaser last season when well placed to win two Grade 2 races, most notably beating subsequent Grade 1 winner Millers Bank in the Pendil at Kempton; pulled up behind that rival in a Grade 1 at Aintree after jumping errors.

Pied Piper

4 ch g New Approach - Pure Fantasy (Fastnet Rock)

Gordon Elliott (Ire) — Caldwell Construction

PLACINGS: 1131d- RPR **141+h**

Starts	1st	2nd	3rd	4th	Win & Pl
4	2	1	1	-	£78,318

1/22	Chel	2m1f Cls1 Gd2 Hdl 4yo good	£34,170
12/21	Punc	1m7½f Mdn Hdl 3yo heavy	£6,321

Notably strong traveller who was a leading juvenile hurdler last season without quite delivering in top races; hacked up in a Grade 2 at Cheltenham but managed only third back there in the Triumph Hurdle and was demoted to second at Aintree after dead-heating with Knight Salute.

Pink Legend

8 b m Midnight Legend - Red And White (Red Ransom)

Venetia Williams — Francis Mahon

PLACINGS: 42/14F24221/1P61F22- RPR **144c**

Starts	1st	2nd	3rd	4th	Win & Pl
25	6	7	1	4	£133,289

	1/22	Hntg	2m4f Cls1 List Ch gd-sft	£42,713
129	11/21	Asct	2m5f Cls2 127-142 Ch Hcap good	£13,008
127	4/21	Chel	2m4½f Cls1 Nov List 106-130 Ch Hcap good	£15,377
	11/20	Bang	2m4½f Cls4 Ch soft	£4,874
119	12/19	Sthl	1m7½f Cls3 116-123 Hdl Hcap heavy	£5,894
	3/19	Catt	1m7½f Cls4 Nov Hdl soft	£4,484

Progressive mare who ran a big career-best when second in the Mares' Chase at the Cheltenham Festival last season; had won on only previous run at Cheltenham in 2021 and added further victories at Ascot and Huntingdon last term, though inconsistent at other times.

Porticello (Fr)

4 b g Sholokhov - Chinawood (Chichicastenango)

Gary Moore — O S Harris

PLACINGS: 1/12116- — RPR **135+h**

Starts	1st	2nd	3rd	4th	Win & Pl
6	4	1	-	-	£101,737

	Date	Course	Race	Prize
	2/22	Hayd	1m7½f Cls2 Hdl 4yo heavy	£13,615
	12/21	Chep	2m Cls1 Gd1 Hdl 3yo soft	£39,865
	10/21	Weth	2m Cls1 List Hdl 3yo gd-sft	£11,390
	4/21	Autl	1m7f Hdl 3yo v soft	£22,286

Smart juvenile hurdler last season and did best of the British runners when sixth in the Triumph Hurdle at Cheltenham; outpaced that day and had seemed better suited to softer ground, notably when running away with a weak Grade 1 on soft at Chepstow.

Proschema (Ire)

7 ch g Declaration Of War - Notable (Zafonic)

Dan Skelton — Empire State Racing Partnership

PLACINGS: 314/2P51/152F-3 — RPR **150h**

Starts	1st	2nd	3rd	4th	Win & Pl
12	3	2	2	1	£44,218

	Date	Course	Race	Prize
140	5/21	Aint	2m4f Cls2 119-141 Hdl Hcap good	£8,169
129	4/21	Chel	2m4½f Cls2 114-140 Hdl Hcap good	£8,195
	2/21	Newc	2m½f Cls4 NHF std-slw	£4,549
	1/21	Newc	2m½f Cls4 NHF std-slw	£4,679
	11/19	Weth	2m Cls3 Nov Hdl soft	£6,173

Classy Flat performer who has developed into a useful stayer over hurdles; finished second in a 3m Grade 2 last season but missed the rest of the season after falling at Cheltenham (still in contention); solid third at Haydock on only subsequent hurdles run in May.

Protektorat (Fr)

7 b g Saint Des Saints - Protektion (Protektor)

Dan Skelton — Sir A Ferguson, G Mason, J Hales & L Hales

PLACINGS: 57/22130/11221/2134- — RPR **172+c**

Starts	1st	2nd	3rd	4th	Win & Pl
18	5	6	2	1	£274,165

	Date	Course	Race	Prize
	12/21	Aint	3m1f Cls1 Gd2 Ch soft	£44,775
	4/21	Aint	2m4f Cls1 Nov Gd1 Ch gd-sft	£42,285
	11/20	Chel	2m4f Cls2 Nov Ch gd-sft	£12,820
	10/20	Carl	2m Cls3 Ch gd-sft	£7,018
	1/20	Chel	2m4½f Cls1 Nov List Hdl soft	£14,238

Top British contender for last season's Cheltenham Gold Cup in the betting and the race, finishing an honourable third behind A Plus Tard; two previous best runs at Aintree, including a Grade 1 novice win in 2021, but managed only fourth when favourite for the Bowl there.

Queens Brook (Ire)

7 b m Shirocco - Awesome Miracle (Supreme Leader)

Gordon Elliott (Ire) — Bective Stud

PLACINGS: 3/113/123/2122- — RPR **144+h**

Starts	1st	2nd	3rd	4th	Win & Pl
9	3	4	2	-	£72,055

	Date	Course	Race	Prize
	11/21	Fair	2m4f Hdl yield	£8,165
	10/20	Fair	2m Mdn Hdl yield	£6,500
	2/20	Gowr	2m1f NHF 4-7yo heavy	£5,500

Fine second in last season's Mares' Hurdle at Cheltenham, finishing placed at the meeting for the second time after the 2020 Champion Bumper; has been very lightly raced in the meantime, missing nearly a year through injury, but improved with every run last term.

Quel Destin (Fr)

7 ch g Muhtathir - High Destiny (High Yield)

Paul Nicholls — Martin Broughton & Friends

PLACINGS: /F12111115/18512/2P/ — RPR **154h**

Starts	1st	2nd	3rd	4th	Win & Pl
18	8	3	-	1	£201,021

	Date	Course	Race	Prize
	2/20	Sand	2m Cls1 List Hdl heavy	£17,286
	10/19	Chel	2m½f Cls2 Hdl 4yo heavy	£25,024
	2/19	Hayd	1m7½f Cls2 Hdl 4yo gd-sft	£12,996
	12/18	Chep	2m Cls1 Gd1 Hdl 3yo soft	£37,018
	12/18	Donc	2m½f Cls1 Gd2 Hdl 3yo good	£28,135
	11/18	Chel	2m½f Cls1 Gd2 Hdl 3yo good	£18,006
	10/18	Kemp	2m Cls3 Hdl 3yo good	£6,498
	5/18	Autl	1m7f Hdl 3yo heavy	£19,115

Smart hurdler at his peak and built on Grade 1 juvenile success by winning a strong Listed hurdle at Sandown in 2020 (unlucky not to also land a Grade 2 at Fontwell); disappointing in two runs over fences the following season and missed last term through injury.

Quick Wave (Fr)

9 b m Gentlewave - Magicaldoun (Kaldoun)

Venetia Williams — Ms Sharon Kinsella

PLACINGS: 4244/2/P212/F5165/1- — RPR **150+c**

Starts	1st	2nd	3rd	4th	Win & Pl
17	3	4	-	3	£52,045

	Date	Course	Race	Prize
133	1/22	Ludl	3m1½f Cls3 122-140 Ch Hcap soft	£7,951
130	2/21	Catt	3m1f Cls3 107-130 Ch Hcap heavy	£7,018
118	2/20	Leic	2m4f Cls3 111-132 Ch Hcap heavy	£7,668

Hugely impressive on sole run last season when a 14-length winner of a 3m1f handicap chase at Ludlow, apparently rejuvenated by wind surgery having lost her way in early 2021; had won twice (by eight lengths) and finished second twice in first four chase runs in Britain prior to that.

Red Rookie

7 ch g Black Sam Bellamy - Auction Belle (Auction House)

Emma Lavelle — The Hawk Inn Syndicate 3

PLACINGS: 3/11/514/2F1F- RPR **149+c**

Starts	1st	2nd	3rd	4th	Win & Pl
9	4	1	-	1	£21,255

	Date	Course	Race	Prize
	1/22	Hrfd	2m Cls3 Nov Ch gd-sft	£9,367
	2/21	Sand	2m Cls4 Nov Hdl heavy	£3,769
	3/20	Uttx	2m Cls5 NHF 4-6yo heavy	£2,859
	1/20	Extr	2m1f Cls5 NHF 4-6yo heavy	£2,274

Developed into a useful novice chaser last season despite getting round only twice; won at Hereford and finished a neck second at Chepstow either side of a fall at Ascot; far from disgraced in the Arkle at Cheltenham, outrunning odds of 80-1 until falling at the last.

Remastered

9 ch g Network - Cathodine Cayras (Martaline)

David Pipe — Brocade Racing

PLACINGS: 2/052P33/1115/3F249- RPR **155+c**

Starts	1st	2nd	3rd	4th	Win & Pl
22	5	5	3	1	£69,254

	Date	Course	Race	Prize
	2/21	Asct	3m Cls1 Nov Gd2 Ch soft	£16,819
	12/20	Weth	3m Cls4 Nov Ch heavy	£4,289
	11/20	Carl	2m4f Cls3 Nov Ch heavy	£7,018
	11/18	Ffos	2m Cls4 Nov Hdl heavy	£4,159
	2/18	Chep	2m Cls5 NHF 4-6yo heavy	£2,274

Useful staying chaser who looked a big threat when falling four out in the Ladbrokes Trophy last season but finished weakly when again shaping promisingly on next two runs at Haydock; had wind surgery after final chase run, though disappointed back over hurdles subsequently.

Revels Hill (Ire)

7 b g Mahler - Chlolo Supreme (Supreme Leader)

Harry Fry — Noel Fehily Racing Syndicates-Revels Hil

PLACINGS: U1/604P1/42U11- RPR **143+c**

Starts	1st	2nd	3rd	4th	Win & Pl
10	3	1	-	2	£21,847

	Date	Course	Race	Prize
129	3/22	Tntn	3m4½f Cls3 113-132 Ch Hcap soft	£7,951
122	2/22	Tntn	2m7f Cls3 113-132 Ch Hcap gd-sft	£7,951
116	4/21	Wwck	2m5f Cls4 101-118 Hdl Hcap good	£3,159

Progressive young chaser who finished novice campaign on a high last season when easily winning last two races at Taunton; particularly impressive when stepped up to 3m4f on final run and should have bigger staying handicaps on his agenda.

Riviere D'Etel (Fr)

5 gr m Martaline - Angesse (Indian River)

Gordon Elliott (Ire) — Bective Stud

PLACINGS: 2137/1112253- RPR **152+c**

Starts	1st	2nd	3rd	4th	Win & Pl
11	4	3	2	-	£111,976

	Date	Course	Race	Prize
	12/21	Navn	2m1f Nov Gd3 Ch yield	£17,121
	11/21	Punc	2m1f Nov Gd2 Ch yield	£18,438
	10/21	Fair	2m Ch good	£5,795
	12/20	Punc	2m Mdn Hdl 3yo heavy	£6,000

Smart mare who flourished when sent chasing as a four-year-old last season, winning three times before the turn of the year; twice second at Grade I level but proved less effective in the spring when only fifth in the Arkle at Cheltenham and third at Punchestown.

Ronald Pump

9 ch g Schiaparelli - Fruit Yoghurt (Hernando)

Matthew Smith (Ire) — Laois Limerick Syndicate

PLACINGS: 2242/F2/3525752F-723 RPR **157c**

Starts	1st	2nd	3rd	4th	Win & Pl
34	5	7	3	6	£246,072

	Date	Course	Race	Prize
	11/19	Fair	2m5f Ch heavy	£6,389
136	4/19	Fair	3m Nov 112-136 Hdl Hcap gd-yld	£29,234
123	3/19	Cork	3m 108-130 Hdl Hcap soft	£9,989
108	1/19	Fair	3m 81-108 Hdl Hcap good	£6,659
102	12/18	Cork	2m4f Nov 80-102 Hdl Hcap sft-hvy	£5,996

Four-time runner-up at Grade I level, chasing home Honeysuckle in the last two runnings of the Hatton's Grace Hurdle; very nearly took advantage of lower chase mark when second in the Leinster National last spring and ran well in the Irish Grand National until falling at the last.

Rouge Vif (Fr)

8 b g Sageburg - Rouge Amour (Cadoudal)

Harry Whittington — Kate & Andrew Brooks

PLACINGS: 113/14213/1349/434-F RPR **152c**

Starts	1st	2nd	3rd	4th	Win & Pl
21	7	3	4	4	£187,432

	Date	Course	Race	Prize
156	10/20	Chel	2m Cls2 135-161 Ch Hcap good	£30,029
	2/20	Wwck	2m Cls1 Nov Gd2 Ch gd-sft	£22,780
	10/19	MRas	2m1f Cls3 Nov Ch gd-sft	£7,988
	3/19	Kels	2m2f Cls1 Nov Gd2 Hdl gd-sft	£28,475
	1/19	Newc	2m Cls4 Nov Hdl soft	£4,094
	12/18	Sthl	1m7½f Cls4 Mdn Hdl gd-sft	£4,094
	3/18	Ludl	2m Cls4 NHF 4-6yo soft	£4,809

One-time promising young chaser for Harry Whittington, finishing third in the Tingle Creek in 2020, but nowhere near that level since then, including for Paul Nicholls last season; now back with Whittington after £40,000 sale in June off much-reduced handicap mark.

Royal Rendezvous (Ire)

10 b g King's Theatre - Novacella (Beyssac)

Willie Mullins (Ire) — Dr S P Fitzgerald

PLACINGS: 111/P1351/2/01112P-1 — RPR **165+c**

Starts	1st	2nd	3rd	4th	Win & Pl
17	9	2	1	-	£300,782

160	4/22	Punc	2m5f 134-160 Ch Hcap gd-yld	£49,580
	10/21	Gowr	2m4f Gd2 Ch good	£19,063
153	7/21	Gway	2m6½f 140-158 Ch Hcap good	£131,696
	5/21	Baln	2m2f Hdl sft-hvy	£6,058
	3/20	Naas	2m4f Nov Gd3 Ch soft	£16,250
	11/19	Thur	2m2f Ch soft	£6,389
	10/18	Gway	2m½f Mdn Hdl yield	£7,632
	10/18	Tipp	2m NHF 4-7yo good	£7,087
	8/18	Dpat	2m3f NHF 4-7yo gd-yld	£5,451

Held up by injury through his career but has still developed into a very smart chaser over the last 18 months; gained his biggest win in the 2021 Galway Plate and went on to add a Grade 2 at Gowran and a valuable handicap at Punchestown; prefers good ground.

Royale Pagaille (Fr)

8 b g Blue Bresil - Royale Cazoumaille (Villez)

Venetia Williams — Mrs S Ricci

PLACINGS: /F5U2/23/1116/21255- — RPR **171+c**

Starts	1st	2nd	3rd	4th	Win & Pl
21	5	5	2	-	£256,209

163	1/22	Hayd	3m1½f Cls1 Gd2 143-163 Ch Hcap soft	£42,713
156	1/21	Hayd	3m1½f Cls1 Gd2 136-156 Ch Hcap heavy	£27,036
140	12/20	Kemp	3m Cls2 129-147 Ch Hcap soft	£25,024
	12/20	Hayd	2m5½f Cls2 Nov Ch heavy	£12,021
	1/18	Pau	2m½f Hdl 4yo heavy	£13,593

High-class staying chaser who has won his last four races on soft/heavy ground, including a brilliant victory under top weight in last season's Peter Marsh; not quite at that level on a quicker surface, though still second in the Denman Chase and fifth in the Cheltenham Gold Cup.

Run Wild Fred (Ire)

8 ch g Shantou - Talkin Madam (Talkin Man)

Gordon Elliott (Ire) — Gigginstown House Stud

PLACINGS: 31F1/3455222/2122FF- — RPR **157+c**

Starts	1st	2nd	3rd	4th	Win & Pl
21	5	6	3	1	£225,369

145	11/21	Navn	3m 124-149 Ch Hcap good	£42,143
	2/20	Punc	3m Nov Gd3 Hdl heavy	£17,500
	12/19	Navn	2m4f Mdn Hdl soft	£7,188
	3/19	Limk	2m NHF 5-7yo heavy	£6,382
	1/19	Fair	2m NHF 5-7yo good	£5,827

Smart staying chaser who deservedly landed a valuable handicap chase in last season's Troytown having finished second in the Thyestes and Irish Grand National in 2021; didn't quite build on that back in novice company (second when favourite at Leopardstown and Cheltenham).

Saint Calvados (Fr)

9 b g Saint Des Saints - Lamorrese (Pistolet Bleu)

Paul Nicholls — Kate & Andrew Brooks

PLACINGS: 4/1336/1422/4U/3P51- — RPR **165+c**

Starts	1st	2nd	3rd	4th	Win & Pl
22	9	2	3	3	£376,180

	4/22	Sand	2m6½f Cls1 Gd2 Ch good	£45,560
155	10/19	Chel	2m Cls2 129-155 Ch Hcap heavy	£37,164
	11/18	Naas	2m Gd3 Ch yield	£17,688
	2/18	Wwck	2m Cls1 Nov Gd2 Ch soft	£22,780
147	1/18	Newb	2m½f Cls3 Nov 135-147 Ch Hcap soft	£7,343
143	12/17	Newb	2m½f Cls3 Nov 127-143 Ch Hcap heavy	£8,656
	3/17	Autl	2m2f Hdl 4yo v soft	£28,718
	12/16	Cagn	2m1½f Hdl 3yo soft	£15,882
	11/16	Fntb	2m2f Hdl 3yo heavy	£8,118

Gained a first win for two and a half years when winning the Oaksey Chase at Sandown in April; hasn't convinced with his stamina in three runs over 3m (best run when third in last season's King George) but trainer convinced he stays and plans to campaign him in top staying races.

Saint Felicien (Fr)

5 br g Saint Des Saints - In Race (Sageburg)

Gordon Elliott (Ire) — Robcour

PLACINGS: 1/12P- — RPR **153+h**

Starts	1st	2nd	3rd	4th	Win & Pl
4	2	1	-	-	£30,965

	11/21	Gowr	2m Nov Hdl 4yo yield	£7,112
	3/21	Autl	2m1½f Hdl 4yo v soft	£19,304

Lightly raced and highly rated French recruit who was sent off favourite for last season's Coral Cup on just his fourth run only to be pulled up; had made a winning Irish debut at Gowran before a solid second behind Darasso when stepped up in class at Naas.

Saint Palais (Fr)

5 b g Saint Des Saints - Ladies Choice (Turgeon)

Richard J Bandey — Tim Syder

PLACINGS: 8/2322/11141- — RPR **154+c**

Starts	1st	2nd	3rd	4th	Win & Pl
10	4	3	1	1	£48,709

145	3/22	Uttx	3m Cls2 Nov 124-145 Ch Hcap soft	£20,931
135	12/21	Newb	3m2f Cls3 115-135 Ch Hcap soft	£10,130
125	12/21	Weth	3m Cls3 115-137 Ch Hcap gd-sft	£6,100
118	10/21	Worc	2m7f Cls4 Nov 111-122 Ch Hcap soft	£3,594

Smart and progressive novice chaser last season; won four out of five races, all in handicaps to climb 35lb in the weights; suffered sole defeat when last of four behind Ahoy Senor at Wetherby but got back on track when winning a good novice handicap at Uttoxeter.

Saint Roi (Fr)

7 br g Coastal Path - Sainte Vigne (Saint Des Saints)

Willie Mullins (Ire) — John P McManus

PLACINGS: 3/511/1244/344-43 — RPR **159h**

Starts	1st	2nd	3rd	4th	Win & Pl
13	3	1	3	5	£168,974

	10/20	Tipp	2m Gd3 Hdl good	£17,500
137	3/20	Chel	2m1f Cls1 Gd3 133-150 Hdl Hcap soft	£56,270
	1/20	Tram	2m Mdn Hdl soft	£5,760

Looked a Champion Hurdle horse at one time, notably when winning the County Hurdle in 2020, but has come up short in seven attempts at Grade I level; third behind Sharjah first time out last season and fourth behind Honeysuckle three times, failing to get within seven lengths of her.

Saint Sam (Fr)

5 b g Saint Des Saints - Ladeka (Linda's Lad)

Willie Mullins (Ire) — Edward Ware

PLACINGS: 9112422/513U-6 — RPR **153+c**

Starts	1st	2nd	3rd	4th	Win & Pl
12	3	3	1	1	£81,126

1/22	Fair	2m1f Ch soft	£8,165
7/20	Claf	2m1f Hdl 3yo soft	£10,983
6/20	Diep	2m1f Hdl 3yo soft	£8,258

Highly talented chaser who might well have won a Grade I novice chase last season but for suspect jumping; finished third at Leopardstown despite several mistakes and held every chance when blundering two out at Punchestown, both times behind Blue Lord.

Saldier (Fr)

8 b g Soldier Hollow - Salve Evita (Monsun)

Willie Mullins (Ire) — Mrs S Ricci

PLACINGS: 1531/F/1/667/8115P6- — RPR **155h**

Starts	1st	2nd	3rd	4th	Win & Pl
15	5	-	1	-	£276,045

	10/21	Tipp	2m Gd3 Hdl yield	£18,438
155	7/21	Gway	2m 132-155 Hdl Hcap good	£131,696
	11/19	Punc	2m½f Gd1 Hdl soft	£53,153
	4/18	Punc	2m Gd1 Hdl 4yo yld-sft	£52,212
	2/18	Gowr	2m Mdn Hdl 4yo heavy	£7,359

One-time Champion Hurdle favourite who has proved largely disappointing since a year layoff following 2019 Morgiana Hurdle win; bounced back to land the Galway Hurdle last summer but no better than fifth in three runs through the winter.

Salvador Ziggy (Ire)

6 b g El Salvador - Doncisha (Westerner)

Gordon Elliott (Ire) — William Hurley & Mrs Aisling Hurley

PLACINGS: 34/28178-1111 — RPR **146+h**

Starts	1st	2nd	3rd	4th	Win & Pl
11	5	1	1	1	£40,678

8/22	DRoy	3m Hdl good	£7,685
7/22	Gway	2m4½f Nov Hdl good	£10,908
7/22	Rosc	2m4f Nov Hdl good	£8,181
5/22	Punc	2m3½f Mdn Hdl good	£5,950
9/21	List	2m4f NHF 5-7yo good	£5,268

Proved a revelation this summer having moved to Gordon Elliott following two modest runs in novice hurdles for James Fahey; completed a four-timer when giving 6lb to more experienced

hurdlers at Down Royal in August, relishing a step up to 3m; looks a smart novice.

Sam Brown

10 b g Black Sam Bellamy - Cream Cracker (Sir Harry Lewis)

Anthony Honeyball — T C Frost

PLACINGS: 11/41/11P/3/732P1- RPR **162+c**

Starts	1st	2nd	3rd	4th	Win & Pl
13	6	1	2	1	£116,609

147	4/22	Aint	3m1f Cls1 Gd3 130-155 Ch Hcap gd-sft	£56,319
	1/20	Hayd	2m4f Cls1 Nov Gd2 Ch heavy	£18,793
	1/20	Ling	2m7½f Cls4 Nov Ch heavy	£4,289
	12/17	Plum	2m4½f Cls4 Nov Hdl soft	£3,249
	3/17	Newb	2m½f Cls5 NHF 4-6yo soft	£2,599
	2/17	Winc	1m7½f Cls6 NHF 4-6yo heavy	£1,949

Fragile gelding who remains very lightly raced for his age but underlined his ability when finally getting a clear run last season, notably when hacking up in a 3m1f handicap chase at Aintree on Grand National day; likely to return this season for the National itself.

Samarrive (Fr)

5 b g Coastal Path - Sambirane (Apeldoorn)

Paul Nicholls — Mrs Johnny De La Hey

PLACINGS: 11/71P91- RPR **144+h**

Starts	1st	2nd	3rd	4th	Win & Pl
7	4	-	-	-	£58,451

137	4/22	Sand	2m4f Cls2 121-141 Hdl Hcap good	£18,211
130	12/21	Sand	2m Cls1 List 123-149 Hdl Hcap gd-sft	£28,475
	4/21	Kemp	2m Cls4 Nov Hdl good	£3,159
	12/20	Ange	2m1f Hdl 3yo heavy	£8,258

Arrived with a big reputation from France and has gone some way to justifying the billing by winning three times in Britain; disappointing in valuable handicaps at Ascot and Sandown last term but seemed to relish step up to 2m4f when winning in calmer waters on final run.

Santa Rossa (Ire)

8 b m Jeremy - Panther Moon (Almutawakel I)

Dermot McLoughlin (Ire) — Mrs P J Conway

PLACINGS: 113/53/1/12-516 RPR **148+h**

Starts	1st	2nd	3rd	4th	Win & Pl
11	5	1	2	-	£120,883

	6/22	Tipp	2m Gd3 Hdl yield	£34,706
	3/22	Limk	2m Hdl gd-yld	£6,941
	3/21	Navn	2m Mdn Hdl yld-sft	£6,321
	2/19	Leop	2m Gd2 NHF 4-7yo good	£46,509
	12/18	Fair	2m NHF 4yo gd-yld	£6,542

Lightly raced mare who won a Grade 2 bumper in 2019 but has twice had hurdling career punctuated by absences of more than a year; returned with a win at Limerick in March and has continued to progress since, notably landing a Grade 3 at Tipperary in June.

Sceau Royal (right): classy operator over fences and hurdles at around 2m

Scarlet And Dove (Ire)

8 b m Jeremy - Dark Mimosa (Bahri)

Joseph O'Brien (Ire) — Gigginstown House Stud

PLACINGS: /514/221F115/223P3-1 RPR **152+c**

Starts	1st	2nd	3rd	4th	Win & Pl
17	6	4	2	1	£140,051

	4/22	Punc	2m5f Gd2 Ch gd-yld	£39,664
	3/21	Limk	2m6½f Nov Gd2 Ch heavy	£22,388
	3/21	Navn	2m Nov Gd3 Ch soft	£18,438
	12/20	Limk	2m3½f Ch heavy	£6,250
	3/20	Navn	2m Mdn Hdl heavy	£6,750
	11/18	Limk	2m NHF 4-7yo yield	£5,451

Smart mare who gained an overdue win when slamming Elimay by 15 lengths in a Grade 2 at Punchestown last season; hadn't won since scoring in the same grade as a novice in 2021 but ran well several times in defeat last term, including a half-length third at the Cheltenham Festival.

Sceau Royal (Fr)

10 b g Doctor Dino - Sandside (Marchand De Sable)

Alan King — Simon Munir & Isaac Souede

PLACINGS: 25/1124F153/1136232- RPR **168c**

Starts	1st	2nd	3rd	4th	Win & Pl
44	16	9	6	3	£627,619

	11/21	Winc	1m7f Cls1 Gd2 Hdl good	£34,170
	10/21	Kemp	2m Cls1 List Hdl good	£22,780
	2/21	Newb	2m½f Cls1 Gd2 Ch gd-sft	£25,628
	11/20	Winc	1m7½f Cls1 Gd2 Hdl good	£27,336
150	10/20	Ffos	2m Cls2 134-154 Hdl Hcap gd-sft	£25,024
	11/18	Chel	2m Cls1 Gd2 Ch good	£42,203
	1/18	Donc	2m½f Cls1 Nov Gd2 Ch soft	£19,933
	12/17	Sand	1m7½f Cls1 Nov Gd1 Ch gd-sft	£29,810
	11/17	Wwck	2m Cls3 Nov Ch 4-5yo gd-sft	£9,384
	10/17	Wwck	2m Cls4 Nov Ch good	£5,198
149	11/16	Winc	1m7½f Cls1 Gd2 133-149 Hdl Hcap good	£35,772
	10/16	Chel	2m½f Cls2 Hdl 4yo good	£21,977
	1/16	Hntg	2m Cls2 Hdl 4yo soft	£12,512
	12/15	Chel	2m1f Cls2 Hdl 3yo soft	£12,628
	11/15	Wwck	2m Cls4 Hdl 3yo gd-sft	£3,249
	3/15	Bord	2m½f Hdl 3yo v soft	£7,814

Has failed to win in 15 attempts at Grade 1 level outside novice company but has done well over hurdles and fences just below that level, including when winning last season's Elite Hurdle; stayed well enough into third when trying 2m4f for the first time in the Melling Chase at Aintree.

Screaming Colours (Ire)

11 b g Dubai Destination - Colour Scheme (Perrault)

William Durkan (Ire) — Ms M Durkan

PLACINGS: 61/58/15/12224/214-P RPR **155+c**

Starts	1st	2nd	3rd	4th	Win & Pl
15	3	4	-	2	£147,200

142	3/22	Uttx	4m2f Cls1 List 133-159 Ch Hcap soft	£84,405
116	11/20	Punc	3m1½f 90-116 Ch Hcap heavy	£5,500
	4/18	Fair	2m½f Ch sft-hvy	£8,177

Veteran stayer who thoroughly deserved last season's win in the Midlands National at Uttoxeter having finished second four times since previous victory at Punchestown in 2020; hit hard by the handicapper but ran another big race when fourth in the Irish Grand National.

Seabank Bistro (Ire)

5 gr g Walk In The Park - Sigh Of Relief (Old Vic)

Willie Mullins (Ire) — Jodmart Construction

PLACINGS: 14-6 — RPR **130b**

Starts	1st	2nd	3rd	4th	Win & Pl
3	1	-	-	1	£10,310

	1/22	Naas	2m3f NHF 5-7yo yield	£5,206

Not far off the best bumper horses last season, finishing fourth in the Champion Bumper at Cheltenham on just his second run before disappointing at Punchestown; had won over 2m3f first time out and should prove a strong stayer over hurdles.

Secret Investor

10 b g Kayf Tara - Silver Charmer (Charmer)

Paul Nicholls — Hills Of Ledbury

PLACINGS: 721/1122411/202/101/ — RPR **167c**

Starts	1st	2nd	3rd	4th	Win & Pl
19	7	8	-	1	£145,798

	2/21	Newb	2m7½f Cls1 Gd2 Ch gd-sft	£25,748
153	10/20	Chep	2m7½f Cls2 137-156 Ch Hcap good	£15,825
	4/19	Ayr	2m4½f Cls1 Nov Gd2 Ch good	£25,979
	3/19	Winc	2m4f Cls4 Nov Ch good	£5,523
	10/18	Chep	2m3½f Cls1 Nov Gd2 Hdl gd-sft	£22,780
	5/18	Kemp	3m½f Cls4 Nov Hdl good	£4,194
	4/18	Strf	2m6f Cls4 Nov Hdl gd-sft	£6,758

Missed last season through injury but had been in career-best form when last seen, winning the Denman Chase at Newbury by a neck from Clan Des Obeaux; tends to be lightly raced in search of good ground (has never won on soft).

Serious Charges (Ire)

5 b g Soldier Of Fortune - South West Nine (Oscar)

Anthony Honeyball — Potwell Racing Syndicate III

PLACINGS: 2/21116- — RPR **138+h**

Starts	1st	2nd	3rd	4th	Win & Pl
5	3	1	-	-	£19,575

120	3/22	Uttx	2m7½f Cls3 114-126 Hdl Hcap soft	£7,788
	2/22	Font	2m5½f Cls4 Nov Hdl gd-sft	£5,827
	1/22	Extr	2m½f Cls4 Mdn Hdl gd-sft	£4,085

Lightly raced gelding who won his first three races over hurdles last season, including an impressive handicap debut at Uttoxeter when stepped up to 3m for the first time; only sixth when favourite to follow up at Aintree's Grand National meeting; likely to go novice chasing.

Shadow Rider (Fr)

8 ch g Martaline - Samansonnienne (Mansonnien)

Willie Mullins (Ire) — John P McManus

PLACINGS: 1/3173/1- — RPR **140+c**

Starts	1st	2nd	3rd	4th	Win & Pl
5	2	-	2	-	£15,799

	3/22	Gowr	2m4f Ch heavy	£6,445
	12/20	Limk	2m4f Mdn Hdl heavy	£6,000

Talented but fragile gelding who has run just five times under rules since point-to-point win in February 2018; failed to build on maiden win over hurdles but instantly looked better over fences on sole run last season, easily making all when odds-on at Gowran in March.

Shakem Up'Arry (Ire)

8 b g Flemensfirth - Nun Better (Presenting)

Ben Pauling — Harry Redknapp

PLACINGS: 3/F220/14280/U1323- — RPR **144+c**

Starts	1st	2nd	3rd	4th	Win & Pl
15	2	4	3	1	£45,941

131	12/21	Hayd	2m½f Cls3 121-131 Ch Hcap soft	£7,624
	11/20	Ffos	2m Cls4 Nov Hdl soft	£3,769

Finished second in the Tolworth over hurdles and expected to do much better as a chaser last term but couldn't quite build on impressive win at Haydock; still a fair second in a good novice handicap at Newbury and third in the Red Rum at Aintree; open to further improvement.

Shan Blue (Ire)

8 b g Shantou - Lady Roberta (Bob Back)

Dan Skelton — Colm Donlon

PLACINGS: 3/2F1326/111252/F62- — RPR **166+c**

Starts	1st	2nd	3rd	4th	Win & Pl
16	4	5	2	-	£127,186

	12/20	Kemp	3m Cls1 Nov Gd1 Ch gd-sft	£45,774
	10/20	Weth	3m Cls4 Nov Ch gd-sft	£4,289
	10/20	Weth	2m3½f Cls4 Nov Ch gd-sft	£4,289
	12/19	Sthl	1m7½f Cls5 Mdn Hdl heavy	£2,794

Looked a big improver first time out last season only to fall heavily three out when well clear in the Charlie Hall Chase; out for more than four months before disappointing in the Ryanair at Cheltenham but did much better when second in handicap company at Aintree.

Shantreusse (Ire)

6 b g Shantou - Shocona (Oscar Schindler)

Henry de Bromhead (Ire) — Anthony Head

PLACINGS: 21/2110- — RPR **138+h**

Starts	1st	2nd	3rd	4th	Win & Pl
6	3	2	-	-	£33,013

	2/22	Clon	3m Nov Gd3 Hdl heavy	£17,353
	1/22	Cork	3m Mdn Hdl heavy	£6,321
	4/21	Clon	2m NHF 4-7yo yld-sft	£5,268

Very useful staying novice hurdler last season; won a maiden at Cork by 17 lengths before comfortably following up in a Grade 3 at Clonmel, both on heavy ground; possibly unsuited by quicker ground when well beaten in the Albert Bartlett; likely to go novice chasing.

Shishkin: brilliant 2m performer who has won twice at the Cheltenham Festival

Sharjah (Fr)

9 b g Doctor Dino - Saaryeh (Royal Academy)

Willie Mullins (Ire) — Mrs S Ricci

PLACINGS: 31311B/4162/132/211- — RPR **161+**h

Starts	1st	2nd	3rd	4th	Win & Pl
23	9	3	3	2	£779,878

	12/21	Leop	2m Gd1 Hdl yld-sft	£79,018
	11/21	Punc	2m Gd1 Hdl gd-yld	£52,679
	12/20	Leop	2m Gd1 Hdl soft	£50,000
	12/19	Leop	2m Gd1 Hdl yield	£66,441
	12/18	Leop	2m Gd1 Hdl gd-yld	£65,265
	11/18	Punc	2m Gd1 Hdl good	£52,212
146	8/18	Gway	2m 135-146 Hdl Hcap soft	£156,637
	11/17	Gowr	2m Nov Hdl 4yo heavy	£8,161
	9/17	Gowr	2m Mdn Hdl 4yo heavy	£6,844

Top-class 2m hurdler who matched Istabraq and Hurricane Fly with a fourth successive Matheson Hurdle at Leopardstown last Christmas, making it six Grade I wins overall; missed the Champion Hurdle with a hip injury having finished second in the two previous runnings.

Shishkin (Ire)

8 b g Sholokhov - Labarynth (Exit To Nowhere)

Nicky Henderson — Mrs J Donnelly

PLACINGS: 3/11/F111/11111/11P- — RPR **181+**c

Starts	1st	2nd	3rd	4th	Win & Pl
13	11	-	-	-	£391,521

1/22	Asct	2m1f Cls1 Gd1 Ch soft	£85,425
12/21	Kemp	2m Cls1 Gd2 Ch soft	£56,950
4/21	Aint	2m Cls1 Nov Gd1 Ch gd-sft	£42,701
3/21	Chel	2m Cls1 Nov Gd1 Ch soft	£73,854
1/21	Donc	2m½f Cls1 Nov Gd2 Ch soft	£14,682
12/20	Kemp	2m Cls1 Nov Gd2 Ch soft	£18,224
11/20	Kemp	2m2f Cls4 Ch good	£4,394
3/20	Chel	2m½f Cls1 Nov Gd1 Hdl soft	£70,338
2/20	Hntg	2m3½f Cls1 Nov List Hdl gd-sft	£17,286
1/20	Newb	2m½f Cls4 Nov Hdl heavy	£4,549
3/19	Kemp	2m Cls5 Mdn NHF 4-6yo gd-sft	£3,119

Brilliant 2m chaser who took unbeaten record over jumps to ten races when winning an epic clash with Energumene in last season's Clarence House Chase at Ascot; pulled up early in the Champion Chase and subsequently found to be suffering from a rare bone condition.

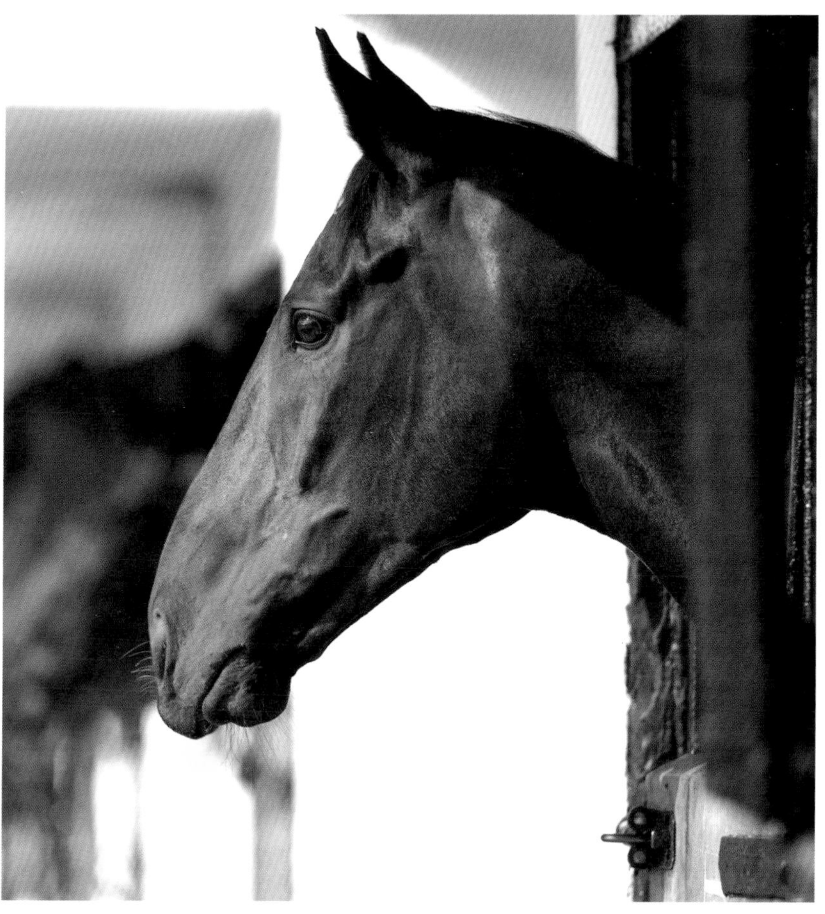

Silent Revolution (Ire)

6 b g Sholokhov - Watson River (Presenting)

Paul Nicholls — Colm Donlon

PLACINGS: 213/1P1- — RPR **133+h**

Starts	1st	2nd	3rd	4th	Win & Pl
6	3	1	1	-	£12,854

4/22	Chep	2m Cls4 Nov Hdl good	£5,446
11/21	Newb	2m½f Cls4 Nov Hdl good	£4,085
12/20	Hntg	2m Cls5 NHF 4-6yo soft	£2,274

Won two out of three in novice hurdles last season, with sole defeat coming when thrown in at the deep end in the Supreme at Cheltenham (pulled up); bounced back at a more realistic level when winning at Chepstow and looks one for good handicaps.

Silver Forever (Ire)

8 gr m Jeremy - Silver Prayer (Roselier)

Paul Nicholls — Colm Donlon

PLACINGS: 11312/1131/11- — RPR **151+c**

Starts	1st	2nd	3rd	4th	Win & Pl
10	7	1	2	-	£69,723

12/21	Newb	2m7½f Cls1 List Ch gd-sft	£15,661
11/21	Newb	2m6½f Cls3 Ch good	£7,080
1/20	Sand	2m4f Cls1 List Hdl soft	£12,529
11/19	Newb	2m½f Cls2 Nov Hdl gd-sft	£12,996
10/19	Chep	2m3½f Cls4 Nov Hdl soft	£4,159
2/19	Asct	1m7½f Cls4 NHF 4-6yo gd-sft	£4,549
11/18	Chep	2m Cls5 NHF 4-6yo soft	£2,274

Smart and lightly raced mare who won a Listed novice chase at Newbury last December to match hurdles win in the same grade at the start of 2021; had the Mares' Chase at Cheltenham as her aim at the time but missed the rest of the season with a recurrence of a pelvis injury.

Simply The Betts (Ire)

9 b g Arcadio - Crimson Flower (Soviet Lad)

Paul Nicholls — Kate & Andrew Brooks

PLACINGS: /1184/11211/6/6P252- — RPR **160c**

Starts	1st	2nd	3rd	4th	Win & Pl
20	7	4	1	2	£156,067

149	3/20	Chel	2m4½f Cls1 Gd3 140-157 Ch Hcap soft	£61,897
140	1/20	Chel	2m4½f Cls2 Nov 121-147 Ch Hcap soft	£17,204
132	11/19	Newc	2m½f Cls3 Nov 125-132 Ch Hcap heavy	£7,018
125	11/19	Chep	2m Cls3 Nov 109-127 Ch Hcap soft	£7,018
	10/18	Hexm	2m Cls4 Nov Hdl soft	£4,159
	5/18	Wwck	2m Cls5 Mdn Hdl good	£3,249
	9/17	MRas	2m½f Cls6 NHF 4-6yo good	£1,560

Pulled off a big double at Cheltenham two seasons ago, winning two novice handicap chases including at the festival; hasn't quite built on that since, though did finish second in two more handicaps over the same course and distance last term; prefers soft ground.

Sir Gerhard (Ire)

7 b g Jeremy - Faanan Aldaar (Authorized)

Willie Mullins (Ire) — Cheveley Park Stud

PLACINGS: 1/111/3111-3 — RPR **157+h**

Starts	1st	2nd	3rd	4th	Win & Pl
8	6	-	2	-	£223,692

	3/22	Chel	2m5f Cls1 Nov Gd1 Hdl soft	£76,030
	2/22	Leop	2m Nov Gd1 Hdl yld-sft	£74,370
	12/21	Leop	2m Mdn Hdl soft	£7,902
	3/21	Chel	2m½f Cls1 Gd1 NHF 4-6yo gd-sft	£31,652
	12/20	Navn	2m List NHF 4-7yo sft-hvy	£11,250
	10/20	DRoy	2m½f NHF 4-7yo soft	£5,000

Dual Cheltenham Festival winner, adding last season's Ballymore to 2021 Champion Bumper victory; coped with step up to 2m5f that day, though had been more impressive over 2m at Leopardstown; subsequently beaten at odds-on at Punchestown for second successive year.

Sire Du Berlais (Fr)

10 b g Poliglote - Royale Athenia (Garde Royale)

Gordon Elliott (Ire) — John P McManus

PLACINGS: 618/4941/132/2P401-4 — RPR **165h**

Starts	1st	2nd	3rd	4th	Win & Pl
24	5	3	3	5	£370,107

	4/22	Aint	3m½f Cls1 Gd1 Hdl gd-sft	£140,325
	11/20	Navn	2m4f Gd2 Hdl sft-hvy	£17,500
152	3/20	Chel	3m Cls1 Gd3 131-152 Hdl Hcap soft	£56,270
145	3/19	Chel	3m Cls1 Gd3 134-148 Hdl Hcap gd-sft	£56,270
	5/16	Comp	2m1f Hdl 4yo v soft	£7,765

Veteran staying hurdler who landed a first Grade 1 win when brilliantly beating Flooring Porter at Aintree last season; below his best otherwise and managed only 11th when going for a third win in the Pertemps Final at Cheltenham having won back-to-back runnings in 2019 and 2020.

Sizing Pottsie (Fr)

8 b/br g Kapgarde - Line Salsa (Kingsalsa)

David Pipe — Ann & Alan Potts Limited

PLACINGS: 33U11F/521F5P/3U210- — RPR **153c**

Starts	1st	2nd	3rd	4th	Win & Pl
21	5	2	4	1	£102,307

	3/22	Navn	2m Gd2 Ch soft	£18,097
149	12/20	Fair	2m 132-156 Ch Hcap sft-hvy	£20,000
	3/20	Navn	2m Nov Gd3 Ch heavy	£21,250
	2/20	Fair	2m1½f Ch heavy	£8,500
	3/18	Leop	2m NHF 4yo soft	£6,269

New recruit for David Pipe having been bought for 95,000gns in May; had been a smart 2m chaser for Jessica Harrington, beating Master McShee in a Grade 2 at Navan last season having twice finished second at that level in the past.

Skytastic (Fr)

6 b g Way Of Light - Verzasca (Sadler's Wells)

Sam Thomas — Walters Plant Hire

PLACINGS: 11/110- — RPR **134+h**

Starts	1st	2nd	3rd	4th	Win & Pl
5	4	-	-	-	£23,002

	2/22	Asct	2m3½f Cls2 Nov Hdl soft	£13,008
	1/22	Donc	2m3½f Cls4 Mdn Hdl 4-7yo good	£5,446
	2/21	Donc	2m½f Cls5 NHF 4-6yo gd-sft	£2,274
	11/20	Newb	2m½f Cls5 NHF 4-6yo good	£2,274

Exciting prospect who has won four out of five races under rules, including his first two novice hurdles last season at Doncaster and Ascot; lost unbeaten record when below par in a 3m Grade 1 at Aintree on sharp rise in class; likely to go novice chasing.

Snow Leopardess

10 gr m Martaline - Queen Soraya (Persian Bold)

Charlie Longsdon — A Fox-Pitt

PLACINGS: 31/1/92/321246/111P- — RPR **154+c**

Starts	1st	2nd	3rd	4th	Win & Pl
20	9	3	3	1	£225,644

	2/22	Extr	3m Cls1 List Ch soft	£18,596
140	12/21	Aint	3m2f Cls1 Gd3 136-162 Ch Hcap soft	£84,195
135	11/21	Bang	3m Cls2 125-147 Ch Hcap soft	£13,528
126	11/20	Hayd	3m1½f Cls2 122-142 Ch Hcap soft	£25,117
	9/17	Autl	2m3½f Hdl 5yo v soft	£20,513
123	3/17	Newb	2m4½f Cls1 Nov Gd2 116-132 Hdl Hcap gd-sft	£22,780
	11/16	Donc	2m3½f Cls4 Nov Hdl good	£4,549
	9/16	Gowr	2m List NHF 4-7yo good	£14,697
	2/16	Donc	2m½f Cls6 NHF 4-6yo good	£1,949

Smart staying mare who enjoyed a brilliant campaign last season, winning three times before being pulled up when just 10-1 for the Grand National; had won over the National fences in the Becher Chase before reverting to mares' company to land a Listed chase at Exeter.

Silver Forever: could continue to prove progressive over fences if returning to her best following injury

Soaring Glory (Ire)

7 b g Fame And Glory - Hapeney (Saddlers' Hall)

Jonjo O'Neill — P Hickey

PLACINGS: 112/12F314/1435- — RPR **152h**

Starts	1st	2nd	3rd	4th	Win & Pl
13	5	2	2	2	£141,145

143	10/21	Asct	1m7½f Cls1 List 118-144 Hdl Hcap soft	£23,919
133	2/21	Newb	2m½f Cls1 Gd3 129-152 Hdl Hcap gd-sft	£70,338
	10/20	Chep	2m Cls4 Nov Hdl good	£3,769
	11/19	Asct	1m7½f Cls4 NHF 4-6yo soft	£4,549
	10/19	Wwck	2m Cls5 NHF 4-6yo good	£2,599

Has a fine record in big-field handicap hurdles, landing a second valuable pot at Ascot last season after the 2021 Betfair Hurdle; again ran well in the Betfair when a close fifth last term (mistake two out) having finished third at Grade 1 level in the Christmas Hurdle.

Soldier Of Destiny (Ire)

6 b g Presenting - Sagarich (Sagamix)

Jamie Snowden — Sir Chips Keswick

PLACINGS: 342/145131- — RPR **141+c**

Starts	1st	2nd	3rd	4th	Win & Pl
7	2	1	1	2	£21,043

131	3/22	Hayd	2m4f Cls3 Nov 126-133 Ch Hcap good	£8,169
122	2/22	Ffos	2m3½f Cls4 Nov 109-122 Ch Hcap soft	£8,169

Exuberant front-running chaser who flourished following wind surgery last season, winning two of his last three races at around 2m4f; also ran well when third at Newbury in between after a final-fence blunder (stamina starting to fade at 3m); still very lightly raced.

Solo (Fr)

6 b g Kapgarde - Flameche (Balko)

Paul Nicholls — Mrs Johnny De La Hey

PLACINGS: 2118/45040/22367- — RPR **144c**

Starts	1st	2nd	3rd	4th	Win & Pl
14	2	3	1	2	£69,125

	2/20	Kemp	2m Cls1 Gd2 Hdl 4yo gd-sft	£17,085
	11/19	Autl	2m1½f Hdl 3yo heavy	£19,459

Looked a future star when hacking up in a Grade 2 at Kempton on British debut in 2020 but has failed to win since, proving bitterly disappointing; came closest when beaten a nose on chase debut last season and at least ran with credit twice more over fences.

Sounds Russian (Ire)

7 b g Sholokhov - Reevolesa (Revoque)

Ruth Jefferson — Claxby & Co

PLACINGS: 22241112- — RPR **152+c**

Starts	1st	2nd	3rd	4th	Win & Pl
8	3	4	-	1	£37,258

132	2/22	Kels	2m7½f Cls3 Nov 116-132 Ch Hcap heavy	£7,407
121	12/21	Kels	2m6½f Cls3 Nov 108-125 Ch Hcap heavy	£9,040
111	12/21	Sedg	2m5f Cls4 103-119 Ch Hcap soft	£3,594

Prolific novice chaser in modest company last season, winning three times by an aggregate of 48 lengths; ran a cracker when second to Dusart at Ayr on sharp step up in class, proving effectiveness on good to soft ground (all three wins on softer and most impressive on heavy).

Sporting John (Ire)

7 b/br g Getaway - Wild Spell (Oscar)

Philip Hobbs — John P McManus

PLACINGS: 1/1117/31FP/141- — RPR **157+h**

Starts	1st	2nd	3rd	4th	Win & Pl
11	6	-	1	1	£81,993

151	1/22	Wwck	3m1f Cls2 132-158 Hdl Hcap soft	£15,609
146	11/21	Chel	3m Cls1 List 125-146 Hdl Hcap good	£17,085
	2/21	Sand	2m4f Cls1 Nov Gd1 Ch heavy	£20,026
	2/20	Asct	2m3½f Cls2 Nov Hdl soft	£15,640
	12/19	Extr	2m1f Cls4 Nov Hdl 4-6yo soft	£4,224
	11/19	Extr	2m1f Cls3 Nov Hdl soft	£6,238

Did well back over hurdles last season having lost his way after winning a Grade 1 novice chase two seasons ago; won handicap hurdles at Cheltenham and Warwick and would have been a contender for the Pertemps Final or Stayers' Hurdle but for a late setback.

Stage Star (Ire)

6 b g Fame And Glory - Sparky May (Midnight Legend)

Paul Nicholls — Owners Group 044

PLACINGS: 123/111PP- — RPR **145+h**

Starts	1st	2nd	3rd	4th	Win & Pl
8	4	1	1	-	£53,920

	12/21	Newb	2m4½f Cls1 Nov Gd1 Hdl soft	£34,331
	11/21	Newb	2m4½f Cls3 Nov Hdl gd-sft	£5,991
	10/21	Chep	2m3½f Cls4 Mdn Hdl good	£4,085
	10/20	Chep	2m Cls5 Am NHF 4-6yo soft	£2,274

Looked the best staying novice hurdler in Britain early last season, completing a hat-trick with a comfortable victory in the Challow; bitterly disappointing at Cheltenham and Aintree when pulled up in both races having raced far too freely; likely to go novice chasing.

State Man (Fr)

5 ch g Doctor Dino - Arret Station (Johann Quatz)

Willie Mullins (Ire) — Mrs J Donnelly

PLACINGS: 2/F11-1 — RPR **156+h**

Starts	1st	2nd	3rd	4th	Win & Pl
5	3	1	-	-	£132,823

	4/22	Punc	2m3½f Nov Gd1 Hdl gd-yld	£61,975
141	3/22	Chel	2m1f Cls1 Gd3 134-152 Hdl Hcap gd-sft	£56,270
	2/22	Limk	2m Mdn Hdl soft	£4,958

Hugely exciting hurdler who defied lack of experience to win at Cheltenham and Punchestown last season having landed only a maiden hurdle beforehand; hacked up in the County Hurdle off 141 and stepped up in class and trip to win a 2m4f Grade 1; Champion Hurdle contender.

Stattler (Ire)

7 br g Stowaway - Our Honey (Old Vic)

Willie Mullins (Ire) R A Bartlett

PLACINGS: 132/3134/3111- RPR **164+c**

Starts		1st	2nd	3rd	4th	Win & Pl
11		5	1	4	1	£119,542
	3/22	Chel	3m6f Cls1 Nov Gd2 Am Ch gd-sft			£60,763
	1/22	Naas	3m1f Nov Gd3 Ch gd-yld			£14,874
	12/21	Fair	2m5f Ch yld-sft			£5,795
	12/20	Leop	2m4f Mdn Hdl soft			£6,000
	1/20	Fair	2m NHF 5-7yo heavy			£5,008

High-class staying novice chaser last season, winning all three starts as he gradually stepped up in trip; particularly impressive when winning the National Hunt Chase at Cheltenham, beating Run Wild Fred by eight lengths; tougher tasks await but could be a Gold Cup horse.

Stolen Silver (Fr)

7 gr g Lord Du Sud - Change Partner (Turtle Island)

Sam Thomas Walters Plant Hire & Potter Group

PLACINGS: U1218P/332P8/124341- RPR **155+c**

Starts		1st	2nd	3rd	4th	Win & Pl
19		4	4	3	2	£98,920
143	4/22	Chel	2m4½f Cls1 Gd2 140-154 Ch Hcap good			£39,466
136	10/21	MRas	2m1f Cls3 Nov 131-142 Ch Hcap good			£7,080
	1/20	Hayd	1m7½f Cls1 Nov Gd2 Hdl heavy			£17,085
	11/19	Ffos	2m Cls4 Nov Hdl soft			£3,769

Lightly raced chaser who finished last season with an impressive wide-margin win in the Silver Trophy at Cheltenham; had run well at Cheltenham twice earlier in the season when second and fourth in major handicaps, latterly in the Plate on ground softer than ideal.

Suprise Package

6 b g Le Fou - Suetsu (Toulon)

Peter Fahey (Ire) Paul Leech

PLACINGS: 20372/124P2729166- RPR **146+h**

Starts		1st	2nd	3rd	4th	Win & Pl
15		2	4	1	1	£114,420
135	3/22	Sand	2m Cls1 Gd3 121-146 Hdl Hcap soft			£56,270
	4/21	Punc	2m4½f Hdl yield			£39,509

Progressive hurdler who ran away with last season's Imperial Cup at Sandown having finished second in a hot handicap at Leopardstown earlier in the season; good sixth in a red-hot County Hurdle but outpaced in a 2m Grade 1 novice hurdle at Aintree on final run.

Tea Clipper (Ire)

7 b g Stowaway - A Plus Ma Puce (Turgeon)

Tom Lacey Jerry Hinds & Ashley Head

PLACINGS: 1/1112/1533/12444- RPR **153+c**

Starts		1st	2nd	3rd	4th	Win & Pl
13		5	2	2	3	£114,382
	10/21	Chep	2m3½f Cls1 Nov List Ch good			£19,933
134	10/20	Chep	2m3½f Cls1 Gd3 127-146 Hdl Hcap good			£22,780
127	12/19	Hntg	2m Cls3 115-128 Hdl Hcap gd-sft			£12,512
	11/19	Kemp	2m Cls4 Nov Hdl good			£4,094
	10/19	Wwck	2m Cls4 Nov Hdl good			£4,549

Lightly raced staying chaser who made the frame at Cheltenham and Aintree for the second successive year last season; had lost his way slightly after an impressive chase debut but did better in the spring when switched to handicaps after wind surgery.

Teahupoo (Fr)

5 b g Masked Marvel - Droit D'Aimer (Sassanian)

Gordon Elliott (Ire) Robcour

PLACINGS: 1112/1110-6 RPR **165+h**

Starts		1st	2nd	3rd	4th	Win & Pl
9		6	1	-	-	£97,583
	2/22	Gowr	2m Gd3 Hdl heavy			£14,874
	12/21	Limk	2m Gd2 Hdl 4yo heavy			£18,438
	11/21	Naas	2m Gd3 Hdl 4yo yield			£14,487
	2/21	Fair	2m Gd3 Hdl 4yo soft			£14,487
	1/21	Fair	2m Hdl 4yo heavy			£8,955
	10/20	Autl	2m2f Hdl 3yo heavy			£18,305

Sharply progressive hurdler for much of last season and hacked up in the Red Mills Trial Hurdle at Gowran on heavy ground; just 9-1 for the Champion Hurdle next time but didn't beat a single rival at Cheltenham or Punchestown when seemingly unable to cope with quicker conditions.

Telmesomethinggirl (Ire)

7 b m Stowaway - Wahiba Hall (Saddlers' Hall)

Henry de Bromhead (Ire) Kenneth Alexander

PLACINGS: 1/350/131131/553B-F RPR **152+h**

Starts		1st	2nd	3rd	4th	Win & Pl
14		4	-	4	-	£74,817
	3/21	Chel	2m1f Cls1 Nov Gd2 Hdl gd-sft			£37,982
	9/20	List	2m4f Hdl good			£9,250
	8/20	Bell	2m4f Hdl soft			£5,750
	6/20	Rosc	2m Mdn Hdl good			£5,000

Won at the Cheltenham Festival in 2021 but suffered rotten luck back at the meeting last season, getting brought down two out when in contention for the Mares' Hurdle; hadn't won in the interim but produced a career-best when a close third behind Royal Kahala at Christmas.

The Big Breakaway (Ire)

7 ch g Getaway - Princess Mairead (Blueprint)

Joe Tizzard Eric Jones, Geoff Nicholas & John Romans

PLACINGS: 1/114/1223P/F23P- RPR **152c**

Starts		1st	2nd	3rd	4th	Win & Pl
12		3	3	2	1	£72,012
	11/20	Chel	3m½f Cls2 Nov Ch soft			£12,628
	12/19	Newb	2m4½f Cls4 Nov Hdl 4-6yo soft			£4,484
	11/19	Chep	2m3½f Cls5 Mdn Hdl soft			£2,794

Widely regarded as a future star in younger days but hasn't won since chase debut at Cheltenham in 2020; finished second and third at Grade 1 level that season but failed to hit those heights last term and pulled up on handicap chase debut at Kempton on final run.

The Galloping Bear

9 b g Shantou - Cheshire Kat (King's Theatre)

Ben Clarke — Adrian Paterson

PLACINGS: 25/2111/211/F11- — RPR **155+c**

Starts	1st	2nd	3rd	4th	Win & Pl
6	4	-	-	-	£80,848

140	2/22	Hayd	3m4½f Cls1 Gd3 135-159 Ch Hcap heavy	£60,067
135	1/22	Ling	3m5f Cls3 109-135 Ch Hcap heavy	£15,843
	3/21	Carl	3m½f Cls5 Am Hunt Ch soft	£2,989
	2/21	Font	3m2f Cls6 Am Hunt Ch soft	£1,949

Prolific staying chaser who successfully graduated out of point-to-points and hunter chases last season by winning two open handicaps, most notably in the Grand National Trial at Haydock; gained both wins on heavy ground and seen by his trainer as very ground-dependent.

The Glancing Queen (Ire)

8 b m Jeremy - Glancing (Kayf Tara)

Alan King — Dingwall, Farrell, Hornsey & Murray

PLACINGS: /1351/8/13125/11271- — RPR **149+c**

Starts	1st	2nd	3rd	4th	Win & Pl
15	7	2	2	-	£115,235

140	4/22	Chel	2m½f Cls2 125-140 Ch Hcap good	£13,008
	12/21	Wwck	2m4f Cls1 Nov List Ch soft	£14,238
	11/21	Bang	2m1½f Cls1 Nov List Ch gd-sft	£14,238
	1/21	Bang	2m½f Cls4 Nov Hdl heavy	£3,769
	11/20	Wwck	2m5f Cls4 Nov Hdl gd-sft	£3,769
	4/19	Aint	2m1f Cls1 Gd2 NHF 4-6yo soft	£25,322
	11/18	Chel	2m½f Cls1 List NHF 4-6yo good	£12,379

Smart mare who won three times last season, twice in Listed novice chases before adding a mares' handicap at Cheltenham; dropped back to 2m that day having twice looked a suspect stayer at around 2m4f at the track, though has won over similar trips at easier tracks.

The Galloping Bear: tough staying chaser who loves a thorough test of his stamina

The Last Day (Ire)

10 b g Oscar - The Last Bank (Phardante)

Evan Williams — Mr & Mrs William Rucker

PLACINGS: /1341/F221/14/56/F1- — RPR **145+c**

Starts	1st	2nd	3rd	4th	Win & Pl
17	6	2	1	2	£104,085

133	4/22	Aint	2m Cls1 Gd3 131-153 Ch Hcap gd-sft	£56,270
131	11/19	Aint	2m Cls3 120-139 Ch Hcap soft	£16,245
	3/19	Carl	2m Cls3 Nov Ch heavy	£9,747
	3/18	Chep	2m Cls4 Nov Hdl heavy	£4,094
	11/17	Chep	2m Cls4 Mdn Hdl soft	£3,899
	1/17	Sthl	1m7½f Cls6 Mdn NHF 4-6yo soft	£1,326

Lightly raced gelding who won last season's Red Rum Chase at Aintree to reward connections' patience after a difficult couple of years; had looked progressive in 2019 only to suffer a long injury layoff and then fall when in front at the last on reappearance last season.

The Nice Guy (Ire)

7 b g Fame And Glory - Kilbarry Beauty (Saffron Walden)

Willie Mullins (Ire) — Malcolm C Denmark

PLACINGS: 1111-1 — RPR **156+h**

Starts	1st	2nd	3rd	4th	Win & Pl
5	5	-	-	-	£160,207

4/22	Punc	3m Nov Gd1 Hdl gd-yld	£61,975
3/22	Chel	3m Cls1 Nov Gd1 Hdl gd-sft	£78,680
1/22	Naas	2m3f Mdn Hdl gd-yld	£7,437
12/21	Leop	2m NHF 4-7yo yld-sft	£6,848
11/21	Fair	2m NHF 4-7yo good	£5,268

Unbeaten in five races under rules after a wonderful season culminating in Grade 1 wins at Cheltenham and Punchestown, staying on most impressively to land the Albert Bartlett; has plenty of chasers in his pedigree and should make a fine staying novice.

Third Time Lucki: made his mark over fences last season with three novice chase successes

The Shunter (Ire)

9 b g Stowaway - Tornado Lady (Gulland)

Emmet Mullins (Ire) — John P McManus

PLACINGS: P/411413112/34UP-786 — RPR **147c**

Starts	1st	2nd	3rd	4th	Win & Pl
34	5	1	6	7	£198,351

140	3/21	Chel	2m4½f Cls1 Gd3 130-154 Ch Hcap gd-sft	£46,423
135	3/21	Kels	2m Cls2 124-150 Hdl Hcap gd-sft	£46,920
128	11/20	Chel	2m½f Cls1 Gd3 128-154 Hdl Hcap soft	£45,560
	9/20	Punc	2m5f Ch yld-sft	£6,250
	9/20	Dpat	2m3f Mdn Hdl good	£5,000

Massive improver two seasons ago and landed a plunge in the Plate at the Cheltenham Festival, pulling off a rare course double having won the Greatwood that campaign; has found higher marks beyond him.

The Widdow Maker

8 ch g Arvico - Countess Point (Karinga Bay)

Joe Tizzard — Sax Purdie

PLACINGS: 9/783110/156123- — RPR **146c**

Starts	1st	2nd	3rd	4th	Win & Pl
13	4	1	2	-	£44,103

	2/22	Extr	2m3f Cls3 Nov Ch soft	£9,040
128	12/21	Winc	1m7f Cls3 112-128 Hdl Hcap good	£8,169
118	3/21	Tntn	2m½f Cls4 105-118 Hdl Hcap soft	£3,769
	2/21	Tntn	2m½f Cls4 Mdn Hdl heavy	£3,769

Began chasing in February and instantly proved better over fences; made an impressive start at Exeter on soft ground (has also won on heavy) and ran two solid races on quicker, including when third in a weak Grade I at Aintree.

Theatre Glory (Ire)

5 b m Fame And Glory - Native Beauty (King's Theatre)

Nicky Henderson — Canter Banter Racing

PLACINGS: 113111- — RPR **136+h**

Starts	1st	2nd	3rd	4th	Win & Pl
6	5	-	1	-	£55,694

	4/22	Chel	2m4½f Cls1 Nov List Hdl good	£14,238
129	3/22	Kels	2m Cls2 Nov 103-129 Hdl Hcap good	£26,015
	1/22	Wwck	2m3f Cls3 Nov Hdl gd-sft	£6,671
	11/21	Hntg	2m Cls4 Nov Hdl good	£4,085
	5/21	Worc	2m Cls5 Mdn NHF 4-6yo good	£1,906

Exciting and prolific mare who won four out of five races over hurdles last season; suffered sole defeat in a Listed race at Newbury but progressed subsequently and won easily in Listed company at Cheltenham on final run, having also landed a valuable mares' handicap at Kelso.

Thedevilscoachman (Ire)

6 br g Elusive Pimpernel - Hagawi (Selkirk)

Noel Meade (Ire) — John P McManus

PLACINGS: 1/15117/321- — RPR **160+h**

Starts	1st	2nd	3rd	4th	Win & Pl
9	5	1	1	-	£57,592

	2/22	Navn	2m5f Gd2 Hdl heavy	£18,097
	2/21	Punc	2m½f Nov List Hdl soft	£14,487
	1/21	Navn	2m1½f Nov Hdl heavy	£8,429
	11/20	Cork	2m Mdn Hdl 4yo heavy	£6,000
	1/20	Naas	2m NHF 4yo gd-yld	£5,591

Didn't jump well in two runs over fences last season but produced a career-best effort when reverting to hurdles, winning the Boyne Hurdle on heavy ground; didn't run again with quicker conditions against him in the spring; should stay 3m.

Third Time Lucki (Ire)

7 br g Arcadio - Definite Valley (Definite Article)

Dan Skelton — Mike & Eileen Newbould

PLACINGS: 3114/1121464/113123- — RPR **158c**

Starts	1st	2nd	3rd	4th	Win & Pl
17	8	2	3	3	£139,470

	1/22	Donc	2m½f Cls1 Nov Gd2 Ch good	£23,674
	11/21	Chel	2m Cls1 Nov Gd2 Ch good	£30,280
	10/21	Chel	2m Cls2 Nov Ch good	£13,008
	12/20	Kemp	2m Cls2 Nov Hdl gd-sft	£10,047
	10/20	Weth	2m Cls3 Nov Hdl gd-sft	£5,913
	10/20	Uttx	2m Cls4 Nov Hdl 4-6yo gd-sft	£3,769
	1/20	Hntg	2m Cls5 NHF 4-6yo soft	£2,274
	12/19	MRas	2m½f Cls5 Mdn NHF 4-6yo soft	£2,274

Quickly developed into a smart novice chaser last season, winning three times including twice at Cheltenham; just came up short against the very best, finishing third in Grade I races at Sandown and Aintree either side of a well-beaten second behind Edwardstone at Warwick.

Third Wind

8 b/br g Shirocco - Act Three (Beat Hollow)

Hughie Morrison — Mouse Hamilton-Fairley

PLACINGS: 1211/714/5251P/7331- — RPR **149+h**

Starts	1st	2nd	3rd	4th	Win & Pl
18	6	2	3	1	£175,483

141	3/22	Chel	3m Cls1 Gd3 134-156 Hdl Hcap soft	£56,270
	2/21	Hayd	3m½f Cls1 Gd2 Hdl soft	£17,085
137	12/19	Winc	2m5½f Cls2 120-146 Hdl Hcap heavy	£11,574
131	3/19	Sand	2m4f Cls1 Nov Gd3 123-138 Hdl 4-7yo Hcap soft	£42,203
	2/19	Tntn	2m3f Cls4 Nov Hdl soft	£5,133
	12/18	Plum	2m4½f Cls4 Mdn Hdl soft	£4,094

Gutsy winner of the Pertemps Final at Cheltenham, extending tremendous record in big handicaps having won the EBF Final and never failed to make the frame in six handicap runs; has largely come up short in Graded company but did win a Grade 2 at Haydock in 2021.

Thomas Darby (Ire)

9 b g Beneficial - Silaoce (Nikos)

Olly Murphy — Mrs Diana L Whateley

PLACINGS: 312/2313/3303/414P4- — RPR **157h**

Starts	1st	2nd	3rd	4th	Win & Pl
19	5	3	6	3	£166,903

	11/21	Newb	3m Cls1 Gd2 Hdl gd-sft	£34,170
151	1/20	Asct	2m3½f Cls1 Gd3 125-151 Hdl Hcap heavy	£28,475
	1/19	Tntn	2m½f Cls4 Nov Hdl gd-sft	£5,133
	10/18	Chel	2m½f Cls3 Mdn Hdl good	£9,285
	5/18	Hntg	2m Cls5 Am Mdn NHF 4-6yo good	£2,274

Has developed into a very useful staying hurdler despite tending to come up short in the top races; did win last season's Long Distance Hurdle at Newbury and has made the frame three times in 3m Grade I races; struggled in two runs over fences in 2019.

Three Stripe Life (Ire)

6 br g Leading Light - Hirayna (Doyoun)

Gordon Elliott (Ire) — K Haughey & Laura Haughey & Kieran T Byrne

PLACINGS: 14/12221-3 — RPR **148h**

Starts	1st	2nd	3rd	4th	Win & Pl
8	3	3	1	1	£148,888

	Date	Course	Race	Prize
	4/22	Aint	2m4f Cls1 Nov Gd1 Hdl gd-sft	£56,319
	11/21	Fair	2m Mdn Hdl yield	£5,268
	1/21	Navn	2m NHF 4-7yo heavy	£5,268

Classy and consistent novice hurdler last season who thoroughly deserved Grade I victory at Aintree having finished second three times at that level, including in the Ballymore; again just came up short against the very best novices when only third behind State Man at Punchestown.

Threeunderthrufive (Ire)

7 b g Shantou - Didinas (Kaldou Star)

Paul Nicholls — McNeill Family

PLACINGS: 21/11161/211116- — RPR **156+c**

Starts	1st	2nd	3rd	4th	Win & Pl
13	9	2	-	-	£134,190

	Date	Course	Race	Prize
	1/22	Wwck	3m Cls1 Nov Gd2 Ch soft	£31,691
	12/21	Donc	3m Cls1 Nov Gd2 Ch gd-sft	£24,489
	11/21	Chel	3m½f Cls2 Nov Ch good	£15,624
	11/21	Extr	3m Cls2 Nov Ch gd-sft	£12,725
	4/21	Prth	3m Cls1 Nov List Hdl gd-sft	£11,960
	2/21	Muss	3m Cls2 Nov Hdl soft	£12,512
	11/20	Ludl	2m5f Cls2 Hdl good	£9,747
	10/20	Ling	2m3½f Cls4 Mdn Hdl soft	£3,769
	1/20	Chep	2m Cls5 NHF 4-6yo heavy	£2,274

Prolific stayer who won four novice chases last season to go with four novice hurdles in the previous campaign; came up short at the Cheltenham Festival for the second year in a row, finishing a well-beaten sixth in the Brown Advisory.

Thunder Rock (Ire)

6 b g Shirocco - La Belle Sauvage (Old Vic)

Olly Murphy — McNeill Family & Ian Dale

PLACINGS: 2/31/211191- — RPR **137+h**

Starts	1st	2nd	3rd	4th	Win & Pl
8	5	1	1	-	£40,201

	Date	Course	Race	Prize
	4/22	Ayr	2m4½f Cls3 Nov Hdl gd-sft	£8,714
123	2/22	Hntg	2m3½f Cls2 123-145 Hdl Hcap soft	£15,833
	12/21	Muss	2m4f Cls4 Nov Hdl 4-6yo gd-sft	£4,629
	11/21	Weth	2m3½f Cls3 Nov Hdl gd-sft	£6,535
	2/21	Extr	2m1f Cls5 NHF 4-6yo heavy	£2,274

Prolific novice hurdler last season when winning four of his last five races, most notably on handicap debut at Huntingdon; sole disappointment when well beaten in the EBF Final (reported not to have acted on the track); likely to go novice chasing.

Thyme Hill

8 b g Kayf Tara - Rosita Bay (Hernando)

Philip Hobbs — The Englands & Heywoods

PLACINGS: 123/1114/121/5225- — RPR **163h**

Starts	1st	2nd	3rd	4th	Win & Pl
14	6	4	1	1	£329,041

	Date	Course	Race	Prize
	4/21	Aint	3m½f Cls1 Gd1 Hdl gd-sft	£84,195
	11/20	Newb	3m Cls1 Gd2 Hdl good	£28,475
	12/19	Newb	2m4½f Cls1 Nov Gd1 Hdl soft	£25,929
	11/19	Chel	2m5f Cls1 Nov Gd2 Hdl soft	£18,006
	10/19	Chep	2m3½f Cls1 Nov Gd2 Hdl gd-sft	£19,933
	10/18	Worc	2m Cls5 NHF 4-6yo good	£2,274

Dual Grade I winner but just came up short against the top staying hurdlers last season; still ran big races when second behind Champ in the Long Walk Hurdle and Flooring Porter in the Stayers' Hurdle at Cheltenham; looks a fine prospect for novice chases.

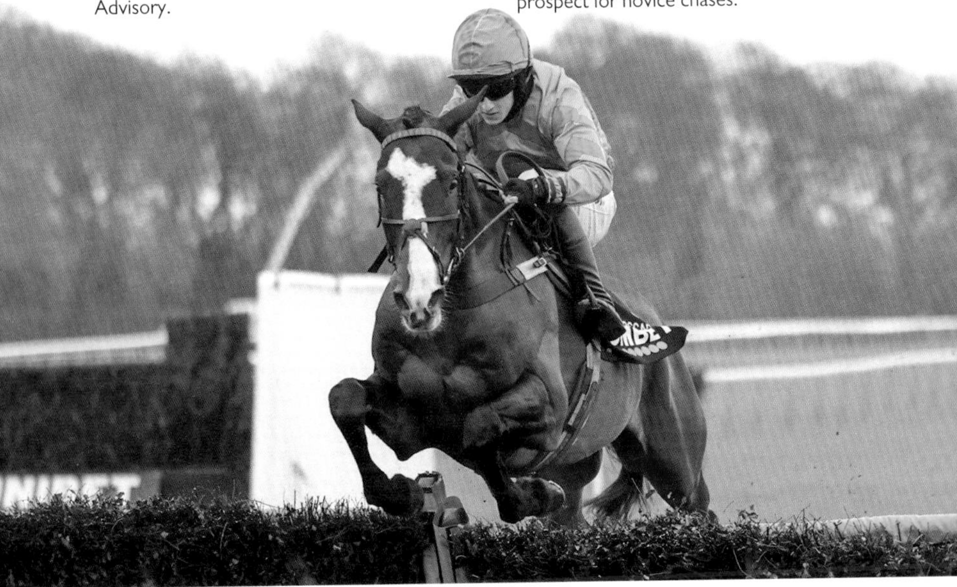

Thyme White (Fr)

6 b g Anodin - Jane (Samum)

Paul Nicholls — The Stewart Family & Michael Blencowe

PLACINGS: 2210/1U907/2U12F- RPR **145c**

Starts	1st	2nd	3rd	4th	Win & Pl
14	3	4	-	-	£56,934

134	12/21	Donc	2m½f Cls3 Nov 123-134 Ch Hcap soft	£5,882
130	10/20	Chep	2m Cls2 119-136 Hdl 4yo Hcap good	£10,397
	2/20	Muss	1m7½f Cls1 List Hdl 4yo soft	£19,933

Lightly raced chaser who won a novice handicap at Doncaster last season but proved slightly disappointing in the spring after an 8lb rise; beaten favourite at Ascot, though still a fair second, and fell three out in the Red Rum at Aintree having jumped poorly.

Time To Get Up (Ire)

9 ch g Presenting - Gales Return (Bob's Return)

Jonjo O'Neill — John P McManus

PLACINGS: 2/42/3411/0330- RPR **140c**

Starts	1st	2nd	3rd	4th	Win & Pl
11	2	2	3	2	£113,526

138	3/21	Uttx	4m2f Cls1 List 132-154 Ch Hcap gd-sft	£67,524
130	2/21	Winc	3m1f Cls3 122-140 Ch Hcap heavy	£10,234

Hugely progressive two seasons ago, winning the Midlands National in just his fourth chase, but suffered a fruitless campaign last term; couldn't qualify for the Grand National after a setback and disappointed anyway in the spring, though still a fair third defending Uttoxeter crown.

Tommy's Oscar (Ire)

7 b g Oscar - Glibin (Luso)

Ann Hamilton — Ian Hamilton

PLACINGS: /3121112613/2311119- RPR **159+h**

Starts	1st	2nd	3rd	4th	Win & Pl
15	8	3	2	-	£138,076

	1/22	Hayd	1m7½f Cls1 Gd2 Hdl soft	£42,713
150	1/22	Muss	1m7½f Cls2 124-150 Hdl Hcap gd-sft	£15,609
147	12/21	Donc	2m½f Cls2 121-147 Hdl Hcap gd-sft	£9,626
138	11/21	Hayd	2m3f Cls2 123-145 Hdl Hcap good	£26,015
132	3/21	Kels	2m Cls2 122-148 Hdl Hcap gd-sft	£15,432
124	1/21	Muss	1m7½f Cls3 104-130 Hdl Hcap soft	£6,238
	12/20	Newc	2m Cls4 Nov Hdl soft	£3,769
	12/20	Sedg	2m1f Cls4 Mdn Hdl gd-sft	£3,769

Big improver last season when graduating from handicaps into a legitimate Champion Hurdle dark horse, despite managing only ninth at Cheltenham (only one British runner priced shorter); had earlier won four 2m hurdles in a row, including the Champion Hurdle Trial at Haydock.

Tommy's Oscar: stepped on to the big stage over hurdles last season with victory in the Champion Hurdle Trial at Haydock

Top Dog (Ire)

5 b g Leading Light - Princess Leya (Old Vic)

Emma Lavelle — Nicholas Mustoe

PLACINGS: 2/231P- RPR **122+ b**

Starts	1st	2nd	3rd	4th	Win & Pl
5	1	2	1	-	£19,769

	2/22	Newb	2m½f Cls1 List NHF 4-6yo gd-sft	£11,390

Useful and consistent in good bumpers last season, winning a Listed race at Newbury having finished second and third at Cheltenham and Ascot; reportedly hated heavy ground when pulled up in the Champion Bumper; nice prospect for hurdles, though not particularly big.

Topofthegame (Ire)

10 ch g Flemensfirth - Derry Vale (Mister Lord)

Paul Nicholls — Chris Giles & Mr& Mrs P K Barber

PLACINGS: 1/142/F412/2212/ RPR **167c**

Starts	1st	2nd	3rd	4th	Win & Pl
11	3	5	-	2	£240,041

	3/19	Chel	3m½f Cls1 Nov Gd1 Ch soft	£98,473
142	2/18	Sand	2m7½f Cls1 Gd3 123-147 Hdl Hcap soft	£56,270
	12/16	Asct	2m5½f Cls3 Mdn Hdl gd-sft	£7,798

Has missed the last three seasons through injury just as he looked to have developed into a top staying chaser, winning what proved a red-hot RSA Chase in 2019 (Santini and Delta Work behind); Grand National a likely aim if injury stands up to training.

Tornado Flyer (Ire)

9 b g Flemensfirth - Mucho Macabi (Exceed And Excel)

Willie Mullins (Ire) — T F P Partnership

PLACINGS: /411P35/22543/51P-77 RPR **172+c**

Starts	1st	2nd	3rd	4th	Win & Pl
21	6	2	3	2	£332,604

	12/21	Kemp	3m Cls1 Gd1 Ch soft	£143,045
	12/19	Navn	2m1f Nov Gd3 Ch soft	£19,932
	11/19	Naas	2m3f Ch sft-hvy	£7,720
	12/18	Punc	2m4f Mdn Hdl good	£7,087
	4/18	Punc	2m½f Gd1 NHF 4-7yo yield	£52,212
	1/18	Fair	2m NHF 5-7yo soft	£5,451

Shock winner of last season's King George when achieving only victory since 2019; probably flattered by how that race was run (held up as main rivals did too much up front) and has come up short in ten other runs at Grade 1 level (placed three times).

Tritonic

5 ch g Sea The Moon - Selenography (Selkirk)

Alan King — McNeill Family & Ian Dale

PLACINGS: 115/251400- RPR **145+h**

Starts	1st	2nd	3rd	4th	Win & Pl
9	3	1	-	1	£100,435

141	12/21	Asct	1m7½f Cls1 Gd3 133-153 Hdl Hcap gd-sft	£59,798
	2/21	Kemp	2m Cls1 Gd2 Hdl 4yo good	£12,814
	1/21	Asct	1m7½f Cls3 Hdl 4yo soft	£6,173

Looked an exciting prospect when winning first two hurdle races in 2021 (sent off 4-1 when fifth in the Triumph Hurdle that year) but largely disappointing since; won a handicap hurdle at Ascot last season but then well beaten in the Christmas Hurdle and two more big handicaps.

Truckers Lodge (Ire)

10 b g Westerner - Galeacord (Accordion)

Paul Nicholls — Gordon & Su Hall

PLACINGS: 1221/24121/U77/5336- RPR **153c**

Starts	1st	2nd	3rd	4th	Win & Pl
22	6	5	2	4	£187,833

141	3/20	Uttx	4m2f Cls1 List 131-157 Ch Hcap heavy	£84,478
	10/19	Chep	2m7½f Cls3 Ch gd-sft	£7,018
	3/19	Extr	2m7f Cls4 Nov Hdl gd-sft	£4,224
123	12/18	Chep	2m7½f Cls3 110-129 Hdl Hcap heavy	£6,758
	5/18	Sthl	2m4½f Cls5 Mdn Hdl good	£3,444
	4/17	Chep	2m Cls6 NHF 4-6yo good	£1,949

Won the Midlands National as a novice in 2020 only to find life much more difficult after a subsequent 14lb rise; steadily fell in the weights and did much better again last winter, finishing third in the Welsh National at Chepstow and a Listed handicap at Ascot.

Two For Gold (Ire)

9 b g Gold Well - Two Of Each (Shernazar)

Kim Bailey — May We Never Be Found Out Partnership

PLACINGS: 14/1112/2P313U/112P- RPR **165c**

Starts	1st	2nd	3rd	4th	Win & Pl
21	10	3	2	2	£224,174

	1/22	Ling	2m6f Cls2 Ch heavy	£79,725
150	12/21	Donc	3m Cls2 124-150 Ch Hcap gd-sft	£11,707
149	2/21	Wwck	2m4f Cls2 129-155 Ch Hcap soft	£21,896
	1/20	Wwck	3m Cls1 Nov Gd2 Ch soft	£19,933
	12/19	Kels	2m7½f Cls3 Nov Ch soft	£12,116
132	11/19	Carl	2m4f Cls3 Nov 117-135 Ch Hcap soft	£8,123
	1/19	Bang	2m7f Cls4 Nov Hdl gd-sft	£4,094
	12/18	Weth	2m5½f Cls4 Nov Hdl soft	£4,224
	2/18	Donc	2m½f Cls5 NHF 4-6yo gd-sft	£2,599
	12/17	Sthl	1m7½f Cls5 Am NHF 4-6yo good	£2,599

Massively improved chaser last season and had his finest hour when edging out Dashel Drasher in a valuable new 2m4f chase at Lingfield's new Winter Million card; stepped forward again when second in the Ascot Chase but a clear non-stayer in the Grand National.

Undersupervision (Ire)

6 ch g Doyen - Dances With Waves (Presenting)

Nigel Twiston-Davies — Anne-Marie & Jamie Shepperd

PLACINGS: 1142/2F3641P- RPR **143+c**

Starts	1st	2nd	3rd	4th	Win & Pl
10	2	2	1	2	£46,092

132	3/22	Donc	3m2f Cls2 129-147 Ch Hcap soft	£28,780
	12/20	Hrfd	3m1½f Cls4 Nov Hdl heavy	£3,769

Useful staying chaser who won last season's Grimthorpe Chase at Doncaster as a novice; had run well in defeat earlier in the season, twice finishing in the first three at Cheltenham, but was pulled up when favourite back there on final run.

Unexpected Party (Fr)

7 gr g Martaline - Reform Act (Lemon Drop Kid)

Dan Skelton — O'Reilly, Maclennan, Tynan, Carthy & Shanahan

PLACINGS: 2/41221P- RPR **141+h**

Starts	1st	2nd	3rd	4th	Win & Pl
7	2	3	-	1	£28,675

130	1/22	Asct	2m3½f Cls2 125-143 Hdl Hcap soft	£15,609
109	10/21	Weth	2m5½f Cls4 Nov 84-110 Hdl Hcap gd-sft	£3,159

Progressive novice hurdler last season, flourishing in good handicaps; deservedly won at Ascot after finishing second at Cheltenham and Wetherby (favourite every time); pulled up when 8-1 for the Coral Cup; likely to go novice chasing.

Vanillier (Fr)

7 gr g Martaline - Virgata (Turgeon)

Gavin Cromwell (Ire) — Mrs H M Keaveney

PLACINGS: P/1/21201/431333-6 RPR **151c**

Starts	1st	2nd	3rd	4th	Win & Pl
12	3	2	4	1	£120,690

11/21	Punc	2m6½f Nov Gd2 Ch yield	£18,438
3/21	Chel	3m Cls1 Nov Gd1 Hdl gd-sft	£55,127
11/20	Naas	2m3f Mdn Hdl sft-hvy	£7,000

Strong stayer who was a wide-margin winner of the Albert Bartlett in 2021 but failed to hit the same heights over fences last season, winning just once; step up in trip and return to Cheltenham yielded no improvement when a distant third in the National Hunt Chase.

Vauban (Fr)

4 ch g Galiway - Waldfest (Hurricane Run)

Willie Mullins (Ire) — Mrs S Ricci

PLACINGS: 211-1 RPR **150+h**

Starts	1st	2nd	3rd	4th	Win & Pl
4	3	1	-	-	£201,949

4/22	Punc	2m Gd1 Hdl 4yo yield	£61,975
3/22	Chel	2m1f Cls1 Gd1 Hdl 4yo gd-sft	£75,965
2/22	Leop	2m Gd1 Hdl 4yo yield	£61,975

Outstanding juvenile hurdler last season, winning three Grade 1 races including the Triumph Hurdle at Cheltenham; extended that superiority over Fil Dor when following up at 4-11 at Punchestown, showing a stunning change of gear; looks a Champion Hurdle horse.

Velvet Elvis (Ire)

6 br g Shirocco - Treen (Charnwood Forest)

Thomas Gibney (Ire) — Derek Kierans

PLACINGS: 1/4021130/43516- RPR **149c**

Starts	1st	2nd	3rd	4th	Win & Pl
12	3	1	2	2	£54,888

133	3/22	Navn	3m Nov 116-138 Ch Hcap soft	£29,748
	2/21	Thur	2m4f Nov Hdl heavy	£8,429
	1/21	Cork	3m Mdn Hdl sft-hvy	£6,321

Improved hugely when stepped up in trip and sent handicapping last spring; got off the mark in a 3m novice chase at Navan and ran a big race when sixth in the Irish Grand National; has scope for improvement after just five runs over fences.

Walking On Air (Ire)

5 b g Walk In The Park - Refinement (Oscar)

Nicky Henderson — Mrs Doreen Tabor

PLACINGS: 2/1P- — RPR **134+h**

Starts	1st	2nd	3rd	4th	Win & Pl
3	1	1	-	-	£4,752

	1/22	Newb	2m½f Cls4 Nov Hdl gd-sft	£4,085

Ran only twice last season but made a big impression when winning by 13 lengths on hurdles debut at Newbury; had been as short as 7-1 for the Ballymore at Cheltenham before waiting for Aintree but well below par in that 2m4f Grade 1 and pulled up.

War Lord (Ger)

7 gr g Jukebox Jury - Westalin (Sternkoenig)

Joe Tizzard — The Wychwood Partnership

PLACINGS: 13418/213047/112142- — RPR **153c**

Starts	1st	2nd	3rd	4th	Win & Pl
18	6	3	2	3	£151,137

	1/22	Ling	2m Cls2 Nov Ch heavy	£26,015
	11/21	Carl	2m Cls2 Ch gd-sft	£26,015
135	10/21	NAbb	2m½f Cls3 Nov 128-135 Ch Hcap gd-sft	£6,753
131	11/20	Hayd	2m3f Cls2 121-143 Hdl Hcap soft	£25,024
120	2/20	Tntn	2m½f Cls4 111-120 Hdl Hcap soft	£4,809
	10/19	Plum	2m Cls4 Mdn Hdl soft	£4,094

Smart novice chaser last season, leaving hurdles form behind to win three times and run well at Grade 1 level on all three other runs; belied 50-1 odds when a strong-finishing fourth in the Arkle and finished a solid second behind Millers Bank over 2m4f at Aintree.

West Balboa (Ire)

6 b m Yeats - Rostellan (Flemensfirth)

Dan Skelton — Bullen-Smith & Faulks

PLACINGS: 2/12- — RPR **130h**

Starts	1st	2nd	3rd	4th	Win & Pl
2	1	1	-	-	£17,339

	11/21	Wwck	2m5f Cls4 Nov Hdl gd-sft	£4,357

Missed the second half of last season but had already proved a very useful mare in just two runs over hurdles; won by 17 lengths on hurdles debut at Warwick and coped well with sharp rise in class when second behind Stage Star in the Challow.

West Cork

8 b g Midnight Legend - Calamintha (Mtoto)

Dan Skelton — Mike & Eileen Newbould

PLACINGS: 1/22112/1542-F — RPR **145h**

Starts	1st	2nd	3rd	4th	Win & Pl
10	3	4	-	1	£95,939

134	11/21	Chel	2m½f Cls1 Gd3 130-147 Hdl Hcap good	£56,270
	1/20	Hntg	2m Cls4 Nov Hdl soft	£4,224
	12/19	Hntg	2m Cls4 Nov Hdl gd-sft	£5,523

Lightly raced and progressive hurdler who did well in delayed first season out of novice company last term; defied long layoff to win the Greatwood Hurdle and continued to run well in big handicaps off rising marks, notably when second in the Scottish Champion Hurdle.

Whatdeawant (Ire)

6 b g Aizavoski - Hidden Reserve (Heron Island)

Willie Mullins (Ire) — Sean & Bernardine Mulryan

PLACINGS: 13/153- — RPR **139h**

Starts	1st	2nd	3rd	4th	Win & Pl
5	2	-	2	-	£35,442

	12/21	Navn	2m4f Mdn Hdl yield	£6,321
	1/21	Fair	2m½f NHF 5-7yo heavy	£5,268

Very highly tried in novice hurdles last season, running exclusively in Grade 1 company after a winning debut and emerging with some credit; stuck on for a fair third in the Ballymore at Cheltenham and should be well suited by further.

Win My Wings (Ire)

9 b m Gold Well - Telstar (Montelimar)

Christian Williams — Sue Howell

PLACINGS: 2231668/231/15P111F- — RPR **155+c**

Starts	1st	2nd	3rd	4th	Win & Pl
21	7	3	3	-	£179,691

140	4/22	Ayr	4m Cls1 Gd3 121-147 Ch Hcap gd-sft	£84,405
132	2/22	Newc	4m1½f Cls2 120-144 Ch Hcap gd-sft	£41,624
129	1/22	Extr	3m Cls3 115-130 Ch Hcap soft	£11,219
	5/21	Comp	2m2f Hdl heavy	£19,286
123	4/21	Chel	3m2f Cls3 100-123 Ch Hcap good	£6,556
	9/19	Worc	2m4f Cls4 Nov Hdl soft	£3,769
	4/19	Ffos	2m6f Cls5 Mdn Hdl good	£3,119

Progressive mare who won three in a row last season including a couple of major staying handicaps in the Eider and Scottish Grand National, hacking up by seven lengths in the latter race; up 14lb but might have still been placed but for falling two out in the bet365 Gold Cup.

Windsor Avenue (Ire)

10 b g Winged Love - Zaffarella (Zaffaran)

Brian Ellison — Phil & Julie Martin

PLACINGS: 12/112F/2P360/2P1PP- — RPR **155+c**

Starts	1st	2nd	3rd	4th	Win & Pl
21	7	5	1	1	£120,665

144	1/22	Donc	3m Cls1 List 129-155 Ch Hcap good	£56,950
	11/19	Carl	2m4f Cls3 Nov Ch soft	£7,473
	10/19	Sedg	2m3½f Cls4 Ch soft	£4,614
	1/19	Sedg	2m4f Cls4 Nov Hdl 4-7yo gd-sft	£4,094
	11/18	Hexm	2m4f Cls4 Mdn Hdl good	£4,094
	2/18	Carl	2m1f Cls5 NHF 4-6yo heavy	£2,599
	1/18	Sedg	2m1f Cls5 NHF 4-6yo soft	£2,274

Hugely inconsistent but classy staying chaser on his day, winning last season's Sky Bet Chase at Doncaster at 40-1; had also finished second in a competitive handicap at Bangor but was pulled up on all three other runs last term, including in the Topham.

Wonderwall (Ire)

6 b g Yeats - Rock Me Gently (Sulamani)

Richard Spencer — Rebel Jumping II

PLACINGS: 137/21F- — RPR **136+h**

Starts	1st	2nd	3rd	4th	Win & Pl
6	2	1	1	-	£13,416

1/22	Donc	2m5f Cls4 Mdn Hdl gd-sft	£5,446
11/20	Asct	1m7½f Cls4 NHF 4-6yo soft	£3,899

Very lightly raced hurdler who showed promise in just three runs last season; beat dual subsequent winner City Chief at Doncaster and held every chance when falling at the last in a Listed novice at Huntingdon (sent off favourite); open to further progress.

Zambella (Fr)

7 b m Zambezi Sun - Visby (Irish Wells)

Nigel Twiston-Davies — Simon Munir & Isaac Souede

PLACINGS: U44/71112F2/4112143- — RPR **148+c**

Starts	1st	2nd	3rd	4th	Win & Pl
19	8	3	1	4	£167,736

2/22	Uttx	2m4f Cls2 Ch soft	£14,503
12/21	Donc	2m4½f Cls1 List Ch soft	£33,762
12/21	Aint	2m4f Cls1 List Ch soft	£16,346
1/21	Leic	2m Cls1 List Ch soft	£14,682
12/20	Wwck	2m4f Cls1 Nov List Ch soft	£11,746
11/20	Bang	2m1½f Cls1 Nov List Ch soft	£14,238
4/19	Comp	2m2f Hdl 4yo v soft	£19,459
3/19	Fntb	2m2f Hdl 4yo v soft	£8,649

Smart and consistent mare who has won five Listed chases against her own sex across the last two seasons; game fourth in the Mares' Chase at Cheltenham and would have filled a similar position in that race in 2021 but for falling three out.

Zanahiyr (Ire)

5 ch g Nathaniel - Zariyna (Marju)

Gordon Elliott (Ire) — Bective Stud

PLACINGS: 1114/212223F- — RPR **161h**

Starts	1st	2nd	3rd	4th	Win & Pl
11	4	4	1	1	£206,610

10/21	DRoy	2m1f Gd2 Hdl soft	£26,339
12/20	Leop	2m Gd2 Hdl 3yo soft	£17,500
11/20	Fair	2m Gd3 Hdl 3yo soft	£13,750
10/20	Baln	2m2f Mdn Hdl 3yo soft	£5,000

Tough and consistent hurdler who ran well in a string of top races last season, finishing second in three Grade 1 races and third in the Champion Hurdle; likely to appreciate further but looked to be coming off worse against Epatante when falling at the last over 2m4f in the Aintree Hurdle.

Zanza (Ire)

8 b g Arcadio - What A Bleu (Pistolet Bleu)

Philip Hobbs — Louisville Syndicate Elite

PLACINGS: 6F60/421FP6/362PP8P- — RPR **153c**

Starts	1st	2nd	3rd	4th	Win & Pl
25	5	2	1	1	£88,487

138	11/20	Newb	2m½f Cls2 134-147 Ch Hcap good	£19,028
136	11/19	Newb	2m½f Cls3 120-136 Cond Hdl Hcap gd-sft	£6,433
131	3/19	Newb	2m½f Cls2 122-134 Hdl Hcap gd-sft	£9,747
	12/18	Tntn	2m3f Cls4 Nov Hdl gd-sft	£5,133
	11/18	Chep	2m Cls4 Nov Hdl soft	£4,094

Has won only once over fences but has been a regular presence in top handicaps in the last two seasons, often proving unlucky in running; finished second in last season's Racing Post Gold Cup at Cheltenham but lost his way subsequently (pulled up in three of last four runs).

KEY HORSES LISTED BY TRAINER

Kim Bailey
Does He Know
Espoir De Romay (Fr)
First Flow (Ire)
Happygolucky (Ire)
Imperial Aura (Ire)
Two For Gold (Ire)

Richard Bandey
Mister Malarky
Saint Palais (Fr)

Peter Bowen
Mac Tottie

Martin Brassil
Fastorslow (Fr)
Longhouse Poet (Ire)

Charles Byrnes
Blazing Khal (Ire)

Jennie Candlish
Cheddleton

Ben Case
Cobblers Dream (Ire)

Ben Clarke
The Galloping Bear

Barry Connell
Enniskerry (Ire)

Paddy Corkery
Master McShee

Gavin Cromwell
Darver Star (Ire)
Flooring Porter (Ire)
My Mate Mozzie (Ire)
Vanillier (Fr)

Rebecca Curtis
Lisnagar Oscar (Ire)
Pats Fancy (Ire)

Henry Daly
Fortescue
Hillcrest (Ire)

Henry de Bromhead
A Plus Tard (Fr)
Ballyadam (Ire)
Bob Olinger (Ire)
Captain Guinness (Ire)
Chris's Dream (Ire)
Coeur Sublime (Ire)
Dancing On My Own (Ire)
Eklat De Rire (Fr)
Envoi Allen (Fr)
Guily Billy (Fr)
Honeysuckle
Jason The Militant (Ire)
Journey With Me (Ire)
Life In The Park (Ire)
Magic Daze (Ire)
Minella Indo (Ire)
Monalee (Ire)
Shantreusse (Ire)
Telmesomethinggirl (Ire)

Pat Doyle
Flame Bearer (Ire)

William Durkan
Screaming Colours (Ire)

Stuart Edmunds
Gentleman At Arms (Ire)

Gordon Elliott
Abacadabras (Fr)
Absolute Notions (Ire)
American Mike (Ire)
Andy Dufresne (Ire)
Ash Tree Meadow (Fr)
Braeside (Ire)
Commander Of Fleet (Ire)
Conflated (Ire)
Delta Work (Fr)
Escaria Ten (Fr)
Farclas (Fr)
Fil Dor (Fr)
Floueur (Fr)
Frontal Assault (Ire)
Fury Road (Ire)
Galvin (Ire)
Grand Paradis (Fr)
Grand Roi (Fr)
Hollow Games (Ire)
Iberique Du Seuil (Fr)
Mighty Potter (Fr)
Minella Crooner (Ire)
Mount Ida (Ire)
Off Your Rocco (Ire)
Party Central (Ire)
Pied Piper
Queens Brook (Ire)
Riviere D'Etel (Fr)
Run Wild Fred (Ire)
Saint Felicien (Fr)
Salvador Ziggy (Ire)
Sire Du Berlais (Fr)
Teahupoo (Fr)
Three Stripe Life (Ire)
Zanahiyr (Ire)

Brian Ellison
Windsor Avenue (Ire)

Peter Fahey
Suprise Package

Pat Fahy
Dunvegan (Fr)

Lorna Fowler
Colonel Mustard (Fr)

Harry Fry
Dubrovnik Harry (Ire)
Gin Coco (Fr)
Love Envoi (Ire)
Metier (Ire)
Might I (Ire)
Revels Hill (Ire)

Tom George
Clondaw Castle (Ire)

Thomas Gibney
Velvet Elvis (Ire)

Harriet Graham & Gary Rutherford
Aye Right (Ire)

Alex Hales
Millers Bank

Ann Hamilton
Bavington Bob (Ire)
Nuts Well
Pay The Piper (Ire)
Tommy's Oscar (Ire)

Shark Hanlon
Hewick (Ire)

Jessica Harrington
Ashdale Bob (Ire)
Lifetime Ambition (Ire)

KEY HORSES LISTED BY TRAINER

Sizing Pottsie (Fr)

Milton Harris
Knight Salute

Nicky Henderson
Ahorsewithnoname
Allart (Ire)
Balco Coastal (Fr)
Buzz (Fr)
Caribean Boy (Fr)
Champ (Ire)
Chantry House (Ire)
City Chief (Ire)
Constitution Hill
Doddiethegreat (Ire)
Dusart (Ire)
Epatante (Fr)
First Street
Fusil Raffles (Fr)
Jonbon (Fr)
Marie's Rock (Ire)
Mister Coffey (Fr)
Mister Fisher (Ire)
No Ordinary Joe (Ire)
Pentland Hills (Ire)
Shishkin (Ire)
Theatre Glory (Ire)
Walking On Air (Ire)

Philip Hobbs
Campond (Fr)
Celebre D'Allen (Fr)
Musical Slave (Ire)
Sporting John (Ire)
Thyme Hill
Zanza (Ire)

Richard Hobson
Lord Du Mesnil (Fr)

Anthony Honeyball
Sam Brown
Serious Charges (Ire)

Chris Honour
Grumpy Charley

Ruth Jefferson
Sounds Russian (Ire)

Nick Kent
Erne River (Ire)

Alan King
Edwardstone
Harbour Lake (Ire)
Major Dundee (Ire)
North Lodge (Ire)
Sceau Royal (Fr)
The Glancing Queen (Ire)
Tritonic

Neil King
Lookaway (Ire)
Onemorefortheroad

Tom Lacey
Adrimel (Fr)
Glory And Fortune (Ire)
Lossiemouth
Tea Clipper (Ire)

Emma Lavelle
Killer Clown (Ire)
Paisley Park (Ire)
Red Rookie
Top Dog (Ire)

Charlie Longsdon
Snow Leopardess

Tony Martin
Good Time Jonny (Ire)

Donald McCain
Mackenberg (Ger)
Minella Drama (Ire)
Minella Trump (Ire)

John McConnell
Bardenstown Lad
Mahler Mission (Ire)

Oliver McKiernan
Gatsby Grey (Fr)
Meet And Greet (Ire)

Dermot A McLoughlin
Lord Lariat (Ire)
Santa Rossa (Ire)

Noel Meade
Beacon Edge (Ire)
Diol Ker (Fr)
Jeff Kidder (Ire)
Thedevilscoachman (Ire)

Gary Moore
Authorised Speed (Fr)
Botox Has (Fr)
Editeur Du Gite (Fr)
Goshen (Fr)
Nassalam (Fr)
Porticello (Fr)

Mouse Morris
French Dynamite (Fr)
Gentlemansgame

Hughie Morrison
Not So Sleepy
Third Wind

Emmet Mullins
Cape Gentleman (Ire)
Noble Yeats (Ire)
The Shunter (Ire)

Willie Mullins
Adamantly Chosen (Ire)
Allaho (Fr)
Allegorie De Vassy (Fr)
Appreciate It (Ire)
Ashroe Diamond (Ire)
Asterion Forlonge (Fr)
Billaway (Ire)
Blue Lord (Fr)
Blue Sari (Fr)
Brandy Love (Ire)
Bring On The Night
Bronn (Ire)
Burrows Saint (Fr)
Capodanno (Fr)
Carefully Selected (Ire)
Chacun Pour Soi (Fr)
Champ Kiely (Ire)
Ciel De Neige (Fr)
Cilaos Emery (Fr)
Classic Getaway (Ire)
Dark Raven (Ire)
Dinoblue (Fr)
Dysart Dynamo (Ire)
Easy Game (Fr)
Echoes In Rain (Fr)
El Barra (Fr)
El Fabiolo (Fr)
Elimay (Fr)
En Beton (Fr)
Energumene (Fr)
Facile Vega (Ire)
Ferny Hollow (Ire)
Fighter Allen (Fr)
Franco De Port (Fr)
Gaelic Warrior (Ger)
Gaillard Du Mesnil (Fr)
Galopin Des Champs (Fr)
Gentleman De Mee (Fr)
Grangeclare West (Ire)
Ha D'Or (Fr)
Haut En Couleurs (Fr)
Hors Piste (Fr)
Hunters Yarn (Ire)
Icare Allen (Fr)
Il Etait Temps (Fr)
Impulsive Dancer (Ire)
James Du Berlais (Fr)
James's Gate (Ire)
Janidil (Fr)
Jon Snow (Fr)
Jungle Boogie (Ire)
Kemboy (Fr)
Kilcruit (Ire)
Klassical Dream (Fr)
Madmansgame
Minella Cocooner (Ire)
Mt Leinster (Ire)
Royal Rendezvous (Ire)
Saint Roi (Fr)
Saint Sam (Fr)
Saldier (Fr)
Seabank Bistro (Ire)
Shadow Rider (Fr)
Sharjah (Fr)
Sir Gerhard (Ire)
State Man (Fr)
Stattler (Ire)
The Nice Guy (Ire)
Tornado Flyer (Ire)
Vauban (Fr)
Whatdeawant (Ire)

Amy Murphy
Kalashnikov (Ire)

Ciaran Murphy
Enjoy D'Allen (Fr)

Olly Murphy
Brewin'Upastorm (Ire)
Copperless
Go Dante
Gunsight Ridge
Itchy Feet (Fr)
Thomas Darby (Ire)
Thunder Rock (Ire)

Paul Nicholls
Bravemansgame (Fr)
Broken Halo
Clan Des Obeaux (Fr)
Complete Unknown (Ire)
Dolos (Fr)
Enrilo (Fr)
Frodon (Fr)
Gelino Bello (Fr)
Greaneteen (Fr)
Hacker Des Places (Fr)
Henri The Second (Fr)
Hitman (Fr)
Knappers Hill (Ire)
McFabulous (Ire)
Monmiral (Fr)
Pic D'Orhy (Fr)
Quel Destin (Fr)
Rouge Vif (Fr)
Saint Calvados (Fr)
Samarrive (Fr)
Secret Investor
Silent Revolution (Ire)
Silver Forever (Ire)
Simply The Betts (Ire)
Solo (Fr)
Stage Star (Ire)
Threeunderthrufive (Ire)
Thyme White (Fr)
Topofthegame (Ire)
Truckers Lodge (Ire)

Paul Nolan
Mrs Milner (Ire)

Fergal O'Brien
Alaphilippe (Ire)
Bonttay (Ire)
Imperial Alcazar (Ire)
Paint The Dream

Joseph O'Brien
A Wave Of The Sea (Ire)
Banbridge (Ire)
Darasso (Fr)
Early Doors (Fr)
Fakir D'Oudairies (Fr)
Fire Attack (Ire)
Home By The Lee (Ire)
Scarlet And Dove (Ire)

Jonjo O'Neill
Annie Mc (Ire)
Anyharminasking (Ire)
Easysland (Fr)
Petit Tonnerre (Fr)
Soaring Glory (Ire)
Time To Get Up (Ire)

Ben Pauling
Global Citizen (Ire)
Shakem Up'Arry (Ire)

David Pipe
Adagio (Ger)
Gericault Roque (Fr)
Main Fact (USA)
Make Me A Believer (Ire)
Remastered

Nicky Richards
Nells Son

Padraig Roche
Brazil (Ire)

Lucinda Russell
Ahoy Senor (Ire)
Corach Rambler (Ire)
Haute Estime (Ire)
Mighty Thunder

Jeremy Scott
Dashel Drasher

Michael Scudamore
Do Your Job (Ire)

Dan Skelton
Allmankind
Ashtown Lad (Ire)
Ballygrifincottage (Ire)
Doctor Parnassus (Ire)
Flegmatik (Fr)
Langer Dan (Ire)
Molly Ollys Wishes
My Drogo
Nube Negra (Spa)
Proschema (Ire)
Protektorat (Fr)
Shan Blue (Ire)
Third Time Lucki (Ire)
Unexpected Party (Fr)
West Balboa (Ire)
West Cork

Matthew Smith
Ronald Pump

Jamie Snowden
Ga Law (Fr)
Soldier Of Destiny (Ire)

Richard Spencer
Wonderwall (Ire)

Sam Thomas
Al Dancer (Fr)
Before Midnight
Good Risk At All (Fr)
Iwilldoit
Skytastic (Fr)
Stolen Silver (Fr)

Sandy Thomson
Dingo Dollar (Ire)

Colin Tizzard
Amarillo Sky (Ire)
Eldorado Allen (Fr)
Elixir De Nutz (Fr)
Fiddlerontheroof (Ire)
Jpr One (Ire)
Lostintranslation (Ire)
Oscar Elite (Ire)
The Widdow Maker
War Lord (Ger)

Joe Tizzard
The Big Breakaway (Ire)

Nigel Twiston-Davies
Beauport (Ire)
Bristol De Mai (Fr)
Fantastikas (Fr)
Good Boy Bobby (Ire)
Gowel Road (Ire)
Guard Your Dreams
I Like To Move It
Undersupervision (Ire)
Zambella (Fr)

Lucy Wadham
Martello Sky

Ted Walsh
Any Second Now (Ire)

Paul Webber
Indefatigable (Ire)

Christian Williams
Kitty's Light
Win My Wings (Ire)

Evan Williams
Annsam
Coole Cody (Ire)
The Last Day (Ire)

Ian Williams
Party Business (Ire)

Nick Williams
One For The Team

Venetia Williams
Brave Seasca (Fr)
Chambard (Fr)
Cloudy Glen (Ire)
Commodore (Fr)
Espoir De Guye (Fr)
Fanion D'Estruval (Fr)
Frero Banbou (Fr)
Fuji Flight (Fr)
Funambule Sivola (Fr)
Green Book (Fr)
L'Homme Presse (Fr)
Pink Legend
Quick Wave (Fr)
Royale Pagaille (Fr)

Michael Winters
Chatham Street Lad (Ire)

2023 BRITISH FIXTURES

GB Flat meetings in capitals; *=Floodlit; *=Evening

JANUARY

1 Sun Cheltenham, Catterick, Exeter, Fakenham, Musselburgh, SOUTHWELL[AW]
2 Mon LINGFIELD[AW], *NEWCASTLE[AW], Ayr, Plumpton
3 Tue CHELMSFORD CITY[AW], *WOLVERHAMPTON[AW], Musselburgh
4 Wed NEWCASTLE[AW], *KEMPTON[AW], Hereford
5 Thu WOLVERHAMPTON[AW], *CHELMSFORD CITY[AW], Ffos Las
6 Fri KEMPTON[AW], *SOUTHWELL[AW], Ludlow
7 Sat *KEMPTON[AW], LINGFIELD[AW], Newcastle, Sandown, Wincanton
8 Sun SOUTHWELL[AW], Chepstow
9 Mon *WOLVERHAMPTON[AW], Taunton, Ayr
10 Tue *SOUTHWELL[AW], Exeter, Doncaster
11 Wed *KEMPTON[AW], LINGFIELD[AW], Leicester
12 Thu *CHELMSFORD CITY[AW], NEWCASTLE[AW], Bangor, Catterick
13 Fri *NEWCASTLE[AW], LINGFIELD[AW], Huntingdon, Sedgefield
14 Sat *CHELMSFORD CITY[AW], LINGFIELD[AW], Kempton, Warwick, Wetherby
15 Sun SOUTHWELL[AW], Kelso
16 Mon *WOLVERHAMPTON[AW], Fontwell, Hereford
17 Tue KEMPTON[AW], *SOUTHWELL[AW], Chepstow
18 Wed *SOUTHWELL[AW], Newbury, Plumpton
19 Thu *KEMPTON[AW], Newcastle, Ludlow, Wincanton
20 Fri *NEWCASTLE[AW], SOUTHWELL[AW], Lingfield, Market Rasen
21 Sat Ascot, *WOLVERHAMPTON[AW], LINGFIELD[AW], Haydock, Taunton
22 Sun Lingfield, Fakenham
23 Mon KEMPTON[AW], SOUTHWELL[AW], *WOLVERHAMPTON[AW]
24 Tue *SOUTHWELL[AW], Exeter, Leicester
25 Wed *KEMPTON[AW], NEWCASTLE[AW], Warwick, Catterick
26 Thu *NEWCASTLE[AW], SOUTHWELL[AW], Wetherby, Wincanton
27 Fri *WOLVERHAMPTON[AW], LINGFIELD[AW], Doncaster, Huntingdon
28 Sat Cheltenham, *KEMPTON[AW], LINGFIELD[AW], Doncaster, Uttoxeter
29 Sun Fontwell, Sedgefield
30 Mon *WOLVERHAMPTON[AW], Hereford, Plumpton
31 Tue *SOUTHWELL[AW], Ffos Las, Newcastle

FEBRUARY

1 Wed *KEMPTON[AW], Ayr, Exeter, Leicester
2 Thu *CHELMSFORD CITY[AW], SOUTHWELL[AW], Fakenham, Wincanton
3 Fri *NEWCASTLE[AW], LINGFIELD[AW], Catterick, Chepstow
4 Sat *KEMPTON[AW], LINGFIELD[AW], Musselburgh, Sandown, Wetherby
5 Sun Hereford, Musselburgh
6 Mon *WOLVERHAMPTON[AW], Carlisle, Fontwell
7 Tue *SOUTHWELL[AW], Market Rasen, Taunton
8 Wed *KEMPTON[AW], Ludlow, Sedgefield
9 Thu *NEWCASTLE[AW], Doncaster, Ffos Las, Huntingdon
10 Fri *CHELMSFORD CITY[AW], SOUTHWELL[AW], Bangor, Kempton
11 Sat Newbury, LINGFIELD[AW], *WOLVERHAMPTON[AW], Uttoxeter, Warwick
12 Sun SOUTHWELL[AW], Exeter
13 Mon *WOLVERHAMPTON[AW], Catterick, Plumpton
14 Tue *NEWCASTLE[AW], Ayr, Lingfield
15 Wed *KEMPTON[AW], Hereford, Wetherby
16 Thu *CHELMSFORD CITY[AW], Newcastle, Leicester, Sandown
17 Fri *SOUTHWELL[AW], LINGFIELD[AW], Fakenham, Kelso
18 Sat *NEWCASTLE[AW], LINGFIELD[AW], Ascot, Haydock, Wincanton
19 Sun Newbury, Musselburgh
20 Mon *NEWCASTLE[AW], Carlisle, Lingfield
21 Tue *SOUTHWELL[AW], Market Rasen, Taunton
22 Wed *KEMPTON[AW], NEWCASTLE[AW], Doncaster, Ludlow
23 Thu *NEWCASTLE[AW], SOUTHWELL[AW], Huntingdon, Sedgefield
24 Fri *WOLVERHAMPTON[AW], LINGFIELD[AW], Exeter, Warwick
25 Sat *CHELMSFORD CITY[AW], LINGFIELD[AW], Chepstow, Kempton, Newcastle
26 Sun Fontwell, Hereford
27 Mon *WOLVERHAMPTON[AW], Ayr, Plumpton
28 Tue *SOUTHWELL[AW], Catterick, Leicester

MARCH

1 Wed *KEMPTON[AW], LINGFIELD[AW], Musselburgh, Wincanton
2 Thu *CHELMSFORD CITY[AW], NEWCASTLE[AW], Ludlow, Taunton
3 Fri *NEWCASTLE[AW], LINGFIELD[AW], Doncaster, Newbury
4 Sat *WOLVERHAMPTON[AW], LINGFIELD[AW], Doncaster, Kelso, Newbury
5 Sun Huntingdon, Ffos Las
6 Mon *WOLVERHAMPTON[AW], Wetherby, Southwell
7 Tue *SOUTHWELL[AW], Newcastle, Sandown
8 Wed *KEMPTON[AW], LINGFIELD[AW], Catterick, Fontwell
9 Thu *NEWCASTLE[AW], SOUTHWELL[AW], Carlisle, Wincanton
10 Fri *KEMPTON[AW], Ayr, Exeter, Leicester
11 Sat *CHELMSFORD CITY[AW], WOLVERHAMPTON[AW], Ayr, Hereford, Sandown
12 Sun Warwick, Market Rasen
13 Mon *WOLVERHAMPTON[AW], Plumpton, Stratford, Taunton
14 Tue Cheltenham, *NEWCASTLE[AW], *SOUTHWELL[AW] Sedgefield
15 Wed Cheltenham, *KEMPTON[AW], *NEWCASTLE[AW], Huntingdon
16 Thu Cheltenham, *CHELMSFORD CITY[AW], *SOUTHWELL[AW], Hexham
17 Fri Cheltenham, *NEWCASTLE[AW], *WOLVERHAMPTON[AW], Doncaster, Fakenham
18 Sat *WOLVERHAMPTON[AW], Fontwell, Kempton, Newcastle, Uttoxeter
19 Sun Chepstow, Carlisle
20 Mon Southwell, Taunton
21 Tue Market Rasen, Plumpton, Wetherby
22 Wed Warwick, Ffos Las, Haydock
23 Thu Chepstow, Ludlow, Sedgefield
24 Fri *NEWCASTLE[AW], Hereford, Musselburgh, Newbury
25 Sat *WOLVERHAMPTON[AW], LINGFIELD[AW], Bangor, Kelso, Newbury
26 Sun Carlisle, Exeter
27 Mon LINGFIELD[AW], *WOLVERHAMPTON[AW], Wincanton
28 Tue *WOLVERHAMPTON[AW], Huntingdon, Hexham
29 Wed *KEMPTON[AW], LINGFIELD[AW], Market Rasen, Newcastle

New Year's Day action at Cheltenham

2023 BRITISH FIXTURES

30 Thu *WOLVERHAMPTON^{AW}, Taunton, Warwick, Sedgefield

31 Fri SOUTHWELL^{AW}, *NEWCASTLE^{AW}, LINGFIELD^{AW}, Wetherby

APRIL

1 Sat DONCASTER, *CHELMSFORD CITY^{AW}, KEMPTON^{AW}, Stratford, Uttoxeter

2 Sun DONCASTER, Ascot

3 Mon *NEWCASTLE^{AW}, LINGFIELD^{AW}, Ludlow

4 Tue THIRSK, *SOUTHWELL^{AW}, Fontwell

5 Wed *KEMPTON^{AW}, WOLVERHAMPTON^{AW}, NOTTINGHAM, Wincanton

6 Thu *SOUTHWELL^{AW}, CHELMSFORD CITY^{AW}, Hereford, Wetherby

7 Fri LINGFIELD^{AW}, NEWCASTLE^{AW}, BATH

8 Sat KEMPTON^{AW}, *WOLVERHAMPTON^{AW}, Carlisle, Haydock, Newton Abbot, MUSSELBURGH

9 Sun SOUTHWELL^{AW}, Ffos Las, Market Rasen, Plumpton

10 Mon REDCAR, WOLVERHAMPTON^{AW}, Chepstow, Fakenham, Huntingdon, Plumpton

11 Tue PONTEFRACT, *WOLVERHAMPTON^{AW}, Exeter

12 Wed *KEMPTON^{AW}, CATTERICK, NOTTINGHAM, Southwell

13 Thu Aintree, *CHELMSFORD CITY^{AW}, NEWCASTLE^{AW}, Taunton

14 Fri Aintree, *SOUTHWELL^{AW}, LEICESTER, Sedgefield

15 Sat Aintree, YARMOUTH^{AW}, *WOLVERHAMPTON^{AW}, Chepstow, Newcastle

16 Sun Huntingdon, Wincanton

17 Mon *KEMPTON^{AW}, REDCAR, WINDSOR, Kelso

18 Tue *SOUTHWELL^{AW}, LINGFIELD^{AW}, NEWMARKET, Newton Abbot

19 Wed BEVERLEY, *KEMPTON^{AW}, NEWMARKET, Cheltenham

20 Thu *CHELMSFORD CITY^{AW}, NEWMARKET, RIPON, Cheltenham

21 Fri Ayr, *BATH, NEWBURY, *Exeter, Fontwell

22 Sat Ayr, *BRIGHTON, NEWBURY, *NOTTINGHAM, THIRSK, Bangor

23 Sun Stratford, Plumpton

24 Mon PONTEFRACT, WINDSOR, Hexham, *Kempton

25 Tue EPSOM, *WOLVERHAMPTON^{AW}, YARMOUTH, Ffos Las

26 Wed CATTERICK, *LINGFIELD^{AW}, Ludlow, Perth

27 Thu BEVERLEY, *CHELMSFORD CITY^{AW}, Perth, *Taunton, Warwick

28 Fri SANDOWN, DONCASTER^{AW}, *Chepstow, Perth, *Southwell

29 Sat Sandown, *DONCASTER, HAYDOCK, LEICESTER, RIPON, *WOLVERHAMPTON^{AW},

30 Sun WETHERBY, MUSSELBURGH

MAY

1 Mon BATH, WINDSOR, BEVERLEY, Kempton, Warwick

2 Tue *NEWCASTLE^{AW}, BRIGHTON, NOTTINGHAM, YARMOUTH

3 Wed ASCOT, *KEMPTON^{AW}, *BRIGHTON, PONTEFRACT, WOLVERHAMPTON^{AW}

4 Thu AYR, *CHELMSFORD CITY^{AW}, *LINGFIELD^{AW}, REDCAR, SALISBURY

5 Fri NEWMARKET, *NEWCASTLE^{AW}, GOODWOOD, MUSSELBURGH, *Cheltenham

6 Sat NEWMARKET, *DONCASTER, GOODWOOD, THIRSK, *Hexham, Uttoxeter

7 Sun NEWMARKET, HAMILTON, SALISBURY

8 Mon AYR, SOUTHWELL^{AW}, *WINDSOR, Worcester

9 Tue LINGFIELD^{AW}, *Ludlow, Fakenham, Ffos Las

10 Wed CHESTER, *KEMPTON^{AW}, *Fontwell, Kelso, Newton Abbot

11 Thu CHESTER, *THIRSK, *CHELMSFORD CITY^{AW}, SOUTHWELL^{AW}, Huntingdon

12 Fri CHESTER, ASCOT, *NOTTINGHAM, *RIPON, *WOLVERHAMPTON^{AW}, Market Rasen

13 Sat HAYDOCK (mixed), ASCOT, LINGFIELD, NOTTINGHAM, *LEICESTER, Hexham, *Warwick

14 Sun Ludlow, Plumpton

15 Mon MUSSELBURGH, CATTERICK, *WINDSOR, WOLVERHAMPTON^{AW}, *Southwell

16 Tue BEVERLEY, CHEPSTOW, *SANDOWN, *WETHERBY, Sedgefield

17 Wed YORK, *BATH, Newton Abbot, *Perth, Worcester

18 Thu YORK, *NEWMARKET, SALISBURY, *Fontwell, Perth

19 Fri YORK, *HAMILTON, NEWBURY, NEWMARKET, *Aintree

20 Sat *DONCASTER, NEWBURY, NEWMARKET, THIRSK, *Uttoxeter, Bangor

21 Sun RIPON, Stratford

22 Mon CARLISLE, REDCAR, *WINDSOR, *Market Rasen, Ffos Las

23 Tue *AYR, BRIGHTON, WOLVERHAMPTON^{AW}, *Hexham, Huntingdon

24 Wed AYR, *KEMPTON^{AW}, YARMOUTH, *Southwell, Warwick

25 Thu CATTERICK, *CHELMSFORD CITY^{AW}, WOLVERHAMPTON^{AW}, *SANDOWN, HAYDOCK

26 Fri BATH, HAYDOCK, GOODWOOD, *PONTEFRACT, *Worcester

27 Sat GOODWOOD, HAYDOCK, CHESTER, *SALISBURY, YORK, *Ffos Las, Cartmel

28 Sun Fontwell, Kelso, Uttoxeter

29 Mon LEICESTER, REDCAR, WINDSOR, Cartmel, Huntingdon

30 Tue *NOTTINGHAM, BRIGHTON, LEICESTER, *LINGFIELD, REDCAR

31 Wed BEVERLEY, HAMILTON, Newton Abbot, *Warwick, *Cartmel

JUNE

1 Thu *CARLISLE, LINGFIELD, RIPON, YARMOUTH, *Market Rasen

2 Fri EPSOM, CARLISLE, *CATTERICK, CHEPSTOW, *DONCASTER, *Stratford

3 Sat EPSOM, DONCASTER, *LINGFIELD, MUSSELBURGH, Hexham, *Stratford, Worcester

4 Sun NOTTINGHAM, Fakenham

5 Mon THIRSK, *WINDSOR, AYR, *WOLVERHAMPTON^{AW}

6 Tue LEICESTER, *LINGFIELD^{AW}, *WETHERBY, Southwell

7 Wed NEWBURY, *KEMPTON^{AW}, NOTTINGHAM, *RIPON, Newton Abbot

8 Thu *YARMOUTH, *CHELMSFORD CITY^{AW}, HAMILTON, Ffos Las, Uttoxeter

9 Fri THIRSK, *BATH, BRIGHTON, *GOODWOOD, *HAYDOCK, Market Rasen

10 Sat BEVERLEY, CATTERICK, *CHEPSTOW, HAYDOCK, *LINGFIELD, Bangor

11 Sun GOODWOOD, Perth

12 Mon LINGFIELD, *PONTEFRACT, *WINDSOR, Southwell

13 Tue *AYR, *WETHERBY, BRIGHTON, SALISBURY

2023 BRITISH FIXTURES

- 14 Wed *HAMILTON, HAYDOCK, *KEMPTON[AW], YARMOUTH, Newton Abbot
- 15 Thu *HAYDOCK, NEWBURY, NOTTINGHAM, YARMOUTH, *Worcester
- 16 Fri CHEPSTOW, *GOODWOOD, SANDOWN, YORK, *Aintree, *Fontwell
- 17 Sat BATH, *LEICESTER, SANDOWN, YORK, CHESTER, Hexham, *Uttoxeter
- 18 Sun DONCASTER, SALISBURY
- 19 Mon CARLISLE, LINGFIELD[AW], *NOTTINGHAM, *WINDSOR, WOLVERHAMPTON[AW]
- 20 Tue ROYAL ASCOT, *BEVERLEY, *BRIGHTON, THIRSK, Stratford
- 21 Wed ROYAL ASCOT, *NEWCASTLE[AW], HAMILTON, *RIPON, Worcester
- 22 Thu ROYAL ASCOT, CHELMSFORD CITY[AW], *LINGFIELD[AW], RIPON, *Uttoxeter
- 23 Fri ROYAL ASCOT, *MUSSELBURGH, *GOODWOOD, *NEWMARKET, REDCAR, Market Rasen
- 24 Sat ROYAL ASCOT, AYR, *HAYDOCK, *LINGFIELD, NEWMARKET, REDCAR, Perth
- 25 Sun PONTEFRACT, FFOS LAS, Hexham
- 26 Mon CHEPSTOW, *WINDSOR, *WOLVERHAMPTON[AW], Southwell
- 27 Tue BEVERLEY, BRIGHTON, *NEWBURY, *Newton Abbot
- 28 Wed *BATH, CARLISLE, *KEMPTON[AW], SALISBURY, Worcester
- 29 Thu *HAMILTON, *LEICESTER, NEWCASTLE[AW], NEWMARKET, NOTTINGHAM
- 30 Fri *CHESTER, DONCASTER, *NEWCASTLE[AW], *NEWMARKET, YARMOUTH, Cartmel

JULY

- 1 Sat CHESTER, *DONCASTER, *LINGFIELD, NEWCASTLE[AW], NEWMARKET, WINDSOR
- 2 Sun WINDSOR, Cartmel, Uttoxeter
- 3 Mon *MUSSELBURGH, PONTEFRACT, *WINDSOR, Southwell
- 4 Tue BRIGHTON, HAMILTON, *FFOS LAS, *Stratford
- 5 Wed *BATH, MUSSELBURGH, THIRSK, *EPSOM, Worcester
- 6 Thu *KEMPTON[AW], HAYDOCK, *NEWBURY, YARMOUTH, Perth
- 7 Fri *BEVERLEY, DONCASTER, *HAYDOCK, SANDOWN, Newton Abbot
- 8 Sat BEVERLEY, *CARLISLE, HAYDOCK, LEICESTER, *NOTTINGHAM, SANDOWN
- 9 Sun AYR, CHELMSFORD CITY[AW], Market Rasen
- 10 Mon *CHEPSTOW, AYR, *RIPON, Worcester
- 11 Tue *BRIGHTON, PONTEFRACT, WOLVERHAMPTON[AW], *Uttoxeter
- 12 Wed *BATH, CATTERICK, *KEMPTON[AW], LINGFIELD, YARMOUTH
- 13 Thu NEWMARKET, CARLISLE, DONCASTER, *EPSOM, *NEWBURY
- 14 Fri NEWMARKET, ASCOT, *CHEPSTOW, *CHESTER, YORK
- 15 Sat NEWMARKET, ASCOT, CHESTER, *HAMILTON, *SALISBURY, YORK
- 16 Sun Perth, Stratford
- 17 Mon AYR, *WINDSOR, *WOLVERHAMPTON[AW], Newton Abbot
- 18 Tue LINGFIELD, BEVERLEY, *NOTTINGHAM, *Southwell
- 19 Wed CATTERICK, BATH, *WOLVERHAMPTON[AW], *YARMOUTH, Uttoxeter
- 20 Thu CHEPSTOW, *EPSOM, HAMILTON, LEICESTER, *Worcester
- 21 Fri *HAMILTON, HAYDOCK, NEWBURY, *NEWMARKET, NOTTINGHAM, *PONTEFRACT
- 22 Sat *DONCASTER, *HAYDOCK, NEWBURY, NEWMARKET, RIPON, Market Rasen, Cartmel
- 23 Sun REDCAR, Newton Abbot, Stratford
- 24 Mon AYR, *BEVERLEY, *WINDSOR, Cartmel
- 25 Tue *CHELMSFORD CITY[AW], MUSSELBURGH, *WOLVERHAMPTON[AW], Southwell
- 26 Wed BATH, CATTERICK, *LEICESTER, LINGFIELD, *SANDOWN
- 27 Thu *DONCASTER, *NEWBURY, SANDOWN, YARMOUTH, Worcester
- 28 Fri ASCOT, *CHEPSTOW, *NEWMARKET, THIRSK, *YORK, Uttoxeter
- 29 Sat ASCOT, *WINDSOR, NEWCASTLE[AW], NEWMARKET, *SALISBURY, YORK
- 30 Sun PONTEFRACT, Uttoxeter
- 31 Mon AYR, *FFOS LAS, *LINGFIELD, Newton Abbot

AUGUST

- 1 Tue GOODWOOD, BEVERLEY, YARMOUTH, *Perth, *Worcester
- 2 Wed GOODWOOD, *LEICESTER, REDCAR, *SANDOWN, Perth
- 3 Thu GOODWOOD, *EPSOM, NOTTINGHAM, *NEWCASTLE[AW], Stratford
- 4 Fri GOODWOOD, *BATH, *MUSSELBURGH, *NEWMARKET, WOLVERHAMPTON[AW], Bangor
- 5 Sat GOODWOOD, DONCASTER, *HAMILTON, *LINGFIELD, NEWMARKET, THIRSK
- 6 Sun CHESTER, Market Rasen
- 7 Mon AYR, *CARLISLE, RIPON, *WINDSOR
- 8 Tue *RIPON, CATTERICK, *CHELMSFORD CITY[AW], FFOS LAS
- 9 Wed BATH, BRIGHTON, *KEMPTON[AW], PONTEFRACT, *YARMOUTH
- 10 Thu *SALISBURY, BRIGHTON, NOTTINGHAM, *SANDOWN, YARMOUTH
- 11 Fri BRIGHTON, *HAYDOCK, MUSSELBURGH, *NEWMARKET, THIRSK
- 12 Sat ASCOT, *AYR, HAYDOCK, *LINGFIELD, NEWMARKET, REDCAR
- 13 Sun LEICESTER, WINDSOR
- 14 Mon KEMPTON[AW], *WINDSOR, WOLVERHAMPTON[AW], *HAMILTON
- 15 Tue *NEWCASTLE[AW], *CHELMSFORD CITY[AW], LINGFIELD, NOTTINGHAM
- 16 Wed BEVERLEY, *FFOS LAS, *KEMPTON[AW], SALISBURY, YARMOUTH
- 17 Thu *AYR, BEVERLEY, WOLVERHAMPTON[AW], *LINGFIELD, SALISBURY
- 18 Fri NEWBURY, *NEWMARKET, WOLVERHAMPTON[AW], *THIRSK, EPSOM
- 19 Sat *BATH, DONCASTER, NEWBURY, NEWMARKET, RIPON, *Market Rasen, Perth
- 20 Sun SOUTHWELL[AW], PONTEFRACT
- 21 Mon CATTERICK, *WINDSOR, BRIGHTON, *Bangor
- 22 Tue *Worcester, Newton Abbot
- 23 Wed YORK, *LEICESTER, BATH, CARLISLE, *KEMPTON[AW]
- 24 Thu YORK, *CHELMSFORD CITY[AW], CHEPSTOW, *Fontwell, Stratford

2023 BRITISH FIXTURES

25	Fri	YORK, FFOS LAS, *HAMILTON, NEWMARKET, *GOODWOOD YORK
26	Sat	YORK, GOODWOOD, NEWMARKET, *REDCAR, *WINDSOR, Cartmel
27	Sun	BEVERLEY, GOODWOOD, YARMOUTH
28	Mon	CHEPSTOW, EPSOM, RIPON, SOUTHWELL^{AW}, Cartmel
29	Tue	NEWBURY, *MUSSELBURGH, RIPON, *Worcester
30	Wed	CATTERICK, *KEMPTON^{AW}, LINGFIELD, MUSSELBURGH, *Sedgefield
31	Thu	CARLISLE, CHELMSFORD CITY^{AW}, BATH, *NEWCASTLE^{AW}, *Stratford

SEPTEMBER

1	Fri	*FFOS LAS, *SALISBURY, CARLISLE, THIRSK, *WOLVERHAMPTON^{AW}, Fontwell
2	Sat	BEVERLEY, *CHELMSFORD CITY^{AW}, CHESTER, *WOLVERHAMPTON^{AW}, SANDOWN, Newton Abbot
3	Sun	BRIGHTON, Worcester
4	Mon	BRIGHTON, CHEPSTOW, *SOUTHWELL^{AW}
5	Tue	*HAMILTON, *RIPON, GOODWOOD, Bangor
6	Wed	*KEMPTON^{AW}, BATH, LINGFIELD, WOLVERHAMPTON^{AW}, *Hexham
7	Thu	*WINDSOR, *CARLISLE, HAYDOCK, SALISBURY, Sedgefield
8	Fri	ASCOT, HAYDOCK, *KEMPTON^{AW}, NEWCASTLE^{AW}
9	Sat	ASCOT, HAYDOCK, KEMPTON^{AW}, THIRSK, *WOLVERHAMPTON^{AW}, Stratford
10	Sun	YORK, Fontwell
11	Mon	*NEWCASTLE^{AW}, BRIGHTON, Newton Abbot, Perth
12	Tue	CATTERICK, LEICESTER, *Kelso, Worcester
13	Wed	*KEMPTON^{AW}, CARLISLE, BATH, Uttoxeter
14	Thu	DONCASTER, *CHELMSFORD CITY^{AW}, FFOS LAS, EPSOM
15	Fri	DONCASTER, CHESTER, *SALISBURY, SANDOWN
16	Sat	DONCASTER, BATH, CHESTER, LINGFIELD, *MUSSELBURGH
17	Sun	DONCASTER, MUSSELBURGH
18	Mon	*KEMPTON^{AW}, BRIGHTON, THIRSK, Worcester
19	Tue	REDCAR, YARMOUTH, *NEWCASTLE^{AW}, Uttoxeter
20	Wed	BEVERLEY, SANDOWN, YARMOUTH, *Kelso
21	Thu	AYR, *CHELMSFORD CITY^{AW}, PONTEFRACT, YARMOUTH
22	Fri	AYR, *KEMPTON^{AW}, NEWBURY, Newton Abbot
23	Sat	AYR, CATTERICK, NEWBURY, NEWMARKET, *WOLVERHAMPTON^{AW}, YORK
24	Sun	HAMILTON, Plumpton
25	Mon	*WOLVERHAMPTON^{AW}, HAMILTON, LEICESTER, Warwick
26	Tue	BEVERLEY, *NEWCASTLE^{AW}, LINGFIELD^{AW}, NOTTINGHAM
27	Wed	*KEMPTON^{AW}, GOODWOOD, REDCAR, Perth
28	Thu	*SOUTHWELL^{AW}, NEWMARKET, PONTEFRACT, Perth
29	Fri	*NEWCASTLE^{AW}, HAYDOCK, NEWMARKET, Worcester
30	Sat	*CHELMSFORD CITY^{AW}, HAYDOCK, NEWMARKET, RIPON, CHESTER, Market Rasen

OCTOBER

1	Sun	EPSOM, FFOS LAS
2	Mon	BATH, *NEWCASTLE^{AW}, HAMILTON, Newton Abbot
3	Tue	AYR, *WOLVERHAMPTON^{AW}, Sedgefield, Southwell
4	Wed	*KEMPTON^{AW}, CATTERICK, NOTTINGHAM, Bangor
5	Thu	*CHELMSFORD CITY^{AW}, LINGFIELD^{AW}, SALISBURY, Warwick
6	Fri	ASCOT, *NEWCASTLE^{AW}, Fontwell, Hexham
7	Sat	ASCOT, NEWMARKET, REDCAR, *WOLVERHAMPTON^{AW}, Fontwell
8	Sun	Kelso, Uttoxeter
9	Mon	*WOLVERHAMPTON^{AW}, PONTEFRACT, WINDSOR, Stratford
10	Tue	*SOUTHWELL^{AW}, BRIGHTON, LEICESTER, Huntingdon
11	Wed	*KEMPTON^{AW}, NOTTINGHAM, Ludlow, Sedgefield
12	Thu	AYR, *CHELMSFORD CITY^{AW}, Exeter, Worcester
13	Fri	*NEWCASTLE^{AW}, NEWMARKET, YORK, Chepstow
14	Sat	*CHELMSFORD CITY^{AW}, NEWMARKET, YORK, CHESTER, Chepstow, Hexham
15	Sun	GOODWOOD, Ffos Las
16	Mon	*KEMPTON^{AW}, MUSSELBURGH, WINDSOR, YARMOUTH
17	Tue	*NEWCASTLE^{AW}, LEICESTER, Hereford, Huntingdon
18	Wed	BATH, *KEMPTON^{AW}, NOTTINGHAM, Wetherby
19	Thu	*CHELMSFORD CITY^{AW}, BRIGHTON, Carlisle, Wincanton
20	Fri	*NEWCASTLE^{AW}, HAYDOCK, REDCAR, Fakenham, Uttoxeter
21	Sat	ASCOT, CATTERICK, *WOLVERHAMPTON^{AW}, Market Rasen, Newton Abbot, Stratford
22	Sun	Kempton, Sedgefield
23	Mon	*SOUTHWELL^{AW}, PONTEFRACT, WINDSOR, Plumpton
24	Tue	*WOLVERHAMPTON^{AW}, YARMOUTH, Exeter, Hereford
25	Wed	*KEMPTON^{AW}, NEWMARKET, Fontwell, Worcester
26	Thu	*WOLVERHAMPTON^{AW}, SOUTHWELL^{AW}, Carlisle, Ludlow
27	Fri	DONCASTER, NEWBURY, *WOLVERHAMPTON^{AW}, Cheltenham
28	Sat	*CHELMSFORD CITY^{AW}, DONCASTER, NEWBURY, Cheltenham, Kelso
29	Sun	Aintree, Wincanton
30	Mon	*SOUTHWELL^{AW}, LEICESTER, REDCAR, Huntingdon
31	Tue	*NEWCASTLE^{AW}, CATTERICK, Bangor, Chepstow

NOVEMBER

1	Wed	*KEMPTON^{AW}, NOTTINGHAM, Lingfield, Fakenham
2	Thu	*CHELMSFORD CITY^{AW}, LINGFIELD^{AW}, Stratford, Worcester
3	Fri	*NEWCASTLE^{AW}, NEWMARKET, Uttoxeter, Wetherby
4	Sat	*SOUTHWELL^{AW}, NEWMARKET, Ascot, Ayr, Wetherby
5	Sun	Carlisle, Huntingdon
6	Mon	*WOLVERHAMPTON^{AW}, KEMPTON^{AW}, Hereford, Plumpton
7	Tue	*NEWCASTLE^{AW}, REDCAR, SOUTHWELL^{AW}, Warwick
8	Wed	*KEMPTON^{AW}, Chepstow, Musselburgh, Warwick
9	Thu	*CHELMSFORD CITY^{AW}, Ludlow, Newbury, Sedgefield
10	Fri	*NEWCASTLE^{AW}, Exeter, Fontwell, Hexham
11	Sat	DONCASTER, *CHELMSFORD CITY^{AW}, Aintree, Kelso, Wincanton
12	Sun	Ffos Las, Sandown
13	Mon	*WOLVERHAMPTON^{AW}, Carlisle, Kempton
14	Tue	*WOLVERHAMPTON^{AW}, NEWCASTLE^{AW}, Huntingdon, Lingfield
15	Wed	KEMPTON^{AW}, *SOUTHWELL^{AW}, Ayr, Bangor
16	Thu	*CHELMSFORD CITY^{AW}, Market Rasen, Sedgefield, Taunton
17	Fri	Cheltenham, *WOLVERHAMPTON^{AW}, NEWCASTLE^{AW}, Southwell

2023 BRITISH FIXTURES

18 Sat Cheltenham, LINGFIELD^AW, *WOLVERHAMPTON^AW, Uttoxeter, Wetherby
19 Sun Cheltenham, Fontwell
20 Mon *KEMPTON^AW, Exeter, Leicester, Plumpton
21 Tue *CHELMSFORD CITY^AW, Fakenham, Hereford, Lingfield
22 Wed *SOUTHWELL^AW, Ffos Las, Hexham, Warwick
23 Thu *WOLVERHAMPTON^AW, Market Rasen, Newcastle, Wincanton
24 Fri *SOUTHWELL^AW, Ascot, Catterick, Chepstow
25 Sat LINGFIELD^AW, *WOLVERHAMPTON^AW, Ascot, Haydock, Huntingdon
26 Sun Exeter, Uttoxeter
27 Mon Kempton, Ludlow
28 Tue Sedgefield, Southwell
29 Wed Kelso, Hereford, Wetherby
30 Thu Musselburgh, Lingfield, Taunton

DECEMBER

1 Fri Doncaster, Newbury, Musselburgh
2 Sat Newbury, Newcastle, Bangor, Doncaster
3 Sun Carlisle, Leicester
4 Mon *WOLVERHAMPTON^AW, Ayr, Plumpton
5 Tue LINGFIELD^AW, *WOLVERHAMPTON^AW, Southwell
6 Wed *KEMPTON^AW, LINGFIELD^AW, Haydock, Ludlow
7 Thu *CHELMSFORD CITY^AW, Leicester, Market Rasen, Wincanton
8 Fri *NEWCASTLE^AW, Exeter, Sandown, Sedgefield
9 Sat *NEWCASTLE^AW, *WOLVERHAMPTON^AW, Aintree, Chepstow, Sandown, Wetherby
10 Sun Huntingdon, Kelso
11 Mon *CHELMSFORD CITY^AW, Ayr, Lingfield
12 Tue *SOUTHWELL^AW, Fontwell, Uttoxeter
13 Wed *KEMPTON^AW, LINGFIELD^AW, Hexham, Leicester
14 Thu *CHELMSFORD CITY^AW, Newcastle, Taunton, Warwick
15 Fri Cheltenham, *SOUTHWELL^AW, Bangor, Doncaster
16 Sat Cheltenham, NEWCASTLE^AW, *WOLVERHAMPTON^AW, Doncaster, Hereford
17 Sun Carlisle, Southwell
18 Mon *WOLVERHAMPTON^AW, Musselburgh, Plumpton
19 Tue *WOLVERHAMPTON^AW, Catterick, Fakenham, Wincanton
20 Wed *KEMPTON^AW, LINGFIELD^AW, Ludlow, Newbury
21 Thu *CHELMSFORD CITY^AW, SOUTHWELL^AW, Exeter, Ffos Las
22 Fri *WOLVERHAMPTON^AW, SOUTHWELL^AW, Ascot, Uttoxeter
23 Sat LINGFIELD^AW, Ascot, Haydock, Newcastle
24 & 25 *No racing*
26 Tue Kempton, Fontwell, Aintree, Market Rasen, Sedgefield, Wetherby, Wincanton, WOLVERHAMPTON^AW
27 Wed Chepstow, Kempton, *WOLVERHAMPTON^AW, Wetherby
28 Thu *NEWCASTLE^AW, Catterick, Leicester
29 Fri *SOUTHWELL^AW, Doncaster, Kelso
30 Sat *WOLVERHAMPTON^AW, Haydock, Newbury, Taunton
31 Sun LINGFIELD^AW, Uttoxeter, Warwick

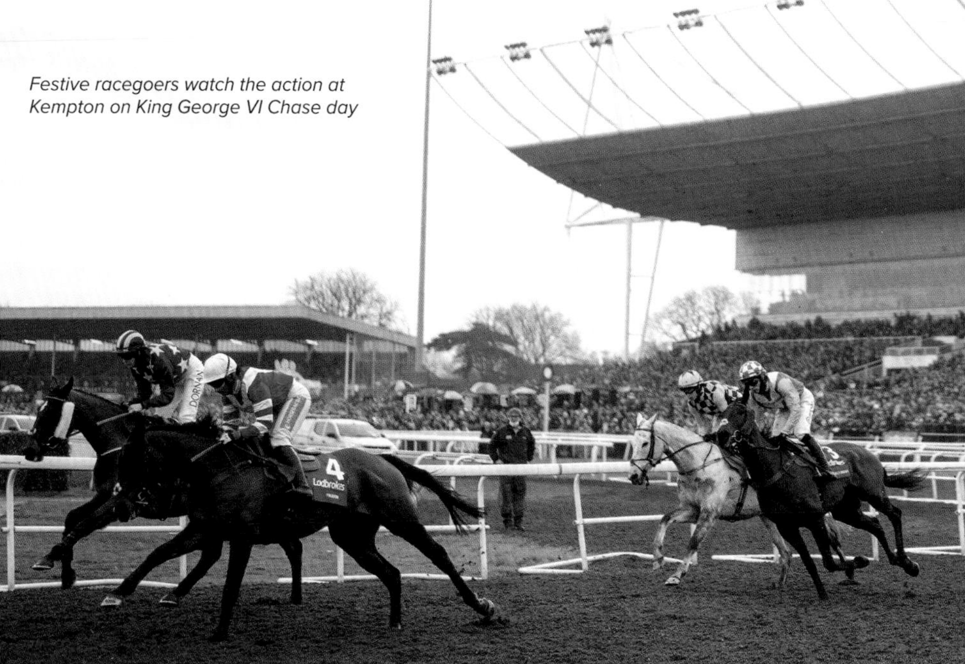

Festive racegoers watch the action at Kempton on King George VI Chase day

INDEX OF HORSES

A Dream To Share 106
A Plus Tard 84, 92, 94, 111, 146, 171, 178
A Wave Of The Sea 111
Abacadabras 111
Absolute Notions 111
Adagio 111
Adamantly Chosen 111
Adrimel 111-112, 166
Aeronisi 80, 102
Ahorsewithnoname 20, 21, 112
Ahoy Senor 89, 112, 116, 122, 145, 162, 174, 181
Al Dancer 112
Alaphilippe 112
Allaho 100, 113, 128, 146, 160
Allart 19, 113
Allegorie De Vassy 113
Allmankind 86, 113-114, 160
Almazhar Garde 41, 42
Altobelli 10-11
Amarillo Sky 114
Amarillobymorning 63
American Mike 92, 114
Amrons Sage 20
Andy Dufresne 114
Annie Mc 114
Annsam 75, 77, 114
Any News 166
Any Second Now 114
Anyharminasking 90, 115
Appreciate It 115
Ardbraccan 42-44
Ash Tree Meadow 115
Ashdale Bob 115-116
Ashroe Diamond 116
Ashtown Lad 116
Ask Me Early 8
Asterion Forlonge 117
Attacca 20
Authorised Speed 117
Aye Right 117
Balco Coastal 20, 117
Ballyadam 117
Ballycamus 102
Ballygrifincottage 116, 117
Ballyhigh 20
Banbridge 117
Bardenstown Lad 118
Bavington Bob 118
Beacon Edge 92, 118
Bear Ghylls 89-90
Beau Balko 55
Beauport 118
Bebraveforglory 80
Before Midnight 118
Bellatrixsa 86
Between Waters 21
Bill Jack 70
Billaway 118
Black Poppy 102-103
Blazing Khal 120, 146
Blue Lord 120, 128, 182
Blue Sari 120
Blueking D'Oroux 55
Bob Olinger 89, 94, 100, 120, 121, 124, 146
Bold Plan 75, 78-79
Bold Reaction 20
Bombay Sapphire 21
Bonttay 121
Boom Boom 20
Boothill 10
Bothwell Bridge 19
Botox Has 121
Bowtogreatness 58-59
Braeside 121
Brandy Love 7, 113, 121, 165
Brave Seasca 86-87, 122
Bravemansgame 47, 52, 112, 122, 160
Brazil 122, 146
Breaking Cover 26
Brewin'Upastorm 122
Bring On The Night 122
Bristol De Mai 122
Broken Halo 123
Bronn 123
Broomfield Burg 20
Burrows Saint 123
Buzz 124
Byorderofthecourt 53
Cadell 20
Camprond 124
Cape Gentleman 124
Cape Vidal 26
Capodanno 124, 163
Captain Guinness 125
Captain Morgs 20
Captain Teague 53
Carefully Selected 125
Caribean Boy 19, 125
Carrigmoorna Rowan 11
Castle Robin 40, 41
Castleward 53
Celebre D'Allen 125
Chacun Pour Soi 125, 135
Chambard 84, 125
Champ 18, 100, 126, 194
Champ Kiely 90, 91, 126
Chantry House 18, 19, 106, 126
Chatham Street Lad 127
Cheddleton 127
Chris's Dream 127
Christopher Wood 86
Ciel De Neige 127
Cilaos Emery 127
City Chief 20, 127, 198
Clan Des Obeaux 47, 48, 54, 100, 128, 184
Classic Getaway 128
Clondaw Castle 128
Cloudy Glen 128, 142
Cobblers Dream 128
Coeur Sublime 120, 128
Colonel Harry 70
Colonel Mustard 130
Commander Of Fleet 130, 142
Commodore 131
Complete Unknown 51-52, 131
Conflated 131, 137
Constitution Hill 6, 7, 14-17, 20, 90, 96, 98, 115, 131, 161, 170
Coole Cody 75-77, 130, 131
Copperless 131
Corach Rambler 131
Craigneiche 20
Credrojava 11
Current Mood 78
Dancing On My Own 132
Dancingontheedge 54
Dans Le Vent 77-78
Darasso 132-133, 181
Dark Raven 133
Darver Star 133
Dashel Drasher 133, 196
De Rasher Counter 32, 33
Deeper Blue 10
Del La Mar Rocket 59
Delta Work 133, 195
Densworth 59
Didero Vallis 84, 85
Dingo Dollar 133, 170
Dinoblue 133
Diol Ker 134, 161
Divilskin 53
Do Your Job 134, 171
Doc McCoy 70
Doctor Parnassus 134
Doddiethegreat 135
Does He Know 135
Dolos 135
Doyen For Money 29
Doyen Star 80
Dream In The Park 36
Dubrovnik Harry 10, 135
Dunvegan 135
Dusart 19, 135, 188
Dysart Dynamo 135-136
Early Doors 136
Easy Game 136
Easy Rider 20
Easysland 136
Echoes In Rain 136
Editeur Du Gite 136
Edwardstone 98, 120, 122, 136, 147, 193
Eklat De Rire 137
El Barra 137, 144
El Fabiolo 96, 137, 153, 161
Eldorado Allen 86, 94, 137
Elimay 137, 183
Elixir De Nutz 137
En Beton 137
Energumene 18, 85, 98, 100, 125, 138, 143, 185
Enjoy D'Allen 138
Enniskerry 138
Enrilo 138
Envoi Allen 85, 138
Epatante 16-18, 138-140, 198
Erne River 140
Escaria Ten 140
Espoir De Guye 140
Espoir De Romay 106, 140
Everyonesgame 41
Fable 21
Facile Vega 90-92, 114, 117, 140, 141
Fairy Gem 10
Fakir D'Oudairies 94, 140, 155
Fanion D'Estruval 86, 141
Fantastic Lady 21
Fantastikas 141
Farclas 141
Farmer's Gamble 103
Farouk D'Alene 92, 118
Fastorslow 141-142
Ferny Hollow 98, 142
Fiddlerontheroof 108, 113, 128, 142, 144
Fighter Allen 142
Fil Dor 98, 142-143, 196
Fine Casting 59-60
Fire Attack 143
Fire Flyer 54
Firestep 19, 20
Firestream 26-27
First Flow 143
First Street 143
Flame Bearer 106, 107, 143, 153
Flash Collonges 52
Flegmatik 143
Flemenstide 55

INDEX OF HORSES

Flooring Porter 100, 143, 187, 194
Floueur 144
Fontaine Collonges 87
Forever Blessed 11
Fortescue 144
Fortuitous Favour 29
Fortunes Melody 11
Franco De Port 144
French Dynamite 144
Frero Banbou 84-85, 144-145
Frodon 47-48, 94, 145
Frontal Assault 145
Fuji Flight 145
Full Of Light 20
Funambule Sivola 85-86, 145
Fury Road 145
Fusil Raffles 19, 145
Ga Law 69-70, 146
Gaelic Park 41-42
Gaelic Warrior 122, 146
Gaillard Du Mesnil 100, 146
Galopin Des Champs 92-94, 100, 106, 120, 146, 163, 167
Galvin 140, 146
Gatsby Grey 146
Gelino Bello 50, 120, 146-147, 154
Gentleman At Arms 147
Gentleman De Mee 98-100, 136, 147, 153
Gentlemansgame 106, 147
Gericault Roque 147
Gin Coco 7-8, 10, 147
Git Maker 67, 69
Glimpse Of Gala 40
Global Citizen 56, 57-58, 147
Glory And Fortune 147
Go Dante 148
Golden Son 54-55
Good Boy Bobby 148
Good Risk At All 148
Good Time Jonny 148-150
Goodtimecrew 11
Goshen 150
Gowel Road 150
Grand Paradis 150
Grand Roi 150-151
Grangeclare West 151
Greaneteen 48, 94, 151, 155
Green Book 86, 151-152
Grivetana 55
Grumpy Charley 152
Guard Your Dreams 152
Guetapan Collonges 44
Guily Billy 153
Gunsight Ridge 153
Gustavian 26, 27
Ha D'Or 153
Hacker Des Places 54, 153
Hang In There 32-34
Happygolucky 153
Harbour Lake 153
Hardy Du Seuil 67, 68-69, 70
Harper's Brook 60
Haut En Couleurs 153
Haute Estime 154
Hector Javilex 44
Henri The Second 54, 154
Henry's Friend 60
Hermes Allen 53
Hewick 155
High Fibre 10
Hillcrest 155
Hitman 48, 94, 95, 155
Holetown Hero 54
Hollow Games 155
Home By The Lee 155
Honeysuckle 14, 15, 16, 17, 90, 140, 155, 180, 182
Hors Piste 156
Hot Rod Lincoln 10
Howdyalikemenow 79-80
Huflower 55
Hunters Yarn 156
Hunting Brook 36
Hurricane Danny 54
Hurricane Highway 80
Hymac 10
I Giorni 29
I Like To Move It 156
Iberico Lord 20
Iberique Du Seuil 156-158
Icare Allen 158
Il Etait Temps 158
Il Ridoto 49
Iliade Allen 54
Iliko D'Olivate 55
Immortal 20
Imperial Alcazar 158
Imperial Aura 158
Impose Toi 20
Impulsive Dancer 158
Inca De Lafayette 55
Indefatigable 158
Iolaos Du Mou 20
Irish Hill 55
Isaac Des Obeaux 54
Issuing Authority 20
Itchy Feet 160
Ivaldi 55
Iwilldoit 160
James Du Berlais 160
James's Gate 160
Janidil 160
Jason The Militant 160
Jeff Kidder 160
Jemima P 36
Jemura 20
Jenny Wyse 52
Jet Powered 20
Joe Dadancer 63
Jon Snow 161
Jonbon 7, 20, 21, 90, 94-96, 161
Journey With Me 161
JPR One 161
Jungle Boogie 108, 161
Just Toby 103
Kalashnikov 161
Kemboy 161
Kilbeg King 26
Kilcruit 106, 162
Killer Clown 32, 35, 162
Kiltealy Briggs 64, 65, 67-68, 69
Kincardine 20
King Orry 104
Kitty's Light 162
Klassical Dream 106, 111, 116, 143, 147, 162
Knappers Hill 54, 162
Knight Salute 162, 177
Lady Adare 8
Lady D'Arbanville 21
Langer Dan 163
L'Astroboy 79
Legends Ryde 67, 70
L'Homme Presse 70, 82, 84, 87, 89, 92, 112, 162-163
Libberty Hunter 80
Life In The Park 163
Lifetime Ambition 163
Lightfoot Lady 20
Lilith 24-25
Lisnagar Oscar 163-164
Little Bruce 44-45
Longhouse Poet 164
Lookaway 164
Loop Head 80
Lord Du Mesnil 165
Lord Lariat 165
Lossiemouth 165
Lostintranslation 165
Love Bite 21
Love Envoi 4-5, 7, 121, 165
Luccia 20
Mac Tottie 165
Mackenberg 166, 167
Madmansgame 166
Magic Daze 166, 173
Mahler Mission 166
Maid O'Malley 108
Main Fact 166
Major Dundee 166
Make Me A Believer 166
Malinello 60
Marco Island 26
Marie's Rock 7, 18, 167
Martello Sky 167
Master McShee 167, 187
McFabulous 50-51, 167-168
Meet And Greet 108, 168
Metier 7, 168
Might I 6, 7, 90, 170
Mighty Potter 146, 170
Mighty Thunder 170
Milldam 70
Millers Bank 170-171, 177, 197
Minella Cocooner 108, 171
Minella Crooner 171
Minella Drama 171
Minella Indo 111, 131, 171
Minella Trump 171
Mister Coffey 19, 171
Mister Fisher 19, 172
Mister Malarky 172
Molly Ollys Wishes 172
Mollycoddled 70
Monalee 172
Monmiral 50, 51, 173
Morozov Cocktail 104, 105
Mount Ida 173
Mrs Milner 173
Mt Leinster 173
Mumbo Jumbo 35
Musical Slave 173
My Drogo 173
My Mate Mozzie 174
Nassalam 174
Nells Son 174, 175
Nestor Park 60-61
Nickle Back 108
No Ordinary Joe 20, 174
No Questions Asked 63
Noble Yeats 100, 174
North Lodge 117, 174
Norton Hill 26
Not At Present 62-63
Not So Sleepy 174
Nube Negra 175
Nuts Well 175
Off Your Rocco 175
On My Command 21
On The Platform 104
One For The Team 175
One Touch 61-62
Onemorefortheroad 176
Oscar Elite 176
Paint The Dream 176

INDEX OF HORSES

Paisley Park 30-32, 176
Park Hill Dancer 20
Park This One 70
Parramount 40
Party Business 176
Party Central 176
Passing Well 70
Pats Fancy 177
Pay The Piper 177
Pentland Hills 20, 21, 177
Persian Time 20
Petit Tonnerre 177
Petrossian 20
Pic D'Orhy 48, 177
Pied Piper 162, 177
Pink Legend 86, 177
Pisgah Pike 66, 67, 70
Porter In The Park 36
Porticello 178
Prime Venture 75, 80
Private Ryan 20
Proschema 178
Protektorat 178
Puddles In The Park 80
Queens Brook 178
Queens Rock 21
Quel Destin 178
Quick Wave 178
Quinta Do Mar 62
Rare Edition 40-41
Rathmacknee 20
Realisation 45
Red Rookie 34-35, 180
Redemption Day 92
Ree Okka 10
Regal Encore 27-29
Regarde 70
Remastered 180
Revels Hill 8-10, 180
Riviere D'Etel 120, 180
Roger Pol 70
Ronald Pump 180
Rouge Vif 180
Royal Max 20
Royal Rendezvous 181
Royale Pagaille 82, 84, 181
Run Wild Fred 181, 190
Russian Ruler 19
Sabrina 55
Saint Calvados 48, 181
Saint Felicien 181
Saint Palais 181
Saint Roi 182
Saint Sam 182
Saldier 182
Salvador Ziggy 182-183
Sam Brown 22, 24, 183
Samarrive 51, 183
Santa Rossa 183
Santini 195
Scarlet And Dove 183
Sceau Royal 183
Scene Not Herd 40, 41
Screaming Colours 183
Seabank Bistro 184
Secret Investor 184
Secret Reprieve 72-75
Seeyouinmydreams 53
Serious Charges 25-26, 27, 184
Severance 62
Shadow Rider 184
Shakem Up'Arry 58, 59, 184
Shan Blue 145, 184
Shang Tang 34
Shantreusse 184
Sharjah 182, 185
Shishkin 18-19, 100, 138, 143, 185
Silent Revolution 51, 186
Silver Forever 186
Silver Hallmark 108
Simply The Betts 187
Sir Gerhard 98, 187
Sire Du Berlais 143, 187
Sizing Pottsie 167, 187
Sky Pirate 122
Skytastic 187
Slip Of The Tongue 108
Slipway 58-59
Snow Leopardess 38-40, 187
Soaring Glory 188
Soldier Of Destiny 70, 188
Solo 188
Sonigino 55
Sounds Russian 188
Sporting John 188
Stage Star 10, 51, 188, 197
State Man 106, 143, 188, 194
Stattler 7, 142, 190
Statuaire 174
Stay Away Fay 52-53
Stolen Silver 190
Storminhome 63
Stringtoyourbow 104-105
Stroll On By 45
Super Survivor 68, 70
Suprise Package 190
Surrey Quest 20
Swapped 19-20
Tallow For Coal 70
Tarahumara 34
Tea Clipper 190
Tea For Free 45
Teahupoo 190
Tedwin Hills 35-36
Telmesomethinggirl 190
The Big Breakaway 190
The Bomber Liston 20
The Brew Master 20
The Galloping Bear 191
The Glancing Queen 191
The Last Day 78, 192
The Mighty Arc 45
The Nice Guy 96-97, 108, 171, 192
The Shunter 193
The Widdow Maker 193
Theatre Glory 21, 193
Thedevilscoachman 193
Third Time Lucki 193
Third Wind 193
Thomas Darby 193
Three Stripe Life 7, 106, 170, 174, 194
Threeunderthrufive 49, 194
Thunder Rock 194
Thyme Hill 194
Thyme White 195
Tightenourbelts 36
Time To Get Up 195
Timeforatune 54
Tommy's Oscar 194, 195
Top Dog 34, 35, 121, 195
Topofthegame 49, 195
Tornado Flyer 195
Touchy Feely 20-21
Treyarnon Bay 21
Tritonic 195-196
Trojan Horse 29
Truckers Lodge 196
Tweed Skirt 21
Two For Gold 196
Undersupervision 196
Unexpected Party 196
Up For Parole 70
Valsheda 19
Vanillier 92, 196
Vauban 98, 99, 142, 158, 196
Velvet Elvis 196-197
Voice Of Calm 34-35
Walking On Air 18, 197
War Lord 197
Warriors Story 105
West Balboa 197
West Cork 197
Western Zephyr 45
Westwood Ryder 20
Whatdeawant 197
Will Carver 20
Win My Wings 197
Windsor Avenue 197
Wiseguy 18
Wonderwall 198
World Of Dreams 28, 29
Wouldubewell 35
Wrappedupinmay 53
You Wear It Well 70
Young Butler 34
Zambella 198
Zanahiyr 160, 198
Zanza 198